The Theater of Tony Kushner

Studies in Modern Drama
Kimball King, *Series Editor*

The Theater of Tony Kushner

Living Past Hope

James Fisher

Routledge
New York   London

Published in 2002 by
Routledge
29 West 35th Street
New York, NY 10001

Published in Great Britain by
Routledge
11 New Fetter Lane
London EC4P 4EE

Routledge is an imprint of the Taylor & Francis Group.
Copyright © 2001 by Routledge

First Routledge paperback edition, 2002.
Printed in the United States of America on acid-free paper.

10 9 8 7 6 5 4 3 2 1

Library of Congress Cataloging-in-Publication Data

Fisher, James
    The theater of Tony Kushner: living past hope / by James Fisher
        p.   cm.
    Includes bibliographical references and index.
    ISBN 0-8153-3150-9 (hb) — 0-415-94271-3 (pbk.)
    1. Kushner, Tony—Criticism and interpretation. I. Title.
PS3561.U778 Z64 2001
812'.54—dc21

For Dana, Daniel, and Anna

Contents

Preface

In the ten months since the hardback edition of this book was first published, the world has changed. The tragic events in New York City, Washington, D.C., and the skies over western Pennsylvania on the morning of September 11, 2001, and the resulting "war" on terrorism, have transformed the international community. Outcomes may not be known for many months or years, if ever, but it is certainly true that the United States has been obliged to face some sobering and deeply disturbing realities. It is becoming evident that as a nation the United States, obsessed for the past decade with its unprecedented prosperity, must seriously examine the way it deals with its virtually unchallenged predominance in the world. Our wealth and overwhelming military might have not solved many of our social problems or provided the security we believe existed before 9/11. As Tony Kushner suggests, this is the moment not only for looking at ourselves, but also for examining differences: "Even a country at war has a moral imperative to think about the people with whom they are fighting and ask questions about them" (Poniewozik).

Kushner has seen his newest play, *Homebody/Kabul*, which he began writing nearly four years ago, become, as his two-play epic *Angels in America* did a decade ago, a lightning rod for social and political debate on questions of immediate import. Prior to 9/11, a drama about a middle-class British woman's fascination with the past and present of Afghanistan might have been instructive for an audience comparatively unaware of this troubled corner of the world. After 9/11, *Homebody/Kabul* appears prophetic in shaping the questions that suddenly face us as we try to comprehend a culture so utterly different from our own. These troubling questions challenge our values and suggest the precipice on which we stand.

Were the tragedies of 9/11 in part the result of a long history of American foreign policy gaffes extending back to the Vietnam era or before? Is the conversion of other countries to our way of life necessary for our ultimate survival? What of other cultures and values can coexist with our own? How do we deal with the inevitable incompatibilities? Will the world grow smaller and essentially become one culture? Can we learn to coexist with values that we have traditionally mistrusted and feared?

Focusing on a fractured, dysfunctional British family, in *Homebody/Kabul* Kushner argues for a deeper level of Western engagement with the struggles of the Afghan people. The Homebody insists that those living in comfort and luxury are obliged to assist those without the same level of security and ease, and that we must strive to truly comprehend the "other." The critical success of *Homebody/Kabul* underscores aspects of Kushner's work that this book attempts to address, not only in the play's themes, but also in the very nature of theater itself. His work inspires numerous questions: What is the future of the American theater? How much will Kushner's politically driven, boldly imaginative, highly theatrical, lyrical, and controversial work mean to the development of American drama in coming decades? Is Kushner the equal of those seriously minded playwrights immediately preceding him? Albee? Mamet? Shepard? McNally? Whom has Kushner inspired? Who among Kushner's contemporaries equal his already impressive achievement? Is Kushner's role that of a contrarian on the American scene—is he an outspoken neosocialist in an era of neoconservatism stretching back to the Reagan Revolution—offering an opposing view to that of the mainstream, a voice of liberal conscience in a period of self-interest masquerading as individualism? What seems certifiably true is that Kushner has emerged as an exemplar of what the theater can be at its most effective and affecting. With *Homebody/Kabul*, he proves for the second time that the drama can be at the center of national debate, whether the subject is the social progress of homosexuals or the complicated tangle of politics, culture, and violent upheaval inspired by the ramifications of 9/11. In both cases, and despite the obvious differences in subject matter, these plays offer pleas for compassion, understanding, and the insistence that we, as a society, *must* learn to live with differences, whether these differences reside within our own sovereign borders or outside.

Among his contemporaries, Kushner seems likely to be the one who remains committed to live theater. Despite his identification as a "gay" dramatist, his true persona is that of a "political" writer. Bold political statements are rare in mainstream American film and television, and, as such, Kushner truly requires the immediacy inherent in the platform live theater provides. For him, serious dramatists fall into two distinct categories: "the ones who ask small questions but give great answers (the traditionalists) and the ones who ask huge questions and often, as a consequence of the ambitiousness of their questioning, fail to give good answers or even any answers at all (the experimentalists, the vessel breakers); both are necessary" (Kushner, e-mail). There is little doubt as to which category Kushner aspires to.

As with virtually all of his plays, in *Homebody/Kabul* Kushner expands the private into the public; his play is full of grief-stricken ruminations on the tragic fracturing of this mysterious city that is a product of both his research and his imagination. History and culture intersect in Kushner's epic theatrical fusing of the past, current events, and his own vivid imaginings. Theater as a transformative force is in full evidence as Kushner proposes compassion, love, and a willingness to take the journey toward greater understanding as the only hope for redemption and salvation. The play, James Reston Jr. writes, is for "those who can see through the fog of patriotism to the finer distinctions, who are finally ready to ask how on earth do we get out of this godforsaken place, who can bear to contemplate the thought that we have participated to some extent in our own tragedy" (Reston 53). Kushner can bear to contemplate it and, at the same time, to ask the more generalized questions inherent in momentous changes. Is it possible for individuals to belong to and contribute to such moments? Can we only be defeated and silenced by the unstoppable sweep of history? Can we honestly face our own culpability or, as the play's Homebody wonders, are we "succumbing to luxury" (*Homebody/Kabul* 1). The play insists that there are consequences to everything—whether it be the Homebody's catalytic decision to go to Afghanistan or the choices made as part of American foreign policy.

A one-act version of *Homebody/Kabul* was originally staged at the small Chelsea Centre in London during the summer of 1999, a production examined in chapter six of this book. Since then, Kushner has expanded it into a three-and-a-half-hour, three-act drama extending beyond the hour-long monologue delivered by the Homebody, an otherwise unnamed woman, in the one-act version. Fascinated by the vast history of Afghanistan, the Homebody concludes her highly imaginative monologue as the play shifts from her comfortable London living room to various locations around the wounded city of Kabul. Milton Ceiling, a repressed middle-aged British computer specialist and the Homebody's husband, arrives in Kabul with their troubled grown daughter, Priscilla. They hope to either find the Homebody or claim her remains. Milton convinces himself that his wife has been killed—she has, after all, flaunted herself by wearing a Walkman to listen to Sinatra on the public streets—but Priscilla refuses to accept this scenario. Covered in a burka, she slips into the exotic and profoundly dangerous environs of Kabul under the Taliban.

In depicting the Taliban, Kushner exposes the frightening face of religious fanaticism, demonstrating his aversion to any brand of fundamentalism and its inherent intolerance. At the same time, he humanizes other Afghan characters trapped within the harsh oppression of the Taliban. Searching Kabul, Priscilla finds herself a guide, an old poet who shows her the world her mother has apparently embraced, a city, Kushner suggests, that may be cursed by the myth that the grave of Cain is there. The grave's purported location is now a Taliban minefield. Priscilla learns that her mother may be living in this tragic city as the wife of a well-to-do Muslim, a character who is never seen. His Afghan wife, Mahala, is seen, however,—and her rage is terrifying. A former librarian who, like the Homebody, loves language and books, she begs Priscilla to help her escape from Afghanistan. She is, she fears, forgetting the alphabet and seems to hover on the brink of madness as she spews her rage in various dialects. Priscilla, growing in wisdom as she continues her journey through Kabul's streets, ruefully notes that Mahala "isn't mad, she's fucking furious. It isn't at all the same" (Kushner, *Homebody/Kabul* 80), that a life of fear and oppression can only lead to total resignation or a fury that true survivors must have to fight on. Mahala's fiery confrontation with Priscilla is only one dramatic highlight in Kushner's Brechtian, episodically cinematic drama. Whether the Homebody is dead or alive is never confirmed, but this is not what interests Kushner. The collision of cultures, as the Homebody explains it, is what intrigues him: "Ours is a time of connection; the private, and we must accept this, and it's a hard thing to accept, the private is gone. All must be touched. All touch corrupts. All must be corrupted" (*Homebody/Kabul* 2).

The corrupting touch is immersion in another world, another life—a plunge into a culture at once alien, inviting, and frightening. Priscilla's yearning, desperate search is not only for her missing mother, but for comprehension and for the connection that the Homebody insists is necessary, both among nations and between people. As John Heilpern writes, the play is a "journey without maps to the ravaged, symbolic center of a fucked-up universe," a towering drama about:

> lost civilizations and unsolvable paradoxes, furious differences and opposites and disintegrating, rotting pidgin cultures. It's about desolation and love in landmined places, child murderers and fanatics, tranquilized existence and opium highs, travel in the largest sense of the word—travel of the mind and soul. To where? An unknowable mystery, perhaps, where all confusion is banished. (Heilpern)

Homebody/Kabul's haunting timeliness has impressed its first critics and audiences, but Kushner eschews the label of prophet. His mission is to incite in his audience an emotional, humanizing response to the harrowing moments of existence and survival, as well as to prod vigorous discussion of strategies for navigating the political, social, and intellectual minefields of our time. *Homebody/Kabul* is much more than a mere dramatic response to a horrifying moment in time; through the potency of metaphor Kushner explores the process of humanizing the "enemy" and redeeming ourselves. His metaphors are most effectively delivered through language; the Homebody basks in language, which is her only friend. Priscilla is comparatively inarticulate, rejecting the luxurious language that her mother uses to fill an otherwise empty life. Priscilla's Afghan guide, the old poet, writes what may be poetry or intelligence for the Northern Alliance in Esperanto, the universal language that Kushner describes as a language without cultural history—a blameless mode of expression by which to communicate without inherent cultural oppression and the burdens of history. Mahala's anger cannot be fully expressed, even through the range of dialects she employs to express her rage against the Taliban and the West, both of which, in her view, have visited much suffering on her country.

Critics generally applauded *Homebody/Kabul* in its initial New York run, which was extended twice from its originally scheduled four weeks, as the play improbably became the hottest ticket in New York next to the hit musical *The Producers*. Some critics found this elegiac work less effective because it lacked the white-hot rage that burnished Kushner's first great drama, *Angels in America*. Negative or mixed reviews quibbled about the play's politics or its length, suggesting that the Homebody's first-act monologue was superior to the two acts set in Kabul. Despite these few complaints, virtually all reviewers praised Kushner's mastery of language, imaginative theatricalism, thematic ambition, and prophetic insights. Michael Phillips, writing in *The Los Angeles Times*, called *Homebody/Kabul* an "uneven, often inspired play" (Phillips), while *The Boston Globe*'s Fred Kaplan effused about this "audacious play" (Kaplan). Comparing Kushner to Brecht, *The Nation*'s reviewer, Elizabeth Pochoda, quoted Brecht's dramatic advice: "Try to discover the best way for people to live together," wondering, "How many living dramatists other than Tony Kushner would know how to begin to do that?" (Pochoda). *Variety*'s Charles Isherwood stressed Kushner's ambition in writing a "Dense, thorny, eloquent, troubling and a little troublesome" play (Isherwood), while *The New York Time*'s Ben Brantley applauded "this lumbering yet compelling evening" that proved Kushner could "still deliver his sterling brand of goods: a fusion of politics, poetry and boundless empathy transformed through language into passionate, juicy theater" (Brantley). It is a work, Brantley notes, that expresses a love of the world despite its bloody tragedies, and that is "infused with that contradictory, impossible love, a reminder of how essential and heartening Mr. Kushner's voice remains" (Brantley). Nancy Franklin, writing in *The New Yorker*, lauded Kushner's "essentially political nature and his concomitant interest in history—his insistence on history, really" (Franklin), while *The New York Observer*'s John Heilpern simply proclaimed *Homebody/Kabul* "the most remarkable play in a decade—without doubt the most important of our time" (Heilpern).

Kushner's immediate future looks bright indeed. After its extended New York engagement, *Homebody/Kabul* moved to runs at both Trinity Repertory Theatre and Berkeley Repertory Theatre, with a production at London's Young Vic planned for late 2002, as well as publication of the script by the Theatre Communications Group. He continues to revise and polish his next epic drama, *Henry Box Brown*, for its anticipated first productions at the National Theatre of Great Britain and the New York Public Theatre. *Brandibar*, a children's book by Kushner, with illustrations by Maurice Sendak, will be published in 2002, a project that connects to Kushner's early children's plays discussed in this book's introduction. In March 2002, Kushner directed a New York Public Theatre staging of Ellen McLaughlin's play *Helen*, a comedy inspired by the legend of Helen of Troy, with a cast featuring Donna Murphy, Phylicia Rashad, and Marian Seldes. Under Mike Nichols's direction, a six-part HBO television miniseries version of *Angels in America* went before the cameras in April 2002, with a stellar cast led by Al Pacino, Meryl Streep, Emma Thompson, Mary Louise Parker, and Jeffrey Wright. Late 2002 is expected to bring the premiere of Kushner's *Caroline or Change* (examined in chapter seven) at New York's Public Theatre. With original music by Jeanine Tesori, this tale of a precocious little boy living in Louisiana at the time of John F. Kennedy's assassination and the Civil Rights movement sets some Kushner autobiography to music. He has also spoken of being at work on a new play about gay men and women, but has yet to offer further specifics on that project. International theaters and regional and repertory stages around the United

States continue to stage Kushner's earlier works, and he remains a sought-after lecturer on everything from his own drama to various political and gay issues.

Kushner's activism is firmly tied to his art—he believes that good politics can produce good aesthetics and, as always, he remains alert to the raw edges of contemporary life and those pressure points of history that relate to our current dilemmas. Perhaps most important, he respects his audience by challenging it. Speaking of *Homebody/Kabul*, Kushner explains that no audience member goes to a play about Afghanistan expecting an easy night. He counts on, he says, "an audience really wanting to ask a lot of questions and be asked to do a certain amount of thinking" (Peyser). In *Homebody/Kabul*, Kushner raises questions about love, war, guilt, family dysfunction, and the complex maze of history viewed through rich language, metaphor, intimate exploration of character, and politics. He reveals much about the compelling questions of the present moment and the lessons of the past, but he also underscores the needs of his audience, as he explained in a recent interview:

> I think that people do go to art in general as a way of addressing very deep, very intimate, very mercurial and elusive, ineffable things in a communal setting. It ends a certain kind of inner loneliness. Or it joins one's own loneliness with the inner loneliness of many other people. And I think that that can be healing. (Barrett)

Kushner, the dramatic healer, will certainly continue his distinctly individual dramatic journey by continuing to ask the great, unanswerable questions and to imagine fantastic worlds as he provides his audience with strategies for living past old hopes and creating new ones.

James Fisher
April 2002

Introduction

The Feathers and the Mirrors and the Smoke

> Art is necessary in order that man should be able to recognize and challenge
> the world. But art is also necessary by virtue of the magic inherent in it.
> —Ernst Fischer (14)

Tony Kushner's sudden and conspicuous arrival on the international stage in the early 1990s was as surprising and jolting as the abrupt celestial appearance at the end of *Millennium Approaches*, the first of Kushner's two *Angels in America* plays. Together, these plays comprise a theatrical epic that critics compared favorably to the greatest plays of the twentieth century. In an era of increasing devaluation of the arts—and of the theater in particular—Kushner's self-described "gay fantasia on national themes" moved international audiences, generated controversy, and inspired activists and artists.

Kushner's apparently sudden prominence was not so sudden. He was established in regional theaters as a director, adaptor, and dramatist throughout the United States and England since the mid-1980s. *Angels* represented a remarkable culmination for a playwright laboring to develop a way of presenting political drama on American stages in the late twentieth century. Kushner writes that "since it's true that everything is political (though not exclusively so) it becomes meaningless to talk about political and nonpolitical theatre, and more useful to speak of a theatre that presents the world as it is, an interwoven web of the public and the private" ("Notes About Political Theatre" 22). Imagining a political theater is difficult, Kushner believes, because the theater is "a world that's many things but has always been tainted, tawdry, and superfluous. It's very important not to devalue the tainted, the tawdry, and the superfluous and indeed, the essential tackiness and falseness of the theatre is its greatest aesthetic asset and political strength" ("Notes About Political Theatre" 25). The theater, he believes, presents the sole realm in contemporary life where it is possible to explore the fact

1

that things are not always what they seem to be; that the unpredictability and vibrancy of actual human presence contains an inimitable power and a subversive potential; that there is an impurity, a fluidity at the core of existence—these secrets speak to the liberationist, revolutionary agenda of our day. I continue to believe in this usefulness, and the effectiveness, of this increasingly marginalized profession and art. But I believe that for theatre, as for anything in life, its hope for survival rests in its ability to take a reading of the times, and change. ("Notes About Political Theatre" 34)

Angels in America examined these intangible but essential aspects of existence and, as a result, emerged as that rarest of theatrical ventures—a must-see event capturing many of the central issues of its time. It introduced a bold new theatricality to the American stage, as well as demonstrating a bracing intellectualism, lyricism, seriousness (tempered with the outrageously hilarious), and political activism. The tensions between popular mainstream theater and a drama of high purpose (a division that Kushner calls "invidious" [Vorlicky 64]) blends together in *Angels*, as well as in the rest of Kushner's dramatic work, in unique ways, and he recognizes the importance of the blending of art and the wonderment of the stage:

The theater always has to function as popular entertainment. Or at least the theater that I do, because I don't have the talent for doing anything else, I think . . . it has to have the jokes and it has to have the feathers and the mirrors and the smoke. (Vorlicky 63)

The feathers and the mirrors and the smoke, as well as the dynamic seriousness of *Angels*, thrust Kushner into the theatrical forefront, inviting comparison with earlier titans of American drama from Eugene O'Neill, Clifford Odets, and Thornton Wilder to Tennessee Williams and Edward Albee, while also making him a highly visible political and social activist both within the theater and outside its usual borders.

Comprised of two long plays, *Millennium Approaches* and *Perestroika*, *Angels* encompasses a complex and emotionally charged portrait of life in the United States in the midst of Ronald Reagan's presidency. Kushner presents this America as a place where present, past, and future intersect in a blur of reality, fantasy, and guardedly hopeful imagination. Written by Kushner during a time in which he despaired about America's sharp swing to the political right and its homophobic response to the mounting devastations of the AIDS crisis, *Angels* presents the mid-1980s as a critical transitional period in the history of the nation in which complicated questions about the future of American society are raised.

In *Angels*, as in most of his other plays, Kushner raises hard questions about morality in a diverse nation increasingly conflicted over moral, political, sexual, and spiritual views and values. Can we reckon with the past and constructively embrace the inevitability of change as we move into the future? Is America rushing headlong toward apocalypse or, despite failures and betrayals of its ideals, is it bound for a bright tomorrow? Kushner asks these questions through what has become his trademark mix of the hilarious and the tragic; his view is frequently dark, even frightening, but there is always a redeeming—and hard won—sense of hope. He is a cautious and questioning optimist, aware that there are no easy answers or completely happy endings, but always noting the possibility for change and progress. Examining individuals at moments of significant personal crisis (influenced, to a great extent, by societal conditions and the specters of the past and the future), Kushner probes the national conscience in ways that not only show him to be the equal of his dramatic predecessors and peers on the American stage, but also demonstrate his singularity in creating profoundly emotional and intellectually charged encounters with history, politics, and the personal.

In *Angels*—and in Kushner's lesser-known but equally challenging dramas—disparate, frequently self-contradictory characters are caught up in tragic personal situations that coincide with periods of significant social change. Their self-contradictions and the conflicts among the characters who, in Kushner's plays, always represent a mixed bag of classes, races, cultural backgrounds, and ideological principles, are explored in the plays. Kushner closely examines the contrasts and parallels between the characters and vividly establishes issues to debate on both the personal and universal levels. Like George Bernard Shaw and Bertolt Brecht, Kushner uses the stage as a platform for social, political, and religious argument, but in ways that neither Shaw nor Brecht, nor any other American dramatist, has. In Kushner's plays ideological debate emerges from a composite of rhetorical rationality, literary and cultural imagery drawn from the dogmas of the past, and wildly imaginative fantasy to unfold the complex crosscurrents of history. Of history, Kushner acknowledges having "a kind of dangerously romantic reading of American history. I do think there is an advantage to not being burdened by history the way Europe is. This country has been, in a way, an improvisation of hastily assembled groups that certainly have never been together before and certainly have a lot of trouble being together" (Szentgyorgyi 19). It is, he believes, a "mongrel" nation made up of "the garbage, the human garbage that capitalism created: the prisoners and criminals and religiously persecuted and the oppressed and the slaves that were generated by the ravages of early capital" (Szentgyorgyi 19). Within the tensions inherent in these relationships, Kushner finds the pressure points of his drama:

> There are moments in history when the fabric of everyday life unravels, and there is this unstable dynamism that allows for incredible social change in short periods of time. People and the world they're living in can be utterly transformed, either for the good or for the bad, or some mixture of the two. I think that Russia in 1917 was one of the times, Chile under Allende was one of those times. It's a moment when the ground and the sky sort of split apart, and there's a space, a revolutionary space. During these sorts of periods all sorts of people— even people who are passive under the pressure of everyday life in capitalist society—are touched by the spirit of revolution and behave in extraordinary ways. (Szentgyorgyi 16)

Kushner found such a moment for *Angels* in the rise of the "new conservatism" of the late twentieth century. Kushner seeks out similar historical moments in all of his plays, finding them in the premodern rise of capitalism in the late seventeenth century in *Hydriotaphia, or The Death of Dr. Browne*, in the collision of the old world shtetls of Eastern Europe and the new technologies of the modern world in his adaptation of the Yiddish theater classic *A Dybbuk*, in the Nazi Party's seizure of power in 1930s Germany in *A Bright Room Called Day*, in the American Deep South of the 1960s in *Caroline, or Change*, in the collapse of the Soviet Union in *Slavs!*, and in the struggles for survival in the decaying American infrastructures of the late twentieth century in *Grim(m)*.

Kushner's seemingly inexhaustible imagination, informed and fueled by a breathtakingly wide range of literary, cultural, historical, and religious sources, establishes his uniqueness within the traditions of U.S. drama. He is perhaps more successful than any of his predecessors or contemporaries in melding together an aesthetic drawn from aspects of postnaturalistic European theater, with elements of the traditions of America's lyrical dramatic realism. Influences from literature, art, and thought of the ancient world on through to the Renaissance blend together in Kushner's work, along with socialist politics inspired by Karl Marx and Leon Trotsky. In literary and dramatic terms, these political influences derive from Kushner's reading of Walter Benjamin and Brecht, his most important dramatic inspiration. Kushner's study of the great religions, from Christianity and Judaism (his own faith) to a variety of eastern religions, mingles with his love of a broad range of modern and postmodern literary influences including writers from the classical realm to nineteenth-century German classicism: poets ranging from Rilke to Stanley Kunitz; French Renaissance to Yiddish theater; modern dramatists from Brecht, O'Neill, and Williams to such contemporaries as John Guare, Richard Foreman, Maria Irene Fornes, Charles Ludlam, Robert Patrick, Harvey Fierstein, Larry Kramer, Terrence McNally, Suzan-Lori Parks, Paula Vogel, Connie Congdon, Mac Wellman, Ellen McLaughlin, Holly Hughes, David Greenspan, and their British counterparts like Edward Bond, Caryl Churchill, David Edgar, Howard Brenton, and David Hare, among others—all of whom Kushner refers to as part of "a kind of a weird little sort of tarnished golden age" (Vorlicky 210) of late-twentieth-century drama. From Williams to Hare, modern playwrights have attempted to find expressive ways to bring the fantasies and images of the historical past together with the real or imagined earlier lives of their characters, but few have done it with the dramatic potency, humor, and scope Kushner brings to the task.

An understanding of Kushner's political beliefs is essential to fully understanding his drama, as his socialist politics are never far from the surface. Although most critics and audiences think of Kushner almost solely as a "gay dramatist," it is truly the case that he is a "political dramatist" who happens to be gay. Kushner calls for a new brand of socialism that might better be labeled progressivism, a politics that he has called a "socialism of the skin," and one that honors the values and traditions of the past without a slavish adherence to belief systems whose traditions have excluded or oppressed diversity in culture, sexual orientation, and politics. For Kushner, socialism is about beginning to struggle in a really, really powerful way with why economic justice and equality are so incredibly uncomfortable for us, and why we still define our worth by how much money we individually can make at the expense of other people, and why we find sharing and collective enterprise and motivations that are not competitive so phenomenally difficult. It's a tremendously difficult struggle that one has to undertake. It has to do with unlearning privilege; it has to do with examining what sort of events and activities make you feel worthwhile as a human being. But I really believe that the world is doomed unless we can re-create ourselves as social beings as opposed to little ego-anarchists. (Vorlicky 70)

Kushner insists that unshakable dogmas of any variety are dangerous and that viewing the world solely in rational ways is potentially catastrophic. Rather, he believes it is through the unspoken, the unseen, and a faith in the hard progress built of compassion and humanism that society can proceed most effectively into the unknowable future. Imagination is the true source of revelation for Kushner, particularly an imagination informed by an exposure to the workings of history, and the ways in which history has been understood, distorted, and manipulated over the centuries. Kushner engages with history, reevaluates its evidence and its ruins, its theories and its dictums, and its human toll, with the aim of illuminating those overlooked and misunderstood elements which might offer a valuable lesson for moving forward. Kushner is convinced that

the only politics that can survive an encounter with this world, and still speak convincingly of freedom and justice and democracy, is a politics that can encompass both the harmonics and the dissonance. The frazzle, the rubbed raw, the unresolved, the fragile and the fiery and the dangerous. (*Thinking About the Longstanding Problems of Virtue and Happiness* 10–11)

As an American playwright, Kushner's overt political voice makes him a nearly unique figure. Few contemporary dramatists in the United States, whatever their personal politics, examine political issues, theories, and historical figures as Kushner does, although collectives like the San Francisco Mime Troupe and the Bread and Puppet Theater offer interesting parallels to Kushner (whose own early experiences as a director and writer were in collective-style theater groups).

Contemporary British writers Caryl Churchill and David Hare attempt, in their different ways, to mount a similar assault on the collisions of history and politics with the personal and, as such, are obvious contemporaries of Kushner, although both British writers work on a smaller dramatic canvas. And despite the fact that there is little similarity in the theatrical styles employed, the work of Nobel Prize–winning playwright and commedia dell'arte–inspired actor Dario Fo is connected to Kushner in that both draw their themes from left-wing politics and both have chosen, in their highly individual ways, to provide a voice for the oppressed and marginalized. Like Fo, Kushner tends toward inclusiveness in both his personal politics and in his art, and this extends even into the ways in which he makes plays. Kushner's plays borrow aspects of expressionism, Brechtian epic theater, realism/naturalism, fantasy, poetic drama, a rich brand of popular culture theatricalism, and a historical, linguistic, and universal thematic scope belonging more to classical and Renaissance dramatic traditions than to much of the theater of the twentieth century.

Much has been written about the importance of Brecht to Kushner's work: Kushner himself has frequently acknowledged the significance of Brecht to his evolution as a writer and theater artist. Reading Brecht's theories and plays "was a kind of revelation to me" (Weber 68), he recalls, and offered the first evidence that led him to believe

> that people who are seriously committed political intellectuals could have a home in the theater, the first time I believed that theater, really good theater, had the potential for radical intervention, for effectual analysis. The things that were exciting me about Marx, specifically dialectics, I discovered in Brecht, in a wonderful witty and provocative form. I became very, very excited about doing theater as a result of reading Brecht. (Weber 68)

As he began to write plays himself in the early 1980s, Kushner was profoundly influenced by Brecht's techniques, as well as the content of his plays. It might reasonably be expected that Kushner would be viewed as a logical heir to those few American dramatists with a political identity (Clifford Odets, Arthur Miller), but Kushner seems instead to descend directly from Ibsen, Shaw, and especially Brecht, believing deeply that "all theater is political" (Blanchard 42).

Kushner's political awakening had begun during his college days after reading Ernst Fischer's *The Necessity of Art. A Marxist Approach*, as well as the writings of Walter Benjamin, especially *Understanding Brecht*. From these writings, and from Brecht's plays themselves, Kushner gained a sense of the social responsibility of the artist. However, Kushner's initial response to Fischer was "incredibly angry, because I thought it was Stalinist and dangerous" (Vorlicky 247). Fischer, an Austrian who joined the Communist Party in 1934, was once described by Kenneth Tynan as the Aristotle of Marxism, and in *The Necessity of Art* he explores not only the nature of art, but the reasons it is needed by society. Fischer seems to be describing the impact of *Angels* while setting out Kushner's raison d'être when he writes:

> In the alienated world in which we live, social reality must be presented in an arresting way, in a new light, through the "alienation" of the subject and the characters. The work of art must grip the audience not through passive identification but through an appeal to reason which demands action and decision. (Fischer 10)

Fischer points out that even "a great didactic artist like Brecht does not act purely through reason and argument, but also through feeling and suggestion," with the goal of "*enlightening* and *stimulating action*" (Fischer 14). Kushner has obviously drawn on Fischer's concept of art and its purposes, and on Benjamin's conception of history. Kushner explains that his initial anger in response to Fischer's ideas led him to look at other works about art and Marxism, a choice that led him directly to Brecht and Benjamin. Widely regarded as the outstanding German literary critic of the twentieth century, Benjamin was described by Hannah Arendt as "the most peculiar Marxist" of his time, "whose spiritual existence had been formed and informed by Goethe," but who found in Brecht "a poet of rare intellectual powers and, almost as important for him at the time, someone on the Left who, despite all talk about dialectics, was no more of a dialectical thinker than he was, but whose intelligence was uncommonly close to reality" (Benjamin 11–15). Kushner shares these characteristics with Benjamin, and in Benjamin's essay, "Theses on the Philosophy of History," Kushner finds some grounding for his approach to historical drama. As Benjamin writes:

> There is no document of civilization which is not at the same time a document of barbarism. And just as such a document is not free of barbarism, barbarism taints also the manner in which it was transmitted from one owner to another. A historical materialist therefore dissociates himself from it as far as possible. He regards it as his task to brush history against the grain. (256–57)

This brushing against the grain of history is a guiding notion in those instances in which Kushner dramatizes actual events and characters, from the life and death of seventeenth-century writer and physician Sir Thomas Browne in *Hydriotaphia* to mid-twentieth-century political operative and ultraconservative lawyer Roy Cohn in *Angels*. It is perhaps too simple to suggest that Kushner's drama provides an alternative history—certainly with Cohn, his depiction seems not to depart very far from the realities of Cohn's life even as he fictionalizes specific events. Instead, Kushner probes into the unexplored corners of the historical figure and situation. He skews the angle of the life to crisis moments (the day of Browne's death or the moment at which Cohn learns that he has AIDS) and from this tilt, fresh visions of the history spill out.

Kushner—who for a time considered a career as a teacher of the literature and history of the Middle Ages—shares Benjamin's belief that history (social, political, and personal) teaches profound lessons and he understands that the concepts of apocalypse and the afterlife are fraught with the same struggles, confusions, and pain encountered in real life. Kushner is inspired by Benjamin's assertion that, as he describes it, one is "constantly looking back at the rubble of history. The most dangerous thing is to become set upon some notion of the future that isn't rooted in the bleakest, most terrifying idea of what's piled up behind you" (Savran 300). While Kushner looks to the past to help frame eternal questions about existence, he does not propose to simply recommit to old values. For Kushner, American society is in an age of intellectual stagnation and profound political and social crisis, but he views the greatest threats as internal—a moral emptiness stemming from what he views as a fundamental abandonment of commitment to justice, compassion, love, and mercy that is a requirement for moral survival in his universe.

There is little doubt that ideas from Benjamin's *Understanding Brecht* and other essays on art, theater and film, and literature permeate Kushner's work as a dramatist. "Theses on the Philosophy of History" not only provides central imagery for *Angels*, but it, along with Brecht's writings, illuminates all of Kushner's plays thus far. Kushner has also spoken of feeling intimidated by

Brecht's dramatic achievement, that if he could not write a play equal to *Mother Courage and Her Children,* he did not want to write at all. However, while reading Shakespeare and Brecht at the same time, he found a dialectical method in the structure of the historical plays of these two vastly different dramatists and strove, at the beginning of his playwriting career, to emulate the lyricism and scope of Shakespeare while, at the same time, drawing on the epic qualities of Brecht. Even as a graduate student, Kushner wrote a couple of things that were heavily influenced by Brecht. Seeking an image of a politicized artist who successfully merged art and politics, Kushner found that Brecht offered "a really brilliant marriage of Marxist theory as theater practice" (Vorlicky 248). Brecht, who believed that "if we want a truly popular literature [and here, in regard to Kushner, one might interject theater], alive and fighting, completely gripped by reality and completely gripping reality, then we must keep pace with reality's headlong development" (Brecht 112), seems to imagine a Kushner carrying a Marx-inspired battle against oppression into the future.

Kushner's Brechtian style took fuller shape in his first two important plays, *A Bright Room Called Day* and *Hydriotaphia,* and flowered fully in *Angels* and in his own adaptation of Brecht's *The Good Person of Setzuan.* Kushner, however, has adapted Brecht's methods to suit his own particular voice, embellishing the method with his own devices. Kushner's major plays adopt a structure that is at once both cinematic (he has said that Robert Altman's 1974 epic film *Nashville* provided structural ideas for *Angels*) and Brechtian, but he couples the alienation techniques of Brecht with a fully realized emotional and personal strain drawn more from American lyrical realism than from Brecht (whose character's emotional struggles are often downplayed in his effort to keep the audience focused on the issues). These techniques combine with an often outrageous sense of humor (again, far bolder than the typical dry Brechtian ironies, owing much to Kushner's queering of his subjects), and a phantasmagoric theatricality (extending well beyond anything Brecht contemplated) to offer a completely original brand of American political theater. Much of this originality is already evident in Kushner's earliest plays, but it comes to full fruition between the writing of his first important play, the overtly Brechtian *A Bright Room Called Day,* and his masterfully original *Angels.*

As previously noted, the political dramatist is a comparative rarity in the American theater. Kushner's predecessors with political aims, including Odets and Miller, seem to have had little direct influence on Kushner, although he directed a production of Odets's *Golden Boy* at the Repertory Theatre of St. Louis in 1986. The profound influence of European politics, literature, and theater on Kushner is important, but he is, despite this, a quintessentially American figure. The stunning ambition (and length) of Kushner's plays calls to mind Eugene O'Neill, a dramatist whose life and work "excited and impressed" him, and, to a lesser extent, Wilder, but Kushner is closer in spirit to Tennessee Williams, "all-in-all my favorite playwright and probably all-in-all our greatest playwright" (Vorlicky 235).

Kushner also acknowledges some debt to contemporary gay dramatists like Larry Kramer and Harvey Fierstein, but they are less significant to Kushner's development as a dramatist than Williams. There are obvious similarities between Williams and Kushner in the lyricism of both writers and in the sexual identities that inform their work. Perhaps more significantly, Kushner and Williams present views of a changing sociopolitical environment—their characters are generally caught between two worlds: one that is dying and one that is being born. The friction of such transitions—and the attempt to survive in the confusing netherworld created by them—amplifies the emotions and struggles of their characters.

Of his predecessor, Kushner has said, "I've always loved Williams. The first time I read *Streetcar*, I was annihilated. I read as much Williams as I could get my hands on until the late plays started getting embarrassingly bad.... I'm really influenced by Williams" (Savran 297). Kushner is also drawn to the seriocomic plays of John Guare, who, like Williams, "has figured out a way for Americans to do a kind of stage poetry. He's discovered a lyrical voice that doesn't sound horrendously twee and forced and phony" (Savran 297). Kushner aims for a similar sort of lyricism in *Angels*, both in language and in theme, weaving a tapestry of the crushing human and spiritual issues of the Reagan era—and beyond—with poignance (in the Williams and Guare senses) and epic stature (in both the differing O'Neillian and Brechtian senses). Kushner's less familiar but no less effective other plays, both full-length and one-act, are similar to *Angels* in this regard. Williams's passion for illusion, in his appreciation of the fragility of beauty and in the profound heartbreak of his most memorable characters, is certainly evident in Kushner's work. Prior Walter (who gets his name from Walter Benjamin) of *Angels* is a logical heir to Williams's delicate souls and Kushner, who gives Prior a famous Williams line to repeat in *Perestroika*, the second of the *Angels* plays, makes certain that the connection will not be missed—even if Prior turns out, despite his gentleness, to be a survivor, while Williams's Blanche DuBois cannot cope. The influence of Williams on Kushner could hardly be overlooked in the illusory and lyrical aspects of Kushner's work, as critic John Lahr writes:

> Not since Williams has a playwright announced his poetic vision with such authority on the Broadway stage. Kushner is the heir apparent to Williams' romantic theatrical heritage: he, too, has tricks in his pocket and things up his sleeve, and he gives the audience "truth in the pleasant disguise of illusion." And, also like Williams, Kushner has forged an original, impressionistic theatrical vocabulary to show us the heart of a new age. ("Earth Angels" 133)

An important connection between Kushner and Williams also lies in their homosexuality. Williams, who was guardedly open about his sexuality from the 1960s until his death, and featured gay characters in his drama from nearly the beginning of his playwriting career, could not be as "out" as Kushner can be. Still, a gay sensibility fuels the work of both writers. One of the great ironies of the success of *Angels* (and, for that matter, the plays of Williams) has been the enormous mainstream audience that has embraced it despite the fact that its politics, moral universe, and sexuality are, at least as measured by many of those elected to public office in the United States, incompatible with the beliefs of

American society. It is perhaps in this irony that some of the questions that both Williams and Kushner explore meet: "What is the relationship between sexuality and power? Is sexuality merely an expression of power? Is there even such a thing as 'sexuality'?" (Savran 308).

As is true for Williams, not all—or even most—of Kushner's plays are *about* homosexuality. Even *Angels*, a play widely regarded as a milestone in gay drama—and in the movement for gay rights and the war against AIDS—is not simply a gay play. It is about many facets of American life, of which sexuality and homophobia are traditionally, and certainly currently, divisive issues. Gay characters are usually present in Kushner's other plays, but often in secondary roles. However, regardless of the significance of a given character, sexuality informs Kushner's work, much as it does Williams's. If Williams can be said to sexualize American drama, Kushner queers it and the historical events he examines.

Kushner came of age in an era of dizzying changes in the American cultural landscape. Following some abortive efforts to find a "cure" for his sexual orientation, Kushner came to terms with his homosexuality and was inspired by gay activist writers and artists like Williams, and, even more so by those emerging from the Stonewall generation and after. Kushner's identity as a gay man not only led to the dramatic work for which he is most known, but has permeated all of his dramatic work and an increasing commitment to social activism, from a variety of leftist political issues to gay rights and AIDS to the role of controversial art in a society. Kushner was especially inspired by such gay rights organizations as ACT UP and Queer Nation, whose chant "We're here, we're queer, we're fabulous" pervades his drama, especially *Angels*. The social and political battles of the last four decades of the twentieth century are as important to understanding Kushner as are his literary and theatrical influences.

Kushner's reverence for great dramatic works of the past, many of which examine questions of religious faith in conflict with social reality, the complexities of politics, and the meeting of past and present, is important. As a gay man, Kushner also acknowledges some debt to pioneering gay dramatists Robert Patrick, Kramer, and Fierstein, as well as their logical predecessor, Williams, who dealt more frankly with this topic in later dramas—*Cat on a Hot Tin Roof* (1955), *Suddenly Last Summer* (1958), *Small Craft Warnings* (1972), *Something Cloudy, Something Clear* (1981), and *The Notebook of Trigorin* (1981). Williams paved the way for other gay dramatists to delve into gender matters with greater purpose, as with the outrageous camp sensibilities of Charles Ludlam and Charles Busch or in the politicized dramas of Kramer—and, ultimately, Kushner's plays. Kushner recognizes that Williams, with lyricism and compassion, brought sexuality out of the American theatrical closet.

Kushner's political activism is of central importance to an understanding of his work. It is also important to appreciate that he is both unmistakably American and strongly connected to his Eastern European roots and its cultural masterworks. As a Jew, Kushner is part of an ethnic heritage that has experienced harrowing losses—and has survived. He identifies parallels between the Jewish experience and what gays have contended with in American society. Kushner struggles with an ambivalence toward Judaism due to homophobic traditions within his faith. However, for him, the connections between Jews and homosexuals are most important in that he believes both groups have a shared a history of "oppression and persecution" that offers "a sort of false possibility of a kind of an assimilation" (Vorlicky 278). Kushner insists that "as Hannah Arendt says, it's better to be a pariah than a parvenu. If you're hated by a social order, don't try and make friends with it. Identify yourself as other, and identify your determining characteristics as those characteristics which make you other and unliked and despised" (Vorlicky 218).

Kushner began his dramatic career in earnest as the terrifying devastation of AIDS became all too clear, and it is against this background that Kushner emerged as a playwright and director. However, to see Kushner solely as a gay dramatist—either in *Angels* or Kushner's "queering" of history in other works— is far too limiting for a writer whose work is diverse in its subjects and characters. Other influences on him are at least as significant. Some of these can be seen in *Angels*, but they come into sharper relief in his lesser-known works written and produced both before and after the *Angels* phenomenon.

There is a sense of classical fatality in Kushner's plays, but there is also an unmistakable Ibsenite element—the idea that humanity may be proceeding on the wrong moral road and that the souls of the past and future will exact retribution. Kushner believes that tragedy—both real and fictional—teaches and changes people, a sentiment he shares with many modern dramatists and, in America, especially with the generation of post–World War II playwrights. American dramatists also supplied Kushner with a strong sense of the personal in drama. In bringing his own autobiography on to the stage, Kushner emphasizes that life is loss: "You can't conquer loss. You lose. To suggest otherwise would be to suggest a fantasy. . . . Life is about losing. Things are taken from you. People are taken from you. You just have to face it" (Pacheco 17). As a gay man, a Jew, and a political leftist, Kushner strives to express a capacity for forgiveness in the human spirit, but adds that the losses suffered by the groups of which he is a part make a forgiving spirit difficult. As he says, "Loss and forgiveness go hand in hand, and it's tricky" (Vorlicky 63).

If Williams provides Kushner with a powerful model of a dramatist struggling with issues of loss and forgiveness, other American dramatists offer different sorts of inspiration. Miller's plays share the Ibsenite moral quandaries, but Kushner professes not to admire much of Miller's drama except, grudgingly, the raw force of *Death of a Salesman*, despite his feeling that it is "melodramatic, and it has that awful, fifties kind of Herman Wouk-ish sexual morality that's disgusting and irritating" (Savran 296). However, at least on one level Kushner shares some thematic turf with Miller in questioning America's embracing of commerce—the relentless selling of a product, an image, or an idea as the measure of success—and that, for better or worse, this has been, and will likely continue to be, the driving aspect of the American national persona.

Like *Death of a Salesman* and its contemporary counterparts in David Mamet's *American Buffalo* and *Glengarry Glen Ross*, *Angels* sees the selling of America more in terms of a selling out—of the abandonment of principle, of the loss of compassion for the less fortunate, of a failure to believe in the fundamental connectedness of all members of humanity, despite the vast racial, ethnic, religious, and cultural diversity. Miller and Mamet both focus on the white heterosexual male as the center of society, while Kushner reflects the ever-changing American demographic, expanding it to include the full spectrum of American society. Miller's drama was born out of the crucible of the social struggles of the turbulent 1930s, an era in which America came closest to a socialist society and, as such, an era of significance to Kushner. However, Kushner's own formative era coincided with the turbulent late 1960s and early 1970s. The internalized moral battles of Miller's age, which exploded in the early 1950s during the witch hunts of the House Un-American Activities Committee, surely seem too constricting—even too narrow—for Kushner, an artist inspired to examine diverse issues on a broader and bolder level.

Angels, of course, provided Kushner with numerous awards and a fame usually unavailable to working American dramatists during the last half of the twentieth century. It also made him a leading spokesperson for gay rights and leftist politics in a contentious era for both. *Angels*, which has elicited both enthusiasm and controversy in productions around the world, is, at the very least, a defiant indictment of the hypocrisy of the American moral compass. Regarding politics, it is ironic that Kushner is perhaps the best-known dramatist of his generation in the United States as the result of representing viewpoints seemingly incompatible with a post-Reagan neoconservative age. Understanding Kushner's dramatic output, his conceptions of stage technique, his views of politics, religion, sexuality, and much else, may offer some insights into not only the drama of the past century, but also into the complex contradictions of American life at the dawn of a new millennium.

Much about Kushner's theatrical achievement, as well as his social and political beliefs, can be found in *Angels*. However, despite its remarkable impact, *Angels* is only a part of the rich and impressively diverse dramatic output of a still youthful playwright. The twentieth-century American theater has produced only a few plays equal to *Angels: Long Day's Journey into Night, Our Town, A Streetcar Named Desire, Death of a Salesman, A Raisin in the Sun,* and *Who's Afraid of Virginia Woolf?* It is perhaps too soon to imagine Kushner's ultimate influence on American drama—and society—for at least a couple of reasons. Certainly, there is much more to come from his pen. More significantly, American theater at the dawn of the twenty-first century seems to be moving in several different directions at once. While it is obvious that Kushner provides a boldly epic, highly theatrical, politically engaged, and richly emotive model as a true alternative to the minimalist, densely constructed, and small-scale plays of such other leading contemporary dramatists as Albee, Mamet, McNally, and Sam Shepard, there is little doubt that Kushner has been a revitalizing force in American drama during the last decade of the twentieth century. His influence on the development of the American theater may ultimately equal that of O'Neill or Williams. His drama daringly mixes fantasy and reality—as well as tragedy and comedy—to blend together elements of the past, present, and future of the world of his play, the lives of his characters, and the society in which he lives.

The Theater of Tony Kushner: Living Past Hope is the first study to examine Kushner's entire dramatic output thus far. The phenomenon of *Angels*, while catapulting Kushner to prominence, has, at times, somewhat obscured the rest of his work as a dramatist (in both the full-length and one-act forms), adaptor, screenwriter, and librettist. His plays, produced and unproduced, offer a more staggering range of themes and characters than even the titanic *Angels* can encompass. In his own plays and his free adaptations, Kushner examines the nature of love as understood through the prisms of diverse cultures from seventeenth-century France to the shtetls of Eastern Europe, the rise of capitalism at the dawn of the industrial age, issues of spirituality and religion, the moral dilemmas of the Holocaust, the collapse of the Soviet Union, environmental catastrophe, psychoanalysis, grassroots tax revolt, the experience of immigrants coming to the United States, the struggles of gays within a homophobic society, the nature of art, and the meanings of death and the afterlife.

This book will examine all of these plays in an attempt to shed some light on the techniques and themes of Kushner's work and his place in millennial American and international drama. In exploring the profound moral, social, religious, and political questions that will shape the future of the United States in the world community, Kushner's ambitious output extends well beyond the impressive *Angels*. Single chapters are devoted to each of his produced full-length plays (*A Bright Room Called Day, Hydriotaphia, or The Death of Dr. Browne, Angels in America,* and *Slavs! Thinking About the Longstanding Problems of Virtue and Happiness*). Other chapters will examine a number of his one-act plays and his numerous adaptations including *The Illusion* (from Pierre Corneille's *L'Illusion comique*), *Stella* (from Goethe's play), *St. Cecilia, or The Power of Music* (adapted from a story by Heinrich von Kleist), *A Dybbuk* (from S. Ansky's Yiddish theater classic, *The Dybbuk*), Brecht's *The Good Person of Setzuan,* and *Widows*, adapted in collaboration with Chilean novelist and political activist Ariel Dorfman. Kushner has also completed a number of unpublished and/or unproduced works that will be examined in this study, including the opera libretto *Caroline, or Change*, the screenplay *Grim(m)*, and a number of works-in-progress, including a three-play cycle on economic history, the first play of which, *Henry Box Brown, or The Mirror of Slavery*, is expected to debut at the Royal National Theatre of Great Britain. Attention will also be paid to Kushner's essays, poetry, and political activism.

The Theater of Tony Kushner: Living Past Hope draws its subtitle from part of a speech spoken by Prior Walter in *Perestroika*, the second of the *Angels* plays: "We live past hope" (136). This line, more than any other in Kushner's oeuvre, captures the intent of his drama: a belief that despite centuries of historical and personal tragedy, we must progressively face the inevitabilities of a future we cannot know while, at the same time, learning from an often tragic and destructive past we know only too well. Belief in progress, in compassion, in the transformative power of love, in true community is the religion Kushner offers for the new millennium.

The Great Work Begins: A Short Biography

> Tony Kushner is drunk on ideas, on language, on the possibility of changing
> the world. His talent and his heart are incendiary, combustible, explosive,
> heartbreakingly vital and on-target.
>
> —Larry Kramer (Roca 32)

Tony Kushner was born in New York City on July 16, 1956, the second of three
children of William and Sylvia (Deutscher) Kushner, both classically trained
musicians who encouraged their son's interests in art and literature (they even
named him after popular singer Tony Bennett as an added encouragement).
From his parents, "New York–New Deal liberals transplanted to the Deep South,"
he inherited "a healthy appetite for politics, for history, for political theory," a
hunger they, in turn, inherited from their parents, "all of us indebted to the insa-
tiable curiosity, skepticism, pessimistic optimism, ethical engagement, and
ardent pursuit of the millennium that is, for me, the most valuable heritage of
nearly two thousand years of Diasporan Judaic culture" ("Notes About Political
Theatre" 20).

Kushner spent most of his childhood in Lake Charles, Louisiana ("No one
asked me if I wanted to go," Kushner jokes [Szentgyorgyi 18]), where his mother,
a professional bassoonist, "one of the first American women to hold a principal
chair in a major orchestra (the New York City Opera orchestra at the age of
eighteen)" ("Notes About Political Theatre" 19), and an amateur actress, frequently performed in local plays, including *Death of a Salesman*, *The Diary of
Anne Frank*, and *A Far Country*. It was in Louisiana, in "the culture of 'genteel'
post-integration bayou-county racism" (*Thinking About the Longstanding Problems of Virtue and Happiness* 50), that Kushner became entranced by the emotional power of the theater and the arts in general—he would return to this
setting for a semiautobiographical libretto, *Caroline, or Change*, and other of his
works include similarly autobiographical strains most touchingly demonstrated
in the sad bassoon music he employs in some in honor of his mother's memory.
The stage, a place of "hysterical and historical conversion" ("Notes About
Political Theatre" 20), provided an appealing world for a child who knew, even at
an early age, that he was different: "I grew up very, very closeted, and I'm sure
that the disguise of theater, the doubleness, and all that slightly tawdry stuff
interested me" (Savran 293). As a child, he also acted occasionally in plays himself, but resisted the off-stage gay life of the theater which frightened him,
becoming instead a high school debater because, "I had decided at a very early
age that I would become heterosexual" (Savran 293). This painful struggle with
his true self continued into Kushner's twenties.

Kushner moved to New York in 1974 to begin his college education at
Columbia University, where he completed a Bachelor of Arts degree in English
Literature in 1978. During his time at Columbia, he immersed himself in the
New York theater scene, taking in as many Broadway shows as possible, as well as
more experimental works by Spalding Gray, Lee Breuer, JoAnne Akalaitis, and
especially Richard Schechner's production of *Mother Courage and Her Children*

("which I still think is the greatest play ever written") and Richard Foreman's staging of *The Threepenny Opera* ("which I saw about ninety-five times and which is one of my great theater experiences" [Savran 294]). Kushner's taste in theater began to mature, as did his "fairly standard liberal politics" (Savran 294) influenced by faculty and fellow students at Columbia, but more importantly through his growing interest in Brecht. He read Brecht's dramatic works, as well as his seminal essay, "A Short Organum for the Theater," along with Marx, Arnold Hauser, and Benjamin's *Understanding Brecht*. He was also drawn into study of medieval literature, including *Beowulf*, finding the "magic and the darkness of it very appealing" to his "fantastical, spiritual side" (Savran 295). His study of the classics included the Greeks and he found himself moved to realize that ancient plays by Aeschylus or Euripides did not seem at all primitive. Although he claims not to believe in fundamental universal truths, he discovered in reading ancient and medieval works that "there are certain human concerns" (Savran 295) that have always been part of the human experience.

In this period, Kushner grappled intensely with his sexual orientation, seeking therapy to find a so-called cure for his homosexuality, before facing it in various ways. One involved calling his mother from a New York City phone booth in September 1981 to tell her that he was gay, a scene he would powerfully recreate in *Angels*. In experiences recognized by many homosexuals, Kushner found himself struggling with his father's initial disapproval, though their battles eventually subsided as the senior Kushner accepted his son's orientation. Kushner himself came to embrace his sexuality and, as a dramatist, especially in the wake of *Angels*, became a prominent activist in the movement for gay and lesbian rights.

Following the completion of his degree at Columbia, Kushner worked as a switchboard operator at the United Nations Plaza Hotel beginning in 1979. During this period, he also directed small-scale theater productions of very big plays, ranging from stagings of Shakespeare's *The Tempest* and *A Midsummer Night's Dream* to Brecht's *The Baden-Baden Play for Learning*. Accepted to New York University's Tisch School of the Arts to pursue a Master of Fine Arts degree in directing, Kushner staged a short Brecht play as his audition for entrance into the program. At Tisch, he was trained under the guidance of Brecht specialist Carl Weber and aspired to follow the paths of such forerunning theatrical artists as Richard Foreman, Joanne Akalaitis, and Liz LeCompte, whose productions he found exceptional.

Kushner continued to work the switchboard to pay the rent, but in the summers he also worked at a school for gifted children in Louisiana, writing plays for them to perform and others which he produced with his fellow students at Tisch prior to completing his degree in directing in 1984. Some of these plays were also staged by the Imaginary Theatre Company at the Repertory Theatre of St. Louis and elsewhere. Kushner's plays from this period, beginning around 1982, demonstrate the breadth and virtuosity of his later playwriting, including a range of genres and styles, including an opera (*La Fin de la Baleine: An Opera for the Apocalypse* [1982]), some childrens' theater plays (*Historiomax* [1985], *Yes Yes No No* [1985], *The Protozoa Review* [1985], *The Heavenly Theatre: Hymns for*

Martyred Actors [1985], *In Great Eliza's Golden Time* [1986]), one-act and full-length plays (*The Age of Assassins* [1986], *Last Gasp at the Cataract* [1986], and *Hydriotaphia, or The Death of Dr. Browne* [1987]), and an adaptation (Goethe's *Stella* [1987]). They also demonstrate elements of his later works in their lyricism, thematic sweep, and bold theatricality. For example, one of his earliest works, the 1982 *La Fin de la Baleine: An Opera for the Apocalypse* (translated from the French, the title means *The End of the Whale*), a theater-dance piece, features a scene in which a woman with a tuba dances on point while spouting water from her mouth. Imagination, ambition, and political commitment were Kushner's most evident traits as a beginning dramatist.

Grief Pushes Outward: *Yes Yes No No*

> It might be argued that, perhaps,
> Civilization would collapse
> Without us feeling that we had
> Collectively done something bad.
> —Actor 1, *Yes Yes No No* (5.19)

An especially illuminating example of Kushner's early works is his children's play, *Yes Yes No No* (subtitled *The Solace of Solstice Apogee/Perigee Bestial/Celestial Holiday Show*), which demonstrates that even within the often debased form of children's theater, and even at the beginning of his work as a dramatist, Kushner's imaginative poetic gifts and thematic ambition are present and, to a great extent, fully formed. Directed and designed by Kushner for the Repertory Theatre of St. Louis's Imaginary Theatre Company, and performed in shopping malls and hospitals from December 2–21, 1985 (with a brief December 23–27, 1985 run on the Rep's main stage), *Yes Yes No No* features a cast of four women, played in the original production by Kari Eli, Maggie Lerian, Lisa Raziq, and Jeanne Trevor. The roles can also be played by an all-male cast merely by changing a few pronouns in the text, but in either case cast members each play numerous roles.

Set during the winter solstice (at "various places around the universe" [stage directions]), *Yes Yes No No* announces that it is no ordinary children's play as its prologue establishes a seriocomic tone, an actor-centered technique, and explores themes no less significant than the creation of the universe and the meaning of good and evil. Beginning with a typically Kushnerian question, a tape-recorded voice (God?) asks, "Is it not wonder?" (Prologue.1), as actors, playing shepherds and angels, ruminate on the beauty of the winter environment and remark that they are looking on

> The Face
> Of God, the Face
> Of Heaven, miracle face
> Of angels announcing in a language of Awe
> To a cold frightened hilltop
> Open vowels of . . . (Prologue.1)

At which point they are interrupted by a chorus of sheep "ooh-ooh"-ing "The First Noel." This abrupt mixture of the portentous and the comic is a Kushner trademark that, along with his characteristically poetic language, is in ample evidence in this imaginative trip through religious myth and science. In the play's first part, God and Space converse about the creation of the first atom, and God has an idea:

> It will be VERY small.
> It will be VERY light.
> It will be HARD TO SEE
> And HARD TO TOUCH.
> It will not be much but
> It will be Something. (1.4)

Space thanks God for the atom's creation, noting that

> This could be the start
> Of Something b-b-b-
> Big. (1.5)

In part 2, the actors reflect on the multiplication of atoms and gases fusing to create the universe, with Kushner implanting a little political theory, as when all four actors proclaim

> From grains of sand to giant stars all things share one condition.
> The world we see would never be except for OPPOSITION. (2.8)

The complications of the making of the universe—and the existence of the human lives created ("Life is confusing" [3.8])—reveal, to some extent, Kushner's own childhood confusions and struggles, as in some counterpoint speeches in part 3:

> Sometimes, when I am
> sad, I can't remember what
> it's like to be happy, and I
> think I'll never be happy
> again. (3.9)

> Sometimes when I am
> happy, I can't remember what
> it's like to be sad, and I
> think I'll never be sad again. (3.10)

Part 4 explores the "contrariness" inherent in existence, as the angels, who are "very very nice," share a feast at the Table of Elements with the devils, who "live in Hell" (4.13). When a devil and an angel get into a fight, the angel's wings are broken off. God intervenes with a way of reinventing this damaged angelic being:

> I
> Have an idea.

> I will name it
> Something new.
> I will call it
> Human. (4.14–15)

The devil, feeling guilty, wants to know how he might atone for his sin, but begs the Human not to take his "badness" which "is all I have" (4.15), so the Human instead takes his guilt:

> While the angel, who was now
> A human being, was left
> Feeling guilty,
> And so became more human
> Than before. (4.16)

In part 5, Kushner examines the nature of guilt and its relation to human affairs ("Even the President feels guilty" [5.17]), which allows his young audience to experience the ways they feel when mistakes and their differences cause disturbance. Responses to guilt, apologizing, praying, talking to an analyst, singing, and eating are tested and found wanting, so Kushner proposes that it is possible that civilization might end without a collective human feeling of guilt. Even Santa Claus, it is revealed, feels guilty sometimes. One of the actors tells a tale in which a group of Santas give up their joyful dancing in the snow because they are too fat. Feeling greatly depressed:

> They all ate like little piggies
> Faster than they could digest.
> Ate the puddings, pears and figgies;
> Then they didn't feel depressed! (5.20)

At least not for the moment, until they are overwhelmed by feelings of despair much worse than what they felt before: "Why won't it ever let me be?" (5.21). Part 6 explores the meaning of despair, as Devil-Tempters play on human guilt, with the result that their souls are "slamming shut" (6.22) and

> Grief pushes outward
> And down to
> A dreamless deep slumber,
> Heavy and hollow
> And endlessly sad. (6.22)

For the final scene, the actors play "a BUSH, a PERSON, and two RAVENS" (6.23) crying at the coming of the sad, cold, and lonely winter. Person pricks his finger on a thorn from the Bush, leading all to marvel at the beauty of the "drop of red" (7.25) blood that, they imagine, is like the berries that come with springtime. They all feel better that "winter doesn't last forever" (7.25) and understand, as one of the actors explains in a final speech, that the spring is impossible without the winter:

> Because this is a world that depends on FRICTION,
> The Yes and the No and the CONTRADICTION.
> The seed and the plant and the plant and the seed,
> And is it not a wonder
> Indeed? (7.27)

Yes Yes No No was described by Don Shewey, who served on a panel selecting plays for an anthology of children's plays, as "the maddest piece of kid-lit I'd read since Ionesco's story for toddlers in which all the characters are named Jacqueline" (Shewey 32). Certainly few children's plays would attempt to deal, however lightheartedly and lyrically, with the issues in *Yes Yes No No*. Kushner typically takes his audience—even the young one this play is aimed at—into the depths of despair and pain from which he finds, through a belief in the wonder of existence, the essential spinning forward of progress and a hope earned through suffering and difficulty.

Yes Yes No No and Kushner's other early works explore themes and dramatic techniques that would remain evident, if more masterfully employed, in his plays through the end of the twentieth century. Beginning in the mid-1980s, Kushner's work, both as a director and a playwright, and as the artistic director of the Heat & Light Company, a political theater group, brought him awards and the support of several prestigious grants, including the Seidman Award in Directing from the New York University Tisch School of the Arts in 1983–84, a Directing Fellowship from the National Endowment for the Arts in 1985, the Princess Grace Award in 1986, a Playwriting Fellowship from the New York State Council for the Arts in 1987, and a Fellowship from the National Endowment for the Arts in 1988.

Kushner became assistant director of the St. Louis Repertory Theatre in 1985–86, and in 1987–88 he became artistic director of the New York Theatre Workshop. For NYTW he staged early versions of *A Bright Room Called Day* and his Goethe adaptation, *Stella*, and, that same year, directed the first version of his play, *Hydriotaphia, or The Death of Dr. Browne*, for the Home for Contemporary Theatre and Art in New York. Kushner also worked as Director of Literary Services for the Theatre Communications Group during 1989 and regularly taught at an array of universities, ultimately joining the permanent faculty of the Tisch School in 1996. However, Kushner's efforts as a director and teacher were superseded by his writing, adapting, and political activism in the late 1980s. Along with his own plays and adaptations, Kushner exercised his writing skills in a variety of ways, including contributing a narration to replace Paul Green's original text of *Johnny Johnson* to accompany Kurt Weill's music in a concert performance of the piece performed by Larry Kert on a program called *Voices of Change. American Music of Protest, Politics and Persuasion* in September 1989. This breadth of activity suggests that in all aspects of his work—even from its beginnings—Kushner merged politics, literature, and music, as would be amply evident in all of his dramatic work.

In this period, Kushner lost his mother to cancer and he completed and produced his first important plays. It is at this point that *The Theater of Tony Kushner: Living Past Hope* begins, with the goal of serving as an introduction to

Kushner's complete dramatic works to date and placing them beside the extraordinarily acclaimed *Angels*. Some of these works feature themes Kushner explored in *Angels*, while others move in different directions, both thematically and dramaturgically. Setting *Angels* within the context of Kushner's entire output as a working dramatic artist during an era of new energy, broader ethnic and gender diversity, and conspicuous theatricality on American stages will hopefully deepen understanding and appreciation of his dramatic journey to, as critic John Lahr describes it, "that most beautiful, divided, and unexplored country—the human heart" ("Angels on Broadway" 137).

CHAPTER ONE

Past Heaven, Through the Earth, to Hell

A Bright Room Called Day

> As Walter Benjamin wrote, you have to be constantly looking back at the
> rubble of history. The most dangerous thing is to become set upon some
> notion of the future that isn't rooted in the bleakest, most terrifying idea of
> what's piled up behind you.
>
> —Tony Kushner (Savran 300)

Kushner severely tests his faith in hope in *A Bright Room Called Day*, a dark,
despairing work illuminating issues of political engagement (past and present),
survival, and fear in an era of great social evil—in this case, the rise of Adolf
Hitler. Kushner presents this period of time as an unstoppable wave of political
upheaval and sets the political upheavals against the life of a lone woman unable
to cope with a social madness she can barely comprehend. Employing an epic
structure and expanded by Kushner's abundant theatricality, lyricism, and, as
Harold Bloom writes, "authentic gift for fantasy" (109), Kushner's play leaps
into the darkest of dark nights, an era he described in 1991 as like few others in
history. Written at a point in American history—the height of Ronald Reagan's
presidency—that he considered as bleak as the early days of the Nazi regime in
Germany, *Bright Room* highlights Germany in 1933 and America in 1985 in
ways that generated considerable controversy and critical division when the
play was performed.

In his published afterword to *Bright Room*, Kushner agrees with some critics
of the play that it is "immature," particularly in its invitation for an audience "to
consider comparisons between Ronald Reagan and Adolf Hitler" (172), but to
Kushner, "Leaders like Reagan and Bush are essentially as morally debased as the
people who followed Hitler" (Szentgyorgyi 15). This most Brechtian of Kushner's
plays "is supposed to be about morbidity and mysticism in the face of political
evil, [but] is actually to an extent a manifestation of the kind of reaction it seeks
to describe" (180). Kushner stresses that *Bright Room's* bold collision of past and
present—the aspect of the play most frequently criticized by critics—is intended

as a warning signal, not a prediction, but I often ask myself: Is it politically effective? Will it galvanize an audience to act or, less ambitiously, will it make an audience think, argue, examine the present through the example of the past? Or will it merely confirm and voice for them what they may already suspect: that something unstoppable and horrendous is right around the corner? (180)

Such questions inevitably arise from any drama aiming to address with directness—and even with accusation—political issues, especially for American audiences who, in the late twentieth century, became increasingly less accustomed to, or welcoming of, political debate in the theater.

First produced in 1985, *Bright Room* was published in an anthology called *Seven Different Plays* (New York: Broadway Play Publishing, 1988), edited by playwright Mac Wellman, and later published on its own by Broadway Play Publishing and the Theatre Communications Group in 1994 with an afterword by Kushner. It envisions the harrowing perils of the Nazi rise in a profoundly grim and intellectually probing drama, uniquely combining an intimate and realistic portrait of the lives of some German filmmakers in the early 1930s with an epic scope encompassing not only the Holocaust, but contemporary issues as well. These are introduced and contextualized by Zillah Katz, a present-day Jewish political activist and ardent feminist who points out parallels between the Nazi era and her own time, the mid-1980s. A fringe radical leftist exile in Reagan's America, Zillah seeks revelations from the past.

Zillah's paranoid rants in the face of Reagan's 1984 reelection mirror Kushner's own fear in what he calls "a season of calamity," adding that "the desolate political sphere mirrored in an exact and ugly way an equally desolate personal sphere" (173) that he himself was experiencing at the time. Deaths of friends and family and the decline of political liberalism in the face of Reagan's conservative mandate led to what Kushner himself called the "outrageous comparison" (176) between Reagan (and in subsequent updates of the play, Bush) and Hitler. This comparison led to "outrage" (176) from critics when the play was produced in America and London, where Zillah's rants were rewritten as attacks on conservative Prime Minister Margaret Thatcher (who Kushner viewed as Britain's Reagan).

Critics either bitterly condemned the play or scoffingly dismissed it, labeling the offending comparison as childish, a charge to which Kushner felt "highly susceptible," while insisting that his hyperbole is "a response to the Right's cynical underestimation of every genuine social evil" (177). For Kushner, the rise of Reagan stemmed from problems inherent in both ends of the political spectrum: the "Left characterizes the Right's nostalgia as senescent; the Right characterizes the Left's demands for change as adolescent" (171). As Kushner explains it, "The Left—the true, progressive Left—has taken increasingly to looking longingly towards time of less-unjust injustices, less-toxic toxicity, as the Right continues to careen human society forward into a future nobody wants" (171–172). Reagan's "unimaginable" (175) visit to the Nazi cemetery at Bitburg, Germany, and his refusal to acknowledge or respond seriously to the growing death toll from AIDS in the mid-1980s horrified Kushner who, in retrospect, believes that the play's "experiment remains useful and entertaining. And while I am wary of a tendency, given the absence of God, to substitute the judgment of History for the judgment of Heaven, I believe that History will judge Reagan and Bush harshly; not occupying the same circle of Hell as Hitler, but numbered among the damned" (178).

In response to the criticisms of the analogies between the Nazis and the political right in the 1980s–90s in America and England spoken by Zillah, Kushner explained that "we're so allergic to politics in the theater and I wanted to treat that. I wondered, while I was writing it, what if, in the middle of this well made, little four-wall drama someone stood up and said well, what's the most obnoxious thing anyone could say in 1985? 'You've just reelected Adolf Hitler'" (Szentgyorgyi 17).

Kushner wrote *Bright Room* during 1984 and 1985 within a framework of the political currents of the mid-1980s, and several difficult personal crises. The play's title originated in Kushner's mishearing of a videotape of choreographer Agnes DeMille describing a dance called "A Bridegroom Called Death." It is "about Germans, refugee and otherwise, caught on the cusp of the historic catastrophe about to engulf them" (174) and was first staged in an April 1985 workshop production presented by the Heat & Light Company at Theater 22 in New York City with Kushner directing. Heat & Light, a group patterned to some extent on the British groups 7:84 and Monstrous Regiment as well as on such American collectives as Mabou Mines and the Wooster Group, started following the break-up of 3P (poetry, politics, and popcorn) Productions, a small theater group Kushner worked with as a playwright and director. The traumatic ending of 3P—which led to several members of that group forming Heat & Light—is reflected in the unraveling of the personal and professional connections among the film artists in the play.

The first cast of *Bright Room* included Kushner's close friend Kimberly Flynn, who he credits with teaching him how to read literature, in the role of Rosa Malek. Kushner also dedicated the play to Flynn, who had been seriously injured in a car accident while he was writing the play, as well as to Carl Weber, his mentor in the study of Brechtian theater, and his aunt, Florence Kushner, who provided inspiration for the character of Agnes. Other cast members included Stephen Spinella, who would later achieve acclaim and a Tony Award as Prior Walter in the New York production of *Angels*, as well as Priscilla Stampa, Alexandra Rambusch, Maria Makis, Peter Guttmacher, Jonathan Rosenberg, Theresa Reeves, David Warshofsky, Roberta Levine, and in roles eliminated in subsequent rewrites, Tracy Martin and Michael Mayer (who later directed the national tour of *Angels* and is one of Kushner's closest friends). This workshop staging led to the professional premiere of *Bright Room* at San Francisco's Eureka Theatre in October 1987, under the direction of Oskar Eustis and featuring a cast including Sigrid Wurschmidt, Jeff King, Carmalita Fuentes, Abigail Van Alyn, Michael McShane, Ann Houle, David Warshofsky, and Lorri Holt. This was followed by a 1988 production at London's Bush Theatre. In 1990, Kushner received the Whiting Foundation Writers Award and playwriting fellowships from the

New York State Council on the Arts and the National Endowment for the Arts and, in January 1991, *Bright Room* was produced at the Joseph Papp Public Theatre by the New York Shakespeare Festival. Michael Grief directed a strong cast, including Frances Conroy (Agnes), Henry Stram (Baz), Ellen McLaughlin (Paulinka), Joan MacIntosh (Annabella), Olek Krupa (Husz), Angie Phillips (Rosa), Kenneth L. Marks (Traum and Roland), Marian Seldes (Die Alte), Frank Raiter (Swetts), and Reno (Zillah).

In the revised version of *Bright Room* produced by the New York Public Theatre in 1991, the action cuts back and forth between the 1930s and 1990. The contemporary references by Zillah have been updated by Kushner from the 1985 workshop version (they were also updated for the English production) and, with his permission, additional interruptions are invited in order to keep the focus on the intersection of past evils with current ones. These changes retain Kushner's notion that "one of History's lessons, taught as eloquently and awfully through the Holocaust as any other event in human history, is that we must be wary of our attachment to the illusory comfort of our rooms, the enormous familiar weight of everyday life—we must be wary of overvaluing stability" (179). This dilemma is depicted most vividly in *Bright Room* through the central character, Agnes Eggling.

The published version of *Bright Room* divides the drama into two parts, each consisting of several scenes, as well as a prologue and an epilogue. Kushner represents his dramatic treatise on individuals caught up in the larger sweep of historical, political, and social change—and the ways in which human beings succeed or fail at adapting themselves to such transitions—through the experiences of a small group of bohemian artists. Dealing with the paralysis and fear of German citizens in facing Nazism and the subsequent persecution of Jews, homosexuals, gypsies, and other "undesirables," *Bright Room* converges time and history, in this case through the recurring image of the ghostly Die Alte, and, more startlingly, an appearance by the Devil himself.

Bright Room, inspired to some extent by Brecht's *Fear and Misery of the Third Reich* (a play Kushner does not like; *Bright Room* is, in some ways, a response to it), reflects on the need for average people to recognize evil and unite to battle it, even when the obstacles seem unimaginably strong. In facing this difficult subject matter, Kushner also faces Brecht's theories and his example as a dramatist, attempting to maintain those aspects of Brecht's style that might serve him while struggling to move beyond Brecht in establishing his own individual dramatic voice. Brecht offered Kushner a powerful model for addressing political ideas in the drama—a model that would continue to inspire Kushner through the 1990s—while also allowing Kushner a fluid structural technique.

Christopher Bigsby writes that *Bright Room* is "a startlingly original work, it is allusive and lyrical, displaying that mixture of sensual delight and the unpleasant that he had seen in *The Threepenny Opera*" (Bigsby 92), but it is important to note that it is also a nightmare borne out of catastrophic social upheaval. In *Bright Room* Kushner creates a drama in which the central character suffers so completely from paralyzing fear that she cannot respond to the evils around her.

Kushner has made the most undramatic of human traits the source of his drama. He accomplishes this, in part, by creating an immense historical panorama around the intimate lives of a few characters. Like the later *Angels*, *Bright Room* is inspired by Brecht, but is purely Kushnerian in its theatrics: in the juxtaposition of different times and places; in the lyrical realism in the dialogue exchanges among the characters; and in a sense of inevitability regarding change, loss, and the survival of hope. The imagery of the theater itself is critical to the effectiveness of *Bright Room*—not only in the fact that some of its key characters are performers, but in the transcendent theatricality of the social, sexual, and political background of their lives.

Bright Room explores the links among all kinds of evil, whether of the overtly horrific brand offered by Hitler or the less obvious varieties Kushner identifies within late-twentieth-century political conservatism as represented by Reagan, Bush, and Thatcher. Kushner warns that alienation, as depicted in his main character's agonizing inaction (her name, Eggling, suggests the protective shell—albeit easily broken—she creates around herself), leads to catastrophe, through an Orwellian depiction of the slow and steady closing in of her existence during the years 1932–33, in which the Weimar Republic falls and the Nazis seize power. As critic M. G. Lord writes, in pitting the extreme evil of Hitler against a "kinder, gentler" evil, Kushner "raises some unanswerable questions: Is there radical evil in the world? Or is evil workaday and banal?" (5).

The tragically misaligned characters of Kushner's play do not fully recognize Hitler's depravities at first—or the emotional and political exhaustion of the Weimar period that permitted Hitler's rise, the disintegration of the status quo, and the politicizing of ordinary individuals, most of whom recognize the evil too late to stop it. An emotionally wrenching Brechtian history lesson, *Bright Room* filters the twilight of the Weimar era through Zillah's despairing reaction to the abrupt shift to the extreme right in American politics in the 1980s. History is not merely a simple recounting of facts; for Kushner, the historical is inextricably bound to the personal and, as such, can perhaps be best understood through the experiences of ordinary individuals living through the storm of event, chaos, and change.

Like all of Kushner's plays, *Bright Room*, deals with the spiritual—not in the sense of traditional religious beliefs, but in something that is sensed outside of the obvious realities of day-to-day human experience. He invokes Christian and Judaic imagery, sometimes to provide a mysterious sense of the past, sometimes for humor, and, most importantly, to raise the troubling questions about what may be lost—or even violently destroyed—as one world, one culture, and one faith die. These are all issues he later investigates in other ways in his adaptation of Ansky's early modern Yiddish theater play, *A Dybbuk*, which, in his hands, emphasizes the collision of ancient traditions with the onslaught of modernism.

Bright Room begins as the political and social conditions paving the way for Hitler's rise to power in Germany coalesce. Agnes Eggling, a moderately successful bit player in German films, struggles for fulfillment and survival with a group of close friends who worry, to varying degrees, about what is happening so suddenly in their country. Agnes is unable to respond in the face of the rising evil. She is a pliant woman of good will who expresses the powerlessness of individuals faced with the juggernaut of fascism in Germany. Her inaction is mirrored by the somewhat more engaged Zillah, who, in the 1980s, shares a feeling of hopelessness about the political situation in which she is trapped. Her reactions—however futile—include writing hate mail to Reagan, the only way she, as a powerless member of her society, can find to respond. The play, however, is not unrelentingly grim, as Kushner's own fundamental optimism expresses a belief that some may have enough courage to contemplate their role in a time of cataclysm. Agnes's moral lassitude ultimately succumbs to passivity—she grows emotionally paralyzed, a response symbolized by the diminishment of the physical environment around her. The characters, of course, have good reason to dread Hitler's rise, even if most of them fail to see the depth of the tragedies to come. Others are susceptible to the seductions of Nazism mostly because it represents a new status quo.

Agnes's tightly knit group includes Baz, a gay man who works for the Berlin Institute for Human Sexuality; Paulinka, a featured player and budding star in commercial films; Annabella Gotchling, a Communist who works as a graphic designer; and Husz, a one-eyed cinematographer from Hungary and a Trotskyite. Disorientation from the brisk and brutal change in the political winds leads all of the characters toward some kind of escape into their own individual form of exile. Each offers a differing observation of ways to respond, personally and politically, to the rising tide of evil. Die Alte, a specter of an old woman presumably dead for over twenty years, haunts Agnes to deliver ominous poetic statements suggesting she may be an image of what Agnes is to become.

As Kushner explains, *Bright Room* "ends before the worst nightmare begins, but its ending looks to the camps, the bombings, and even to the Bomb" (180). The prologue, named "Evening Meal in a Windstorm," is set on January 1, 1932, as Agnes and her friends usher in the New Year. Zillah is, simultaneously, seen reading, separate from the play's main action. The friends are debating politics, with Gotchling noting that "Capitalism is a system of . . . ," with Paulinka sarcastically completing her statement: "Digestion. A digestive system" (3–4). The debate is good-humored and the characters do not yet seem to grasp what is on the horizon, as Agnes expresses when she exults: "We live in Berlin. It's 1932. I feel relatively safe" (5).

The friends sit quietly for a time and Paulinka says, "And in the silence, an angel passed over" (6), but it is no angel hovering over these slightly intoxicated bohemians. To while away the evening, they drink and together compose a story about a night watchman who has spent his last few coins on a woolen coat to protect him against the harsh night wind. This is a sufficient response, he thinks, but the wind wails, "Just you wait" (8). Ultimately, the watchman realizes the coat is not enough protection against the bitter cold and, as he dies from exposure, he hears the wind repeat, "Just you wait" (8).

In the next scene, Agnes and her lover, Husz, are seen in typical domestic circumstances. Husz returns home with a lemon as a gift for Agnes, but feels too anxious to make love and both complain about the lack of interesting film projects. Agnes is doing extra work on a film whose director is only interested in her "jolly twinkle" (10), which she must deliver in crowd scenes, while Husz laments having ever left his native Hungary. "All Day in the Rain," the next scene, finds Agnes discussing psychotherapy with Paulinka, who visits a Dr. Bloom, feeling that "psychoanalysis makes more sense than Communism," which Agnes has begun to flirt with. Paulinka is not impressed with Agnes's new-found passion for Communism: "You'll recover" (15), she smirks, adding, "You don't have a political bone in your body" (14). The apolitical Paulinka's mocking angers Agnes, who insists, "If we go red the whole world will follow us. Everything bad and dangerous will be swept away" (16). This scene is set in counterpoint with Zillah's first interruption in which she is writing a furious tirade to Reagan, adding the postscript that she plans to purchase a computer to keep up the flow of mail protesting the "toxin" spreading from his administration, claiming, "For me and my cause, money is no object" (17–18).

With the main characters and their circumstances established, Kushner's addition of a contemporary perspective is intended to "polarize an audience, separating those who saw the value in holding a miscreant like Reagan up to an agreed-upon standard of Evil from those who felt such an exercise to be preposterous and jejune" (178). Zillah—like Kushner—believes that Hitler set a standard of evil so great that subsequent villains have paled by comparison, but still do much evil. For her, Reagan—the conservative zeitgeist of the mid-1980s—is her Hitler. Critic Linda Winer points out that Zillah dismisses

> the notion that Hitler's evil was different—in more than degree—from evil today. She wants to be somewhere where she can see the danger. "If there's any safety anywhere, it is there." Kushner believes the devil is most dangerous when he becomes invisible. Whether one agrees with Kushner's politics or even his dramaturgy, it's a hell of a good point. (69)

It is May 1932 in the next scene, "Late Night Struggles on Towards Dawn." As the scene opens, Agnes is working on a skit about a "Red Baby," using a puppet she employs to represent the Communist future and a Hitler puppet as her antagonist. Husz tries to lure her to bed, but before she retires she cuts into another lemon he has brought her, tasting its "sour fruit" (20). Agnes falls asleep at her work table and Die Alte, a "very old but hard to tell how old" woman "somewhere between 70 and dead-for-20 years" (viii), appears and the ironic juxtaposition of the two worlds of Agnes and Zillah is now given a third dimension, with Die Alte representing those who have suffered in bleak times before Agnes's and who seems an embodiment, not only of the past, but a symbol of the grimly isolated present and futures of Agnes and Zillah. Die Alte reflects on the coming of an earlier, unnamed war, remembering the excitement—"the snap of the flags," but laments that now she is "Hungry. Always. Never enough" (22).

The next scene, "Cold and Brutal But Exact and True," set several days later on June 2, 1932, finds Agnes struggling to read Marx's *Das Kapital*. She is interrupted by Baz and Gotchling, who, to her horror, have just returned from a Nazi rally. Baz explains that "You must have an intimate knowledge of the enemy," and proceeds to describe the rally—and his fellow countrymen—with some disdain, believing that the enthusiasm for the Nazis has to do with "desperately trapped sexual energies" (24–25). Annoyed by this argument, Gotchling dismissively points out, "If sexual frustration was the cause, everyone would be a fascist" (25). For Gotchling, the Nazis are merely a "shabby collection of borrowings from all over—a bad collage," to which Baz insists that "Hitler simply offers a lot of very confused and terrified and constipated people precisely what they want, a means of release," adding, in an ominous premonition, "They want bloody things" (25–26). Agnes is shocked at Baz's hint that he may be sleeping with members of the Nazi Party, but he snaps back to accuse her of sleeping with a Trotskyite.

The action jumps in the next scene to July 21, 1932, at the time of National Reichstag Elections, and Agnes and Paulinka are gossiping about Hitler's sex life. Paulinka recounts Hitler's "incestuous infatuation" (32) for his cousin who subsequently killed herself, and adds that rumors are circulating that Hitler is a "coprophiliac" (32). She asks if Agnes believes in evil or the Devil, who Paulinka claims, in a nightmarish speech, to have actually seen. The next scene, "Demonology," moves the action to September 12, 1932, when Agnes is visited by two Communist Party officials, Rosa Malek and Emil Traum, who are concerned about "Left-deviationist tendencies" (37) in Agnes's Red Baby puppet show, which she has been performing at various functions. The Central Committee, Malek and Traum imply, want Agnes to tone down the skit's content and Malek talks of the nightmares she has had imagining a real red baby, "painted or boiled or something" (44).

The scene shifts to November 6, 1932, revealing Agnes and Gotchling happily discussing Nazi setbacks in the Second Reichstag Elections in which the Communists have gained twelve seats while the Nazis have lost thirty-four. Husz rejoices that "the masses are on the move," and, in a lyrical interlude, he imagines making a film that will "make Trotsky weep" (47–48) for the eye Husz lost in the 1919 Hungarian revolt. As Christopher Bigsby writes, "Having had one eye put out by progressives he [Husz] sees an altogether different world. It is as though Beckett were debating with Brecht" (102), but the story here is more significantly about the cost of political engagement and of the changes resulting from shifting political fortunes.

The joy of the Nazi setback is set against Agnes's first direct encounter with Die Alte, who chillingly recites a childhood tale turned nightmare, "Little Penny Man":

> Just before I fall asleep,
> After God has heard my prayers,
> Things below begin to creep:
> The penny man is on the stairs. (53)

Believing that Die Alte is merely a beggar woman who lives on her fire escape, Agnes gives her a roll, and Zillah interrupts in a scene called "The Politics of Paranoia" to recall Watergate as the happiest time of her life, an era that was "dramatic and garish and incredibly funny," adding that it was not at all like the

"bone-naked terror" of the present in which "I sense parallels" between the present and the rise of Hitler—and in which she has "become a completely convinced, humorless paranoiac" (54–55).

In the next scene, "Love Scene Without Lemon," Husz returns home, but this
time it is Agnes who is too anxious to have sex. It is December 4, 1932, and the
characters now realize that Hitler will become Germany's chancellor. Agnes's
fears are beginning to paralyze her, as when she explains that she feels "like I'm in
a film, all the time. A newsreel. I see all these events already on film, not just
Hitler, but us: no sex, eating and crying. All public events. There is a title:
'PERCHED ON THE BRINK OF A GREAT HISTORIC CRIME'" (57).

Barely a month later, on January 1, 1933, Agnes sits alone ruminating on the
reasons she sees as preventing her from leaving Germany: the low rent on her
modest apartment and a fundamental inability—or disinclination—to move,
despite the obviously mounting danger. Later, Baz acknowledges the "genuine
hopelessness" of their situation and relates the changing of the weather to the
changing "Seasons of History" (60–61). Agnes is "overwhelmed. I feel no connection, no kinship with most of the people I see. I watch them in the underground
come and go and I think, 'Are you a murderer? Are you?' And there are so many
people" (61–62). Baz talks of buying some oranges after seeing the corpse of a
man who has jumped (or been pushed) from a window lying in a street. He
imagines giving one of his oranges to the dead man, who he envisions "sitting
in the snow, holding the orange, and comforted. Still bloody, still dead, but . . .
comforted" (62).

The next scene, "Furct und Elend (Fear and Misery)," set on January 30, 1933,
finds Agnes's friends assembled in her apartment discussing the worsening political situation. Gotchling admits that things may get very tough for a while, but
Husz more cynically observes that it will be for "a very long time. To be replaced
by something that looks like progress but will turn out to be worse than what it
replaced" (64). Commenting on his prior enthusiasm for progress, Husz
recounts his "journey to the home of progress. I gave it an eye. Progress ate it up,
crunch crunch, and said, 'You have two eyes, give me another!' And I said, 'Oh no
thanks, I'm leaving'" (65). He wistfully posits that "the eye I have left looks
clearly at all the shit in front of it, but the eye I gave to the revolution will always
see what it saw then . . . " (65–66). Paulinka calls them all "frightened and faith-
less," but Husz ruefully replies, "This age wanted heroes. It got us instead: carefully constructed, but immobile" (67).

In Zillah's next interruption, "German Lessons," she is haunted by both the
past (as represented by Agnes's world—just as Agnes is haunted by the earlier
world of Die Alte) and her own present. She warns that understanding the late
twentieth century requires "not caution or circumspection but moral exuber-
ance. Overstatement is your friend: use it" (70). Her comparisons of Reagan to
Hitler are part of this overstatement, but she insists that

> just because a certain ex-actor-turned-President who shall go nameless sat idly by
> and watched tens of thousands die of a plague and he couldn't even bother to say
> he felt bad about it, much less try to help, does this mean he merits comparison to

a certain fascist-dictator anti-Semitic mass-murdering psychopath who shall also remain nameless? OF COURSE NOT! I mean I ask you—how come the only people who ever say "Evil" anymore are southern cracker televangelists with radioactive blue eyeshadow? (71)

Zillah also offers observations and advice to the audience about the horrors of both periods: "Don't put too much stock in a good night's sleep. During times of reactionary backlash, the only people sleeping soundly are the guys who are giving the rest of us bad dreams. So eat something indigestible before you go to bed, and listen to your nightmares" (71).

In one of the revised interruptions intended for the New York Shakespeare Festival production in 1991, Zillah speaks of Agnes's dilemma, equating their two eras: "Your Great Communicator spoke and created a whole false history; ours spoke and history basically came down with arteriosclerosis; from the Triumph of the Will to the Triumph of the Brain Dead, from National Socialism to National Senility" (160). Zillah's wrath also turns on Reagan's successor, George Bush, the "Kennebunkport Katastrophe," and the Republican Party in general who "brought you Iran Contra" (160), as well as such ultraconservative figures as Jesse Helms and Pat Buchanan, of whom Kushner has Zillah imagine, "it's 1942; the Goerings are having an intimate soiree; if he got an invitation, would Pat Buchanan feel out of place? Out of place? Are you *kidding*? Pig *heaven*, dust off the old tuxedo, kisses to Eva and Adolf" (70–71).

As the first act of *Bright Room* ends, Kushner shifts, in a scene entitled, "Welcome," into a distinctly phantasmagoric mode, raising the play's nightmarish stakes by introducing the Devil himself as a character. Kushner uses this startling addition to the play to introduce an element of moral parable. Husz, a native of the High Carpathians, calls on "a special understanding" (73) that citizens of his homeland have with the Devil, whose arrival is preceded by the appearance of a red-eyed hell hound set to the finale of Mahler's Second Symphony. Herr Gottfried Swetts, the Devil, who some critics viewed as a Faustian character inspired by David Lynch, represents an evil so subtle and complete that it can hardly be recognized. Swetts explains that he has "taken up temporary residence" (75) in Germany and lyrically relates the darkest and bloodiest eras of the past, ominously adding that the evils of more recent centuries have made him "Very strong! Very hungry!" (79). His lyrical recounting of his "Auto-biography" (77) reveals that

> It's not the danger that you see
> that's the danger.
> I become increasingly diffuse,
> like powdered gas taking to air,
> not less potent, but more,
> spreading myself
> around. (80)

Paulinka laughs that Swetts's pronouncements are "a little grandiose," particularly given the ordinary persona the Devil has adopted for his visit, but he warns

her that she cannot imagine "the scope of what's ahead" and "the great possibilities in the Modern World. The depths . . . have not been plumbed. Yet" (80–81).
Kushner uses this embodiment of pure evil to raise questions about the problems
of understanding genuine historical evil. The dumbfounded, frightened Agnes
can only thank Swetts for his visit as the play's first part concludes.

The second part of *Bright Room* begins with a slide show of images of Hitler
with Zillah ironically singing, to the tune of Eubie Blake's "Memories of You," a
serenade:

> How I wish I could forget
> those happy yesteryears
> That have left a rosary
> Of tears.
> Your face beams in my dreams
> 'Spite of all I do;
> Everything seems to bring
> Memories of you. (86)

The following scene, "Man Isn't Good—He's Disgusting," is set on February
27, 1933, and it features another encounter between Agnes and Die Alte, who
coaxes Agnes to join her in another nightmarish "penny man" verse in which the
parallels with Hitler become obvious:

> When the little penny man
> Bangs the pots and pans about,
> No one dares to go downstairs
> No one dares to throw him out. (88)

Agnes remembers this little song from her childhood, but Die Alte warns that
"memory is like the wind. Tricky. Horrible things forgotten overnight. Pleasant
nothings remembered for years" (88). Their singing is interrupted when Agnes
notices a great fire in the distance—the Reichstag building is burning—as the
scene fades.

Zillah interrupts again in a scene called "Night Bats," recalling an old photograph she has seen of a woman amidst a huge crowd of enthusiastic Nazis. The
woman is the only one not offering the Nazi salute and is seen standing, unsmiling, "both hands . . . clutching her purse" (89). This moves Zillah to acknowledge
an allegiance to this anonymous woman who defies, in her small way, the political juggernaut she alone cannot stop. Thinking about this photograph, Zillah
reaches out "across a long dead time: to touch a dark place, to scare myself a little, to make contact with what moves in the night, fifty years after, and what's
driven, every night, by the panic and the pain . . ." (90).

In the next scene, "Further Demonological Explorations," as the Reichstag
burns, Malek and Traum visit Agnes again, this time to return some of Agnes's
things from the Party office, "before we get closed down" (91). Traum suggests
that they will wait in exile for "fascism to run its course" (92), but Malek
expresses intense bitterness over the German Communist Party allowing "the
Russians to run our revolution!" (93). Malek advises Agnes to "burn everything.

Books, pamphlets, everything" (94) to avoid being arrested. A few weeks roll by
to March 5, 1933, and Paulinka rushes into Agnes's apartment to tell her that her
psychiatrist, a Jew, has apparently fled, leaving her "without a word, without the
courtesy of a final session" (98), actions the self-absorbed Paulinka cannot
understand. She hints of her imminent departure from Berlin, but Agnes says, "I
don't know. I don't know what to do" (100).

A week later, on March 12, 1933, Agnes and Gotchling are making anti-Nazi
posters, which worries Agnes who feels great distress with the present situation,
but cannot make a decision in any particular direction and fears reprisals for her
political involvements. Gotchling angrily responds, "Feel feel feel feel feel. So
much feeling. Hold still. Don't feel. Think for a change" (102). Gotchling tries to
persuade Agnes to allow her apartment to serve as a safe house for escaping Jews
and dissidents, but Agnes resists, concerned about her safety and worrying,
"What are people like me supposed to do if people like you just leave?" (103).
Gotchling, a painter by profession, insists that Agnes's apartment is needed to aid
the cause, while she laments that "art . . . is never enough, it never does enough"
(105), a point Kushner makes throughout the script, especially in the "Red Baby"
skits Agnes presents for meetings of the Communists. As an artist in a society
that, at best, undervalues the importance of art, Kushner's concern about the
power of art to cause action or change is an understandable worry, but theater—
especially Kushner's work—does, at its best, possess the power to pose questions,
change attitudes, and inspire action.

In the next scene, "From the Book," Zillah is seen with a Bible, pointing out
that both Reagan and Thatcher are "afflicted in their right hands with a disease of
the manual ligaments called Dupuytren's contracture, which causes the hand to
shrivel, gradually assuming, and I quote, 'a claw-like appearance.' Claw-like,"
which she relates to the Book of Revelations passage, "And He causes all, the rich
and the poor, the free and the slave, to receive a mark on their right hand, and
none can buy or sell without that mark. The name of the Beast, and the number
of that name" (107). Noting that the number of the Beast is 666, Zillah holds up
a sign revealing the three sixes of Reagan's name: R-O-N-A-L-D W-I-L-S-O-N R-
E-A-G-A-N, adding that upon Reagan's retirement from the presidency he
moved to 666 Mayfair Road, but "he had them change the address because, well,
he reads the Book" (108). Kushner uses Zillah in obvious ways to connect the
evils of the past to those he perceives in the present, but her presence also raises
more complex questions about the meaning of the dark disasters of history on
those who live in the present. How do we live with the memories of the unimaginable brutalities of history and how does an understanding of the past alter our
ways of living?

Back at Agnes's apartment, three days later, Baz recounts the arrest of his colleagues at the Berlin Institute for Human Sexuality and the Institute's abrupt
closing by the Nazis. He tells of his own interrogation during which, he is
ashamed to admit, he cried. Comforting him, Husz says that everyone does, but
Baz quips, "It's different when I do it. The mascara runs" (110). He explains that
because he has a police record an escape to Munich was his plan, but when real-

izing the difficulty of escape he planned to kill himself. Instead, while hiding, he meets a "young Silesian" with whom he has a sexual encounter that makes him desire life "in all its hot, tainted glory" (112). Baz also reveals that he went to a movie theater to watch a Marlene Dietrich film and that Hitler himself arrived with an entourage. He describes in great detail his observation of the Führer only a few rows in front of him and considers the chance he had to use the gun with which he planned to kill himself on Hitler. Husz is infuriated that Baz did not shoot Hitler, but Baz, who describes himself as "a homosexual Sunday anarchist with a loaded gun in his pocket," admits it was because he was afraid "they would have shot me" and "I do not want to die" (114–16). He announces that he has arranged for a fake passport and that he plans to leave Germany in six days.

Zillah's next interruption makes it clearer that she imagines that the unsmiling woman in the photograph of the Nazi rally may be Agnes, who she believes "hears me. No answer. I ask her how she died" (117). Zillah considers the various possible deaths Agnes may have ultimately suffered—in a concentration camp, in an air raid—but finally believes she hears the woman tell her that she died, "not in the camps, and not in the war, but at home, in front of a cozy fire, I died of a broken heart" (118), at which point Agnes gasps, believing she senses the presence of someone as the scene ends. Kushner allows Zillah to recognize that unlike the terrors of past history, the most dangerous place to be is at home, where, as Christopher Bigsby writes, "naive commitments and studious evasions, of indifference deepening to hostility and then to evil" (103) reach a level of absurd, banal horror.

On May 1, 1933, Die Alte appears to Agnes again to tell of a black pillow she once had that caused her to have terrible nightmares and that she, like Agnes, "wound up all alone" (120). Frightened, Agnes reacts violently, but Die Alte cradles her in her arms, pointing out that "time is all that separates you from me," adding that "it's bad to be too much alone" (122). In the next scene, "An Acid Morning Light," it is the next day, and Husz and Paulinka turn up at Agnes's apartment following a riot in which Husz has been injured. He only survives, they explain, because Paulinka uses her screen fame to secure his safety in what she jokingly refers to as the "performance of my career," adding that it was "wasted on a crazed Hungarian and three Nazi thugs" (124). Husz, obviously intending to continue to resist the Nazis, shows Agnes a large kitchen knife he carries with him for that purpose. Fearing for her safety, Agnes demands that Husz leave, and he proclaims that "history repeats itself, see, first as tragedy, then as farce" (126). Later he explains to Agnes that "justice . . . is vanishing. Like all the air in the earth's atmosphere getting used up, like life's blood running freely on the ground, pouring from a wound too big to stop up; you watch it spill, watching yourself die" (128). Husz produces two visas intended for their escape, but Agnes inexplicably refuses to leave. Husz goes without her, sadly explaining, "It will not be hard to leave Berlin. But it will be very hard to leave you" (130), and the following day Agnes sits alone tearing up the visa Husz left for her.

More than a month has elapsed when the next scene begins. In "Revelations and Farewell," Paulinka and Baz say their goodbyes to Agnes as they leave Berlin on June 22, 1933. Paulinka ironically notes that the Communist Husz has gone to America, while she is headed for Russia. Baz lyrically laments the failure of the Communist movement as he departs for Paris, and Agnes bitterly watches them depart, crying that "when a person goes, a whole person just goes away, it would leave a hole, some empty place behind, that's what I thought, I imagined that, but . . . it doesn't. Everyone's going but it isn't like the world has gotten emptier, just much smaller. It contracts, the empty places . . . collapse" (136). Later, Gotchling, who is residing secretly in Berlin as part of the underground resistance, shows up to press Agnes again about using her apartment for those in flight. The increasingly immobile Agnes continues to refuse, causing Gotchling to attack her verbally:

> If you say no to this, Agnes, you're dead to me. And we both need desperately to keep at least some part of you alive. Say yes, and I promise to carry you with me, the part of you that's dying now. I can do that, I'm stronger than you. Say yes, and I will take your heart and fold it up in mine, and protect it with my life. And some day I may be able to bring it back to you. (141)

Shamed, Agnes reluctantly relents and Gotchling warns her to expect someone named Rosa to hide out that evening. Zillah offers a brief, lyrical interruption on the "terror that skips over the mind and out the throat" (141), as the fugitive Rosa turns out to be Comrade Malek of the Communist Party's Berlin committee needing refuge before her clandestine escape in the wee hours of the morning. Realizing that Malek cannot answer, Agnes questions her about what she has been doing: "I just need to know that you'll be working. You and Gotchling. You'll keep doing what needs to be done, underground, I couldn't, I'm not really worth much, I suppose . . . the fear is too great, it makes me stupid, but. . . . It still matters to me" (145).

Malek expresses a belief that things will eventually improve, but perhaps not for many years. This distresses Agnes, whose loneliness and fear prevent her from doing "something to help but I'm simply not able" (145). Malek tells Agnes of a house on the German-Czechoslovakian border used as an escape, adding, "The borders are full of holes" (146). She seems, though, to understand that Agnes will not—or cannot—take advantage of this valuable information.

Agnes's life and circle of friends continues to diminish as she attempts to grasp survival, watching others flee, die, or, like herself, become immobilized by fear. Alone in a dark corner of her apartment, Agnes is little more than a trapped animal, and in the play's epilogue lyrically explains her dilemma:

> I live in a modern flat.
> On one side lives nightmare,
> on the other despair.
> Above me, exhaustion,
> below me, a man
> with the pale face
> and red hands of a strangler. (148)

As *Bright Room* concludes, Die Alte joins Agnes to offer another nightmarish verse conjuring the postwar "ruins of home," where "everyone was patchy, delirious, diseased, and waiting for the end ..." (149), while Agnes awaits the hellish horror to come:

> Clubfoot.
> Smell of sulphur.
> Yellow dog.
> No shadow.
> Welcome to Germany. (151)

The characters in *Bright Room*—in its way, a theatrical history of the victims of fascism not unlike the Chilean peasant women in Kushner's co-adaptation of Ariel Dorfman's *Widows*—only barely glimpse the depths of the evil that victimizes them as they flee, either from the geographic center of the danger or, like Agnes, into an exhausted, forlorn isolation in the eye of the storm. For Agnes, the isolation is physical (she hides in a corner of her small apartment) and, more significantly, psychological as her tragic retreat forces her to close her heart and mind to the events swirling about her. Her meager hope seems only that she might survive until the evil subsides—or moves elsewhere—and there is, as such, safety only in choking off any human interaction.

Critics considered *Bright Room* a challenging, emotionally demanding work, whether or not they liked it or agreed with all of its themes. When *Bright Room* premiered at London's Bush Theatre in 1988, reviewer Michael Coveney found it to be a "melange of Christopher Isherwood and Mnouchkine's *Mephisto*, it charts the stamping out of Communist optimism and acceleration of fugitive paranoia" (17). As previously noted, many critics decried the equating of Nazism with Reaganism, but others, some of whom had problems with the play's grim tone, shared David Richards's view that *Bright Room* "is an ambitious, disturbing mess of a play" and that Kushner "can write nervous, scratchy dialogue streaked with the dark phosphorescence of poetry" (5). *Variety's* critic, Remy., acknowledged the "terrifying inevitability" of the play's story, but found that Kushner's "graspingly literary script lacks the moral weight and dramatic power of other shows whose ghosts are keenly felt," including *Cabaret* and Wallace Shawn's *Aunt Dan and Lemon*, and carped that there was "more posturing in the writing than in the performances" (118). Reviewer Thomas M. Disch described the play as "a gay, American equivalent of David Hare's" (352), but Michael Feingold joined the chorus of disapproval over the play's messiness while also acknowledging that Kushner is "infallible as a word-slinger" (83).

Linda Winer stressed that Kushner's "rage and heart are courageous" when she described *Bright Room* as "a big, dense play of ideas—a welcome rarity after an era of apolitical American isolationist theater," although she also felt that it was "too ambitious to be this unilluminating and too shallow for the enormity of its subject" (44). Critic Howard Kissel found Kushner's writing to be "not without wit or intelligence," but felt that some of the play's characters lack dimension (surely intentional on Kushner's part—beyond Agnes, who is fairly fully developed, the rest of the characters are types and used by Kushner accordingly), while noting that the only one who is not, Agnes, is "a young woman of wavering beliefs, for the most part poignantly played by Frances Conroy" (29). For Kissel, Kushner is "merely a pamphleteer, not a playwright" (29). This, of course, is the sort of criticism traditionally leveled at socially conscious, political dramatists, from Ibsen to Brecht. David Patrick Stearns thought that the play "runs amok" in equating Hitler and Reagan, but "for those not *too* put off, a more credible parallel emerges between the vanquishing of Germany's idealistic, anti-Nazi Communist movement in the 1930s and the death of liberalism in the USA" (4D). Reviewer Gerald Weales recognized the hopeful elements behind Kushner's pessimism, stressing that it "came across to me as a more despairing play than it probably intended to be" (132).

Some critics were brutally critical of Kushner's playwriting, though most of them would make a complete turnabout on this when *Angels* appeared. Roy Sander went so far as to condemn New York's Public Theatre for bothering to produce *Bright Room* at all, a play he felt was merely "a series of lame and poorly structured scenes" demonstrating "an intellectual shallowness that has given sophomores a bad name and the calibre of writing that can give play selection committees a bad reputation" (48). *New York Times* reviewer Frank Rich was most dismissive of all, calling *Bright Room* "a fatuous new drama" and "the most infuriating play of 1991," filled with "speechifying" and spoiled by Kushner's "indiscriminat[e] dumping [of] all present-day ills into Zillah's diatribes until all moral distinctions are blurred and history is rendered meaningless" (C11). It is worth noting that Rich's condemnation of *Bright Room* was omitted from an over-one-thousand-page volume collecting Rich's published drama reviews, perhaps because he subsequently heaped lavish praise on *Angels*.

Publication of *Bright Room* by the Theatre Communications Group in 1994 led some critics to a higher appraisal of the play's worth. Jack Helbig stressed that even if Kushner had not written *Angels*, "this earlier work would guarantee him a place in the pantheon of noteworthy living playwrights ... the play is as compelling on the page as on the stage," for "Kushner the artist outstrips Kushner the heavy-handed polemicist" (87). Among contemporary American dramatists, Kushner's work offers the reader of his plays a full and literate experience that most late-twentieth-century plays do not. Critics of published versions of Kushner's plays often offer praise equal to or greater than that which appears regarding productions of the plays.

Despite largely negative critical response to the New York production of *Bright Room* in 1991, it has had numerous productions in regional and university theaters in recent years, especially since the triumph of *Angels*. *Bright Room* was produced at Atlanta's Actors Express in September 1995 and again met with mixed responses from critics. Critic Dan Hulbert pointed out that Kushner has "a burning vision, of a society whose capitalist triumphs come at the price of its soul," but felt that in this play, the vision was "more fizzle than sizzle" ("Theatre Review: *A Bright Room Called Day*" 5P). Hulbert also reported that the play had been slightly updated (with Atlanta playwright Karen Wurl faxing suggested changes to Kushner for his approval), making connections not only with the Reagan/Bush era, but also with the mid-1990s "Republican Revolution" led by Newt Gingrich. Kushner was friendly to such changes, although he edited them heavily, and, as Hulbert reported, wrote to the Atlanta cast his encouragement to "go with God's speed. The most important thing is to blast the bastards. Do it ferociously. Draw blood" ("Backstage: Express *Room* His Timelier Target" 6L) with the amendments targeting Gingrich, Pat Robertson, and others identified with late-twentieth-century American conservatism.

Bright Room was also staged by Cypress College's Studio Theatre in March 1996, and critic Robert Koehler called it a "remarkable" play, as "quiet and unassuming as tragedy gets" (28). Produced by the Outward Spiral Theatre in Minneapolis, Minnesota in May 1999, critic Rohan Preston wrote that *Bright Room* is an "agitprop play . . . full of unabashed but clumsy political statements. It needs major changes to hold an audience's attention" (7E). An April 2000 production of *Bright Room* at Los Angeles's Theatre of Note, inspired reviewer Jana J. Monji to condemn its "heavy-handed polemics" (F31).

Kushner invites those producing the play to delete the controversial Zillah sequences, which may be an increasingly likely option as the years pass and the specifics of the Reagan-Bush-Thatcher-Gingrich eras fade. The play can certainly function without Zillah, but in many respects her elimination would be unfortunate. The play's political power is, to some extent, in the anger she expresses and that streams from the convergence of past and present evils so central to most Kushner plays. *Bright Room* functions, as Kushner suggests, in the risk run in

> reawakening old nightmares, of being overwhelmed with horror. Conjuring up the future is even more treacherous, because to attempt to envision the future we must resort to what is known, to the past, and if the past as past is nearly unbearable, how much more unbearable to look ahead and see only old nightmares staring back at us. (183)

CHAPTER TWO

The Progress of Death in the Land of Pure Delight

Hydriotaphia, or The Death of Dr. Browne

And here in Heaven
I will never die.
I can say that
And not feel
I'm telling
A lie.
In Heaven I will never die.
Never
Never
Never
Die.

—Browne's Soul, *Hydriotaphia, or*
The Death of Dr. Browne (53)

Political upheavals and the horrors of evil pervade the grim, sensual *A Bright Room Called Day*, but death dominates Kushner's next play, *Hydriotaphia, or The Death of Dr. Browne*, subtitled "An Epic Farce About Death and Primitive Capital Accumulation." Kushner wrote the play in 1987, but it underwent a significant revision prior to its first professional productions a decade later. Kushner frequently points out that "the moments in history that interest me the most are of transition" (Mader 1), something he vividly demonstrates in *Bright Room*. Kushner locates another historical transition in *Hydriotaphia*—one somewhat more obscure but, in its own way, no less important.

Through his imaginative rumination on the life of Sir Thomas Browne in *Hydriotaphia*, Kushner imagines the period in which capitalism was born. Although his interest in historical transitions binds *Bright Room* and *Hydriotaphia* together, there is little else that connects these two plays. In place of the frighteningly real grimness of *Bright Room*, Kushner creates a wild flight of theatrical and

38

intellectual fantasy in *Hydriotaphia* that results from "a certain fascination that I've always had with death and dying, and I've been intrigued by the fact that it seems like a very lively kind of fascination" (Mader 1). *Bright Room's* Agnes certainly fears death in much the way that Browne does in *Hydriotaphia*, but instead of the titanic evil that afflicts Agnes, Browne is in a far more personal struggle with the imminence of his death, the subtler avarice and brutality of his own soul, the greed of his unloving family members and friends, and the ignorant and superstitious time in which he lives. In this play, Kushner asks: what is the effect of unchecked acquisitiveness on an individual's soul, on those around him, and on the society of which he is an integral part? These and related questions are tied to a meditation on the meaning of death, both in its scientific reality and in its spiritual possibility.

Hydriotaphia depicts, with grotesque foreboding, the last day in the life of Sir Thomas Browne (1605–82), a noted seventeenth-century writer and physician and, in Kushner's imagination, a seminal capitalist. This multipronged play mingles the metaphysical with the mundane, explores the complexities of existence and the mysteries of the afterlife and, as such, anticipates themes Kushner explores in more contemporary terms in *Angels*.

The real Sir Thomas Browne was born in London, the son of a successful merchant. His first significant literary work, *Religio Medici* (c. 1635), written sometime before Browne began practicing medicine in Norwich around 1637, was published in 1642 without his consent. *Religio Medici* demonstrates that Browne was a premodern man of science who, despite education at Oxford, Montpelier, and Padua, and a probing intellect, was still bound to many of the superstitions of his day. Three years after its publication, the Catholic Church prohibited the reading of *Religio Medici*, but others, including John Dryden, imitated its style. Browne's contemporaries compared him favorably with Shakespeare, although this comparison rapidly faded in the decades following his death.

Browne married Dorothy, daughter of Edward Mileham of Norfolk, in 1641, and they had eleven children. Following his marriage, Browne completed his most ambitious work, *Pseudodoxia Epidemica* (*Vulgar Errors*), which was published in 1646 and was followed in rapid succession during the 1650s by *The Garden of Cyrus*, *A Letter to a Friend*, and, in 1658, *Hydriotaphia (or Urn-burial)*. Browne was knighted in 1671 by Charles II, although his selection was only by default (the mayor of Norwich had declined the honor) despite the fact that Browne had been a faithful Royalist all of his life.

Later, Browne wrote two more works that were published posthumously: *Christian Morals*, regarded by some scholars as a continuation of *Religio Medici*, and *Certain Miscellany Tracts*, a work on a wide range of topics related to human and natural history. In his *Life of Sir Thomas Browne* (1756), Samuel Johnson describes Browne's writing as "vigorous but ragged, it is learned but pedantick, it is deep but obscure, it strikes but does not please, it commands but does not allure.... It is a tissue of many languages, a mixture of heterogeneous words brought together from distant regions" ("Sir Thomas Browne" 4). His literary influence is especially evident in the works of Swift and Melville, and although

Browne's "appeal has largely been because he inhabits the byways of literary discourse, not the mainroads," writes Jonathan F. S. Post, his "remarkably individual" talents as a writer are in presenting a "countervoice to the expected" in revealing "the dark mysteries of life and human potentiality" (156–57). Since these dark mysteries of life and the possibility of human progress are core themes for Kushner, he was naturally attracted to Browne's work and life.

Specifically focusing on Browne's treatise, *Hydriotaphia*, described by Post as one of "the ripest of any studies written in English" (12), Kushner invents the last day of Browne's life as a metaphor for his theories and what Browne symbolizes in the dialogue on social and economic progress. In *Hydriotaphia*, Browne went beyond the typical archaeological reporting of his day when writing of nearly fifty ancient burial urns discovered in a field near Walsingham. Browne challenges the limits of human knowledge in his treatise; pondering on the bones found in the urns, he questions man's sense of "significance and self-sufficiency" (Post 121), finding that the "certainty of death is attended with uncertainties, in time, manner, places" (*The Major Works*, 290). He also criticizes the burial practices of the ancients and his own time, focusing on "the irrationality of numerous customs and the way fictions—or glosses—of death presume to rationalize the unknown" (Post 126), concluding that God does not necessarily promise immortality to human beings:

> There is nothing strictly immortall, but immortality; whatever hath no beginning may be confident of no end. All others have a dependent being, and within the reach of destruction, which is the peculiar of that necessary essence that cannot destroy it self; And the highest strain of omnipotency to be so powerfully constituted, as not to suffer even from the power of it self. But the sufficiency of Christian Immortality frustrates all earthly glory, and the quality of either state after death, makes a folly of posthumous memory. God who can only destroy our souls, and hath assured our resurrection, either of our bodies or names hath directly promised no duration. (*The Major Works*, 312–13)

Browne's ruminations on death, burials, and the Christian view of eternal life are used by Kushner as a grotesque backdrop for a man facing his own demise. Kushner employs these notions as a jumping-off point for an irreverently whimsical, theatrically baroque exploration of life and death through his argument with Browne's own philosophical questions about existence and the material and spiritual aspects of death. Not binding himself to the strict facts of Browne's life, Kushner's close encounter with Browne is at once both outrageously comic and malevolently macabre.

When he first encountered Browne's writing, Kushner attempted to stage the treatise *Hydriotaphia* itself, but he found that this experience instead inspired a play. Spending three weeks writing *Hydriotaphia* in 1987 for a brief non-Equity production, Kushner worked with the cast, including some members of the first staging of *Bright Room*, and "it ran for one week in a tiny theater in New York. This is a period piece with heavy costumes, . . . and we ran during a very hot summer in an unair-conditioned space" (Evans, "Last Laughs," 10). Obviously, this was not the perfect venue, but Kushner retained an affection for the play over the subsequent years. Following the success of *Angels*, there was a great demand for another Kushner play, so he brought it off the shelf and began revisions.

With Kushner's cooperation, *Hydriotaphia* was given a production in 1997 at the Tisch School of the Arts at New York University, directed by Michael Wilson. The staging led to joint productions at the Alley Theatre in Houston, Texas (also directed by Wilson), and at California's Berkeley Repertory Theatre in 1998. For each of these productions, Kushner made significant revisions. Prior to the Alley's production, Kushner discussed the play's genesis with the theater's dramaturg, Travis Mader. Calling *Hydriotaphia* "semi-historical and semi-biographical," he explained that he found in Browne's *Hydriotaphia* "some of the most beautiful prose I had ever read," and that he particularly responded to "how obscure and strange it is—and being fascinated with the themes it touches on, which are dying and immortality" (Mader 1). The inevitability of death, human conceptions of the possibility of continuing life after death, and the meaning the past holds for the future are all usual Kushnerian concerns. In *Hydriotaphia* they are presented with a seemingly incompatible mixture of illusory invention, expansive humor, and highly charged drama.

Beyond a complex depiction of human existence and death, Kushner argues political and economic issues in *Hydriotaphia* through an amalgam of Brechtian and cinematic techniques. Like *Bright Room*, *Hydriotaphia* is episodic, with one scene seeming to bleed into the next and with projected titles for scenes and comments on the action. Here again, Kushner reinvigorates the Brechtian style, melding Brecht's structural foundation with his own approach to character, linguistic lyricism, and a bold theatricality. Kushner is interested in Browne's life and times as they represent the notion of the revolution of "primitive capital accumulation," a term coined by Marx, who, Kushner writes, is

> making reference to the ugly and vital process whereby a nation which is entering a capitalist phase of economic and social relations dislocates its rural populations in the course of a violent land-grab by aristocratic and entrepreneurial classes intent on accumulating, by any means necessary, the material resources which provide the bases for mercantile, manufacturing and speculatory fortunes; from the devastation consequent upon such officially sanctioned piracy, an impoverished urban and factory workforce emerges, desperate for wages: primitive capital accumulation is the nakedly brutal manner in which money was grubbed from people and land, before the banalization, the normalization of such mayhem, before we learned new words for it, like modernization, Progress, industrialization—before the invention of Spin. ("Three Brief Notes from the Playwright," 5)

Shakespeare, Kushner continues, lived through the end of the "roughest phases" of primitive accumulation in England, and he believes that Shakespeare's plays, as such, "reflect the chaos of the time, their bloodiness, their immense excitement, and the irreconcilable dissonance of such vast material appetite with Christ's asceticism, with His antipathy towards wealth and usury, Christ's preference for the poor" ("Three Brief Notes from the Playwright," 5). In Kushner's view, the resulting human misery caused by the seizure of "common lands, moors and forests, and their transformation into private property, made a social, political revolution inevitable" ("Three Brief Notes from the Playwright," 5), one in which capital brutally triumphed. Kushner adds that Browne lived "after that revolution, during the Restoration of the Old Order Transformed (think Gerald Ford taking over after the dismissal of Nixon) (or perhaps, 'earth-friendly' Al Gore replacing Monica Lewinsky's boyfriend)" ("Three Brief Notes from the Playwright," 5). The connections between the transition era in which Browne lived and that of Kushner's own life are more fully explained by Kushner:

> The play is set just after an extreme time, after Cromwell. It is very similar to the 1990s. Reaganism is to a certain extent a Restoration. Nixon began it: a certain resettling of the terms of the social contract along very conservative lines. And the social revolution of the 1960s is still with us—just witness what is happening in the White House! One wonders why Monica [Lewinsky] was keeping that dress— but let's not get into that. All of this would be inconceivable in the '60s—our blessing and our curse. The '60s were not a time about sexuality, social interrelatedness, politics. Clinton is very much a product of the '60s, as is, in his own bizarre way, Newt Gingrich. In a sense they are a reaction to the '60s. We are very much in this post-revolutionary, post-counterrevolutionary dazedness that you find in Dr. Browne's time in 17th century England. (Roca 32)

Kushner imagines Browne's era as one of transition into modern capitalism, a time in which the powerful could freely seize common lands and accumulate vast holdings of valuable property. Stressing the politics inherent in the situation, Kushner says that *Hydriotaphia* is "about how the political and economic system we live under affects everything, including the way we die. It's about how his [Browne's] death affects the lives of everyone in his household. It also is about the death of a writer and the ramifications of his work" (Evans, "Last Laughs," 10).

Along with the political, it is important to note the personal aspects of *Hydriotaphia*, a "dark comedy with a strain of gallows humor, a kind of madness" (Evans, "Last Laughs," 10), which was partially inspired by Kushner's response to the AIDS pandemic. The loss of many friends, as well as the death of his uncle, Max Deutscher, to whom he dedicated *Hydriotaphia*, were Kushner's first significant experiences with death. Describing himself as "an agnostic Jewish humanist socialist," Kushner's personal identification with the political issues and the unanswerable and frightening questions raised in *Hydriotaphia* leads him to depict "a society that glorifies individuality at the expense of connectedness, that makes a virtue of isolation and pathologizes connectedness, we make our deaths hard. Death is terrifying because we fear extinction, find it inconceivable" (Evans, "Last Laughs," 10). The failure of connectedness—of the denial of a society's accountability for the well-being of all of its citizens—is a theme that comes more fully to the fore in *Angels*, as well as in such later Kushner works as *Slavs!*, the one-act teleplay *East Coast Ode to Howard Jarvis*, and the as-yet unproduced opera libretto *Caroline, or Change*, and the screenplay *Grim(m)*.

Blending realistic and phantasmagoric elements in his seriocomic riff on Browne, Kushner employs human embodiments of Death, Browne's Soul, and witches who roam through this antic and chilling "epic farce" set in the plague-ridden days of the Restoration. The action is presented in Browne's sickroom on April 3, 1667 ("more or less" according to the stage directions, 39), and although *Hydriotaphia* demands no scene changes, its requirements are not minimal. The play is filled with the potential for numerous imaginative scenic and lighting effects, as when Browne's Soul attempts to ascend to Heaven on a golden ladder from above or when Death appears eerily from the shadows to lay "a chilly hand on Dr. Browne's throat" (3) while drawing a huge carving knife from his sleeve. Other visual inspirations are provided by the scene itself, with Kushner calling for a central deathbed with a marble headboard "like a tombstone" (41), and the richly appointed chamber is scattered with the attractions of Browne's life, including books, papers, scientific equipment, musical instruments, nautical tools, writing implements, human skulls, medicine bottles, and "bottles with dead things and necrotic tissues floating inside" (41).

In the play's opening image, wedding death with life, Browne lies semi-comatose on his deathbed while two servants roll on the floor in passionate abandon. Browne is depicted as a grasping, emotionally barren conservative who is physically and spiritually bloated with the excesses of his life. These excesses are symbolically underscored by the bizarre clutter of man-made and natural acquisitions filling his room.

As Browne slips into and out of consciousness, lying in his own filth (he describes himself as "a blossom of putrescence" [117]), Kushner begins *Hydriotaphia* by establishing Browne as the senior partner in a limestone quarry business along with his stuttering pastor, Dr. Leviticus Dogwater, a Protestant cleric who announces to Browne's wife that "once we thought Heaven glowed with the light of divine fire, Dame Dorothy, but now we *know*—it glows with the shine of gold" (67). Dogwater mouths Christian platitudes, claims to believe in its dogmas, but his true ethos, "Accumulate, Accumulate" (143), is avidly shared by Browne.

Browne's London Limestone Quarry Company has seized some Norfolk common lands, forcing the residing peasants off and onto the open road. Pounding engines beat constantly in the distance as the quarry relentlessly fills the pockets of Browne, Dogwater, and the quarry's investors, all of whom hope to expand their holdings in similar fashion with Browne's guidance. Dogwater anxiously monitors Browne's condition, hoping to wrest a controlling interest in the quarry before Browne, suffering from an onion-sized intestinal blockage, succumbs.

Grotesquely bloated from the discomforting blockage—"I'd sell my soul for a bowel movement" (72), he cries—Browne's distension metaphorically underscores his rampant acquisitiveness. Browne at first denies seeing his impertinent, sometimes bawdy Soul, who waits impatiently for his death, much in the manner of Ebenezer Scrooge denying the existence of Jacob Marley's ghost in *A Christmas Carol*. Relations between Browne and his Soul are, however, far more contentious. As Browne fights off death, Soul, striving to avoid pollution from human contact, angrily tells him, "You hoard everything. It's only justice that you should die of constipation" (78). Browne admits glimpsing a point of heavenly light in the blackness of his periodic comas, but Soul is annoyed that Browne, who has shown little interest in that bit of "gold" during his life, now clings

Figure 1: Jonathan Hadary as Sir Thomas Browne in Tony Kushner's *Hydriotaphia, or The Death of Dr. Browne* at Houston's Alley Theatre in April 1998. Photo by T. Charles Erickson.

desperately to it simply because she wants it. He battles the inevitability of his demise, thus preventing Soul's rise to Heaven. "Redeem me then," she demands, "DIE! I want nothing weighty, no ballast when I ascend. Nothing you've touched and polluted. The house, the gold, the quarry, all yours. I only want a small shard of an idea ... " (78). Death, walking the earth in the guise of Browne's long-deceased father, who Browne bitterly remembers as "a granite-hearted drunkard" (165), is prepared to oblige Soul by ending Browne's life, but he is continually— and comically—interrupted as he stalks his victim.

Browne clings to life as those around him begin a fierce battle for his fortune. Dogwater insists, "God hates idle money as much as he hates idle men" (68), and Browne detects "a distinctly mercenary scent in the air tonight. This isn't me dying; it's a great deal of money rolling over" (167). Browne's intimates are vying—through sex, lies, and avarice—for a piece of the quarry, but his long-suf-fering, no-nonsense wife, Dame Dorothy, wants nothing to do with it, explaining the essential difference between her husband and herself by pointing out that "the engines [of the quarry] give me nightmares and headaches. But they tran-quilize him" (89). The fourteen children Dame Dorothy has borne her husband provide little comfort for her since some have died in infancy and those who attained adulthood have been driven away by Browne's harsh criticisms and emotional coldness. He is ultimately able to acknowledge his familial failures when he laments, "I think now I never thought enough about love" (122). This remark points to another significant thread that runs through *Hydriotaphia* and Kushner's other works.

The only small affection Browne can find comes from Babbo, his "imponder-ably old and faithful retainer" (76) whose "charming peasant patois" (118) pro-vides him some measure of comfort. Babbo nursed Browne's father and his grandfather, and notes in the strange dialect Kushner invents for her, that Browne's grandfather "han't bin no babbie, just lonely. He bin da most entertain-ing of da three" (177). As this example indicates, the unbridled anarchy of this appealingly cluttered play carries into its dialogue. To avoid the usual stilted Americanized British stage speech, Kushner creates a crazy quilt language for the play's "bumpkins" that, he writes in the stage directions, is "derived from Yorkshire, Brooklyn and also on Krazy Kat. It is not southern American, Texan, Irish nor African American!!" adding that for the aristocratic characters, a "stan-dard American English, crisp and clear" (42) be employed.

Babbo offers the sweet warmth and comic ribaldry of an old nurse of theatri-cal tradition. She occasionally falls into sexual tomfoolery with Maccabbee, Browne's horny amanuensis, who wears a tin nose in place of the real one he has lost to a virulent case of the clap. Dr. Emil Schadenfreude, Browne's German physician and resident fop, provides little comfort, matter-of-factly expressing Kushner's fascination with "life in death" (58) while finding that his difficult patient is "a regular sack of toxins" (55). Providing further comic complications in the battle for Browne's fortune is Doña Estrelita, his Spanish ex-lover. Constructed of equal parts Carmen Miranda and Eva Peron (with a little Charo thrown in), Doña Estrelita seems to genuinely care for Browne—or at least for the memory of their torrid affair twenty years before—and she wants to take his corpse with her to be buried in Spain. Also drifting in and out is Leonard Pumpkin, Browne's gravedigger, an ambitious young man who sees his way out of poverty through the sexual favors of Browne's lonely wife. Pumpkin hopes that following Browne's death Dame Dorothy will marry him and, using her inherited riches, he can seek a knighthood and leave his peasant status permanently behind him.

Another mysterious figure appears in Magdelina Vindicta, the Abbess of X, who turns out to be Browne's sister thought lost twenty years before in a shipwreck. She is now a militantly subversive nun; "I'm not at liberty to say" (141), she imperiously intones when pressed for details about her particular order. Debating with Dogwater over Browne's fortune, she indicates her disgust with the pompous moralizing masking the cleric's greed, insisting that the "Mysteries of the Faith aren't subservient to market fluctuations!" (143). She expresses a similar disdain for Dogwater's views on religion: "They should never have translated the Bible," she says, "You are the crippled progeny of that labor" (143). Despite her protestations, however, it is clear that she, like the others, has come in hope of inheriting Browne's financial empire. In one of the play's more farcical moments, the Abbess, who Browne himself describes as "ferocious" (165), beats up Dogwater as they battle to replace forged versions of Browne's will in his desk.

The play's other comedic moments emerge in various ways: Browne gives a leech to Dogwater, who shrieks and throws it into the audience—a gag set in counterpoint with the play's more serious ambitions and intended to engage the spectators more directly in the farcical spirit of the plot. There is much joking in the play about the rivalries between Catholicism and Protestantism, as well as a broadly comic scene in which Dogwater and Schadenfreude simultaneously attempt to top each other with their florid eulogies for a profoundly disinterested Browne. Much of the remaining humor involves secondary characters struggling to prevail in winning Browne's fortune. This battle of the wills causes Browne to complain, "I seem to have lost center-stage" (116); about to become "wormfood" (73), he whines that "my later is gone" (82) and realizes there is no way to change this course of events. Dogwater stutteringly comments that "Guh-God moves in mah-mysterious and sometimes ruh-rather malicious ways. To spur us. And we go on. We duh-dare not do otherwise" (208).

Kushner adds three additional characters who represent "da homeless n' afflictet" (80). Sarah, Mary, and Ruth are all members of the Ranters, a radical religious sect that formed in England during the social unrest of the mid-seventeenth century. The Ranters, who collectively called themselves "My one flesh," proposed a unity with mankind and the whole of creation and, in essence, this is how Kushner employs the three members in the play. The historical Ranters questioned God's omnipotence, wondering why He permits evil in the world. Their pantheistic/nature-based beliefs later led many Ranters to convert to Quakerism as their sect vanished. Kushner's three Ranters are among those who have been displaced by Browne's ruthless land acquisition. Dame Dorothy, as Babbo explains, is "partial to heretics" (99), so she has admitted the three women to their house, apparently not aware that one of them, Sarah, is the daughter of a woman hanged as a witch with Browne's assistance. This element of the play is also historically based; in 1664, Browne testified at the trial of two women, Amy Duny and Rose Cullender, accused of bewitching some children. Browne was called upon as an expert witness, but, as Kushner explains, "merely stated that if we believe there is a God, we must also concede the existence of Satan and of witches. He was not attempting to sway the outcome, but to his horror, the women were hanged. There was a sense of guilt that poisoned the remaining years of his life" (Evans, "Last Laughs," 10). Those poisoned years have had a profound effect on the Browne of Kushner's play, and the Ranters are a visible reminder of Browne's culpability. They come to his home to exact revenge (while also stealing food and silver from Browne's kitchen) and provide a vivid image of those harmed, intentionally or not, by Browne's superstitions, mistakes, and acquisitiveness.

Despite the riotously lunatic comic drive of its plot, *Hydriotaphia* does not lose its focus. It is a deeply disturbing meditation on death that explains Kushner's belief in "something vital and electric in morbidity" (Mader 1). He divides the lengthy *Hydriotaphia* into three acts, and each scene is named: "Contemptus Mundis" (act 1, scene 1), "In What Torne Ship Soever I Embarke" (act 1, scene 2), "The Dance of Death" (act 2), "Who Sees Gods Face, That is Self Life, Must Die" (act 3, scene 1), and "Post Mortem" (act 3, scene 2). Although the action seems to proceed continuously, there is an episodic quality to the comings and goings of Browne's death chamber that is decidedly Brechtian.

Kushner's 1998 revision of *Hydriotaphia* strengthens the image of the central character—sardonic, querulous, argumentative, and dismissive of those around him, Browne is a forerunner of Kushner's imagining of Roy Cohn in *Angels*. Kushner characterizes both as extremely odious while still creating sympathy for their sufferings and their fundamental humanity. Browne deserves to have lost the love of his wife and absent children, admitting himself that "I did not live well" (88). He stresses, though, that "I never intended to harm. That was true" (121). His coldness—and the chill he feels from those around him—is part of his attraction to the dead, and his own disenchantment is reflected in his understanding of his archaeological work. When an ancient burial urn from the excavation of his quarry arrives, the prodigiously pedantic Browne reflects on his memories of visiting ancient Roman catacombs where "that fragile stillness" of death hovered, and where he could view the "dry, deflated bodies" and "the disappointed faces of the dead" (162). In moments like those, the play succeeds in foregrounding Kushner's belief that there is something frighteningly alive about Browne's fascination with burials and obsession with death. When Browne orders the urn to be opened, he is shaken when "a spume of dust" rises suddenly from it. Frightened, Browne notes, "See? The dead do rise" (164).

Yet Browne cannot face his own end. Prevented from being celestially freed from Browne's body, his Soul becomes increasingly human, and believes that Browne is "murdering the song" (105) of her delayed ascension. She regards Browne as dead weight that is pulling her down, so, ever the scientist, Browne orders Maccabbee to help him prove the weightlessness of the soul. Maccabbee weighs three live chickens, which are then slaughtered and weighed again. Two of the chickens weigh exactly the same as when they were alive, while the third inexplicably becomes heavier. When the expanding chicken explodes, it is discovered to be filled to overflowing with maggots, another grotesque image Kushner uses to relate Browne's physical bloat to his financial greed.

Reflecting on his own mortality, Browne laments at length on the concept of his own demise. He realizes, "Oh god I'm talking myself to death" (180). Despite a rational awareness that he is at life's final frontier, Browne cannot truly believe it. When Pumpkin arrives to discuss plans for Browne's burial, Kushner brings together many strands of Browne's persona: false modesty, arrogance, pride, morbid fascination with the rituals of death, and an abject fear of the unknown:

> I want to be buried deep. Very deep . . . not too deep. Apart from the mob, but not in a lonely place. Avoid the usual cliches, no willow trees, though I'd like a view, for summer evenings. No pine box. Flimsy. Use that urne. Toss out the previous occupant, or better yet, throw me in there with him and let us mingle. (*Little pause*) No markers, or, well, maybe just a little unpretentious stone. Maybe . . . "Here lies Sir Thomas Browne, scientist." "Here lies Sir Thomas Browne, who made his wife miserable." "Here lies Sir Thomas Browne, no grandchildren . . . BUT A GENIUS! SHAKESPEARE HAD NOTHING ON HIM!" (*He is now bellowing at Pumpkin with wild hatred and immense pride:*) Or maybe an obelisk! Or a pyramid! A pyre! A *sea*-burial, or . . . GET OUT OF HERE! (171)

When Pumpkin persists, Browne becomes hysterical: "I don't need you, wretch! I'M NOT GOING TO DIE. It isn't . . . *conceivable*! I can't . . . IF I DIE . . . THE WORLD ENDS!" (171).

Dame Dorothy makes a final sad attempt at a reconciliation, telling Browne that "I never really wanted anything from you. And you leave behind you only a dreadful lot of woe" (172). Despite this, she offers to stay with him as he faces the end, but he rebuffs her in a gesture true to his basic persona. Browne fears death, but clings to the Christian belief that the end of this life opens a door into the next. Death, comically interrupted in his prior attempts to claim Browne, finally does so in a spine-tingling scene abruptly shifting the play away from its farcical tone. Brutally strangling his helpless victim, Death points out that "there is no mystery to this. It's ugly. A simple murder . . . " (181). Browne tries to see his death in more lyrical literary terms, but Kushner maintains the nightmarish reality by employing a Melvillian seafaring metaphor that is a precursor to a similar speech by Prior Walter in *Millennium Approaches*:

> The ship embarks at first wind. The mast and sails are gilded with blood, on seas of blood we sail, in search of prey. The nets hauled in by mighty hands, up from the red depths to the surface, up come the great black nets, full and heavy of the world's riches, hauled to the stronghold, to the drybone bank of death, with a hiss and suck plucked from the waters, in a ruby mist, in a fine red rain. You . . . who must live through this . . . I pity you. (180)

Figure 2: (Front Left to Right) John Feltch as Dr. Schadenfreunde, Bettye Fitzpatrick as Babbo, and Charles Dean as Dr. Dogwater, and (Back) Alex Allen Morris as Maccabbee in Tony Kushner's *Hydriotaphia, or The Death of Dr. Browne* at Houston's Alley Theatre in April 1998. Photo by T. Charles Erickson.

Once dead, and following some additional machinations over Browne's will, the remaining characters come together to sing the English hymn, "There Is A Land of Pure Delight" (a mild anachronism—this particular hymn, by Isaac Watts, was not written until 1704). The lyrics suggest a beauty in the journey from life to death that is in ironic juxtaposition to its actuality:

> There is a land of pure delight
> Where saints immortal reign.
> Infinite day excludes the night
> And pleasure banish pain.
> There everlasting spring abides,
> And never-withering flowers.
> Death like a narrow sea divides.
> This heavenly land from ours. (197)

The inarticulate characters only understand death as a sad fact of life, and Babbo simply moans that Browne, "Nevah more ta waket" (186), although he does speak further through his will.

In the last act, Browne's true will is finally read. Here Browne's character is illuminated clearly and simply: "My will is to eat. To greedily engorge without restraint and know not eating death" (202). Death has, in fact, devoured him despite his wishes. Babbo, reflecting on Browne's death, fancifully recounts his life and fascination with a mortality he fought unsuccessfully to defeat, concluding, "N'da kid growet up to be a famous doctah wif da power a life n' death, n'den . . . N'den he died, a course" (186). Browne's will reveals that he has left his worldly riches to his wife after all, and, in response to the farcical connivings of the others vying for his fortune, he mocks, "So much fuss and bother . . . I suppose it gave the supporting cast something to do. While waiting for the end" (202). Greedily retentive to the end, Browne refuses even to share any visionary insights with his survivors: "the future. . . . NO. Don't tell them ANYTHING" (203).

Dame Dorothy, who resists the acquisitive tendencies of her late husband, sees things differently. Believing her whole generation to be "cursed by our gold" (210), and to the horror of Dogwater, the Abbess of X, and Schadenfreude, she decides to return the quarry lands "to the people" (193). She has seen too much suffering—and has endured much herself—resulting from her husband's ruthless acquisition of the land, although Kushner makes it obvious that Dame Dorothy's gesture is too little and too late. The acquisition of capital has become the order of the day, despite her resolve to resist it. Kushner's gift for rhetoric serves Dame Dorothy's explanation of her concerns for the displaced, the feelings she harbors about her life with her husband, and the ravages of capitalism:

People sleep on the open road at night. On cold mornings there's some who don't wake up. You see them, ice-crusted . . . I want a thicker skin but it won't grow, at night I hear those machines in the quarry pounding and I think: it's flesh those hammers pound, it's bone. We're immensely rich but we live without luxury. He can't bear to part with anything, even remorse, and I can't bear the accumulation. Thomas is lucky to die. I must live on here for a while yet, and I hate this life. In me there is a bleeding wound, and it never heals, and it's full of blood, and full of light, and there's paradise in there, besieged and unreachable but always beckoning. And the more foul and ugly the world becomes the more it beckons. The more it aches. (135–36)

Browne's world collapses completely after his death when an alcohol-sotted corpse stashed in the kitchen oven by Pumpkin ignites a fire destroying part of his house. More significantly, the thunder of the quarry machines, mated to Browne's final desperate heartbeats, abruptly stops as the machines collapse into an underground catacomb. Browne's Soul enjoys a postmortem cigarette, but Dame Dorothy firmly rejects Pumpkin and resolves to make the crossing to a new—and perhaps better (or at least more hopeful)—world in America.

A primer for appreciating the style and substance of Kushner's later works, *Hydriotaphia*, like *Bright Room*, establishes his lofty ambitions for a revitalized epic theater which, as he himself explains, explores possibilities that "range from a vastly improved world to no world at all" (Mader 1). The Brechtian influences are somewhat less overt in *Hydriotaphia* than in *Bright Room* as Kushner's own aesthetic asserts itself with greater confidence, but the political message of the play seeps through the cracks of its grisly mausoleum slapstick. The episodic, cinematic qualities are also less in evidence, but there is no lessening of the grotesque phantasmagoria that is given free range thanks, in part, to the play's being set in a time of primitive premodern science. The wonders of contemporary science are viewed in their first awkward, unknowing stages and are, as such, frightening in their horrific ignorance. Browne himself is little more than a science experiment, undergoing leechings and enemas with Rube Goldberg machines belonging more to a commedia dell'arte farce than to real life, as well as various other repugnant procedures which only hasten a death that mere decades later would be treated successfully by medical science. Kushner effectively—if, in this case, with outrageous humor and ghoulish imagery—features his recurring fascination with the wrenches of transitions. It is not only the encroachment of capitalism, but also the marriage of superstition to religion and their collision with science that is also central to *Hydriotaphia*. The intersection of the macabre and the comic has not been given such free range in Kushner's subsequent work, although it is always present even if applied with more subtlety. It is, however, the excessive weirdness of *Hydriotaphia* that is its greatest strength; Kushner imagines the seventeenth century in its most backward, uncomprehending awkwardness and so creates a vision of the human condition in its basest form. Here, Restoration comedy meets a Saturday matinee horror movie, Browne meets the Marxes (Karl and Groucho), and the result is a surprisingly bracing, nightmarish romp through church, cemetery, and capitalism.

When *Hydriotaphia* was given its first professional productions, it premiered at the Alley Theatre in Houston, Texas, for a run scheduled March 27–April 25, 1998. The press opening was delayed a week as Kushner, still revising, continued to sharpen the play. According to the local Houston press, Kushner "has made extensive rewrites that will be going into the production this week, and the Alley wanted to give the cast and production crew time to accommodate the changes" (Evans, "Kushner Still Tweaking *Hydriotaphia* Script," 1C). The Houston performances were followed some months later by a September 11–November 1, 1998 run at the Berkeley Repertory Theatre in Berkeley, California, with several cast members held over from the Alley production. Both productions greatly profited from the performance of Jonathan Hadary, who had played Roy Cohn in the national tour of *Angels in America*. Hadary gave a potent performance as Browne, with one critic noting that he gave the character "a blend of mortal suffering and intellectual detachment" (Evans, "Kushner Hits Highs, Lows in Epic Farce," 1D). Other cast members appearing in both productions included longtime San Francisco Mime Troupe member Sharon Lockwood (The Abbess of X), Shelley Williams (Dame Dorothy), Charles Dean (who played Dogwater at the Alley and switched to Schadenfreude at Berkeley), Paul Hope (Death), and Delia MacDougall, Moya Furlow, and Louise Chegwidden as the Ranters.

Critics in both regions were split over the play's merits. Some reviewers felt there were too many themes to allow an audience to grasp them all. This is a frequent criticism of Kushner's plays. Others disagreed on the success with which the balance of farce and seriousness was presented, with one Houston critic describing Kushner's "wildly erratic" and "irreverent" play as abounding "in bright, whimsical ideas" and with a production that was "ingenious, well-paced and full of neat visual effects" (Evans, "Kushner Hits Highs, Lows in Epic Farce," 1D). Others were less impressed, finding it merely a "mildly interesting entertainment, but the play fails as craft, as social commentary and as a measure of Kushner's formidable talent" (Halverson). Another critic stressed that *Hydriotaphia* contained "some very, very funny moments and has a lovely visual, if occasionally visceral, impact," but found the script "wordy" (Arenschieldt 19).

California critics concurred with those in Texas, with one reviewer appreciating the play's "bubbly, profound, historically rooted Monty Python–meets–Ben Jonson tribute to writing. And he [Kushner] has disguised it as a comedy about thanatology, the study of the experience of dying and bereavement" (De La Viña 29). Another reviewer groused about the play's three-and-a-half-hour length, finding that the play was "as bloated as its protagonist," but that it was "eminently worth watching" and that the "heady result is what might have emerged had Bertolt Brecht and Joe Orton collaborated on a Restoration comedy" (Rosenstein). The comparison to Restoration comedy is apt, but another California critic compared the "often smart and funny" play with George Bernard Shaw's *Heartbreak House*, feeling that it also seemed "static and redundant, an ambitious, anxious work by a writer who was warming up to write a masterpiece" (Winn C1). Other critics stressed *Hydriotaphia*'s contemporariness, with one writer arguing that *Hydriotaphia* is "utterly current in its portrayal of the spiritual corruption that can slowly infect the noblest of souls," despite the play's seventeenth-century setting, adding that "the theater world is never more effectively subversive than when making stinging observations about our world through the lens of another" (Stearns 4D). Most critics commented in some way on "Kushner's deep, playful love of language" (De La Viña 29), and even those finding faults with aspects of *Hydriotaphia* felt it was evidence of Kushner's ability to deliver on his impressive ambitions as a playwright.

Kushner himself felt that *Hydriotaphia* is "in some ways the most heterogeneous play I have written, really sprawling. Even for me" (Roca 32). Reflecting on the play in performance, Kushner stressed "it really is about what the subtitle says, about death and primitive capital achievement. But the longer I have been listening to it, the more I realize it is a play about writing" (Roca 32). Whether Kushner means to suggest that he, as a writer, is able to debate with Browne the writer, or that he admires Browne's ability to capture in prose the mysteries of life and death, is unclear, but for Kushner *Hydriotaphia* prefigured his move toward writing about those aspects of human experience not easily grasped and that may never be understood or articulated by the living, despite our innate awareness of things beyond our comprehension.

In fact, *Hydriotaphia* is, like all of Kushner's major works, overflowing with themes and is illustrative of the author's daring as a writer. Kushner's excess and fearlessness may be viewed as virtues or flaws by audiences and critics, but either way *Hydriotaphia*, in its earliest form and as revised, moved Kushner closer to a fuller explication of themes and growth as a dramatist that would permit him to revitalize late-twentieth-century American theater with *Angels in America*.

CHAPTER THREE

Troubling the Waters

Angels in America. A Gay Fantasia on National Themes

> For an angel went down at a certain season into the pool, and troubled the waters.
>
> —John 5:4

Angels have long been symbols of spiritual significance. Residing in a realm somewhere between the Deity and His creations, angels watch over humanity as unspeakably beautiful harbingers of hope and of death. Kushner turned to Walter Benjamin's image of the Angel of History as the guiding metaphor for his ambitious, sweeping epic, *Angels in America. A Gay Fantasia on National Themes*, which is made up of two long plays, *Millennium Approaches* and *Perestroika*. Benjamin writes of a Paul Klee painting, "Angelus Novus," showing

> an angel looking as though he is about to move away from something he is fixedly contemplating. His eyes are staring, his mouth is open, his wings are spread. This is how one pictures the angel of history. His face is turned toward the past. Where we perceive a chain of events, he sees one single catastrophe which keeps piling wreckage upon wreckage and hurls it in front of his feet. The angel would like to stay, awaken the dead, and make whole what has been smashed. But a storm is blowing from Paradise; it has got caught in his wings with such violence that the angel can no longer close them. This storm irresistibly propels him into the future to which his back is turned, while the pile of debris before him grows skyward. This storm is what we call progress. (257–58)

The *Angels* plays, feverish historical dramas about America's immediate and contemporary history, examine many themes, but are held together by Benjamin's conception of the ruins of history as the price of progress. *Angels* depicts, with varying degrees of anger, humor, and empathy, a poignant and epic tapestry of the substantial societal and spiritual issues facing humankind—and Americans in particular—at the dawn of the new millennium. Presenting a moral combat represented at various points—and on numerous fronts—by the opposing poles of conservative and liberal, gay and straight, victimizer and victim, *Angels* also deftly captures a convergence of *past* (dying old values and certainties symbolized by the death of an elderly Jewish woman who has journeyed from the Old World to America and by a diorama of a Mormon pioneer family), *present* (selfishness, faithlessness, and isolation, as typified by the era itself, by archconservative politician Roy Cohn, and by a perceived decline of compassion in American society at the end of the twentieth century), and *future* (represented as a choice between further deterioration or an acceptance of the necessity of change, as exemplified at the end of *Millennium Approaches* by the startling appearance of an angel who may bring news of salvation or of apocalypse).

Gilbert A. Harrison writes that in Thornton Wilder's *The Skin of Our Teeth* (1942), another classic American play surveying a broad historical canvas and perhaps the first American play to combine apocalyptic anxiety with a renewed sense of hope as in *Angels*, Wilder attempts "to chart mankind's wrong turnings, dead ends, pain, treachery, brutality, absurdities while simultaneously underlining the fact of human endurance" (Harrison 195). Wilder's awareness that much mid-twentieth-century literature and drama suggested that modern man was losing faith in the future led him to propose a new optimism in *The Skin of Our Teeth*. It was possible, he felt, to renew faith in the "conviction that the Positive still lies about us in sufficient fragments to live by" (Harrison 196), and this view, informed by the catastrophic developments of the second half of the twentieth century, permeates *Angels*.

Kushner, like Wilder, takes on the mantle of proposing an imaginary future based on the political and social turmoil of the immediate past and the present. *Angels* exemplifies the literary myth of apocalypse that refers to the beginning and end of time by placing individual and societal circumstances within an ever-continuing arch of universal creation and history. As Lois Parkinson Zamora writes, apocalypse is "a myth of radical transformation, a myth of transcendence. Old worlds can be supplanted by new ones, and if man has 'fallen into time' from his original timeless Eden, there is yet hope for a future paradise: time is impelled forward by a moral dialectic, the present always future-tending" (97–98).

In *Angels*, Kushner's apocalyptic harbinger is an Angel and, in the final scene of *Perestroika*, the play's survivors meet at Central Park's Bethesda fountain, which features a statue of the Biblical angel who "troubled the waters." This angel, coincidentally, was the subject of one of Wilder's early one-act plays, *The Angel That Troubled the Waters* (1928). Kushner uses this imagery at the end of *Perestroika* and throughout both *Angels* plays as he "troubles the waters" of American life in order to permit revelation to his characters of a cure to their ills and a possibility of a new beginning. In *The Angel That Troubled the Waters*, Wilder's angel asks the various crippled souls, "Without your wound where would your power be?" (149). This notion similarly empowers Kushner's characters, some of whom grow strong through their great suffering.

Like Kushner, Wilder wrote during a turbulent time of transition away from nineteenth-century attitudes through the cataclysms of the first half of the twentieth century. His first major work for the theater, *The Trumpet Shall Sound* (1926), is about a particularly American disaster, the Civil War. However, it is in Wilder's Pulitzer Prize–winning novel of 1927, *The Bridge of San Luis Rey*, that many of his recurrent themes emerge. In this novel, his characters must face—and even long for—an apocalypse. One character says, "Let me live now. Let me begin again" (86). Wilder explores this concept in both *Our Town*—as the deceased Emily gets to return to life for a day (much as Prior asks the angels for more life in *Perestroika*)—and, more significantly, as the human race gets to start over in *The Skin of Our Teeth*. Bound together by the mythical metaphor of the apocalyptic angel, Kushner and Wilder each attempt to offer humanly redemptive dramas that stimulate both intellect and emotion. Kushner succeeds more fully, in part because he incorporates his political views (which Wilder tends to scrupulously avoid) and uses his rambles through history to illuminate topical social questions, moral dilemmas, and spiritual issues of the late twentieth century.

Kushner is overtly provocative in ways that Wilder is not. Wilder seems to support traditional and mainstream views and values and his plays appear to be nonconfrontational at first glance. Wilder's work, though, is not without strongly stated views on the oppressive moralizing, anti-intellectualism, and hypocrisy of stereotypical small town life. However, this is about as politicized as Wilder's work gets. Kushner's dramatization of the struggle between American conservatives and liberals, and, more specifically, of the conflict over moral and social dilemmas (such as the conflict between religious beliefs and social reality, homosexuality, the AIDS pandemic, and the attempt to locate a moral footing in a broadly multicultural and diverse democratic society) carries *Angels* to a higher plain. It is interesting to note that a significant link between Wilder and Kushner is the influence of Brecht's epic theater, though Wilder seems only interested in the dramatic techniques, not the content. Brecht's dramatic experiments of the 1930s—particularly in plays like *Mother Courage and Her Children* (1939–40)—provide distinct parallels to *The Skin of Our Teeth*. Both plays present the devastation of war and the many aspects of good and evil in the human character exposed by deprivation and suffering. Kushner similarly believes in progress, but the emotional response his characters elicit from an audience seem to be closer to Wilder's humanism than to Brecht's alienation concept.

Wilder and Kushner both share Brecht's view that the stage can function to encourage a progressive society, but Kushner embraces a bolder political approach than does Wilder. Wilder depicts human experience as a cycle of building up and tearing down, but with some slight progress possible. Kushner in *Angels* also believes in progress, but presents a battle of political ideologies in order to explore the deeper anxieties of its characters through their visions of the ways power and the powerful effect and control their lives, and as they discover their own strengths and weaknesses while buffeted by social changes that are sometimes more complex than they can imagine. It is often presumed that political drama cannot, by virtue of its transitory topicality, attain universality. However, Kushner writes:

It is immensely difficult, if not impossible, to write a play intended to enter into public discourse that is free of any reference to current events, to news. It's hard to understand why anyone would want to. There's an old fantasy that if one writes a play void of any reference to the world in which we live, void of all reference to political parties, to popular culture, to money and to global conflict, one will be producing something more able of gliding through this present distasteful moment and up into that hyperborean realm toward which, we are told, all artists aspire: eternity, universality, immortality—the canon. Nothing seems plainer to me than that work that has attained such status was not designed to do so, but rather came out of the *urgent now*; that any such universality as a work may claim must proceed from its particulars to the general, and that art that strives for universality winds up being generic, and dull; and also, finally, that eternity is a very long time, and immortality almost certainly an impossibility. ("Notes About Political Theatre" 29)

Kushner's politics are based in a socialism inspired, in part, by Brecht's dramatic aesthetic, which created for Kushner a template for political drama. *Angels* is certainly inspired by aspects of Brechtian theater, but it is primarily fueled by Walter Benjamin and by British socialist and literary critic Raymond Williams. In his 1985 essay, "Walking Backwards into the Future," Williams describes socialism as "based on the idea and the practice of *a society*" (283). He points to two sources of confidence inspiring socialists: "a moment in history when the world would be changed" (281) and the discovery of "the laws of movement in history" (282). The realm of socialism, Williams posits, is more than merely a place for "stranded utopians and sectarians" (282):

The idea of *a society* was to distinguish one form of social relationships from another, and to show that these forms varied historically and could change. Thus, in thinking about the longstanding problems of virtue and happiness, people who began from the idea of a society did not immediately refer the problems to a general human nature or to inevitable conditions of existence; they looked first at the precise forms of the society in which they were living and at how these might, where necessary, be changed. The first uses of *socialist*, as a way of thinking, were in deliberate contrast to the meanings of *individualist*: both as a challenge to that other way of thinking, in which all human behaviour was reduced to matters of individual character and more sharply as a challenge to its version of human intentions. Was life an arena in which individuals should strive to improve their own conditions, or was it a network of human relationships in which people found everything of value in and through each other? (283)

These questions provide a foundation for aspects of *Angels*. In Williams's essays there is a belief that with socialism, the "power of private capital to shape or influence these decisions is replaced by active and often local social decision, in what is always in practice the real disposition of our lives," and that there is "an immense and widespread longing for this kind of practical share in shaping our own lives. It has never yet been fully articulated politically and it is our strongest resource, if we can learn to deal honestly with it, for a socialist future" (285–86). Williams envisions this future as one in which "the public interest is not singular but is a complex and interactive network of *different* real interests. A sharing plan begins from this acknowledgement of *diversity*, and encourages the true social processes of open discussion, negotiation and agreement" (285–86). Williams's concept of a socialist society significantly shapes Kushner's conception of America under Reagan. For Kushner, Reagan leads an abandonment of the notion of a society concerned with the "longstanding problems of virtue and happiness." *Angels*, like most of Kushner's work, argues for a reordering of American society along lines suggested by Williams's socialist theories. Laced throughout *Angels* is the call for a reevaluation of old certitudes, whether they be political, social, religious (or moral), or personal. A reformed society built on a progressive, compassionately humanist doctrine that draws its strength from the hard lessons of the past is central to both Williams's theories and *Angels*. For the characters in the play, proceeding into the unknown future seems too frightening, too painful, and too confusing. Walking backwards into the future, as Williams suggests, is a possible route—finding in the values of the past both the triumphant and the catastrophic. When Prior Walter invites the audience to imagine more life at the end of *Perestroika*, he does so with his eyes firmly fixed on what is behind him as well as what might be in front. It is a guarded optimism, won through terrible personal ordeals and a belief in the power of humanity to survive its own failings.

Kushner, like Wilder, struggles with a redefinition of the realistic theater. Kushner's imaginative variations extend the borders of the theater to include surreal projections of the interior and exterior lives of the characters (more frequently thought of as belonging to expressionism), and, in *Angels*, as in *Bright Room* and *Hydriotaphia*, Kushner pushes the borders of realistic theater further by combining fundamentally realistic characters and situations with ghosts, historical displacements, and outright fantasy to alter the way audiences experience the characters' ordinary lives. Kushner describes his attraction to Brecht as deriving to some extent from the ways Brecht

> married the illusion/reality paradigm at the heart of all Western theatre since the Italian Renaissance and Shakespeare to its counterpart in Marx. The distinction that Marx makes between the *real* and the *social*, between the world of illusion created by relationships between producers of commodities, and some unknowable *real* of which the *social* is an imaginary reflection, between the real labor which creates goods in a commodity-producing system, and the form of the commodity into which the traces of labor, of human relationship has disappeared. Theatre, like dialectical materialist analysis, examines the magic of perception and the political, ideological employment to which the magic is put. ("Notes About Political Theatre" 27)

Angels demonstrates that Kushner also has a Shavian affection for political digression (an unfolding human drama interrupted by bursts of social theorizing and debate), but it also demonstrates that socially conscious drama has progressed aesthetically from Shaw through Brecht and on. Kushner has a particular skill for bringing together wildly disparate plot lines, political theorems, and aesthetic motifs in original and satisfying ways, mixing the political and social with the sexual and the personal in ways that call to mind writers as diverse as Walt Whitman, Herman Melville, Thomas Pynchon, and, of course, Brecht.

Critics and audiences alike have recognized the unique qualities of *Angels*, both in terms of its aesthetic achievements and in its enormous thematic challenges. Any student of theater history can recount tales of plays that have attempted to push the boundaries of the social, moral, and political discourse of its time. A drama contesting established values is frequently met with a combination of high praise from supporters and bitter condemnation from detractors. Some of Eugene O'Neill's plays of the 1920s challenged audiences on thematic and artistic grounds—and were occasionally met with outrage over content assaulting contemporary mores. Clifford Odets's left-wing agitprop plays, Tennessee Williams's sexually liberated dramas, Edward Albee's assault on middle-class values and the institution of marriage, the antiwar and counterestablishment plays of the late 1960s, Sam Shepard's gritty and ambiguous parables of broken families and decaying American society, Christopher Durang's stinging satires of Catholicism and upper-middle class values, and David Mamet's linguistically minimalistic slices of the dark side of capitalism—not to mention gay and lesbian-themed plays—are but a few examples of playwrights creating dramatic challenges to the status quo. These plays, obviously intended by their authors to inspire strong and diverse reactions, have occasionally fallen victim to more than the intellectual and emotional debate they meant to create in their audiences. Plays have been banned, public and private funding eliminated for theaters producing them, changes in the works have been demanded, and suspicions have been raised about the motives of their writers and presenters.

All of this and more has been true of *Angels*, which crosses over into controversial terrain on several fronts. Kushner's dramatization of America's seemingly eternal struggle between conservative and liberal—"the liberal pluralist solution (everyone do his or her own thing) against the conservative solution (everyone do the conservatives' thing)" (Graff 10)—and, more specifically, the conflict over the moral and social dilemmas of homosexuality have caused the greatest consternation. In fact, the plays deal with a number of sensitive issues in current American society, many of which are of grave significance: religious beliefs in conflict with social reality, the polarity of American politics, homosexuality, the AIDS pandemic, and the attempt to find moral footing in a multicultural and diverse democratic society in which values seem to be constantly shifting.

If his earlier plays did not make it obvious, *Angels* vividly demonstrates that Kushner is a rarity in American theater—a sociopolitical dramatist. European drama has supplied numerous political playwrights, but comparatively few have emerged in a century of American playwriting. A century before Kushner, George Bernard Shaw, who used the stage as a forum for social debate, believed that every play criticizing society "must, if it is an honest play, involve a certain struggle with the public" (Shaw, May 18, 1895, n.p.). Brecht, whose influence on Kushner is profound, held that "without opinions and objectives one can represent nothing at all" (Brecht 196). Kushner's own sense of the conjunction of politics and art is that

> all theater is political. If you don't declare your politics, your politics are probably right-wing. I cannot be a playwright without having some temptation to let audiences know what I think when I read the newspaper in the morning. What I find is that the things that make you the most uncomfortable are the best things to write plays about. (Blanchard 42)

As Kushner began to think about *Angels* in the mid-1980s, there was much making him uncomfortable: the AIDS crisis and its impact on the gay community, the slow response of American society in general to facing its tragic ramifications, and the country's political swing toward conservatism. As such, *Angels* is charged with a potent mixture of the angers, fears, absurdities, and hypocrisies of the times in which it is set.

The Angel of History: *Millennium Approaches*

Following a long period of gestation, the first of the two *Angels* plays, *Millennium Approaches*, was given a workshop performance at the Mark Taper Forum in May 1990 prior to its official premiere at San Francisco's Eureka Theatre, which had commissioned the work thanks, in part, to a special project grant from the National Endowment of the Arts. The Eureka had previously produced *A Bright Room Called Day* and Oskar Eustis, that production's director, had become a close friend of Kushner's. A combination of the aesthetic demands of the play and a fear of the play's potential for controversy kept Broadway producers from optioning the play initially, despite the critical accolades heaped on the Eureka production. Following revisions and some changes in production staff and cast, *Millennium Approaches* moved to Los Angeles's Mark Taper Forum in 1992, where it received more acclaim. This quintessentially American play was also extremely well-received in a Royal National Theatre of Great Britain production in January 1992, before finally opening on Broadway on May 4, 1993 at the Walter Kerr Theatre. Under the direction of George C. Wolfe, the Broadway cast featured members from San Francisco and Los Angeles (Stephen Spinella, Kathleen Chalfant, and Ellen McLaughlin), from Los Angeles (Joe Mantello), and new members (Rob Leibman, David Marshall Grant, Marcia Gay Harden, and Jeffrey Wright). *Millennium Approaches* was enthusiastically received in New York.

From the time that *Millennium Approaches* first moved to the Mark Taper Forum—before the second *Angels* play, *Perestroika*, had been performed—it began to receive international attention, critical praise, and awards. The acknowledgments included two Fund for New American Plays/American Express Awards, the 1991 National Arts Club's Joseph Kesselring Award, and the Bay Area Drama Critics Award for the Best Play of 1991. When *Millennium Approaches* was produced at the Royal National Theatre of Great Britain it won the London

Evening Standard Award, the London Drama Critics Award, and the Olivier Award as Best Play. When *Millennium Approaches* arrived on Broadway, Kushner was awarded the Pulitzer Prize for Drama. *Millennium Approaches* also received the Tony Award as Best Play, as well as awards for cast members, and a host of critics' awards. Approximately six months after *Millennium Approaches* opened on Broadway, *Perestroika*, which had been performed in repertory with *Millennium Approaches* in San Francisco, Los Angeles, and London, was also performed in repertory with *Millennium Approaches* by the same cast. It also won a Tony Award as Best Play and was a contender for another Pulitzer Prize among its many accolades.

Millennium Approaches begins on a somber note as an elderly rabbi stands over the coffin of Sarah Ironson, an old Jewish woman whose turbulent life embodies the struggles of the immigrant experience, and who, as the rabbi explains, was "not a person but a whole kind of person, the ones who crossed the ocean" (10) so that their children could grow up in America. He stresses, however, that "no such place exists" as America, that "the clay of some Litvak shtetl" (10) has been worked into the bones of Sarah's descendants, that their culture must be passed on. The rabbi harangues the congregation about their lack of respect for the past and for the individual journeys of those like the deceased. He ends his oration with the ominous warning that Sarah's passing means that "pretty soon . . . all the old will be dead" (11), and, with them will go the values and certitudes imported to America by their generation.

In the next several short scenes of this episodic play, Kushner alternately shifts his gaze to two couples: a married pair, Joe and Harper Pitt, and a gay couple, Prior Walter and Louis Ironson, the latter of whom is Sarah's grandson. The two relationships are at crisis points. Following Sarah's funeral, Prior (whose last name Kushner takes from the first name of Walter Benjamin), reveals to Louis that he is HIV positive by showing his first lesion, calling it the "wine-dark kiss of the angel of death" (21). Prior, acknowledging sadly that "I'm going to die" (21), is forced to try to calm Louis who, he fears, will be unable to cope with what is coming and will leave him. Meanwhile, Harper and Joe, both Mormons who have moved to New York a year before so that Joe could take a job as a law clerk for a judge, have grown apart. At this point, their lives intersect with one of the play's historical figures, Roy M. Cohn.

Cohn (1927–86), who was born in New York as the son of an affluent, liberal Bronx court judge and a mother with whom he lived for forty of his fifty-nine years, became a lawyer and a post–World War II conservative power broker. He came to national attention as a twenty-three-year-old assistant U.S. attorney, securing the death penalty for Julius and Ethel Rosenberg. The Rosenbergs were convicted of treason for allegedly selling nuclear secrets to the Russians in 1951 and both were subsequently executed. Cohn became even better known as the self-described "strong right arm" of Senator Joseph McCarthy during the infamous House Committee on Un-American Activities Communist "witch hunts" of the early 1950s. McCarthy's overzealousness and dubious tactics (enthusiastically supported by Cohn) ultimately led to his fall from grace, after which Cohn became a powerful behind-the-scenes force in the Republican Party and a successful New York divorce lawyer, although shortly before his death he was disbarred for unethical practices. Spotted frequently in the early 1980s at New York's posh Studio 54 nightclub, Cohn died of AIDS in 1986, although he insisted until the end that he was suffering from liver cancer. Cohn aggressively supported the antihomosexual agenda of McCarthy and frequently spoke against gay rights, so his life provides Kushner with a compelling figure through which to explore issues of the deeply closeted gay male in late-twentieth-century America, as well as the hypocrisies Kushner sees in conservative politics.

Joe Pitt's own conservative politics attract him to Cohn, who, in turn, would like to place Joe in the Justice Department as a "Royboy" (64) in Washington. Joe meets Kushner's Cohn, a rapacious political predator, in his sleek office command module where he is working his multiline telephone like a piano, wishing he had eight arms like "a fucking octopus. Eight loving arms and all those suckers" (11). Kushner uses outrageous, sardonic humor in his characterization of Cohn, whose enthusiastically cynical corruption is at once both comic and frightening. One of the most remarkable aspects of *Angels* is that Kushner achieves sympathetic moments for his most monstrous and misbehaving characters, like Cohn, whose venomous self-loathing is one of the play's most unsettling aspects. Cohn's persona is most vividly demonstrated in his scathing denial of his own homosexuality when, near the end of the play's first act, he learns from his doctor that he is suffering from AIDS:

> Like all labels they tell you one thing and one thing only: where does an individual so identified fit in the food chain, in the pecking order? Not ideology, or sexual taste, but something much simpler: clout. Not who I fuck or who fucks me, but who will pick up the phone when I call, who owes me favors. This is what a label refers to. Now to someone who does not understand this, homosexual is what I am because I have sex with men. But really this is wrong. Homosexuals are not men who sleep with other men. Homosexuals are men who in fifteen years of trying cannot get a pissant antidiscrimination bill through City Council. Homosexuals are men who know nobody and who nobody knows. Who have zero clout. (45)

Cohn claims that one either makes laws or is subject to them, and he insists that power is America's defining force. For him, the world is chaos and terror and can be survived only if the individual becomes a law unto himself. As Belize, a gay African-American nurse, drag queen, and Prior's closest friend, says of Cohn in *Perestroika*: "I'll show you America. Terminal, crazy and mean" (96). Cohn represents a kind of trickle-down morality in *Angels*—Kushner's notion that if corruption, greed, and bad faith exist in the powerful members of a society, it will ultimately seep down to each individual. As Robert Brustein writes, there are "no angels in America, only angles" (30), and *Angels* presents a battle of political angles—conservative and liberal ideologies in moral combat against each other as the historical failures and hypocrisies within each are challenged. The centrality of politics in *Angels* can be found most obviously in Cohn, the exemplar of traditional American conservatism. He revels in his clout and has no room for compassion for the powerless in his vision of the world. Indeed, when Joe confides his feelings of guilt about his decision to leave Harper, Cohn advises that Joe "learn at least this: What you are capable of. Let nothing stand in your way" (58).

Joe eventually decides to leave Harper because he is caught up in a personal struggle with his long-repressed homosexuality. He has lived according to the rules by which he was raised: to be straight, to be a family man, to be devoutly religious, and to be a staunchly conservative Republican. However, he is also miserably unhappy. In an agonized plea to Harper, who demands that Joe tell her whether or not he is, in fact, a homosexual, Joe replies:

> Does it make any difference? That I might be one thing deep within, no matter how wrong or ugly that thing is, so long as I have fought, with everything I have, to kill it. What do you want from me, Harper? More than that? For God's sake, there's nothing left, I'm a shell. There's nothing left to kill. As long as my behavior is what I know it has to be. Decent. Correct. That alone in the eyes of God. (40)

When Joe is finally driven to acknowledge his sexual orientation, he telephones his widowed mother, Hannah, in the middle of the night. He painfully reveals his secret in a scene mirroring the experiences of many gays (Kushner says this scene is reminiscent of his own "coming out"). After some preliminary awkwardness, during which Joe admits to being drunk, he blurts it out: "Mom. Momma. I'm a homosexual, Momma. Boy, did that come out awkward. (*Pause*) Hello? Hello? I'm a homosexual. (*Pause*) Please, Momma. Say something" (75). Shocked, Hannah is unable to reply directly or to even acknowledge what Joe has said, but as it sinks in she ends the call with a burst of sudden anger by shouting, "Drinking is a sin! A sin! I raised you better than that" (76).

Later, Joe encounters Louis, who is in a fearful flight from Prior, who is beginning to suffer the initial stages of full-blown AIDS. Racked with guilt over his faithlessness, the politically liberal Louis reflects on the era, which he sees as a metaphor for his own behavior. He describes himself, and Joe, as "children of the new morning, criminal minds. Selfish and greedy and loveless and blind. Reagan's children" (74). Louis later has a brutal, punishing sexual encounter with a stranger in Central Park. The stranger asks, "You been a bad boy?" Louis can only reply sadly, "Very bad. Very bad" (55).

Meanwhile, Joe's wife Harper, an agoraphobic seriously addicted to Valium, and Prior, a sometime caterer and designer living partly on a trust fund who is often delirious as he becomes sicker, meet in a mutual hallucination. The highly imaginative Harper is prone to fantasies as an escape from her loneliness and unhappiness. Harper's inability to distinguish reality is seen by Kushner as an appealing quality—she, like the drag-loving Prior, has a rich imaginative life. Harper has already begun to imagine journeys away from her problems, and her troubled relationship with Joe, when she is visited by Mr. Lies, an imaginary travel agent, who looks like the African-American travel agent she became innocently attracted to while planning their move to New York. Fantasizing about this man as an escape from her profound sadness, Harper searches for a place without emotional pain and loneliness. She says, "People who are lonely, people left alone, sit talking nonsense to the air, imagining ... beautiful systems dying, old fixed orders spiraling apart ... " (16). As she confesses to Joe in one of their frequent, heartbreaking confrontations, "I have to make up people to talk to me" (40).

Drifting off into a Valium-induced haze, Harper comes upon Prior, a character in whom Kushner combines the improbably mixed traits of wonderment and cynicism, hope and despair. Prior also has a strong taste for camp, and his references to the icons, music, and expressions of popular culture allow Kushner to lighten the play's darkest moments with hilarity. When Harper stumbles on Prior, he is in full and elegant drag, seated at his dressing table intoning, "I'm ready for my closeup, Mr. DeMille" (30). Delirious from AIDS and too many medications, Prior sees Harper at the same time that she sees him, and, on this strange "threshold of revelation" (33), Prior sees Harper's profound unhappiness and she sees that despite the ravages of his illness, "deep inside you, there's a part of you, the most inner part, entirely free of disease" (34). This provides some small comfort to Prior, but their encounter is otherwise comic, as their vastly different backgrounds offer riotous juxtapositions. When Harper notices that Prior is wearing makeup, she explains that she cannot because she is a Mormon; "I'm a homosexual," Prior confesses, and Harper says, "Oh! In my church we don't believe in homosexuals" (32). Prior immediately replies, "In my church we don't believe in Mormons" (32).

Despite their obviously fertile imaginations, Prior and Harper discuss the limitations of the imagination. Harper concludes that "when we think we've escaped the unbearable ordinariness and, well, untruthfulness of our lives, it's really only the same old ordinariness and falseness rearranged into the appearance of novelty and truth. Nothing unknown is knowable" (32). She finds this "the most depressing hallucination" she has ever had, a feeling that is compounded when she encourages Prior to "see things" and he tells her, "Your husband's a homo" (33). She tries to deny it, but knows deep down that this revelation is true. It at least explains Joe's frequent absences, so she asks Prior if "homos take, like, lots of long walks?" (33), to which he sarcastically replies, "Yes. We do. In stretch pants with lavender coifs" (34). She rushes away and Prior hears a voice inviting him to "Look up, look up, prepare the way" (35) as a large feather floats down from above. He sinks into despair from this disturbing intrusion and his realization that Louis may be gone.

Louis is struggling with what to do about his relationship with Prior, so he turns to the rabbi who spoke at his grandmother's funeral to ask, "what does the Holy Writ say about someone who abandons someone he loves at a time of great need?" (25). The rabbi wonders why anyone would do that and the distraught Louis replies:

Maybe because this person's sense of the world, that it will change for the better with struggle, maybe a person who has this neo-Hegelian positivist sense of constant historical progress towards happiness or perfection or something, who feels

Figure 3: Cynthia Mace, as Harper, and Stephen Spinella, as Prior, in the Mark Taper Forum's 1992 production of Tony Kushner's *Angels in America, Part One: Millennium Approaches.* Photo by Jay Thompson.

very powerful because he feels connected to these forces, moving uphill all the time ... maybe that person can't, um, incorporate sickness into his sense of how things are supposed to go. Maybe vomit ... And sores and disease ... Really frighten him, maybe ... he isn't so good with death. (25)

The rabbi offers little comfort, suggesting that if Louis needs to confess, he should find a priest: "Catholics believe in forgiveness. Jews believe in Guilt" (25). Both parts of *Angels* feature characters who are gay and some who are Jewish. The "complicated, contradictory Jewish types—reactionary Roy Cohn, liberal Louis Ironson, dead radical Ethel Rosenberg" are used by Kushner to examine the trajectory of the Jew through American politics and popular imagery, explains critic Alisa Solomon. As such, Solomon proposes, "the image of the Jew tends to become the image of everyone ... the metaphorical Jew" (122). Louis's grandmother, Sarah, represents one version of the metaphorical Jew, tied to her shtetl past and in the American melting pot ("where nothing melted" [10], as the rabbi insists at her funeral), bringing to America the values of nineteenth-century Eastern European culture and, in some respects, influencing American Jews of subsequent generations. These later generations of American Jews are represented by Cohn on one end of the spectrum and Louis on the other.

The Mormon characters of Joe, Harper, and Hannah provide Kushner with another unyieldingly strict religious tradition, one, Kushner stresses, that is "home-grown" American in its belief that "you're judged by your deeds rather than by your intentions. That's something Mormonism and Judaism share: you have to do good to be good" ("The Secrets of *Angels*" H5). As in other Kushner plays, especially his adaptation of *A Dybbuk* and the one-acts *Notes on Akiba* and *An Undoing World*, "the metaphorical Jew," and, to reconfigure Solomon's symbol, "the metaphorical homosexual," provide an exploration of the profound and often contradictory issues of otherness, assimilation, and oppression.

The "metaphorical homosexual" is centrally important in *Angels*. All of the male characters are gay (with the exception, presumably, of the old rabbi, and, perhaps, Cohn's doctor), whether "out" or closeted. Emily, Prior's nurse, is apparently a lesbian, although this peripheral character is not examined in depth. Conservative critics like John Simon tended to dislike the *Angels* plays, objecting to its presumed plea "not just for homosexuality but also and especially for transgression, a life-style of flouted complaisance and flaunted socially unacceptable excess" (130–31). This criticism seriously misunderstands, or at least underestimates, Kushner's probing of the relationships of power, transgression, sex, and love. Kushner wonders, "What is the relationship between sexuality and power? Is sexuality merely an expression of power?" (Savran 308).

The *Angels* plays have been highly acclaimed by any standards, and perhaps surprisingly so as the work of an openly gay dramatist in a society still deeply conflicted about the role of the homosexual. Kushner's "queerness," which is as much a part of his playwriting as is Chekhov's Russian-ness, has contributed to controversy in theaters around the country where the *Angels* plays have been performed. This anger results from Kushner's approach to several issues, but it is primarily due to its homosexual content. Critics have claimed that the frankness of *Angels* promotes moral decline, despite the fact that many plays featuring gays—in America these can be traced back to Mae West's *The Drag* (1926)—have previously found various levels of acceptance. *The Drag* generated so much controversy that it closed before completing a tumultuous pre-Broadway tour in 1927. A few other curiosities appeared in the subsequent decades, most notably Lillian Hellman's *The Children's Hour* (1934), in which the question of a lesbian relationship is at the heart of the plot, although the themes focus on the damaging power of a lie instead of sexual issues. With the appearance of Robert Anderson's *Tea and Sympathy* (1953), in which a sensitive young man is viewed by his peers as a homosexual (even though it later seems that he may not be), gay issues and characters slowly came out of the shadows.

Tennessee Williams was the theater's angel of sexuality. He was the dramatist most responsible for forcefully introducing sexual issues—both gay and straight—to the American stage. The fruit of his labor is particularly evident in the subsequent generations of playwrights who present gay characters and situations with increasing frankness, depth, and lyricism. Kushner represents a culmination of Williams's influence in these areas. There are significant parallels to be found between *Angels* and the plays of Williams: both feature classically inspired epic passions, both depict dark and poetic images of the beautiful and horrifying aspects of existence, both create a stage language that is at once both naturalistic and poetic, both ponder the distance between illusion and reality, both explore the nature of spirituality from a grounding in classical and modern thought, and both deal centrally and compassionately with complex issues of sexuality from a gay sensibility. Although Alfred Kazin has written of homosexuality that "'the love that dare not speak its name' (in the nineteenth century) cannot, in the twentieth, shut up" (38), the emergence of Williams and those later dramatists such as Kushner who follow in his footsteps has led to a body of important work on a subject about which the stage had been silent for too long.

Ambivalence, a central concern in the *Angels* plays as in much of Kushner's work, also connects him to Williams, who, both in dramatic and personal terms, seemed ambivalent about homosexuality. Although his sexuality was widely known in the theatrical community, it is unclear when Williams first "came out" publicly. He told interviewer David Frost in 1970 that "everybody has some elements of homosexuality in him, even the most heterosexual of us" (40). Williams's characters feel the absence of love and a need for human connection—constant themes throughout Williams's work—and these concerns are similarly central to the characters of *Angels*. There is no question that, as a rule, Williams was writing about love, not gender. He found sexual promiscuity a distortion of the impulse of love and, for him, that impulse, in whatever manifestation, was sacred. In this sense Kushner's own various explorations of the love impulse is not at all unlike Williams.

Williams balked at writing overtly gay-themed plays (despite the subject of homosexuality and gay characters appearing in his work). Kushner, on the other hand, says, "I feel very proud that *Angels* is identified as a gay play. I want it to be thought of as being part of gay culture, and I certainly want people to think of me as a gay writer. It does also seem to speak very powerfully to straight people" (Raymond 17). In reflecting on the history of homosexuals in American theater, Kushner believes that "there's a natural proclivity for gay people—who historically have often spent their lives hiding—to feel an affinity for the extended make-believe and donning of roles that is part of theater. It's reverberant with some of the central facts of our lives" (Blanchard 42). It is not surprising that, in a society in which homosexuals were firmly closeted before the 1960s, the illusions of the stage provided a safe haven for gays. Simply put, Williams could not be as open about his sexuality in his era as Kushner can be now, and this societal change resulted in both the acclaim and the controversy inspired by *Angels*.

Openness about homosexuality crept in during the 1950s as other playwrights introduced gay characters and issues, but often not in their most visible work. William Inge, inspired to become a playwright by Williams's example, did not feature openly homosexual characters in any of his major plays, but in a few lesser-known one-acts he does so vividly. Inge's *The Tiny Closet* (1959), for example, features a man boarding in a rooming house where the nosy landlady has been attempting to break into a padlocked closet in his room. As soon as the man goes out, the landlady and her friend manage to break in and discover an array of elegant women's hats. The landlady's violation—and the presumption that she will cause the man public disgrace—leaves his fate in question. Inge's blunt attack on intolerance (his 1962 one-act, *The Boy in the Basement*, makes a similar assault) was written in the aftermath of the McCarthy era and foreshadows later gay plays, particularly those written after the late 1960s, which argue for wider social acceptance for homosexuals.

Mid-twentieth-century dramatists employed various techniques to present gay characters and situations. One device, "transference," the act of hiding gay viewpoints and situations behind a mask of heterosexuality, was frequently noted by critics. Edward Albee, often accused of using transference in the writing of such plays as *Who's Afraid of Virginia Woolf?* (1962), is a gay dramatist who also emerged in the 1950s. With the homosexual triumvirate of Williams, Inge, and Albee dominating the non-musical Broadway stage, and despite the fact that none of them had publicly acknowledged their own sexuality, *New York Times* drama critic Stanley Kauffmann "outed" them in 1966. Although Kauffmann does not give their names, it is clear to whom he is referring. He implies that homosexual writers have no right to write about anything but gay characters—a bizarre attitude that would logically imply that men are unable to write about women and vice versa. Kauffmann's view becomes clearer when he writes that

> Conventions and puritanisms in the Western world have forced them [homosexuals] to wear masks for generations, to hate themselves, and thus to hate those who make them hate themselves. Now that they have a certain relative freedom, they vent their feelings in camouflaged form.... They emphasize manner and style because these elements of art, at which they are often adept, are legal tender in their transactions with the world. These elements are, or can be, aesthetically divorced from such other considerations as character and idea. (1)

Although it is unlikely that these writers consciously used transference as Kauffmann suggests, all of them, especially Williams, realized, as Strindberg did, that there are many aspects of the female in the male—and vice versa. And also like Strindberg, Williams's pained, driven, poetic, and passionate characters are, to some extent, drawn from his own persona regardless of their gender.

The theater in general caught up with Williams's depictions of homosexuality with the appearance of Mart Crowley's *The Boys in the Band* (1968), the first mainstream drama to feature all gay characters. Between 1960 and the 1980s, however, gay characters were often reduced to peripheral status. They were seen most often in musicals like *La Cage aux Folles* (1983), in well-intentioned comedy-dramas like *Torch Song Trilogy* (1981), or as broad stereotypes in "straight" plays. There were exceptions, including Albee's *Everything In the Garden* (1967), LeRoi Jones's *The Toilet* (1964), and the flamboyant grotesquerie of Charles Ludlam's Theatre of the Ridiculous. At the outset of the AIDS epidemic a seismic change occurred in the dramatic depiction of gays. The gay dramatists of this generation, with whom Kushner allies himself, wrote plays that were either scathing indictments of American society's failure to adequately respond to the AIDS crisis, as in the plays of Larry Kramer, or dark depictions of the oppression of gays, as in Martin Sherman's *Bent* (1978), which dramatizes the oppression of homosexuals during the Holocaust. However, no gay dramatist seems to logically follow Williams, who, as Delma Eugene Presley, writes "made serious efforts to explore the subjects of reconciliation and redemption" (579) in their work, until Kushner. Before Williams, only O'Neill faced such questions in non-gay drama. After Williams, only Kushner did.

For Kushner, the AIDS epidemic had, in essence, pushed gay dramatists toward a more politicized view whether they liked it or not—even more than had been inspired by the activists of the Stonewall era in the late 1960s struggling for tolerance for gays. A politicized gay theater, for Kushner, is a positive direction; he believes that "America watching the spectacle of itself being able to accept homosexuality is good for America" (Blanchard 42). Kushner's own description of queerness—what he calls Fabulousness—as it relates to art is illuminating for understanding not only the social and theatrical history of homosexuality, which has had a major impact on his drama, but also for the political inspirations connected to it, from Queer Nation and ACT UP to his own personal drive toward activism growing out of his understanding of gay history. Fabulousness, as Kushner explains, is:

> Irony. Tragic history. Defiance. Gender-fuck. Glitter. Drama. It is not butch. It is not hot—the cathexis surrounding the fabulousness is not necessarily erotic. Fabulousness is not delimited by age or beauty. Style has a dialectical relationship to physical reality. The body is the Real. Style is Theatre. The raw materials are reworked into illusion. For style to be truly fabulous, one must completely triumph over tragedy, age, physical insufficiencies, and just as important, one's audiences must be made aware of the degree of transcendence, of triumph; must see both the triumph and that over which the triumph has been made. In this the magic of the fabulous is precisely the magic of the theatre. The wires show. The illusion is always incomplete, inadequate; the work behind the magic is meant to be appreciated. ("Notes About Political Theatre" 31)

Williams, whose drama certainly shares aspects of Fabulousness, provided a range of perspectives on the gay experience in his *Small Craft Warnings* (1972), but he did not have the freedom of expression Kushner does on these issues. However, Williams and Kushner similarly allow their characters opportunities to share their private journeys of self-discovery within the complexities, contradictions, and hypocrisies of being gay in modern American life.

The modern American life of the deeply closeted gay man is exemplified in *Angels* by Roy Cohn, whom Kushner also portrays as the dark side of conservatism in twentieth-century politics, while Louis, a "literal and figurative word processor" (Clum 316) working in New York City's Federal Court of Appeals (where Joe also works), represents the liberal side of the political spectrum as self-righteous, mostly impotent, and, finally, nearly equally hypocritical. Louis is hypocritical not about his sexuality, but in his tortured inability to act on his progressive and compassionate beliefs and in his emotional insufficiencies. Louis's liberal idealism and intellectual posturings also find no comfort from Belize, who, as an "out" gay man and a nurse, is angry and overwhelmed at the horrors of AIDS and the various forms of bigotry and inaction he sees on both sides of the political and sexual spectrums. Louis himself ruefully realizes that there is no safety net for life, and little helpful guidance in the past American experience, for "There are no angels in America, no spiritual past, no racial past, there's only the political" (92).

In essence, Louis's view is not different enough from Cohn's for Kushner. Kushner's sympathies seem most strongly to rest with Prior's more human and personal politics. Prior grapples with the politics of existence in a profoundly humane and compassionate way, but he, too, fears the future. He recounts for Louis a story of one of his ancestors forced to escape in a lifeboat with seventy other passengers when a ship foundered. Whenever the lifeboat sat too low in the water or seemed about to capsize, crew members hurled the nearest passenger into the sea. Parsing this seafaring metaphor (similar to one spoken by the dying Sir Thomas Browne in *Hydriotaphia*), Prior, who is coming to terms with his own mortality in a society in which he is marginalized, says

> I think about that story a lot now. People in a boat, waiting, terrified, while implacable, unsmiling men, irresistibly strong, seize . . . maybe the person next to you, maybe you, and with no warning at all, with time only for a quick intake of air you are pitched into freezing, turbulent water and salt and darkness to drown. (41–42)

The play proceeds to explore the deep anxieties of its characters through their visions of the forces that effect and control their lives, and as they discover their own strengths and weaknesses. This process reveals that the obviously strong (Cohn) weaken and the seemingly weak (Prior) gain in strength as they face overwhelming adversities. Despite the socialist predilections of its author, *Angels* attempts to allow both political sides to be seen at their best and worst. Its most lovable character is dying of AIDS, but so is its most detestable. Both conservative and liberal characters have admirable moments and reprehensible ones.

Kushner also depicts the aimlessness he believes infects the nation regardless of political ideology. Joe and Louis meet in a courthouse restroom where Louis disturbs Joe by suggesting that he might be gay, although there is an obvious attraction between them. Later, they meet again outside the courthouse and Joe recounts how he accidentally came to work on a Saturday and found no one there:

> And the whole place was empty. And at first I couldn't figure out why, and I had this moment of incredible . . . fear and also. . . . It just flashed through my mind: The whole Hall of Justice, it's empty, it's deserted, it's gone out of business. Forever. The people that make it run have up and abandoned it. (72)

Louis is still vacillating about whether or not he can face staying with Prior, who is becoming sicker—and more in need of help—every day. Despite his love for Prior, Louis finds liberation from justice—license to abandon—attractive. Abandonment and faithlessness are key concerns in the play and are manifested on multiple levels. Will loved ones abandon us in our hour of need? Has God, who religious faiths suggest loves all of humanity, abandoned his creations? The playwright's response to these questions may be most tellingly articulated by Belize: "I still don't understand what love is. Justice is simple. Democracy is simple.

Those things are unambivalent. But love is very hard. And it goes bad for you if you violate the hard law of love" (100). Kushner stresses that America was founded as a haven, not only a land of opportunity, but also a land of compassion whose citizens, regardless of personal beliefs and values, have a historic right to the pursuit of happiness and a moral responsibility to care for each other despite cultural and political differences. For Kushner, the ability to feel compassion and love for others is a required element in making the ideal of American justice function.

It is also the required element in maintaining functional personal relationships. As *Millennium Approaches* continues, the dilemmas of the two central couples become increasingly complicated. As the lines become more intertwined, more parallels emerge in these two very different couples. The closest parallel is reached when Louis belatedly visits Prior in the hospital while Joe, similarly late, returns to Harper after an extended absence. The overlapping dialogue underscores the fact that the problem in each case is the same—each couple has one partner in serious need and another partner who cannot, or will not, respond. Louis clearly cannot cope with Prior's deteriorating physical condition, which now involves disturbing hallucinations of a flaming aleph (the first letter of the Hebrew alphabet, the seed word, the God letter), more heavenly voices, and a midnight collapse that sends him to the hospital and Louis out into the night. Prior also receives disturbing visits from two prior Priors: one from the thirteenth century, the other from the seventeenth century. These dead ancestors warn of the horrors of death and of a mysterious messenger to come. Kushner explains that the importance of Prior's ancestors is that they are both

> from periods of British history when there were terrible outbreaks of plague. Plagues and epidemics are not new. Prior is the only character in the play with a Yankee WASP background; he can trace his lineage back for centuries, something most Americans can't reliably do. African-American family trees have to start after ancestors were brought over as slaves. Jews emigrated from a world nearly completely destroyed by European genocide. And most immigrant populations have been from poor and oppressed communities among which accurate genealogy was a luxury or an impossibility. ("The Secrets of *Angels*" H5)

Disturbed by Prior's decline, Louis wanders aimlessly. In Central Park, he meets an anonymous man and casually agrees to a sexual encounter. The scene becomes rough as Louis's despair and self-destructive impulses become vividly real:

MAN: Relax.

LOUIS (*A small laugh*): Not a chance.

MAN: It . . .

LOUIS: What?

MAN: I think it broke. The rubber. You want me to keep going? (*Little pause*) Pull out? Should I . . .

LOUIS: Keep going.

Infect me.

I don't care. I don't care. (57)

Having abandoned Prior, and, at the same time, his own sense of right and wrong, Louis is in profound emotional agony over his faithlessness. Filled with remorse, he chooses a consciously self-destructive path. At one point in the play he is discovered on a cold winter's day seated on a park bench without a coat. Louis seeks punishment wherever he can find it, as when he invites Belize, whose sympathies lie with the abandoned Prior, to meet him for coffee knowing that Belize will provide the abuse verbally that the nameless Man in the Park provides physically. Belize reluctantly agrees to meet with Louis, despite his loyalties to Prior. Defensively, Louis launches into a lengthy, breathless lecture on racial politics and capitalism. Louis has been reading Alexis de Tocqueville's prophesy about the future of a democratic America and embraces the idea that isolation and solitude have been the result of democracy and technology in the twentieth century. Louis's theorizing infuriates Belize, who understands "the guilt fueling this peculiar tirade," but he points out that "it's no fun picking on you Louis; you're so guilty, it's like throwing darts at a glob of jello, there's no satisfying hits, just quivering, the darts just blop in and vanish" (92–93).

A childish battle in which Louis and Belize hurl accusations and racial slurs at each other, leading Belize to call Louis "an honorary citizen of the Twilight Zone" (95), ensues, while Prior is seen undergoing a physical exam in which he painstakingly explains the things happening to his body as his illness worsens. Emily, Prior's nurse, suddenly seems to be speaking Hebrew, which deeply disturbs Prior. Meanwhile, Louis and Belize continue to battle and when Belize becomes aware that Louis is seeking forgiveness for abandoning Prior, he says, "I can't help you with that. I can't help you, Louis. You're not my business" (100).

Meanwhile, Joe has left Harper, who slips further away from reality and imagines herself with Mr. Lies in Antarctica. Mr. Lies tells her, "Cold shelter for the shattered. No sorrow here, tears freeze" (101). Harper explains she can have some of the things she wants, "even companionship" (102), or the baby she unsuccessfully tries to convince Joe she is expecting. There is no baby, but Harper imagines, "We'll mend together. That's what we'll do; we'll mend" (103).

Shifting back to reality, Joe's mother, Hannah, living off her husband's army pension, sells her modest home in Salt Lake City and arrives in New York looking for Joe. He fails to meet her and she tries unsuccessfully to find her way to Joe and Harper's apartment. Lost in Brooklyn, she encounters a disturbed homeless woman while seeking directions. The woman is not much help at first, but the stressed-out Hannah demands assistance: "So I am sorry you're psychotic but just make the effort—take a deep breath—DO IT!" (105). The woman, who claims to have dated Nostradamus, manages to direct Hannah to the Mormon Visitors Center, but adds, "In the new century I think we will all be insane" (105).

Joe, who is falling into a relationship with Louis, goes to the ailing Cohn to say he cannot take the offered job as Roy's man in Washington. Cohn tells Joe about his involvement in the Rosenberg case and admits his inappropriate ex parte communication with the judge during the trial. Angered by Joe's indecisiveness,

Roy uses the execution of Ethel Rosenberg, who he describes as "that sweet unprepossessing woman, two kids, boo-hoo-hoo, reminded us all of our little Jewish mamas" (108), to make the point that he achieved his goal:

> Me. I did that. I would have fucking pulled the switch if they'd have let me. Why? Because I fucking hate traitors. Because I fucking hate communists. Was it legal? Fuck legal. Am I a nice man? Fuck nice. They say terrible things about me in the *Nation*. Fuck the *Nation*. You want to be Nice, or you want to be Effective? Make the law, or subject to it. Choose. (108)

Disturbed, Joe tries to flee, but Roy continues to goad him until Joe cracks and draws back to strike Cohn. He thinks better of it, but Cohn says, "Transgress a little, Joseph. There are so many laws; find one you can break" (110). Joe does manage to escape, after which Roy collapses in severe pain, calling to his assistant for help. Instead, a ghostly figure appears, Ethel Greenglass Rosenberg (1915–53), Roy's old nemesis. She and her husband, Julius (1918–53), both members of the Communist Party, were found guilty of treason in 1951 in a controversial case accusing them of transmitting atomic military secrets to a Soviet spy. Following several appeals to the United States Supreme Court and a refusal of clemency by President Eisenhower, the Rosenbergs were executed at Sing Sing Prison in Ossining, New York. Nearly fifty years after their execution, the facts of the case, and the significance of Cohn's involvement, remain in dispute, and Kushner imagines that Ethel, a mother of two small children, was on Cohn's conscience.

Ethel's sudden appearance frightens Roy, who asks, "What is this, Ethel, Halloween? You trying to scare me?" (111). She sardonically replies that her husband sends his regards and they exchange some banter. When Roy doubles over in pain again, Ethel calls for an ambulance. Roy tries to maintain his bravado, insisting that "I'm immortal, Ethel. I have *forced* my way into history. I ain't never gonna die," to which she ominously replies, "History is about to crack wide open. Millennium approaches" (112).

Prior, home from the hospital, but alone in bed, is visited again by the ghostly figures of his two ancestors who are busily preparing the way for a heavenly visitor. Frightened, Prior becomes agitated, so the ghosts conjure up the image of Louis, who dances with Prior as one of the ancestors laments, "The twentieth century. Oh dear, the world has gotten so terribly, terribly old" (114). They vanish, and Prior, left alone, hears the sound of beating wings. As he waits in fear, Joe and Louis are seen in a park. Drawn together, despite their political differences, by mutual attraction and by their mutual guilt about abandoning their partners, Louis calls them "strange bedfellows. I don't know. I never made it with one of the damned before" (117). Thinking about his abandonment of Harper, Joe admits he is "a pretty terrible person," to which Louis, reminded of Prior, says, "There? See? We already have a lot in common" (117). As they go off together, Prior writhes in fear as the beating of the wings comes closer. Facing his fear, calling on "the anger, find the … anger, my blood is clean, my brain is fine, I can handle pressure, I am a gay man and I am used to pressure, to trouble, I am tough and strong" (117), at which point he is overcome by "an

Figure 4: The arrival of the Angel (Teri L. Clark) before the "prophet" Prior (Trevor Fanning) in a 1996 Wabash College Theater production of Tony Kushner's *Angels in America, Part One: Millennium Approaches.* Photo by John Zimmerman.

intense sexual feeling" engendered by the approach of an Angel, who arrives in a blaze of light and triumphal music in a Kafkaesque crash through Prior's bedroom ceiling. "God almighty ... very Steven Spielberg" (118), Prior gapes, and the Angel announces:

> Greetings, Prophet;
> The Great Work begins:
> The Messenger has arrived. (119)

Kushner ends *Millennium Approaches* at this momentous point, leaving the audience to wonder if the arrival of the Angel means Prior's death is imminent— or, as will be borne out in *Perestroika*, something more complex is in the works. The Angel refers to Prior as a prophet; Kushner bases this reference on Jonah, the Biblical prophet who refused to be a prophet. Jonah's "book shows us that the prophets suffered as a result of their vision. The idea that a person assumes suffering for the sake of others, for the sake of the world, does not begin with Jesus" ("The Secrets of *Angels*" H5). In Kushner's case, it at least continues with Prior.

As with all of Kushner's plays, *Millennium Approaches* offers a unique mixture of theatrical fantasy and social reality, while in *Perestroika*, Kushner continues, using the same characters, to expand and deepen the thematic and aesthetic levels of this complex drama. As John M. Clum writes, *Millennium Approaches* depicts the "dissolution of relationships and the various unmoorings seem to be the prelude to a revolution, the creation of a new order" (318), while in *Perestroika* the questions shift to what this "new order" may bring.

Living Past Hope: *Perestroika*

Ethel Rosenberg's prediction that history will crack open comes true in *Perestroika*, the more intellectually and thematically complex of Kushner's two *Angels* plays. In this epic drama, Kushner's characters continue their difficult individual journeys of survival, reassessing their lives and struggling toward the future as new alliances emerge and some arrive at momentous, life-changing decisions. Kushner pulls off a remarkable coup de théâtre by expanding and deepening themes and characters one might reasonably have assumed were exhausted in *Millennium Approaches*.

The mood is significantly darkened in *Perestroika*, although without under-cutting the humor Kushner uses in both plays to break the mounting tension and despairing view. However, he also movingly demonstrates the necessity of for-giveness to progress. *Millennium Approaches* is a more conventional naturalistic drama, despite the embellishments of ghosts, angels, and hallucinations, when compared to *Perestroika*, which adds a bolder metaphysical complexity (the idea that angelic orgasms fuel the progress of the universe, for example) and a more complex intertwining of characters and themes as the play contemplates two possibilities: the end of human history or a renewal that brings salvation.

Perestroika, which Kushner began writing in 1989, was first performed as a staged reading in May 1991 at San Francisco's Eureka Theatre, followed by revisions and another workshop at Los Angeles's Mark Taper Forum in May 1992. The play's world premiere came in November 1992 at the Taper, under the direction of Oskar Eustis, when it and *Millennium Approaches*, already running at the Taper, were performed in repertory. *Perestroika* was similarly joined to *Millennium Approaches* at the Royal National Theatre of Great Britain, where it opened on November 20, 1993, and at Broadway's Walter Kerr Theatre on November 23, 1993.

It is difficult to separate the two *Angels* plays, as the ideas and characters in both are so completely interwoven. There are also connections with Kushner's first post-*Angels* play, *Slavs! Thinking About the Longstanding Problems of Virtue and Happiness*, which, in fact, was constructed from scenes, characters, and the-matic issues planned for inclusion in *Perestroika* until its length grew to the point that Kushner put them aside for later use. *Perestroika* begins in 1986 at the Hall of Deputies in the Kremlin with Aleksii Antedilluvianovich Prelapsarianov, "The World's Oldest Living Bolshevik," facing the end of the Soviet Union and the dawning new millennium, wondering, "Are we doomed? The Great Question before us is: Will the Past release us? The Great Question before us is: Can We Change? In Time? And we all desire that Change will come" (13).

In this scene (it is repeated in *Slavs!*) Prelapsarianov warns the reformers about abandoning the old socialist theories: "If the snake sheds his skin before a new skin is ready, naked he will be in the world, prey to the forces of chaos. Without his skin he will be dismantled, lose coherence and die. Have you, my little serpents, a new skin?" (14). How, he wonders, can they proceed without a new social structure: "Change? Yes, we must change, only show me the Theory, and I will be at the barricades, show me the book of the next Beautiful Theory, and I promise you these blind eyes will see again, just to read it, to devour the text. Show me the words that will reorder the world, or else keep silent" (14). As he continues to warn of moving ahead without a plan, *Perestroika* returns to the end of *Millennium Approaches* with the Angel repeating her greeting to Prior, the prophet.

Joe and Louis are also seen together in Louis's new apartment in the neighborhood where immigrant Jews first lived in New York, a place where, as Louis self-accusingly says, "their more seriously fucked-up grandchildren repair. This is progress?" (15). Joe and Louis have been making love and Louis explains to Joe the value of smell—"an incredibly complex and underappreciated physical phenomenon" (17)—in lovemaking. Joe wants to talk, but the usually loquacious Louis, whose words have only caused him pain, is not interested. "Words are the worst things" (18), he says, as he pulls Joe back to bed. Harper is still in Antarctica, where she is freezing cold and sitting beside a pine tree she has "chewed" (19) down like a beaver, intending to use it to build a fire. An eskimo appears in the image of Joe, who claims to have looked for her everywhere, admitting that he is "having an adventure," which causes her to accuse him of falling "out of love with me" (20). She asks Joe to come back to her, but he cannot, so Mr. Lies plays "a brief, wild lament" on an oboe, explaining the tune is "blues for the death of heaven" (21). A flash of light from a police car brings Harper back to reality, and she finds herself alone in Prospect Park with the pine tree she has apparently chewed down in the Botanical Gardens Arboretum.

Hannah has finally found her way to Joe and Harper's apartment, where she gets a call from the police about Harper, while Prior, alone in bed, is on the phone with Belize trying to explain his vision of the Angel and the particularly odd fact that its presence caused him to ejaculate. Prior explains that he feels "wonderful and horrible all at once, like ... like there's a war inside" (23), but their phone conversation is interrupted by a doctor, who announces to Belize that he has just admitted a patient with "liver cancer" to this floor, despite the fact that it is the floor for AIDS patients. The doctor warns Belize that the patient is "a very important man," to which the unimpressed Belize replies, "Oh, OK. Then I shouldn't fuck up his medication?" (25). The annoyed doctor leaves, but when Belize looks at the chart and realizes who the patient is, he calls Prior with "some piping hot dish" (26). He urges Prior to guess who it is: "The Killer Queen Herself. New York's number-one closeted queen" (26). Prior asks, "*Koch?*"; it is Roy Cohn, of course, and Belize declares, "Fetch me the hammer and the pointy stake, girl. I'm a-going in" (26).

The characters face new troubles and great personal losses in *Perestroika*. Where *Millennium Approaches* depicts faithlessness and selfishness with compassion while offering a glimpse of the retreating conscience of American society, *Perestroika* finds Kushner's indomitable characters moving tentatively toward the feared changes while facing very hard realities. Cohn must face the hardest reality of all: his imminent death, though he retains all of the vivacious viciousness he demonstrated in *Millennium Approaches*. Because Cohn finds himself being nursed by Belize, Kushner can balance the play's overall grimness with humor, but the deeply felt humanism typical of Kushner's work predominates even in their highly charged encounters. While there is much hilarity in Cohn's verbal contests with Belize, Kushner also demonstrates the vast differences in their outlooks in ways that reveal the collision of history with the disturbing and confusing present. When Belize appears at Cohn's bedside, Roy demands a white nurse—he calls it "my constitutional right" (26)—but Belize proceeds to do his job despite hateful taunts and threats from his patient. Cohn complains of pain, so Belize offers a painkiller, but it is rejected. "Pain's . . . nothing, pain's life" (27), Cohn insists, as he hectors Belize with his savagely cockeyed analysis of the historical significance of his being nursed by an African-American:

> Jews and coloreds, historical liberal coalition, right? My people being the first to sell retail to your people, your people being the first people my people could afford to hire to sweep out the store Saturday mornings, and then we all held hands and rode the bus to Selma. Not me of course, I don't ride buses, I take cabs. But the thing about the American Negro is, he never went Communist. Loser Jews did. But you people had Jesus so the reds never got to you. (27–28)

Belize tries to ignore this— he quips "Your chart didn't mention that you're delusional" (28)—but Cohn invites him to stay and talk. Belize resists—"I'd rather suck the pus out of an abscess" (28)—but Cohn insists, complaining about his disease: "Course they can't kill this, can they? No. It's too simple. It knows itself" (28). He compares AIDS to some virulent crab lice he once had and which, he claims, he identifies with, "Determined lowlife. Like me" (28).

Surprising himself, Belize offers Cohn advice about procedures and drugs, but the mistrusting Cohn nastily says, "You're a butterfingers spook faggot nurse. I think . . . you have little reason to want to help me," to which Belize wryly retorts, "Consider it solidarity. One faggot to another" (30). Belize tells Cohn about AZT, then in experimental trials, and Cohn uses his political connections (threatening to "ring up CBS and sing Mike Wallace a song: the ballad of adorable Ollie North and his secret contra slush fund" [31]) to get a batch of real AZT, not the placebos Belize warns are being used in the trials. Cohn and Belize develop a relationship built of equal parts mistrust and mutual need: Belize wants some of the AZT for Prior and, as his condition worsens, Roy needs the advice Belize gives in exchange for the drugs. Cohn demands a multiline phone, complaining of the single line in his room, "How am I supposed to perform basic bodily functions on *this*?" (31). As Cohn gets sicker, and is transformed, at least in his own mind, into one of the disenfranchised, he vents his fury at his recurring vision of Ethel Rosenberg:

> The worst thing about being sick in America, Ethel, is you are booted out of the parade. Americans have no use for sick. Look at Reagan: He's so healthy he's hardly human, he's a hundred if he's a day, he takes a slug in his chest and two

days later he's out west riding ponies in his PJ's. I mean who does that? That's America. It's just no country for the infirm. (62)

While Roy's health declines, Hannah cares for Harper and works as a volunteer at New York City's Mormon Visitors Center. Joe and Louis debate politics between sessions of passionate sex, with Joe insisting that the "rhythm of history is conservative. Change is geologically slow. You must accept that. And accept as rightfully yours the happiness that comes your way" (55). But Louis replies, condemning the "religious fanatics" of the conservative movement, "who want to control every breath every citizen takes" and lists "the ego-anarchist-cowboys-shrilling-for-no-government part of the Republicans" (35), including Pat Buchanan, Jesse Helms, and Newt Gingrich, as well as Reagan and Bush. On a more personal level, Joe and Louis are beginning to feel the pull of their abandoned partners, wondering about the well-being of Harper and Prior. Joe, sounding ominously like Cohn, tries to comfort Louis by suggesting that "[you] did what you needed to do," but Louis morosely accepts that "nobody does what I did, Joe. Nobody" and turns back to sex with Joe, seeking "sweet dreams. Or oblivion. Sweet, sweet oblivion" (38–39). As they sleep, Harper appears to Joe in a dream to tell him that he cannot save Louis—"You never saved anyone. Joe in love. Isn't it pathetic"—and Joe suddenly awakens with a bad case of "night chills" (40).

As act 2 begins, Prior and Belize are returning from a funeral of a friend, "one of the Great Glitter Queens" (41), as the toll of AIDS deaths continues to mount. Prior, wearing a long black coat and a scarf as a hood—looking, Belize sneers, like Morticia Addams—reveals to Belize that he has "been given a prophecy" and that every night he has "these horrible vivid dreams" (43), which are revealed in an encounter between Prior and the Angel. The Angel insists that Prior dig up a book improbably buried under the sink in his kitchen, which he does after the Angel reveals that "The Body is the Garden of the Soul" and overwhelms Prior with an intense orgasm—"She fucked me. She has ... Well, she has eight vaginas" (48), the amazed Prior tells Belize. The angels, he explains, are "basically incredibly powerful bureaucrats, they have no imagination, they can do anything but they can't invent, create, they're sort of fabulous and dull all at once" (49). The Angel has come to Prior because "YOU *Think*. And You *IMAGINE!*" (49)—the angels need Prior to find God, who wandered away on the day of the 1906 San Francisco earthquake and did not return. Belize, listening to all this, interjects, "I smell a motif. The man that got away" (51). The Angel, who has progressed from prophetic warnings to erotic metaphors, warns of a coming apocalypse:

> You cannot Understand, You can only Destroy,
> You do not Advance, You only Trample.
> Poor blind Children, abandoned on the Earth,
> Groping terrified, misguided, over
> Fields of Slaughter, over bodies of the slain:
> HOBBLE YOURSELVES!

> There is No Zion Save Where You Are!
> If you Cannot find your Heart's desire . . . (52)

Prior continues, "In your own backyard . . . ," and, with Belize and the Angel, "You never lost it to begin with" (53). Throughout *Perestroika*, Kushner mines considerable humor from such camp cultural references—Judy Garland (a gay icon, whose New York funeral contributed to the 1969 Stonewall riot), *The Wizard of Oz*, Blanche DuBois from *A Streetcar Named Desire*, and so on—not only to relieve the darker aspects of the play, but also to stave off the sorts of pretentiousness one can fall prey to in attempting to address profound spiritual, philosophical, and political questions.

As the visitation from the Angel continues, Prior insists, "I'm not a prophet, I'm a sick lonely man" (53), but the Angel, referring to him as Jonah, insists:

> You Know Me Prophet: Your battered heart,
> Bleeding in the Universe of Wounds. (54)

Prior worries about being crazy, pointing out that "half my friends are dead and I'm only thirty-one, every goddamn morning I wake up and I think Louis is next to me in bed and it takes me long minutes to remember . . . that this is *real*, it isn't just an impossible, terrible dream" (55). Belize, deeply concerned, insists there is no Angel, that Prior is just "afraid of the future, afraid of time" (55). Prior is not so sure, wondering if "maybe the world has driven God from Heaven, incurred the angels' wrath" and, somehow, allowed him to see "the end of things" (55–56).

In act 3, Cohn is in his hospital bed, struggling with terrible physical discomforts and worrying about a disbarment committee hearing looking into his dubious activities. Ethel Rosenberg appears to him again—she has been monitoring the disbarment hearings from her spectral sphere—and she watches silently as Cohn battles with Belize. When Belize loses his temper at Cohn's racial taunts and throws some back, Cohn is pleased with himself at inspiring this outburst and invites Belize to take a bottle of AZT as a reward.

Hannah, meanwhile, is trying to keep Harper from slipping further into a delusionary state. She takes Harper along as she works at the Mormon Visitors Center, but when Harper is left alone with a life-size robotic diorama of a nineteenth-century Mormon pioneer family, she imagines Joe as the "Mormon Father," while pleading for guidance from the "Mormon Mother." Prior arrives with Hannah's assistance, having become faint on the street outside. Harper sees that Prior is "distracted from grief" (64) and Prior thinks she looks familiar, seeming to remember her from their joint hallucination in *Millennium Approaches*. They watch the diorama together. Not only is Joe the Mormon Father, but Louis appears in it, causing Prior to become emotional. Harper closes the diorama curtain, warning that "this isn't a place for real feelings" (68), as Prior realizes that "imagination is a dangerous thing" (70). Prior leaves and Harper watches the diorama again, pleading with the image of the Mormon Mother, "Bitter lady of the Plains, talk to me. Tell me what to do" (71). She

Figure 5: Jeffrey King, as Joe Pitt, and Ron Leibman, as Roy Cohn, in the 1992 Mark Taper Forum production of Tony Kushner's *Angels in America, Part Two: Perestroika*. Photo by Jay Thompson.

confesses that she is "stuck. My heart's an anchor," and the Mormon Mother
miraculously comes to life to advise, "Leave it, then. Can't carry no extra weight"
(71). The figure dourly leads Harper toward the next stage of her personal journey, and Kushner achieves a transcendent meeting of past and present, a unique
realm where the facts and fictions of human history and literature converge with
contemporary reality.

Joe and Louis continue to discuss their relationship, which seems, at times, to
merge with their political ideologies. Louis feels the need to see Prior, realizing
that "I always seem to have forgotten about love" (74) in the schematics that he
has studied in order to make sense of his life. At the same time, Joe tries to draw
Louis into more sex. Joe says he has "no past now. I could give up anything.
Maybe ... In what we've been doing, maybe I'm even infected" (75). Louis
assures him he is not, but Joe tells Louis that he has "a good heart and you think
the good thing is to be guilty and kind always but it's not always kind to be gentle
and soft, there's a genuine violence softness and weakness visit on people.
Sometimes self-interested is the most generous thing you can be" (75). Louis,
true to his liberal ideology, remains unconvinced.

Harper and the Mormon Mother wander the city and Harper asks, "How do
people change?" to which the Mormon Mother replies that "it has something to
do with God and it's not so very nice" (79). God, she explains,

splits the skin with a jagged thumbnail from throat to belly and then plunges a huge filthy hand in, he grabs hold of your bloody tubes and they slip to evade his grasp but he squeezes hard, he *insists*, he pulls and pulls till all your innards are yanked out and the pain! We can't even talk about that. And then he stuffs them back, dirty, tangled and torn. It's up to you to do the stitching. (79)

Harper understands the meaning of this metaphor, adding that following this horror "you get up. And walk around" (79), but you are changed forever.

Act 4 begins with a dual scene, with Joe visiting Cohn while Louis and Prior meet at a park bench. Cohn bestows a paternal blessing on Joe and tells Joe how his mother had a bone spur surgically removed from his nose when he was only three months old. She "wanted to toughen me up. And it worked" (83). Prior is very angry with Louis, who wants to make up—in fact, he seems to want to return to Prior. Prior realizes, thanks to his experience at the Mormon Visitors Center, that Louis is involved with Joe. When Louis cries, Prior wants to cry with him, but cannot sympathize, "You cry, but you endanger nothing in yourself. It's like the idea of crying when you do it. Or the idea of love" (85). Joe, meanwhile, tells Cohn that he has left Harper and become sexually involved with Louis. Cohn becomes hysterical, ripping out his IV drip; he demands that Joe never talk about it "*ever again*" and that he must go "home. With your wife. Whatever else you got going, cut it dead" (87). Joe is confused, but Cohn insists he leave, while Louis tries to convince Prior that he is bruised inside. The skeptical Prior demands that Louis come back only when the bruises are visible.

The next day, Prior and Belize sneak into the courthouse to catch a glimpse of Joe at work, but Joe's attractiveness disturbs Prior—"He's the Marlboro Man" (91), he moans—and Joe sees them and recognizes Belize as Cohn's nurse. When Prior mentions Harper, Joe becomes outraged and wants to know how Prior knows his wife. Trapped, Prior goes into an insane act to escape, leaving Belize to complain, "I am trapped in a world of white people. That's *my* problem" (93). All of this is compounded in the next scene when Belize reluctantly meets with Louis at Central Park's Bethesda Fountain, which is Prior's favorite place. Belize admits that he and Prior checked out Joe at the courthouse, which infuriates Louis, even more so when Belize tells him that he is "sharing your dank and dirty bed with Roy Cohn's buttboy" (94). Louis refuses to believe it—"Not Roy Cohn. He's like the polestar of human evil, he isn't human even" (95)—and accuses Belize of being jealous that Prior loves him. This is ridiculous to Belize (he has a boyfriend), and more importantly, insignificant. He is angry at the horrors of AIDS and the bigotry he sees on both sides of the political spectrum that makes the problem worse. "I hate this country," he tells Louis. "It's just big ideas, and stories, and people dying, and people like you. The white cracker who wrote the national anthem knew what he was doing. He set the word 'free' to a note so high nobody can reach it" (96). Belize remarks that Louis's liberalism has him "up in the air, just like that angel, too far off the earth to pick out the details. Louis and his Big Ideas. Big Ideas are all you love. 'America' is what Louis loves" (96). Belize ends the conversation by saying, "I live in America, Louis, that's hard enough, I don't have to love it" (96) and goes back to work.

Joe finally turns up at the Mormon Visitors Center seeking Harper and encounters Hannah. He tries to elicit some sympathy from her, but she cannot give it and Joe implies that he fled Salt Lake City to get away from her. Hannah suggests that he think about what he is really running from, but Joe rushes away as Prior enters. Thinking about Joe, Hannah asks Prior if he is "a typical homosexual," to which Prior replies, "Me? Oh I'm stereotypical" (99). Feverish, he becomes unsteady, so Hannah rushes him to the hospital where his condition is stabilized. When Prior introduces Hannah to his nurse, Emily, as his "ex-lover's lover's Mormon mother," she can only reply, "Even in New York in the eighties, *that* is strange" (102). Prior continues to insist he has seen an Angel, which also seems strange, although Hannah is prepared to acknowledge that he had "a vision" (103). As she explains the Mormon founder Joseph Smith's vision, Prior finds it "preposterous" and assumes that because he is "a homosexual. With AIDS" that Hannah must be judging him harshly, but she asserts, "You don't make assumptions about me, mister; I won't make them about you" (103). They discuss homosexuality, as she seeks to understand Joe's situation, and she realizes that her only resistance to it is that it is "ungainly" (104), to which Prior notes, "I wish you would be more true to your demographic profile. Life is confusing enough" (104).

Like the Mormon Mother of the diorama, Hannah, too, is coming to life. Concerned about the distance that separates her from her son—resulting in part from rigid religious beliefs that have made his "coming out" difficult—her tolerance grows through her relationship with Prior, who teaches her by example tolerance for the otherness of homosexuality. She stays with Prior as he fears the Angel is approaching again, while Joe, who has found Harper standing in the icy wind on a promenade, brings her back to their apartment. She asks why he closes his eyes during their sexual encounters, assuming correctly that he imagines men, and she says that she imagines too, although "the only time I wasn't imagining was when I was with you" (106). Harper forces him to look her in the eyes and asks what he sees, to which he replies that he sees nothing. She thanks him for "the truth" (107), and Joe flees again, back to Louis, but discovers no comfort there.

Louis confronts Joe about his political beliefs. Louis has done some research at the courthouse, discovering that Joe has been writing the opinions of the judge he clerks for; many of them are, in Louis's estimation, "legal fag-bashing" (110). Louis also wants to know about Joe's involvement with Cohn, and, borrowing on the famous question Army lawyer Joseph Welch posed to Senator McCarthy during the Army-McCarthy hearings, asks, "Have you no decency, at long last, sir, have you no decency at all?" (110). Louis attempts to shame Joe. He tells him that Cohn has AIDS, guessing that they were so closeted they "probably never figured out each other was ... " (111), at which point Joe begins to beat Louis. When he manages to calm himself, he is shocked at what he has done to Louis: "I never did that before, I never hit anyone," and he pleads with Louis to forgive him, but Louis just wants to "lie here and bleed for a while. Do me good" (112).

Figure 6: Prior Walter (John Feltch) grapples with the Angel (Shelley Williams) in the 1995 Alley Theatre of Houston production of Tony Kushner's *Angels in America, Part Two: Perestroika*. Photo by Sheryl Berger.

Back at the hospital, Ethel Rosenberg appears to Cohn, to tell him that the disbarment committee has ruled against him. Roy Cohn is no longer a lawyer. She says, "I came to forgive but all I can do is take pleasure in your misery. Hoping I'd get to see you die more terrible than I did" (114). He seems to become delirious, mistaking her for his mother and insisting that she sing to him. She resists, but when he starts to cry she sings to quiet him. Assuming that he is dead, she starts to leave, but he springs back to life for one more vindictive triumph in fooling his old adversary: "I fooled you Ethel, I knew who you were all along, I can't believe you fell for that ma stuff, I just wanted to see if I could finally, finally make Ethel Rosenberg sing!" (115). However, within moments, he does die, stabbing an imaginary telephone "hold" button as his final gesture.

Act 5 begins with Prior, still in the hospital being tended by Hannah, fearing the Angel's return. When it does reappear with great fanfare of trumpets and thunder, Prior begs Hannah to help him, but she says that he must "wrestle with her till she gives in" (118). The Angel announces that it is the "CONTINENTAL PRINCIPAL-ITY OF AMERICA" (119) and, with more fanfare, a gate to Heaven is opened for Prior who must choose to stay there or return to earth as a prophet. In Heaven, he finds himself in what appears to be the rubble of the 1906 San Francisco earthquake. Harper appears carrying Prior's cat, Little Sheba, who disappeared in *Millennium Approaches*. Pleased to see her "imaginary friend" (121) again, Harper realizes she is now ready to leave Joe—"He's got a sweet hollow center, but he's the nothing man" (122)—and, while Prior simultaneously wanders through Heaven, she comes to some understandings about her religion and God's disappearance: "I think I've finally found the secret to all that Mormon energy. Heartbreak. Devastation. That's what makes people travel, migrate, build things. Heartbroken people do it, people who have lost love. Because I don't think God loves his people any more than Joe loved me. And so their hearts were broken" (122).

In Cohn's hospital room, his corpse awaits removal while Belize enters, dragging along a reluctant Louis, bruised from Joe's beating. Aiming to steal the huge supply of AZT secreted in a locked box in Cohn's room, Belize needs Louis to say the Kaddish over Cohn in gratitude for the AZT. Louis is horrified and resists, but Belize insists, explaining that Cohn "was a terrible person. He died a hard death. So maybe.... A queen can forgive her vanquished foe. It isn't easy, it doesn't count if it's easy, it's the hardest thing. Forgiveness. Which is maybe where love and justice finally meet. Peace, at least" (124). Suggesting that this act is "expiation" for Louis's own sins, Louis begins the prayer, joined by the ghostly Ethel Rosenberg who recites with him. As they conclude the prayer, they both add, "V'imru omain. You sonofabitch" (126). At the same time, returning to his apartment, Joe is startled to encounter Cohn's ghost who warns him that "you'll find, my friend, that what you love will take you places you never dreamed you'd go" (127).

Prior's wanderings in Heaven continue and he finds himself in the Council Room of the Continental Principalities, a congress of angels debating the state of the earth, most particularly the recent nuclear disaster at Chernobyl, noting that they are no more than "impotent witnesses" (130) to the mayhem on earth. Prior wants to return the book of prophecies he found under his kitchen sink, arguing that the progress of life on earth cannot stop (as the angels wish) and that humans cannot wait for God to come back:

> If He ever did come back, if He ever dared to show His face, or his Glyph or whatever in the Garden again . . . if after all this destruction, if after all the terrible days of this terrible century He returned to see . . . how much suffering His abandonment had created, if He did come back you should sue the bastard. That's my only contribution to all this Theology. Sue the bastard for walking out. How dare He. (133)

Insisting that he wants to live, Prior also demands that the plague of AIDS be stopped, but despite sharing his suffering, the angels claim they do not know how to stop it or to repair any of the disasters of history. Prior's Angel cannot believe he wants to go back to the earth:

> With Apocalypse Descending?
> Who Demands: More Life?
> When Death like a Protector
> Blinds our eyes, shielding from tender nerve
> More horror than can be borne. (135)

Despite the warning, Prior wants to be blessed with more life, explaining that it is human to want to live:

I've lived through such terrible times, and there are people who live through much much worse, but. . . . You see them living anyway. When they're more spirit than body, more sores than skin, when they're burned and in agony, when flies lay eggs in the corners of the eyes of their children, they live. Death usually has to *take* life away. I don't know if that's just the animal. I don't know if it's not braver to die. But I recognize the habit. The addiction to being alive. We live past hope. If I can find hope anywhere, that's it, that's the best I can do. It's so much not enough, so inadequate but. . . . Bless me anyway. I want more life. (136)

Prior leaves the council and walks on the streets of Heaven (in a scene Kushner indicates as optional in performance), encountering Louis's deceased grandmother, Sarah, and the rabbi who buried her, playing cards. Prior tells her that Louis is gay ("A *feygele*? Oy" [137], she moans) and wonders why everyone in Heaven seems to be playing cards. The rabbi explains: "Cards is strategy but mostly a game of chance. In Heaven, everything is known. To the Great Questions are lying about here like yesterday's newspapers all the answers. So from what comes the pleasures of Paradise? Indeterminacy!" (137). Sarah sends Louis her forgiveness with Prior, who begins his return to earth, but on the way passes Cohn haggling on the telephone. The Supreme Being apparently wants Cohn to represent him for the crime of his abandonment of humanity, and Cohn, now literally the devil's advocate, willingly becomes God's as well. He tells God, "You're guilty as hell, no question, you have nothing to plead but not to worry, darling, I will make something up" (139).

Prior awakens in his hospital room, watched over by Belize, who welcomes him back from unconsciousness. Hannah and Emily enter and Prior tries to explain his trip to Heaven, where he repeats Dorothy's lines in *The Wizard of Oz*, "Some of it was terrible, and some of it was wonderful, but all the same I kept saying I want to go home. And they sent me home" (140). Louis arrives demonstrating the visible scars (from Joe's beating) Prior had demanded. Hannah, sensing their need to talk, starts to leave. She asks Prior if she should come see him again, and Prior, borrowing Tennessee Williams's most famous line, drawls, "Please do. I have always depended on the kindness of strangers" (141). Hannah, unfamiliar with the reference, can only reply, "Well that's a stupid thing to do" (141). Hannah does return, no longer a stranger either to Prior or herself, for she has been visited by Prior's angel and experienced a transforming orgasmic liberation similar to that which Prior experienced at the end of *Millennium Approaches*.

Louis and Belize show Prior the stash of AZT while Harper and Joe meet again at their apartment. Harper demands Joe's credit card and he pleads with her not to leave him. She slaps him hard across the face and asks if it hurt. He says it did, to which she simply replies, "Remember that" (142). Louis similarly pleads to return to Prior, acknowledging that "I really failed you. But . . . This is hard. Failing in love isn't the same as not loving" (143). Prior admits he loves Louis, but makes it clear that Louis cannot return as his lover, "Not ever" (143). Harper embarks on a "night flight to San Francisco," dreaming she reaches the "tropopause" where she has an "astonishing ability to see things," including the fact that in the hubbub of the world, "Nothing's lost forever. In this world, there is a kind of painful progress. Longing for what we've left behind, and dreaming ahead" (144).

The final scene of *Perestroika* is set at Central Park's Bethesda fountain four years later. It is 1990, and a newly created family made up of Prior, Hannah, Belize, and a repentant Louis relax there enjoying the bracing cold weather. A stronger, wiser Hannah asserts Kushner's view of the interconnectedness of all humanity regardless of race or sexual preference and the primacy of loyalty and commitment to others, while Louis points to a definition of politics: "The world moving ahead. And only in politics does the miraculous occur" (146). Prior, leaning on a cane but still alive, points out the angel of the fountain, his personal favorite in that it is a figure commemorating death but suggestive of "a world without dying" (147). Louis recounts the story of the angel Bethesda who "descended and just her foot touched earth. And where it did, a fountain shot up from the ground" (147), while Belize explains that if "anyone who was suffering, in the body or the spirit, walked through the waters of the fountain of Bethesda, they would be healed, washed clean of pain" (147). Prior, the prophet, stresses that the healing waters of the fountain are not flowing now, but hopes to be around to see the day it flows freely again. In a final statement made directly to the audience, Prior speaks for himself, for those who have come before, and for the future:

> This disease will be the end of many of us, but not nearly all, and the dead will be commemorated and will struggle on with the living, and we are not going away. We won't die secret deaths anymore. The world only spins forward. We will be citizens. The time has come. (148)

As the curtain falls, Prior offers a final benediction reminiscent of a Thornton Wilder play, *Our Town*, in which the deceased small town farm wife, Emily, proclaims from her grave: "Oh, earth, you're too wonderful for anybody to realize you" (100). Prior, terribly ill with AIDS and having won his belief in a new hope in a battle with life far more harrowing than Emily's, says simply:

> Bye now.
> You are fabulous creatures, each and every one.
> And I bless you: *More Life.* (148)

The many strengths of both parts of *Angels* are most evident in the small collection of characters populating the plays. Compellingly drawn, complex, contradictory, often surprising, their dominant characteristics drive the action and exemplify the human and personal aspects of the political, religious, and moral ideas examined in the plays. The deeply troubled and intensely intellectual Louis, a character at once full of self-righteousness and self-loathing, faces his failings, pays for his sins, and progresses toward a new life. Prior's combination of wonderment and cynicism, hope and despair, integrity and camp provides *Angels* with its dramatic heart. Belize's ability to forgive in the face of the heartbreaking tragedies he sees on his job and the bigotries of American society provides a voice for those who worry less about theories than about doing good work.

Harper's imagination and humor balance her aching neediness and loneliness, while the dryly repressed Hannah eventually comes to a deeper understanding of herself when her stiff propriety and lonely despair give way to a fully transformed woman capable of opening herself to those who are different.

Among the other characters, Joe's wrenching struggle between his sexual identity and his ideological conservatism provides sympathy for a character who causes nearly as much pain as he feels. And Cohn, the malevolent center of the plays, is, as critic Anne Marie Welsh writes, "surely the most Shakespearean stage creation of the 1990s" (E7). *New Yorker* critic John Lahr noted that in Cohn Kushner "personifies the barbarity of individualism during the Reagan years, and also the deep strain of pessimism that goes with the territory" (137). Kushner himself seems to subscribe to what Tennessee Williams understood in creating his own characters: "I don't believe in villains or heroes—only right or wrong ways that individuals have taken, not by choice but by necessity or by certain still-uncomprehended influences in themselves, their circumstances, and their antecedents (91–92).

While *Angels* played on Broadway, another play featuring Cohn as a character ran in a downtown theater: Gary Indiana's *Roy Cohn/Jack Smith*, a one-man show featuring Ron Vawter as Cohn. The play included a reworking of an infamous 1978 speech by Cohn condemning homosexuality, set against the life of Smith, the maker of a 1962 film about gays, *Flaming Creatures*, who died of AIDS in 1989. Directed by Gregory Mehrten, *Roy Cohn/Jack Smith* shared with *Angels* a similarly frightening portrait of Cohn. A television film, *Citizen Cohn* (1992), starring James Woods, freely borrowed on Kushner's idea of Cohn being visited at his deathbed by the ghost of Ethel Rosenberg (expanded in the film to also include Cohn's parents, Joe McCarthy, Robert F. Kennedy, J. Edgar Hoover, and others), but despite Woods's fine performance, the film did little to distract from the attention focused on *Angels*.

Critics, even those of a conservative bent likely to resist aspects of *Angels*, were uniform in their praise of the ambition and aesthetic qualities demonstrated. Most rhapsodized with abandon about the plays themselves and Kushner's promise as a dramatist. In 1992, when both parts of *Angels* were in production at the Mark Taper Forum, *Variety* critic Greg Evans called it "a heady swirl of inspired fancy, harrowing realism and outrageous humor, weighed down only by a lack of focus in the second half. Careful tightening is needed if this work is to achieve its considerable potential" (69), but *New York Times* critic Frank Rich, calling Kushner "visionary," suggested that the plays were nothing less than "a fierce call for gay Americans to seize the strings of power in the war for tolerance and against AIDS. But this play, by turns searing and comic and elegiac, is no earthbound ideological harangue," but instead "at times it is mind-exploding, eventually piling on more dense imagery and baroque spiritual, political and historical metaphor than even an entranced, receptive audience can absorb in two consecutive sittings" ("Marching Out of the Closet, Into History" C15). By the time *Angels* reached New York, Rich was no less enthusiastic, stating that *Millennium Approaches* speaks so powerfully because something far larger and more urgent than the future of the theatre is at stake. It really is history Mr. Kushner intends to crack open. He sends his haunting messenger, a spindly, abandoned gay man with a heroic spirit and a ravaged body, deep into his audience's heart to ask just who we are and just what, as the plague continues and the millennium approaches, we intend this country to become. ("Embracing All Possibilities in Life and Art" C16)

Anna Quindlen called *Angels* "a brilliant, brilliant play about love and the human condition at a time when our understanding of what it means to be human and loving has, thankfully, expanded" (A21), while *Newsweek's* Jack Kroll found *Angels* "the most ambitious American play of our time" (83). *The Nation's* Hal Gelb described Kushner's dialogue as "remarkable in the way it reveals the love the characters are requesting, requiring, giving and withholding, and I found myself hurting for them in a way I don't for characters in other plays. He also supplies them with a flood of laugh lines" (247). Critic John Lahr applauded Kushner's "great gifts of humor and empathy" (137) and the *New Republic's* Robert Brustein felt that *Angels* bested many gay-themed plays, which he found either "shrill" or "soggy," through Kushner's

balanced historical sense that helps him avoid both self-righteousness and senti-mentality. His balanced style helps as well—angry but forgiving, tough-minded but warmhearted, ironic but passionate, mischievous and fantastical. Kushner is that rare American thing, an artist-intellectual, not only witty himself but the gauge by which we judge witlessness in others. His very literate play once again makes American drama readable literature. (29)

When the national tour of *Angels* opened at Chicago's Royal George Theatre on September 25, 1994, critic Richard Christiansen enthused:

Reaching back into medieval history and pointing toward the near-distant future, mixing grand visions with gay jokes, drawing on a body of knowledge that touches on everything from photosynthesis to Reaganomics, traveling from Salt Lake City to Washington, D. C., exploring the origins of Christianity and Judaism, and tracing the patterns of domestic turmoil in gay and straight families, *Angels* is an incredible undertaking for the playwright and an astounding journey of dis-covery for his audience. (1)

Numerous other critics referred to either or both parts of *Angels* as a master-piece. In fact, the praise has been high by any standards, perhaps surprisingly so for the work of an outspoken and openly gay dramatist in a society still deeply conflicted about homosexuality. Does the attention paid to *Angels*, at the very least, suggest a conflict within the American soul?

Something unique happened with the appearance of *Angels*: wherever it is performed it seems to touch a raw nerve. As the national tour of *Angels* began its run in Chicago in 1994, *Variety* critic Lewis Lazare prophetically wondered "how a drama as substantive and potent as *Angels in America* will do in the heart of America" (173), while, more to the point, Stephen Peithman said of *Angels*, "Some plays are born controversial and some have controversy thrust upon them" (12). The plays had "removed from the closet once and for all the enlivening relationship of gay culture and American theatre and the centrality of the homosexual gaze in American literature" (Clum 324), while also fueling the contentious culture wars and the ongoing debate on the acceptance of gays in American society. The resulting controversy emerged most powerfully in rural, predominantly conservative communities.

Among the first significant controversies was a showdown in Charlotte, North Carolina, where the Charlotte Repertory Theatre, under Keith Martin's direction, staged both parts of the play. Rev. Joseph R. Chambers, a self-styled antipornography crusader, who "has waged war against the popular children's TV show *Barney & Friends* ('clearly occult') and Disney's injection of 'voodooism' into *The Lion King*" (Drukman 46), led the charge in Charlotte. Chambers admitted he had not seen *Angels*, but had read some excerpts and condemned the play for "blasphemy" for its depiction of "unsafe sex" and its gay thematic content. Having found a legal loophole, the fact that the scene in which Prior disrobes for a physical examination in a doctor's office "is technically against the law in North Carolina" (Drukman 46), Chambers pursued his cause with zeal. *American Theatre* magazine reported that a "handful of protesters decrying 'public nudity' and 'pornography' picketed early performances, facing off with more numerous counter-demonstrators who rallied in support of the production" (Drukman 46).

Kushner himself appeared on the Charlotte Rep's stage on the third night of performances, stating that "on principle he had no problem with altering the scene, but added that he refused to capitulate to production changes made in craven response to 'homophobic bigotry.' Speaking to the *Charlotte Observer*, he called Chambers 'a major-league wacko'" (Drukman 47). The performances went on, they were sold out, and the production was held over due to popular response. However, a few months later, following a Charlotte Rep production of John Guare's *Six Degrees of Separation*, which Chambers and his followers also condemned, the Rep lost some of its funding from the locally run arts council in Charlotte. The situation, as Steven Drukman writes in *American Theatre*, "is a reminder of how thorny questions about politics, morality and sexuality overlap and are ultimately borne by the artist in negotiation with his community and his own conscience" (47).

Angels also inspired controversy on university and college campuses, first at the Catholic University of America where a graduate student, Christopher Bellis, planned to produce *Millennium Approaches*. In August 1996, three months after the decision was made to produce it, the trouble began. Gitta Honegger, head of Catholic University's drama department, was notified by the university's provost, Msgr. John Wippel, and its dean of arts and sciences, Antanas Suziedelis, that there would be an advertising ban on the production, and that no admission could be charged. Why the production had initially been sanctioned and why it took the administration so long to make its feelings known never became clear, but its action came when the department's season brochure, in which *Millennium Approaches* had been prominently announced, had already been sent to the school's in-house printer.

It seems that Catholic University—which is the only university in the United States chartered by the Vatican—had taken a closer look at what *Angels* was about or, more likely, that a vocal contingent of alumni and administrators disapproved of the play's content. When the story broke in Washington's gay newspaper, the *Washington Blade*, Honegger said the production was banned from advertising the play because "publicity for the show might look like an endorsement of the homosexual lifestyle by the university and the Catholic Church" (Wynn 1). Catholic University issued a statement making it clear that the administration "reserves the right to determine the appropriateness of public presentation to ensure consistency with the university's mission" (Swisher C1). The student director wrote that "the university's action, which I personally believe is a form of censorship, has created a climate of fear which is inappropriate for an academic community" (Nunns 46), adding his concern that the university might take additional action. His fears were well-founded. Shortly thereafter, Suziedelis questioned Bellis's judgment in selecting *Angels*, noting that it would be similar to "a student of art at Yeshiva to propose a garden of swastika sculptures as a thesis project. It was not a prudent choice to stage *Angels in America* as a thesis project at Catholic University" (Nunns 46); Bellis replied sardonically that Suziedelis's response must have been "written in haste" (Nunns 46) and demanded a personal apology for the attack on his judgment and the comparison of homosexuality to Nazism. This demand led Suziedelis to issue an ultimatum: "They could either cancel the play altogether, move it off campus, or limit access to only graduate students, faculty and people from the professional theater" (Nunns 46).

As the ruckus at Catholic continued, one gay alumnus was so angered he returned his master's diploma to the university. When Honneger, Bellis, and the cast discussed the options, it was decided to take the play off-campus. Almost immediately, they received a supportive response from Douglas Wager, artistic director of Washington's Arena Stage, who permitted the production to move into the Stage's "Old Vat" theater where *Millennium Approaches* was performed in a full production, while the same cast gave staged readings of *Perestroika*.

Subsequent eruptions occurred at Indiana's Wabash College and Texas's Kilgore College, both in small, fundamentally conservative rural communities, while schools in more urban settings produced the plays with little or no controversy. At Kilgore, the college's president, William Holda, vigorously supported a production of *Millennium Approaches* (while Wabash's president, Andrew T. Ford, did so only with great reluctance), but the local Gregg County Commission cut a $50,000 grant promised to support Kilgore's Texas Shakespeare Festival, which elicited a response from Kushner: "It's always unpleasant to be the target of hatred, bigotry, and stupidity, just as it's always a shock—at least it is to me. I tend towards the naive and optimistic—to experience first hand the vitality and persistence of the American anti-democratic movement" ("Why We Must Fight"

7). At Kilgore, the result was that individuals and other groups sent support to make up the festival's loss, including the Director's Guild of America, which contributed $10,000. The festival went forward despite the controversy and loss of funds, while Kushner offered a reminder of the value of the artist and the privilege of being one: "We know the secret of making art, while they know only the minor secret of making mischief. We proceed from joy; they have only their misery. And while we have to resist them vigorously, we can also pity them, and let compassion as well as anger fuel our work" ("Why We Must Fight" 7).

When New York City Mayor Rudy Giuliani tried to stop a controversial art show at the Brooklyn Museum of Art, causing a controversy, Kushner responded to the situation in the *Nation*, but it was clear he was writing about the controversies *Angels* had inspired as much as he was writing in support of the art show. Kushner asks the censorious voices of the religious right, "Would a God who gave us powers of creation, curiosity and love then command us to avoid the ideas and art these powers produce?" He stressed that the war against art in the name of God, decency, and civic stability "isn't decent; it's thuggish, its unconstitutional, undemocratic and deeply unwise" ("Fighting the Art Bullies" 41).

Barely ten years after the two *Angels* plays had their debuts so much has been written about them that it would seem there was little left to add. At least two collections of essays—*Essays on Kushner's Angels,* edited by Per Brask, and *Approaching the Millennium. Essays on Angels in America,* edited by Deborah R. Geis and Steven F. Kruger—have appeared, as well as a mountain of articles on virtually every aspect of the plays in a vast range of books, journals, and periodicals. Few American plays in living memory have attracted such interest and, along with it, such controversy. In late 1998, *Angels in America* was selected by the Royal National Theatre of Great Britain as one of the greatest plays of the twentieth century, and *Angels* turned up ranked near the top of other similar lists while also turning up in numerous anthologies of representative American dramas.

As *Angels* neared the end of its Broadway run, Kushner began work on a screenplay for a film version that was originally scheduled to be directed by Robert Altman. Altman's involvement was appealing to Kushner, who had long admired the director's work, but he worried about how to convert these two massive plays into one—or even two—films. *Angels*, Kushner found, is "not only structured like a movie—it's literally structured like an Altman movie. Quite literally, the form is stolen from *Nashville*, so I think it's going to seem like an incredible retread unless we come up with something new" ("Anxious in America" 52). Altman hoped to make two films of the plays, but later withdrew from the project. In 2001, it was announced that Mike Nichols would direct *Angels* for HBO.

In 1999, it was announced that the Paris Opera and the Glyndebourne Festival had commissioned composer Peter Eotvos to write an opera based on *Angels* and, in May 2000, soprano Renee Fleming performed composer Ricky Ian Gordon's "Night Flight to San Francisco," a setting of Harper's monologue on the airplane near the end of *Perestroika*, at New York's Alice Tully Hall. Critic

Anthony Tommasini applauded Kushner's "pensive" speech, but found Gordon's "warmed-over pop style terribly cloying" (E3).

While the Broadway run and the U.S. national tour of *Angels* continued, numerous international productions were staged. The Royal National Theatre of Great Britain had played a significant role in launching the plays, and within a short time the plays seemed to be everywhere. In 1993, productions of the plays appeared in theaters in Sydney and Melbourne, Australia, while in 1995, *Millennium Approaches* was staged at the Aarhus Teater and *Perestroika* was mounted at the Det Kongelige Teater in Denmark. There were productions in several German cities, stagings in Canada, Israel, Holland, Japan, France, Switzerland, Brazil, Uruguay, Italy, Belgium, Finland, Hungary, Iceland, Norway, Poland, Spain, and a near riot accompanied performances at a Rumanian theater.

Kushner has spoken of his interest in revisiting the *Angels* characters in future installments, updating their lives and the attendant political and social issues they face. Should he write another *Angels* play, Kushner intends to focus his attention on the Pitts—Hannah, Harper, and Joe—and such a play would undoubtedly feature the emotional sweep and political engagement of *Millennium Approaches* and *Perestroika*.

Defiantly theatrical, unabashedly sprawling, ambitious, provocative, poignant, and hilarious, *Angels* proposes visions of healing through community. The seriocomic insights, emotional sweep and, in its aesthetics as "anti-illusionist Brechtian graffito" (Harvey 99), its convergence of art and activism combine to depict the emotional devastation of a sad time. *Angels* explores questions of tolerance and the inevitability of monumental change, crossing borders from the real to an imaginative realm in dreams, hallucinations, and fantasy to allow its real-life fears to mix with imaginative hope to offer solace. This darkly touching, ominously political, and humanly redemptive drama suggests that betrayal and sin can and must be forgiven; Kushner persuasively insists that faith in a brighter future is essential, despite the harrowing specters of fear and doubt undermining the survival of hope. Kushner offers a beatific vision of a new America for the twenty-first century as millennium arrives.

CHAPTER FOUR

What Is to Be Done?

Slavs! Thinking About the Longstanding Problems of Virtue and Happiness

> Celebrate Design then, let's!
> The intricate arabesques, the curved, flowering branches of
> an improbable symmetrical tree,
>
> word and ritual and public vow,
> timely impositions on
> the ineffable anarchic love
>
> that blossoms madly in these hearts.
> —Tony Kushner, "Design,"
> *Thinking About the Longstanding*
> *Problems of Virtue and Happiness* (192)

In *Angels in America*, Kushner wondered, "How broad is a community's embrace. How wide does it reach? Communities all over the world now are in a tremendous crisis over the issue of how you let go of the past without forgetting the crimes that were committed" (Lahr, "Beyond Nelly," 129). The tragic past depicted in Kushner's next play, *Slavs! Thinking About the Longstanding Problems of Virtue and Happiness* (1994), is no less crushing, despite the comparatively brief running time (eighty minutes) and simpler dramatic structure. *Slavs!* a play more modestly conceived than either of the two *Angels* plays—a choice Kushner must have made in part to diffuse the high expectations for his first post-*Angels* play—is more overtly satiric than *Angels*. However, it revisits themes introduced in those plays. The emphasis is on political debate and governmental failure as seen through the sad consequences of a country—the crumbling Soviet Union of the late 1980s—abandoning the social theories of nearly a hundred years, embracing capitalism too quickly, and facing change without any guiding principles to replace those of the past.

Kushner's revelatory tragicomic vaudeville treats the Kafkaesque transformation of the Russian social landscape as a symbol for the ways in which shifting political winds profoundly effect the lives of ordinary individuals. Although the play is set in Russia, its resonances with late-twentieth-century American life are unmistakable. The familiar Russian joke of the mid-1980s collapse of communism—"What has capitalism accomplished in Russia in one year that communism couldn't accomplish in seventy years? Making communism look good!"—is taken by Kushner and turned on its head. What, he wonders, will the world be like if capitalism rules unchecked, without alternative social theories as a balance.

Following the seven-and-a-half-hour length of the two *Angels* plays, *Slavs!* is an exploration of other directions in the style and structure of Kushner's plays. He certainly demonstrates that he can explore immense themes in an epic style within a narrower framework than his earlier work. While holding to his particular notions of Brechtian episodic structure, Kushner moves further away from the traditional realistic theater in a play that seems on the surface to be a cartoonish satire. It is, however, much more, especially as the play moves to its desolate conclusion. *Slavs!* is a coda to the *Angels* plays, not only because it contains one scene and a character introduced in *Perestroika*. It is, like the satyr plays performed following tragic trilogies in ancient Greece, a palliative—a lighter work reflecting on themes similar to those in the more epic work. *Slavs!*, as much as *Angels*, demonstrates Kushner's utopian impulses mixed with the more somber strains of apocalyptic anxiety.

The inspiration for *Slavs!* comes from Kushner's response to the catastrophic Soviet nuclear disaster at Chernobyl (also referred to in *Perestroika*) and, while making use of the old apparatchik character from *Perestroika*, *Slavs!* also features some characters and situations Kushner had originally intended for *Perestroika* but had eliminated when that play grew too large. *Slavs!* is similar to the *Angels* plays, *A Bright Room Called Day*, and *Hydriotaphia* in the central role played by Kushner's moral outrage, as well as in his desire to draw lessons from the historical events on both personal and political levels. The play's serious questions about the demise of old values in a time of moral, political, racial, and sexual division are issues pervading most of Kushner's major dramatic works.

As a chronicle of a Russian revolution, *Slavs!* is anything but documentary. Kushner makes this clear in his advisory notes to the play, explaining that he has never visited Russia and intends to imagine the situation there rather than to represent it accurately. *Slavs!* is more a seriocomic nightmare, mixing such diverse elements as Chekhovian despair—a Russia of romantic imagination mixed with hard reality and deep emotional disappointment—and broadly drawn, almost stereotypical character types most obviously seen in the apparatchiks of the first act. More like silent movie comics than real people, they fit into familiar systems of imagery, although the ideas they debate are profoundly complex and troubling questions for the Russian—and perhaps international—future: the rupture of the old and fear of the new which contains within it the social dissolution resulting from economic upheaval, moral confusion, and the ongoing catastrophe of polluted land, water, and air. As in *Bright Room* and

Angels, and, to some extent, *Hydriotaphia*, Kushner's characters are ordinary individuals attempting, with varying degrees of success, to survive horrifying tragedies of human history. Kushner poses these philosophical and historical issues in a humorous and sometimes purposely simplistic way, but only to make way for his true message that revolutionary social change continues to challenge existing social structures and hope is difficult to come by when considering the wreckage of the past and the seemingly unsolvable problems facing us.

Slavs! is a parable of the late-twentieth-century American landscape as well. Elements of racial and anti-Semitic prejudice (as in *Angels*, Kushner draws parallels between anti-Semitism and homophobia), corporate damage to the environment, and a general lack of compassion in human affairs are certainly as much American concerns as they are Russian. The only significant difference between the two countries, in Kushner's view, is that the United States is currently economically successful, while the Russian economy lies in ruins. The most radical elements in *Slavs!* are found in the parallels Kushner draws between the Soviet collapse and the ravages of American-style capitalism. Somewhat surprisingly, Kushner identifies many ways in which the long decline and decay of Russia are like the extraordinary prosperity of America: both countries are multiethnic cultures structured by the theoretical underpinnings of great social experiment that have a comparatively short history, both currently suffer (to differing degrees) from a profound political disillusionment based on the failures and corruptions of their governments, and both have experienced a decline in the power and influence of the liberal elements within their political spheres. When Kushner was preparing *Slavs!* for its New York production, he told *New York Times* interviewer William Harris that he was pessimistic about the state of American politics in the wake of the "Republican Revolution" of the mid-1990s, feeling that

> people who have the ability to shape and influence culture, we failed terribly. We haven't addressed the right issues. These are very bleak times. There's a tendency inside of me to sentimentalize and reassure, because I'm a person who is always desperately craving comfort. I think it's a very bad thing to offer reassurance when people shouldn't be reassured. I also believe in entertaining people. That's the struggle in me: the necessity of presenting a sufficiently terrifying vision of the world so that it can galvanize action—which is something art should aspire to—and really wanting people to have a good time and to get solace from what I do. ("In *Slavs!* Are the Echoes of *Angels*" 36)

This is the wellspring of Kushner's art and the key reason that even the grimmest and most frightening issues and visions in his plays are burnished by a hard-won hopefulness, a guarded optimism, and a need, as a dramatist, to find a modicum of progressive possibility in the darkest corners of existence.

In the late twentieth century, Kushner explains, "When I say I'm a Socialist, people look at me as if I had just said I was a Druid" ("In *Slavs!* Are the Echoes of *Angels*" 5). Socialism's disrepute throughout the world comes as a result of many factors. Kushner says that since the collapse of the Soviet Union, "Free-market capitalism is the coming thing, but that doesn't mean we have to assume it's a good thing. I wanted the play to speak about the particular dilemma that we're faced with now, those of us who believe there's still a necessity for the collective, as well as the individual" ("In *Slavs!* Are the Echoes of *Angels*" 5). For Kushner, Russian history "has always been a great other history to examine questions that are significant in my own life. It's a kind of meta-narrative that's always been tremendously important to me, a history and collection of legends that I've always been very moved by" (Dixon 4). Certainly anyone observing historical currents and the stresses of social change would be attentive to the often devastating developments in Russia during the past twenty years.

Kushner also feels a great affinity for Russian writers and artists and for the goals of the Bolshevik Revolution. *Slavs!* is, Kushner believes, "a completely outside-American reading of the collapse" in Russia, "hence the outsizedness of some of the characters and situations—and it's completely intended to be read as metaphoric" (Dixon 4). Kushner also intends to make clear that "there's still an enormous amount in the literature of socialism that's tremendously valid, and that many of the problems facing this country [the United States] are problems that can only be hoped to be addressed once we start to understand the importance of economic as well as social justice, and deepen our understanding of ways in which society is collective as well as individualist" (Dixon 4). Kushner wonders about the possibility for "societies that are not competitive but cooperative ... do we simply give up on the idea that human society is capable of being made better than what it is?" (Harris, "The Road to Optimism," 28).

The play's raison d'être is the question first posed in a nineteenth-century novel by Nikolai Chernyshevsky—and famously repeated by Lenin—"What is to be done?" (185). Kushner introduces characters who attempt to answer this question but fail, paralyzed, to some extent, by the sheer weight of social catastrophe and individual suffering that overwhelms them all. How, they wonder, are we to proceed when the system in which we have lived our entire lives has fallen to bits around us? There are, of course, no obvious answers to this question and some of the characters only seem prepared to proceed tentatively—and mostly blindly—into a frightening future.

A Brechtian structure is again evident in *Slavs!* with Kushner employing elements of macabre wit that call Ghelderode to mind. However, the caricatured presentation of characters in *Slavs!* seems more indebted to George Bernard Shaw's comedies of ideas than to Brecht or Ghelderode. Part cynical political fable, part requiem for the dead socialist experiment in Russia, part intellectual farce, part political tragedy, *Slavs!* questions, in a typically Kushnerian emotionally charged and politically complex examination of the essence of being Slavic, the disillusionment and fear within the wreckage of the Soviet system and the meaning of love and suffering.

The subtitle of *Slavs!*—and some of its theoretical underpinnings—are taken from socialist philosopher Raymond Williams's 1985 essay "Walking Backwards into the Future," discussed above in chapter 3. Williams's desire to seek a definition of society and notions of the ways in which inevitable changes in social structure impinge on individual lives is as significant in *Slavs!* as it was in *Angels*. Kushner's admiration of Williams's assertion of the importance of a social theory opposing capitalism and the worth of socialism as a social principle does not blind him to the fact that such views can only be "made convincingly by looking honestly at the disastrous wreck of the Soviet system" (Dixon 4). Such sweeping political transformations as those made in Russia in the mid-1980s—and continuing with great difficulty into the present—do not happen every day, or even every decade or century. As such, an opportunity to explore these transformations emerges. When a social experiment of such scope suddenly reverses itself, what can be understood about the human costs of both change and stagnation?

A well-constructed tragicomic rumination about life in the rubble of "the evil empire," *Slavs!* offers a series of connected scenes depicting the breakup of the Soviet Union through a few individual lives. It is rife with ideological hyperbole, and is a sometimes touching depiction of the nostalgia Russians feel—sometimes inexplicably—for their blood-soaked past. It is also replete with Kushner's own self-parody, which mocks the trademark portentousness and overstatement typical of his plays, along with his usual collision of comic and tragic moments merged with images of the real and the fantastic. Kushner explains that he intends

> the movement of the play to be a descent from a sort of delirious optimism about the possibility of change to the grim realities standing in the way of progress, how much history endangers the future, examining the truculence of the human heart and mind when faced with accepting the necessities of change; and a consideration of the failure of the Soviet experiment, and of classical socialism, to arrive at a theory and practice by means of which human affairs can be rationally planned and re-ordered so as to accomplish the goals of economic and social justice. (Dixon 3)

To some degree, the Soviet people are shown as being made dupes by their government, as having to pay an overwhelming price for the corrupted brand of socialism that the Communists brought to the fore in Russia. However, Kushner is not in any sense mocking the Russian people—although he does have some fun with stereotypical views of the characters' Slavic gloom drawn from a range of popular culture images. Instead, Kushner finds "a great amount of courage and optimism" in the willingness of the former Soviets to embrace—however tentatively—perestroika, realizing the price the individual within that society must pay for the change: "Things have gotten very bad there now, and it's very scary," he believes, however, he stresses that there is "an absolute necessity for change" (Dixon 3). For a society to move forward and break free of a past that provides some sense—however false—of stability and comfort, is a difficult choice. Kushner views the connections between *Angels* and *Slavs!* as falling within the range of questions of change when he asks, "How much is change possible and what kinds of models for change and transformation do we have beyond the traumatic, beyond the revolutionary, which seem to me to be what the main questions of the historical event of perestroika were" (Dixon 3).

The brief prologue of *Slavs!* features two old babushkas sweeping the continually falling snow from the steps of the Kremlin's Great Hall of the Soviets in March 1985. As they work, the two old women improbably discuss political theory in a highly intellectual debate that is interrupted briefly by the arrival of two elderly high-ranking Politburo members, Vassily Vorovilich Smukov, a "pessimistic man" in his seventies, and Serge Esmereldovich Upgobkin, an "optimistic man" (91) in his eighties. Typically, Kushner's characters are meetings of strange bedfellows (and there are similarly Dickensian names for the characters throughout *Slavs!*), something underscored comedically here, as the two old functionaries appear and talk for a moment with the babushkas. Their condescending attitude to the two old women (intended by Kushner to be played by men in drag) is obvious, so the babushkas immediately transform themselves into what the apparatchiks want to see, "sweet, toothless old ladies, smiling, head-bobbing, forelock-tugging mumblers" (100), deferential and grandmotherly. Comforted by this image, Smukov and Upgobkin enter the hall as the babushkas continue their debate, acknowledging the "big doings today . . ." (102) taking place inside.

Act 1, scene 1 proceeds immediately as Smukov and Upgobkin arrive in an anteroom just steps away from where the debate rages. Kushner calls the first act of *Slavs!* "treacherous" (94), and "more or less a clown show—the characters are highly fantastical, the style heightened—and it's about change and the fear of the future" (Dixon 3). For Kushner it is important for the audience "to think" (94) in the first part of the play, which explains the use of *Verfremdsdung*—the Brechtian concept of alienation and estrangement—which Kushner achieves through broad comedy. Kushner indicates that these early scenes should be played as farce, despite a few clearly indicated serious moments. He also stresses the importance of status among the governmental characters and underscores that the varying ranks of the Politburo members are critical for distinguishing the intricate categories of power that eventually lead to disturbing conclusions later in the play.

As the first scene commences, the two old men debate the rapidly shifting currents of politics in the collapsing Soviet Union, a new, still undefined post-Leninist world: "People are not capable of change" (105), Smukov laments while he and Upgobkin sip tea from a steaming samovar. The masses, he insists, will not tolerate the deprivations they once withstood to create the socialist system, they "would rather die than change" (106)—"Stagnation," he believes, "is our only hope" (106–7). Upgobkin disagrees, countering that he believes "precisely the opposite" and that the Russian people "have been ordered into Motion by History herself"; "We would rather change," he says, "than die" (107). Worrying about staying awake for the endless debate, they reluctantly enter the Great Hall in the next scene, just in time to hear Aleksii Antedilluvianovich Prelapsarianov, "the world's oldest Bolshevik" (107), deliver an oration on the current state of affairs with intense passion. This speech, previously featured as the prologue to *Perestroika*, underscores the connection of *Slavs!* with *Angels*, but, more importantly, it establishes the play's central concept—past foundations of Soviet society have failed, but nothing exists to replace those foundations except the ruins of that failed system or an acceptance of capitalism. *Slavs!* includes three scenes written for inclusion in *Perestroika* aside from Prelapsarianov's speech that were cut due to *Perestroika's* extreme length.

Prelapsarianov, the play's intellectual conscience and its historical witness as a visible reminder of the Russian Revolution of 1917, argues that change cannot proceed without a new social construction—"the Cold Brilliant Light of Theory" (108)—to illuminate the obscure future. Speaking of the great socialist texts used to support the Soviet experiment, of "the sheer grandeur of the prospect we gazed upon," he scoffs at the "Sour Little Age" (108) of the present. What, he wonders, does the present offer to compare with the great theories of the past? He mockingly points out that all they can offer in its place are "Market Incentives? Watered-down Bukharite stopgap makeshift Capitalism? NEPmen! Pygmy children of a gigantic race!" (108). Prelapsarianov does not simply celebrate the past and mock the present, however. Realizing that "we must change," he pleads passionately that, without theory, "we dare not, we cannot move ahead" (108–9).

Scene 3, set in an anteroom of the Kremlin, introduces two "middle-aged deputies," Ippolite Ippolitovich Popolitipov and Yegor Tremens Rodent, both of whom are agitated over the distressing debate, with Popolitipov insisting that while external changes may be inevitable, "the heart is not progressive. The heart is conservative, no matter what the mind may be" (109). He is convinced that the heart will go back to the familiar, to "what it loves. That's the function of the organ, that's what it's there for: to fall in love. And love is profoundly reactionary, you fall in love and that instant is fixed, love is always fixed on the past" (109).

The two deputies are joined by Upgobkin, who leads the exhausted Prelapsarianov to a seat following his tirade at the podium. They all decry the "madness" of the present social circumstances, and discuss everything from a disastrous leak of radioactivity from a plutonium plant to a bizarre rumor that some people have "used black arts to resurrect ... Rasputin" (112). Popolitipov laments that the current mess "cannot be what Lenin intended," while Rodent whines that it is all as if "seventy years of socialism had never happened" and that "Fantasy is the spiritual genius of Slavic peoples" (112–13). As the conversation continues, the fading Prelapsarianov has a sudden revelation about why Evil triumphs and Good is "cast down in the gutter" (113). It is, he believes, because "God ... Is a Menshevik! Because God ... Is a Petty-Bourgeois! Because God is a Reactionary, and Progressive People are THE POLITICAL ENEMIES OF GOD!" (113). With this pronouncement, Prelapsarianov suddenly collapses and dies, symbolizing the finality of the demise of the Soviet experiment. Here again, as in earlier works, Kushner creates a metaphorical convergence of old and new, past and present.

Shortly thereafter, in scene 4, Popolitipov comments that Prelapsarianov's "grieving heart avenged itself on the forward-moving mind," and tells Rodent that "illness is a metaphor, Yegor; the human body, the body politic, the human soul, the soul of the state. Dynamic and immobile all at once, lava and granite, the head and the heart. It's all tension and tearing" (115–16). Smukov disagrees, but concurs with the deceased Bolshevik that "we should not move until we know where we are going" (116). Upgobkin is anxious to make the leap into the unknown future—so anxious, in fact, that he literally begins leaping about the room taunting his recalcitrant colleagues: "Will you never dare? Will you be dead forever?" (117). Finally, the strain of the leaping causes Upgobkin to die, and he collapses to the floor beside Prelapsarianov. There is a smile frozen on Upgobkin's face, leaving Smukov to wonder, "What on earth do you suppose he saw?" (119). Prelapsarianov has died of too much brain, while Upgobkin has expired from too much heart, and much is made of this by their survivors, although one begs, in a moment of Kushnerian self-parody, "no more metaphors, anyone, please" (118), as the act ends.

Kushner describes the second act of *Slavs!*, which is also set in Moscow, as "very Dostoevskian—dark, full of romantic slavic torment and angst and spooky folk-magic" (Dixon 3), and the setting is certainly appropriately bizarre. In scene 1, Katherina Serafima Gleb, a fiery twenty-something Russian Gen-Xer and punked-out lesbian, is working as a guard in a mysterious laboratory containing a gruesome collection of large jars holding the pickled brains of deceased Soviet thinkers: "The great minds of the Party. Political minds. Scientific minds. Even an artist or two" (129). This "dank, dark, dismal room" (123) of the Pan-Soviet Archives for the Study of Cerebro-Cephalognomical Historico-Biological Materialism is entered by Popolitipov, who carries a beaten-up guitar case and attempts to make love to the bored and directionless Katherina, who seems more interested in the pack of cigarettes he has brought her and in complaining about the grotesque environment around her.

Katherina talks of the brains in the jars which, to her, seem to be "slithering" at night, and she confesses that when she is bored she shakes them up and the loose tissues "Whirl like snowflakes in a crystal snowball" (128–29). As Popolitipov boorishly continues to pursue her, Katherina reminds him that "I'm a lesbian," expressing annoyance that "Poppy," as she calls him, makes her "go through this mortifying business over and over and over again" simply because he has set her up in a "soft, *boring* job" (127–28).

Referring to herself as an "anarchist" (132), Katherina discusses the imminent rise to power of Mikhail Gorbachev who, she fears, "will come, trailing free-market anarchy in his wake! Burger King! Pizza Hut! The International Monetary Fund! Billions in aid will flow!" (132). Although she adamantly denies being anti-Semitic, Katherina compares Gorbachev's "crafty and sly" (132) ways with Jews and insists that with his rise, "there will be no more politics, we will become like Americans" (132). She only hopes that the surprises of a Gorbachev future, "most of them unpleasant," may at least lift "the Great Grey Age of Boredom" (132) she sorrowfully acknowledges as the present. "Sorrow," Poppy replies, is "the spiritual genius of Slavic peoples," and he recounts a tale of his own sad and unloved past as "an ugly child, a graceless child" (132–33) as he and Katherina drink vodka. He confesses that, "the Party adopted me. The Party was not Love, but Necessity; it rebuilt the ruined world," and as the vodka continues to flow, they sadly ruminate on love, with Poppy insisting that "even in a degraded, corrupt and loveless world, love can finally be born" (133–34).

Poppy—and the vodka—have succeeded in momentarily moving Katherina, but his hopes of a little romance are suddenly dashed when Dr. Bonfila Bezhukhovna Bonch-Bruevich, a specialist in pediatric oncology, arrives. Katherina runs to the arms of her "girlfriend" (135) and tension mounts as Poppy attempts to come between Katherina and Bonfila, causing Katherina to angrily insult Poppy. She prefers Bonfila, who "cures people," to "an ineffectual aged paperpushing-timeserver-apparatchik-with-a-dacha like you who only bleeds the people dry" (136). Hurt, Poppy prepares to leave and asks Katherina if she will miss him, but she can only reply, "The cigarettes, definitely" (140). Irate, Poppy turns to Bonfila to offer some criticism of Katherina: "She is the Revolution's Great-Granddaughter. She is . . . a barbarian," adding, "We have not made a world that makes people kind" (140–41). He abruptly departs leaving Bonfila to fear that he may exact some bureaucratic revenge.

Only a few hours later, in scene 2, Bonfila and Katherina are both drunk and Bonfila is telling stories about her great-grandfather, the man who embalmed Lenin. Bonfila expresses her love for Katherina, who sadly replies, "Everyone loves me, but I'm unbearable," and, paraphrasing Poppy's earlier statement, she notes that "sadness is the spiritual genius of the Slavic peoples" (143). Bonfila has brought Katherina a present, an old religious icon of St. Sergius of Radonezh, whose face has been painted over with Lenin's, but Katherina is more interested in sex. Bonfila ignores her advances for the moment, insisting that the icon "works miracles" (148), so Katherina prays to the icon to make Bonfila love her, but is absurdly interrupted when a big babushka enters to tell them that a truckload of drunken soldiers has crashed outside. A melee ensued causing a liquor store window to be smashed, and the babushka presents the women with a large bottle of vodka liberated from the store. As she exits, the babushka notices the icon and recognizes it as St. Sergius "with the face of Great Lenin" (150). She crosses herself as the stunned Katherina and Bonfila stand agape grasping the welcome bottle of vodka.

Scene 3 is even later the same long night. Katherina is sound asleep in Bonfila's lap in the dark room with only a flickering candle to provide illumination. Bonfila looks sadly at the St. Sergius/Lenin icon and says, "We have suffered and suffered and Paradise has not arrived. Shouldn't you come back and tell us what went wrong?" and, as she prays, she demands insistently of Lenin that he return: "Pull yourself together, leave your tomb, come claim your brain, remember speech, and action, and once more, having surveyed the wreckage we have made, tell your children: What is to be done?" (151). The only response she receives is a startling vision of a little girl who appears silently in the dim candlelight. Stunned, Bonfila awakens Katherina, who is too drunk to see this vision which is, as it turns out, an omen.

The final act of *Slavs!* is the heart of the play and, as Kushner explains, "addresses the unbelievably awful conditions of life in contemporary Russia" (Dixon 3). Set in Talmenka, Siberia, in 1992, seven years have elapsed and the action proceeds in a medical facility where Bonfila has been transferred by the vengeful Popolitipov following Katherina's insults in the previous act. A little girl, Vodya Domik—the child from Bonfila's vision—is silently seated on a

Figure 7: (Left to Right) Callie Thorne, as Katherina, and Robin Bartlett, as Bonfila, in the 1995 La Jolla Playhouse production of Tony Kushner's *Slavs! Thinking About the Longstanding Problems of Virtue and Happiness.* Photo by Ken Howard.

wooden chair. Rodent, still the "timorous and deferential" hypocritical appa-ratchik of the first act, enters this "white room," but he has hardened in the inter-vening years and become "nasty" (155). He obnoxiously parrots, "Hello little girl" (156), in Vodya's direction, but she does not respond. Bonfila enters and acknowledges that Vodya is mute.

When Vodya's mother, Mrs. Domik, arrives, Bonfila introduces her to Rodent, who, she explains, is there to make a report on the workings of the facility that has been established to treat child victims of nuclear and toxic waste accidents. Bonfila explains that many of the resident children have died before the age of six and that Vodya is "our survivor" (160). The children, she recounts, are all suffering from "nervous-system damage, renal malformation, liver, cataracts at three, bone-marrow problems" (161) and that many, including Vodya, cannot speak or do not learn to walk at appropriate ages. Realizing that Rodent is a representative of a bloated and unfeeling bureaucracy, Bonfila bitterly criticizes the continual dumping of toxic and nuclear materials in the region, but Rodent tries to blame it all on the Stalin era. She insists that this is not so, that the dumping continues and that Vodya is, as a result, a "mutant" (163). "The whole country's a radioactive swamp" (164), Bonfila points out, adding that hundreds of thousands of people have been exposed.

Bonfila launches into a lengthy tirade cataloguing government unresponsiveness to outcries against plutonium dumping in a cave in the immediate area, while adding that poorly stored nuclear waste has been piling up there since 1950. She demands to know why it has not been moved, but Rodent tensely scoffs at Bonfila's invective, adding in a menacing tone: "In the old days you would not speak to me like this" (164). More directly on the subject, Rodent shrugs off the dumping of the toxins, insisting that "there's nothing to be done. We have no place to put it" (164). This only makes Bonfila angrier and she becomes increasingly accusatory, claiming that "now you're offering to process and store radioactive and toxic waste from the West," to which he matter-of-factly replies, "They'll pay us" (165).

Frustrated and infuriated, Bonfila accuses Rodent of complicity in the Soviet government's nuclear testing on its citizenry, but bitterly admits that she is still a socialist: "Isn't that absurd! After all I've seen I still believe . . . And, and I want to know! And you, SOMEONE MUST TELL ME!" (166). How, she demands to know, did these catastrophes happen in a socialist country? "Naïveté," Rodent replies, to which she sardonically retorts, "It's the spiritual genius of Slavic peoples" (166). As Bonfila continues to rant, Rodent dismissively scoffs, "Siberia, doctor, is making you shrill" (168).

If Rodent thinks he has met his match in Bonfila, nothing could prepare him for his encounter with Mrs. Domik, Vodya's mother, in the play's most harrowing sequence. Mrs. Domik wants to know what Rodent, as the representative of the state, intends to do about her terminally ill daughter, whose care she cannot afford and who, in her view, is a victim of Russia's nuclear policy. Rodent can only supply more empty platitudes and excuses ("Austerity measures are necessary . . ." [169]), and he attempts to hide behind a pose of patriotism. Outraged, Mrs. Domik demands that Bonfila and Rodent take responsibility for Vodya: "Take her to Yeltsin! Take her to Gorbachev! Take her to Gaidar! Take her to Clinton! YOU care for her! YOU did this! YOU did this! She's yours!" (171). She storms out, but returns almost immediately to demand that Rodent take his "filthy fucking hands off my child" (171).

Rodent tremulously attempts to explain the current political situation to Mrs. Domik, insisting that the government has fallen into the hands of those more interested in selling out the interests of Russians to foreign dollars. His weak attempt at sympathy is undermined, however, by his efforts to blame these problems on "dark-skinned people from the Caucasus regions, Muslims, Asiatics, swarthy inferior races" (172), including Jews, who, he claims, have flooded into the country. Worse yet, he tries to give Mrs. Domik some literature on the Liberal Democratic Party of Russia. Rodent's unctuous speechifying causes Mrs. Domik to explode. In a fury, she screams that she is not, in fact, a Russian, but a transplanted Lithuanian because

> fucking Stalin sent my grandma here fifty years ago. My grandpa and my great-uncles and great-aunts died tunneling through the Urals on chain gangs. Their father and his brother were shot in Vilnius, their children were shot fighting Germans, my sister starved to death and my brother killed himself under fucking Brezhnev after fifteen years in a psychiatric hospital, I've tried twice to do the same—and my daughter.... Fuck this century. Fuck your leader. Fuck the state. Fuck all governments, fuck the motherland, fuck your mother, your father, and you. (172–73)

Grabbing Vodya by the hand, Mrs. Domik departs, leaving Rodent "ashen with terror" (173). Reflecting on the power of the "impotent rage" of Mrs. Domik, Kushner explains its relation to electoral apathy in America:

> It leads her to reject fascism, as it leads her to reject any form of government. But whether or not she can ever be reached again or be brought to believe in any system again is scary. It's also a situation we're faced with all over the United States. The people who voted in the Newt Gingrich gang are only a fifth of the population. The people who didn't come out and vote are the people who basically decided that there is no hope for them, that there is no government that will serve them, that there is no ideology they can cling to. (Lahr, "Hail Slavonia," 86)

In the wake of Mrs. Domik's fury, Rodent, blandly hailing "the Motherland" (174), departs, offering no solutions to the disastrous situation. Bonfila explains her own persistence in the face of the horrifying problems: "Because I thought I could do some good here. In the face of all of this impossibility, twenty thousand years, that little girl who won't live five more years, I still believe that good can be done, that there's work to be done. Good hard work" (174). Katherina, who at Bonfila's request has followed her to Siberia, arrives to escort Bonfila home, mumbling that "Siberia sucks" (175) as the third act ends.

The epilogue of *Slavs!*, set in a Siberian-style Heaven of eternal stasis and boredom, is a heavenly scene similar to the one Kushner includes as an "optional" sequence in *Perestroika*, wherein Prior Walter finds himself in an encounter with Louis's deceased grandmother and the rabbi whose oration at Sarah's memorial service begins *Millennium Approaches*. That scene, like the one in *Slavs!*, is intended, as Kushner explains, as a "kind of philosophical discussion about what's to be done now. Is there anything in the whole wreckage of the Soviet Union and the history of socialism in the Soviet Union to be recuperated?" (Dixon 3).

This Heaven is a "gloomy, derelict place like a city after an earthquake" (179),

Figure 8: (Left to Right) Ronny Graham and James Greene in the 1995 Baltimore Center Stage production of Tony Kushner's *Slavs! Thinking About the Longstanding Problems of Virtue and Happiness.* Photo by Richard Anderson.

and the deceased Politburo members from the first act, Upgobkin and Prelapsarianov, sit playing cards. Despite the fact that they have been dead for nearly ten years, they cannot find peace. Upgobkin is "bewildered. I expected more from the Afterlife, in the way of conclusive proof, in some form or another ... " (179) of God's existence. Bored with card playing, they consider looking down to see how things are turning out in Russia—or in other troubled places like Cuba, Rwanda, Bosnia, Pakistan, Afghanistan—but decide they would rather not know, with Prelapsarianov sadly realizing that "it is *depressing*" (181). Upgobkin had at least hoped to see the future once he arrived in Heaven, but "there is only a great cloud of turbulent midnight, and not even the dead can see what is to come" (181).

The two old men notice the arrival of a child—Vodya—who can now speak (eloquently, in fact), and Prelapsarianov laments that it is "sad to see a little one wandering Night's Plutonian Shore," to which Vodya responds, "Plutonium? Is there plutonium even here?" (182). Vodya reveals that she has died of cancer caused by her exposure to plutonium, that a "wild profusion of cells; dark flowerings in my lungs, my brain, my blood, my bones; dandelion and morning glory vine seized and overwhelmed the field; life in my body ran riot" (182).

Prelapsarianov reveals that he died from talking too much and that Upgobkin expired from leaping symbolically into the future. No wisdom emerges from the old men, who note that not seeing the new "is bitter," while Vodya posits that maybe the guiding principles of the past were always wrong: "Perhaps it is true that social justice, economic justice, equality, community, an end to master and slave, the withering away of the state: These are desirable but not realizable on the earth" (183). She laments that the failure of socialism in the East may only be the result of "the inadequacy and criminal folly of any attempt to organize more equitably and rationally the production and distribution of the wealth of nations. And chaos, market fluctuations, rich and poor, colonialism and war are all that we shall ever see" (183). The "foul epithet" that socialism has become as a result of Stalin means that to "the ravages of Capital there will be no conceivable alternative" (184). Vodya concludes, "I am inexpressibly sad, grandfathers. Tell me a story" (184), and Upgobkin recounts the tale of one Vladimir Ilyich Ulyanov, a seventeen-year-old boy, who was sad because the secret police had just hung his brother for plotting to kill the Czar. Because he missed his brother, Upgobkin continues, the boy grew up "to become Great Lenin, and read his brother's favorite book, a novel by Chernyshevsky, the title and contents of which asks the immortal question" (185) with which Lenin

> stood the world on its head; the question which challenges us to both contempla-
> tion and, if we love the world, to action; the question which implies: Something is
> terribly wrong with the world, and avers: Human beings can change it; the ques-
> tion asked by the living and, apparently, by the fretful dead as well: What is to be
> done? (185)

Is the end of *Slavs!* a statement of the complete hopelessness of the situation—both in Russia and in regard to the worth of the socialist model—or is it a call to action, demanding a phoenix-like rising from the ruins?

Originally produced at the Actors Theatre of Louisville as part of its annual Humana Festival of New American Plays in March 1994, *Slavs!* featured a cast including Gerald Hiken, Kate Goehring, Mary Shultz, Barbara eda-Young, Steve Culp, Ray Fry, and Michael Kevin, under Lisa Peterson's direction. As with his prior works, Kushner continued rewriting the play during rehearsals and per-formances prior to its New York premiere. The ATL production was followed by a June 6, 1994 staged reading at New York's Walter Kerr Theatre (where *Angels* was still playing) as a benefit for the Lesbian Avengers Civil Rights Organizing Project. Featuring an "all-star" cast including Tracey Ullman, Madeline Kahn, Laurie Metcalf, Olympia Dukakis, Sandra Bernhard, Anne Pitoniak, Ellen McLaughlin, Kathleen Chalfant, and Barbara eda-Young, with Kate Clinton nar-rating, the reading was preserved for an as-yet-unreleased commercial recording.

Over the following months, a series of *Slavs!* productions were staged throughout the United States, including a June 1994 production at Chicago's Steppenwolf Theatre, a November 1994 staging at the New York Theatre Workshop, also directed by Peterson, who later helmed productions at Baltimore's Center Stage in January 1995 and at the Yale Repertory Theatre in February 1995. Prior to those productions, in December 1994, *Slavs!* premiered in England at the Hampstead Theatre Club, followed by other productions throughout Europe and in regional theaters across the United States, including Boston's Trinity Repertory Theatre in April 1995, Washington, D. C.'s Studio Theatre in October 1995, Los Angeles's Mark Taper Forum in October 1995 (under the direction of Michael Greif), the Berkeley Repertory Theatre in March 1996, and Raleigh, North Carolina's Manbites Dog Theatre also in 1996.

Slavs! engendered a wide variety of critical responses, ranging from disdain and disappointment to exclamations of brilliance and genius. Although some critics seemed disappointed that *Slavs!* did not attempt to match the length and epic scope of *Angels*, many were generally approving of the play. *USA Today's* David Patrick Stearns raved of Chicago's Steppenwolf Theatre production that it was a "theatrically compelling" work "peppered with keen, witty political observations" (4D). Of the subsequent New York production, Vincent Canby described it in the *New York Times* as the work of a "brilliant and restless imagination.... Mr. Kushner's words dazzle, sting and prompt belly laughs," adding that it is a "bracing, rational" play that is "rambunctiously funny, seriously moving" (5). Reviewer John Lahr called *Slavs!* "Part intellectual vaudeville, part meditation on the apparent collapse of socialism" and stressed that even in a small play, Kushner "is capable of cajoling us out of our received opinions through the power of his heart and mind" ("Hail, Slavonia" 85, 87). Critic John Simon dismissed the play as "frat-house theatricals," a work that "hops from social farce to political satire, from lesbian love story to humanitarian speechifying, from hell to earth to squalor in Heaven, from bad to worse" (52), while David Richards viewed it more favorably as a "curious, roundabout play" demonstrating the qualities that made *Angels* "distinctive: the playwright's eagerness to engage an audience in lively political discourse, his willingness to follow his imagination wherever it leads him and his ability to undercut himself with wit whenever his pronouncements start turning too serious," concluding that *Slavs!* is "not much more than a cluster of intellectual vaudeville sketches linked to one another only because they happen to have an overlapping character or two" (C17–C18). Gerald Weales called *Slavs!* a "verbal extravaganza" (701), while William Tynan described Kushner's "baroque dialogue" as "too often mind boggling rather than thought provoking," but added that it is "not without wit" (73). Marc Robinson, critic for the *Village Voice*, was far more enthusiastic, stressing that

> Tony Kushner bears the curse of all artists unlucky enough to have captured the zeitgeist. They are expected to continue on their visionary path, explicating the world's mysteries in each new play. Or they are tempted to use the stage as a bully pulpit, indicting the cause of our malaise and dolling out prescriptions to sooth the pain. It is a mark of Kushner's sophistication that in his newest play he refuses to rest on his well-earned moral authority. A lesser writer would have followed *Angels in America* with something smug and sweeping. As though Kushner feared such a fate, he instead has returned to where he started—a place of healthy confusion. A taut play results: Kushner's humor buoys his political anguish, his lyricism draws dry ideas into rhapsodies and elegies, his interest in character won't let even the most vaudevillian individual conform to type. (91)

Kushner's reaction to the mid-1990s shift to the conservative right is surely present in Rodent's admission that his nation is in "the hands of miscreants and fools. The government does not serve the people, but betrays the people to foreign interests" (171), and in the implied hatreds dividing ethnic, racial, and religious groups. Critic Charles Marowitz described *Slavs!* as taking "a broad swipe at a Russian dilemma which in no way diminishes the horror of its subject-matter" (159), while pointing out the connections with current American politics.

J. Wynn Rousuck, reviewing Baltimore's Center Stage production in the *Baltimore Sun*, felt that the "ever-ambitious Kushner has again saddled himself with material that isn't easy to dramatize—much less accept," but that the play "is still intensely thought-provoking" (E1). Of the Yale Repertory Theatre production, critic Christopher Arnott, reporting on it as well as simultaneous Connecticut stagings of *Angels* and Kushner's adaptation of *A Dybbuk*, stressed the difficulty of capturing the experience of a Kushner play in words, because "as much fun as Kushner is to read, he has to be seen to be believed" (26). Arnott's colleague, Malcolm Johnson, felt that *Slavs!* fell short of *Angels*, but that it "still stands high above most contemporary plays—in its humor, its passion and its dramatic force" (E1). The first English production of *Slavs!* at the Hampstead Theatre Club inspired critic Eric Korn to react with a contradictory view of it as "loosely argued, beautifully written, poorly constructed, thrillingly staged and superbly acted" (18). The cast was led by Imelda Staunton, Aisling O'Sullivan, Peter Bayliss, and Ron Cook. Korn described Kushner's hallucinatory vision of a crumbling Russia as a "place of snow and serge and samovars, apparently assembled from great novels and poor movies, his characters hollow dolls in a haze of balalaika music and vodka-sodden sadness. But the despair is real—the despair of the twice-betrayed disciple" (18). Critic Michael Billington appreciated Kushner's ability to write with "hurtling energy" in a "fine and urgent" (T8) play, but Alastair Macaulay condemned Kushner as "a lightweight" and although he applauded the production and the cast, who, he felt, deserved to be seen in the West End, he added that "a play like this should not" (23). Most other London critics were appreciative of the play's merits.

Los Angeles Times critic Laurie Winer praised the La Jolla Playhouse production of *Slavs!* with a cast led by Robin Bartlett, which was produced in the summer of 1995 before moving to Los Angeles's Mark Taper Forum. Winer called Kushner "an intense and poetical writer, a great shaper of words" who "makes the political personal" ("Old Bolshevik Resurfaces" F1). By the time the La Jolla production reached the Taper, however, Winer's reaction was more guarded for "this brittle, short, funny, maddening, sometimes pretentious intellectual vaudeville" ("Questions Unanswered in Kushner's *Slavs!*" F1). Reviewer Michael Phillips found *Slavs!* to be a "highly companionable" followup to *Angels*, adding that Kushner is "a terrific theatrical conversationalist" (E1, E3), while critic Steven Winn applauded the "vigor and implications of the play's issues" (B1). Describing *Slavs!* as a "tragicomic vaudeville," critic Hedy Weiss, writing of an April 2000 European Repertory Company production at Chicago's About Face Theatre, found that Kushner's play is "the very model of how to turn history into magic." Weiss described Kushner as "a writer at once politically caustic and romantically fearless" (32).

While some critics enjoyed the play's humor, others found it far too comic. The play's humor is established from its start, as the two old babushkas discuss Marxist theory, but only when no one is looking. Other humor emerges from cross-gender casting (the babushkas played by men and Prelapsarianov, as in *Perestroika*, may be acted by a woman). Robert Brustein praised Kushner "for being able to create a deteriorating social and political universe so far away and yet so near. *Slavs!* is proof that he is capable of imagining reality through something other than a sexual prism" (119). This last is perhaps a bit unfair, as Kushner had certainly proved capable of dealing with a wide variety of subjects in *Bright Room*, *Hydriotaphia*, and throughout *Angels*. The sexual is always present in Kushner's plays—even in *Slavs!* there are erotic moments, as in Poppy's flirtation with Katherina—"I would like to run my tongue against the salty soft shag covering your upper lip" (124), he says—and more so in Katherina's drunken seduction of Bonfila, her pleading to "let me lick your cunt till my whole face is wet" (145). More thematically, Katharina rejects typical sexual roles in a parallel with her rejection of everything she associates with her country's past. The sexual is always present, but the sociopolitical issues predominate.

Shortly after initial productions of *Slavs!* it received an Obie Award for Best Off-Broadway Play in 1995 and was published in a volume of the Humana Festival plays, by the Broadway Play Publishing Company, and in a Theatre Communications Group book called *Thinking About the Longstanding Problems of Virtue and Happiness*, which also included several Kushner essays, poems, and a prayer for New York's Episcopalian National Day of Prayer for AIDS which he had delivered at the Cathedral Church of St. John the Divine on October 9, 1994.

Slavs! essentially asks: What is lost when a social system collapses? Is the theory upon which it was based automatically rendered worthless, or are there lessons to be taken from both the reality of the failure and the imaginings of a more progressive society inspired by the theories? Robert L. King, writing in the *North American Review*, identified an inherent pessimism in the situations depicted in *Slavs!*, but despite it, King points out, Kushner "cannot abandon all hope for enlightened change" (44). Kushner's tendency is to dramatize problems and raise challenging questions about them without offering pat answers or suggesting specific solutions. Instead, he chooses the Brechtian method of inviting the audience to contemplate the issues—however complicated and disturbing they may be—and to consider, as is literally asked in the play, What next?

When *Slavs!* was first performed, there were criticisms of Kushner's attempt to wed the semicomic attitudes of the buffoonish politicians of the first part of the play with the tragic circumstances in Siberia in the last act. In fact, Kushner creates slow and subtle changes in tone that allow this linear play to accumulate depth and power as it moves forward. The play initially seems less dramatic than dialectic, especially in the earliest scenes in which Kushner's characters debate the pros and cons of the imminent social changes, but as the play develops it becomes an increasingly witty philosophical discussion of revolution and humanity set against the rather more mundane lives of members of a ravaged society. For the play's general mood, Kushner has obviously turned to imagery and language from the great, despairing Russian writers of the late nineteenth and twentieth centuries: Dostoyevsky, Gogol, Chekhov, and Bulgakov—one joke has Katherina aping the three unhappy siblings of Chekhov's *Three Sisters*: "To Moscow, I want to go back to Moscow!" (174).

The other jokes in *Slavs!* are, improbably, drawn from the horrors of Stalin's brutal reign, as when Katherina notes of the grisly repository of dead brains where she works that all of the famous Bolshevik brains are there "except for those which got flushed in the notorious dead-brain Purges of 1937" (130). Aside from the occasionally clownish political debate set against the genuine sufferings of the characters, Kushner's portrait of social catastrophe only uses humor that is pointed at the disintegrating and grotesque bureaucracy of the old Communist regime and at the romantic longings for a past that may or may not have existed, but can certainly not be recaptured.

Focusing on historical rubble and disarray, of the need to find shards of hope in chaotic and tragic situations, of eras of social and political flux, of the co-dependency of the simple and the profound, Kushner's tone in *Slavs!* is, for the most part, ardently serious. He points forward to the possibilities of change and the hope of the future and away from the wreckage and failures of what has gone before. Buried under the debris of the past, and on the verge of tumult, the lack of a guiding theory is depicted by Kushner as the most catastrophic problem of all for Russia. As Prelapsarianov explains, Russia is a snake that is shedding one skin before another is ready, vulnerable to disaster.

This is the heart of the matter for Kushner. As a socialist, he desires to preserve something hopeful from the collapse of the great socialist experiment in the Soviet Union, however corrupted it became. Without another social theory to balance the excesses of capitalism, Kushner insists that a serious look back at Marxism is essential:

> When a very great theory, and Marxism is a very great theory, suffers the outrages of history, as it has—as well as having caused a few outrages of history—then we're left reexamining what that was, why that happened, and what we're going to do now. There are some lessons that the collapse of the socialist experiment in the Soviet Union needs to teach us. (Harris, "The Road to Optimism," 28)

Raymond Williams, writing in *Marxism and Literature*, stresses that "creativity and social self-creation are both known and unknown events, and it is still from grasping the known that the unknown—the next step, the next work—is conceived" (Williams 212). Kushner's cultural analysis and social criticism, his intellectual longing for a theory as potentially valuable as the documents of socialism (or at least a salvage of the best of socialist theorizing) is tempered by his awareness that the struggle for new systems takes an enormous toll in human suffering. It is finally up to us as individuals and as a society to decide what the future will be. As Bonfila tells the despondent Poppy of the sweep and sadness of a hundred years of Russian history, "Life is almost never literally unbearable. We choose whether or not we bear up. We choose" (139).

CHAPTER FIVE

Transformations and Convergences
Kushner's Adaptations

> I feel in a certain sense that the theatre is the closest that I come to a religion.
> —Tony Kushner (Vorlicky 38)

Only a few of Kushner's predecessors among first-rank American dramatists have dabbled in adaptation: O'Neill transformed Aeschylus's *Oresteia* into *Mourning Becomes Electra*, Miller adapted Ibsen's *An Enemy of the People*, Williams refashioned Chekhov's *The Sea Gull* as *The Notebook of Trigorin*, and Albee made Nabokov's novel *Lolita* into a play. Among Kushner's peers, comparatively few, save David Mamet who has adapted Chekhov, work as adaptors—and none with the breadth or boldness of Kushner. His impressively diverse adaptations include plays ranging from the seventeenth century to the present, and include works by Corneille (*L'Illusion comique*), Goethe (*Stella. A Play for Lovers*), Kleist (*Die Heilige Cäcilie*), the Brothers Grimm ("The Two Journeymen"), Ansky (*The Dybbuk, or Between Two Worlds*), and Brecht (*The Good Person of Setzuan*), as well as a politically charged contemporary novel, *Widows*, co-adapted for the stage by Kushner and the novel's author, Chilean expatriate writer Ariel Dorfman.

Kushner's attraction to the plays of the theatrical past undoubtedly stems, in part, from an appropriation of the thematic sweep and emotional scope they offer, rather like Kushner's own plays. Expanding and shaping particular elements within them, and sometimes liberating them from relative obscurity, Kushner contemporizes these works by emphasizing their aspects pertinent to modern audiences and, in most cases, he succeeds in making them his own while honoring their individual qualities. Kushner explores the structure, language, and style of each of these works, inspiring himself to expand on his own brand of theatricality and lyricism. Drawing on the universally human ideas and emotions in the works he adapts, Kushner has experienced as much critical approval in the area of adaptation as he has with his original plays. Most critics applaud his ability to enhance

111

the original and, in some cases, to make it a stronger, more appealing play in both the thematic and theatrical aspects. This chapter examines Kushner's adaptations to date, more or less in the order in which the originals were written.

The Heart Chases Memory: *The Illusion*

> Love is the world's infinite mutability; lies, hatred, murder even, are all
> knit up in it; it is the inevitable blossoming of its opposites, a magnificent
> rose smelling faintly of blood. A dream which makes the world seem . . .
> An illusion.
> —Alcandre, *The Illusion* (82)

Kushner's most frequently and widely produced adaptation, *The Illusion*, is an attenuated fable of love, magic, and despair, adapted from Pierre Corneille's 1636 comedy *L'Illusion comique*. Kushner completed the adaptation in 1988 and it was first staged by the New York Theatre Workshop the same year, followed by a major debut at the Hartford Stage Company in late 1989. This ephemeral little play acknowledging the theater's singular ability to transform was published by both Broadway Play Publishing and the Theatre Communications Group, prior to a major New York production in 1994. There have been numerous productions on stages around the country. It is, in many respects, the most instructive of Kushner's adaptations in the parallels it offers with some of Kushner's characters and recurring themes in his own work. During the late 1980s and early 1990s, the popularity of *The Illusion* in regional and repertory theaters suggested a hunger for classics that might garner popular appeal. *The Illusion* attained a remarkable level of success for an otherwise obscure seventeenth-century comedy—a success significantly heightened following the triumph of *Angels* and the resulting increased interest on the part of an international audience for more works by Kushner.

Corneille (1606–84) wrote *L'Illusion comique* early in a career that began in 1629 with his play *Mélite*. By 1633, Corneille, who had already written a tragedy, a tragicomedy, and several comedies, was presented to Cardinal Richelieu, who provided Corneille with patronage and convinced him to become part of the "Society of the Five Authors." Corneille completed several plays to order for Richelieu, but he chafed under his patron's constrictions. His fortunes took a major turn the year after he completed *L'Illusion comique* with the composition of *Le Cid* (1637), an historically based tragicomedy. Despite the play's enormous popular success, the French Academy assailed its subject matter and especially Corneille's violation of the French neoclassical tenets of verisimilitude and propriety. Corneille, stung by what he regarded as unfair criticism, left the theater until 1640, after which he wrote a dozen varied plays before 1652, when his dramatic interests shifted to the exploration of religious themes. Ironically, by the time of his death, Corneille was a revered member of the French Academy.

Among Corneille's many plays, *L'Illusion comique* has generally been regarded as a lesser effort and is infrequently produced, especially outside France. It is not a typical Corneille play—his most representative works are large-scale tragedies based on heroic stories drawn from history. This rare foray into comedy—albeit tragicomedy—is elevated from the typical comedies of the seventeenth century by a potent comic device—the merging of the theatrical with the real—which is clearly the source of its appeal to Kushner.

In his adaptation, Kushner weaves a darker undercurrent expanding the pathos of a father's aching loneliness for his long-lost son into all aspects of the play, whether it be within the theatrical illusions of some play-within-the-play scenes or in a magician's ironic, cynical, and wondrous rhetoric on the meaning of love. The play presents, in some respects, a Shavian heartbreak house. The pain resulting from the loss of love, and the object of one's love (as symbolized by the father's unexpected tears for his son), can bring a fuller understanding of the meaning of love.

In a 1991 interview with Steven Winn, Kushner resisted making connections between *The Illusion* and *Angels*, but agreed that both involved issues of love and betrayal and both use "magic that you are not meant to take as either entirely imaginary or entirely real" (1). For Kushner the appeal of Corneille's play lay in its depiction of "misogyny and gender warfare," which "put the lie to our condescending notion that pre-modernist writers hadn't discovered that love can be an ugly addiction full of bitterness" (1). As he tells Winn, he was also drawn to the collision of the tempestuous son and his literal-minded father:

> the idea of this arch rationalist father going into a magician's cave to find this son he's brutalized. The way in which parental male violence reappears in the grown child's abuse of both women and men is very compelling to us. (1)

Some critics found Kushner's adaptation an exuberant interplay of theatricality and reality worthy of Pirandello, but tended to give the credit to Corneille when it is, in fact, Kushner who emphasizes those aspects of Corneille's clever stock plot that connect it to the more complex philosophical underpinnings of Pirandello's plays. Like Corneille and other premodern writers, the distinctly modernist Pirandello borrows stock characters from commedia dell'arte and other older theatrical forms and uses them as the basis for the peasant characters who populate his earliest plays. As his works grew in sophistication and depth, he continued to return to theatrical settings, as in *Six Characters In Search of An Author*, *To-night We Improvise*, and *Each In His Own Way*, because he believed his older sources succeeded where even the greatest of Europe's modern theater had not—"in their greater realism and their greater fidelity to life" (25) despite their overt theatricality. Within these older forms he discovered a "vast virgin world of the unexplored life of human personality" (29). This permitted him to transform the *maschere* of *commedia* into his own *maschere nude*, human characters minus the trappings of civilized behavior and social pretensions. As Pirandello borrowed from earlier theatrical traditions, Kushner does the same, borrowing the outlines of Corneille's plot and the play's central conceit and stock characters. However, the language, the psychological evolution of the major characters, and the voluptuous eruptions of lyricism are purely his own.

Kushner extends the sensual aspects of Corneille's play while enlivening its dialogue, which he liberates from a stiffness that many literal translations of the play suffer from. He mixes language structures freely, from free verse, rhymed couplets, and epigrams to varied types of formal and vernacular speeches, and, in doing so, elevates a dusty dramatic artifact into a lively tragicomedy that equals the brilliantly crafted Richard Wilbur translations of Molière that similarly enliven the original by emphasizing its strengths. Kushner goes further with Corneille than Wilbur does with Molière, freely changing scenes, expanding the one-dimensional characters, and adding and removing dialogue and even whole scenes. *The Illusion* features stock characters who evolved from ancient comedy through commedia dell'arte and into eighteenth-century comedy of manners. Passionate and poetic lovers, scheming servants, a braggart soldier, a doddering father, and a magician are all present here, but each are given fuller dimensions, contradictions, contrarieties, and an ironic humor that extends beyond the simple romantic-comic plots of the play's sources.

Corneille's play seems to be the French theater's answer to Shakespeare's love comedies, with similarities to *A Midsummer Night's Dream*, *As You Like It*, and, especially, *The Tempest*. In Kushner's hands, the play is revitalized particularly in the new emphases and dimensions Kushner brings to its explorations of themes of love and illusion. Love is seen in various lights, as both pure and perverted, and the play examines pretense (both meaningful and deluded), faithfulness and betrayal, and the joys and sufferings inherent in love of any kind. In Kushner's hands, the play's illusions collide with reality to the extent that its meanings become, for a time, intriguingly clouded, but, in the final analysis, much clearer and emotionally compelling. Despite its bittersweet ambiguities, its elusive and enigmatic view of human existence, its darker view of humanity, its emphasis on the power of money and in various aspects of relationships—father and son, master and servant, male and female, ruler and subject—Kushner's version of *The Illusion* is about the power of imagination and love, and uses the theatrical metaphor to unfold a very personal domestic drama of the possibility of family reconciliation in a play that, despite its darkness, is affirming and hopeful.

The adaptation begins with Pridamant, a wealthy and cantankerous old man searching for a magician in a dark cave somewhere between the real world and another, more shadowy, realm. He stumbles across the magician's speechless Amanuensis, who leads Pridamant to his master, Alcandre, a Prospero with a decidedly late-twentieth-century ironic attitude. Kushner eliminates Pridamant's friend from Corneille's original play and replaces him with the Amanuensis, who provides a link between the enigmatic world of the magician and reality. Controlled by his master, yet acting on his own at times, he is a dramatic incarnation of the human dilemma of free will trapped within the needs of survival.

When Alcandre appears, he explains that the Amanuensis is mute ("I did the surgery myself. I too have need of privacy. He is my servant: I keep his tongue in a jar" [5]). Pridamant recounts that some years before he had a bitter quarrel with his only child—"I destroyed my son" (5), he cries. Fearing the strong will and the individuality of the rambunctious young man, Pridamant angrily threw his son out of his house: "He seemed uncontrollable, wild, dangerous to me in all sorts of little ways. I loved him so much I wanted to strangle him. I wanted to snap his spine sometimes in a ferocious embrace. Everything about him seemed calculated to drive me to distraction, and did" (5). Now, the regretful old man feels his life fading away and misses his son, despite a stubborn unwillingness to admit his feelings. Unable to find the boy—"I am led to a blank, tall, doorless wall through which he seems to have slipped" (5)—Pridamant wants Alcandre to conjure up visions of his son's life:

> For the first time this year in the early spring I faced death in the form of a sharp, surprising tear at my heart. A warning. Nothing of my life for the past fifteen years is real to me. I can't stop thinking about him. I can't face death until I see him again. I want to tell him I love him. I want to ask him why he never wrote. I want to tell him that the ghost of him has ruined my life, has sucked everything dry, everything, present happiness and memory as well. I want to make him sick with guilt. I want to make him the heir to my fortune. (6)

Alcandre reveals a tableau of beautifully dressed figures who, in a series of interludes, curiously depict the young man at various points under different names: Calisto, Clindor, and Theogenes. Most of these sequences focus on romantic misadventures, with the changes in name and other disjunctures confusing the impatient Pridamant. He wants to speak directly to his son, but Alcandre warns against violating "the boundary between their world and ours," insisting that the old man resign himself to being "a fitful sleeper in the throes of a nightmare, powerless to affect his life, a possibility you relinquished years ago ... " (7). Puzzled by his son being called by different names, Pridamant's confusion mounts, but Alcandre suggests that there are "small discrepancies between vision and memory. Concentrate on the general outline, leave the details to me" (10). Each of the various scenes seem to demonstrate differing aspects of the young man's personality—some innocent and noble, others self-centered, crafty, and even bitter.

Alcandre's visions depict various manifestations of love in both comic and tragic strains—and it is within this aspect of *The Illusion* that it connects with Kushner's own plays, especially *Angels* and *Slavs!* The various meanings of love—romantic and familial—are explored through the contradictions within the variations of the son's shifting personalities (as well as those of other characters in his world) and within the seeming contradictions of Pridamant's conflicted feelings for his son. He longs for his son, disapproves of his actions, fears him, and wants to change him to better suit Pridamant's own powerful will.

While it may become clear to the viewer that Alcandre is showing Pridamant scenes from plays in which the son, now an actor, is performing, the old man completely believes what he is seeing, despite the obvious confusions that occasionally cause him to erupt in anger. When Pridamant insists that Alcandre make things clearer, the magician insists, in a Kushner addition to Corneille's text, "My visions are concocted through a violent synthesis, a forced conflation of light and shadow, matter and gossamer, blood and air. The magic's born of this uneasy marriage; it costs, you see, it hurts, it's dragged unwillingly from the darkest pools ... " (50). Pridamant's anger inflates when he sees foolish behavior on the part of his son in Alcandre's visions and, at times, he fears for his son's safety. Despite this, Alcandre invites Pridamant to give in to "the strange, pulsing warmth; the flow of blood, the flood of time, immediate, urgent, like bathing water in a warm ocean, rocked by currents of disappointment, joy. ... The heart chases memory through the cavern of dreams" (50).

The relations between the son and the women in his life range through three different segments in three different moods, from an innocent romance to manipulations and deceptions in the name of love. Within these plays-within-the-play, the three separate scenes provide vastly differing tones. In the first, the son appears as Calisto, who pines for his beloved Melibea, recounting a fanciful story of how a hawk brought him to her. The unimaginative Pridamant interrupts, annoyed by the poetic tale: "At home he always told stories like that. When I could catch him I'd whip him for telling lies" (8). Calisto's "every thought is of Melibea. My eyes, my eyes are all for her—Like my father's—deep, dark, there's nothing but love in them," to which the increasingly agitated Pridamant shouts, "That's the look! See? In his eyes! The look that said danger to me" (17). It was, however, merely a look of love that frightened Pridamant, unable to see it, even as Calisto shows it to his Melibea. Calisto and Melibea are brought together by her maid, Elicia, but they must contend with Calisto's rival, Pleribo, who is supported by Melibea's father in his suit for her hand. Just as the father is about to enter, Alcandre ends the scene and assures Pridamant, who wants to see more, that more is to come after a passage of some time.

In the second episode, a similar configuration of characters appears with different names. The son is now Clindor, who is in love with Isabelle, daughter of a wealthy father, although Clindor is also involved with Isabelle's maid, Lyse, a trickster of the commedia dell'arte tradition. Clindor is also the servant of the daft warrior, Matamore, another commedia dell'arte figure—a comic megalomaniac who believes he can win the love of Isabelle. Clindor, who loves both women, is a bit more drawn to Isabelle because of the material comforts a marriage with her might provide. As he says to Lyse, "I'm tired of being poor. You have nothing. I have less than that. Two zeros equal zero. It's simple mathematics" (40). Angered by Clindor's rejection, Lyse secretly plots against him, setting him up to be caught with Isabelle by her two suitors.

Pridamant is disturbed by this turn of events and interrupts, shouting at Alcandre, "They're all in league against him! I don't want to watch anymore" (42). However, the scene continues and Clindor is drawn into a duel with Adraste, one of Isabelle's wealthy suitors. He kills Adraste, at which point Alcandre blacks out the scene. Pridamant wants to know the outcome, but Alcandre matter-of-factly states that Clindor is "in prison, of course, where murderers go" (49).

As the scene continues, Lyse is planning to save Clindor while still exacting revenge on him. She beds the jailer to get a key to Clindor's cell and promises the distraught Isabelle that she will save Clindor if Isabelle gives her all of her wealth.

Figure 9: Philip Goodwin, as Matamore, and Bellina Logan, as Lyse, in the 1989 Hartford Stage Company production of Tony Kushner's *The Illusion*. Photo by T. Charles Erickson.

Isabelle readily agrees and Lyse rushes off to release Clindor from jail. Sitting in prison, contemplating his execution, Clindor wonders about his father. When he is dead, he wonders, will his father, "oblivious, half a world away, feel some correspondent shiver in your spine?" (63). Pridamant is deeply disturbed by this, but Lyse liberates Clindor from jail revealing to him that she is the one who is now wealthy.

In the third scene, Alcandre reveals that Pridamant's son, now called Theogenes, is cheating on his wife, Hippolyta, publicly flaunting his love for Rosine, wife of the Prince. Pridamant continues to be disturbed by what he sees, and resolves to keep his thoughts on the first scene in which his son appeared as a more admirable figure. In this final scene, Theogenes is attracted to Rosine's wealth more than anything else and pursues her, failing to anticipate the Prince's anger. When the Prince confronts Theogenes, he stabs Theogenes to death. Pridamant rushes toward the scene as a "great red curtain falls" and his eyes are suddenly clouded: "What's happening to my eyes? Am I bleeding? No, it's clear, not blood. Some kind of liquid. (*He eats the tear*) Mmmm. Salty, but quite delicious" (78). Alcandre plucks a tear from Pridamant's eye and holds it aloft in a wholly original speech by Kushner:

> This, this jewel. This precious leaded crystal pendant. This diamond dolorosa, so hard fought for, so hard won, this food, my sustenance, for this infinitesimal seepage, for this atom of remorse, for this little globe, this microcosm in which loss, love, sorrow, consequence dwell in miniature, for this iota, this splintered particle of grief, for this I turn the gumstuck machinery, erect the rickety carpentry of my illusions. Or this: to see your granite heart soften, just a bit. (79)

Pridamant retorts that his heart hasn't softened, it has broken, "Scar tissue forms. He's dead" (79). Alcandre, realizing that Pridamant has reached an appropriate level of emotional vulnerability, reveals, in Kushner's complete rewriting of the play's ending, that the images of the son's life are actually scenes from various plays. "I don't know that I like that," Pridamant grumbles. The theater, he insists, is "a make-believe world" consisting

> of angel hair and fancy talk, no more substantial than a soap bubble. You are moved at the sight of a foul murder—then the murderer and the murdered are holding hands, taking bows together. A black-magic reconciliation. It's sinister. (81)

Not so, retorts Alcandre, "What in this world is not evanescent? What in this world is real and not seeming?" (81). These theatrical depictions of love show, as Alcandre explains, that

> love, which seems the realest thing, is nothing really at all; a simple gray rock is a thousand times more tangible than love is; and the earth is such a rock, and love only a breeze that dreams over its surface, weightless and traceless. And yet love's more mineral, more dense, more veined with gold and corrupted with lead, more bitter and more weighty than the earth's profoundest matter. Love is a sea of desire stretched between shores—only the shores are real, but how much more compelling is the sea. (81–82)

The illusion of love is tied to the pasteboard and gossamer theatrical illusion, Alcandre explains, for "the art of illusion is the art of love, and the art of love is the blood-red heart of the world" (82). As Pridamant staggers off to find his son, Matamore returns to the stage, describing himself as "lost and mapless, a wanderer through the world ... " (83) seeking a road that "seems to be going uphill" (83). In dreaming of a better world, Kushner transforms this buffoon into a heartsick romantic, while the Amanuensis, finding his tongue back in his head, says that Matamore will not find a better world "in this life, but in the next" (83). He turns out the lights and the play ends with a typically Kushnerian invitation to the journey toward hope.

This ending—vastly different from that of Corneille's original play, which concludes with a comic scene of the son and his fellow actors splitting up the proceeds from that evening's performance—underscores the play's themes in more lyrical language. It also provides, as Mel Gussow noted in reviewing a 1989 Hartford Stage Company production directed by Mark Lamos, a "more cynical and realistic" (C21) tone. Kushner will have none of the traditional theatrical notion of love as a reward, culmination, or happy ending. Rather, he presents love as a process that is not easy—at various points the characters compare it to a sarcophagus or a catastrophe. Through his own particular emphases, Kushner reworks Corneille's three different love scenes into an exploration of facets of romantic love, ranging from innocence and passion to bitterness and disillusionment, and of familial love, through which he shows in Pridamant that self-delusion and the incapacity for change may cost one the love of a child.

The battle between illusion and reality in the theater, as well as in life, is also explored in *The Illusion*. It is a play in which Kushner makes an important point about the stage's ability to transmute the trivial into the significant. *Angels* is a play overladen with issues of such weight and significance that the bittersweet reflections on love in *The Illusion* seem, on the surface, comparatively insignificant. However, what Kushner refers to as the "tawdry" aspects of the theater are in full flower in *The Illusion*. It is a play that seems to dissolve before your eyes as you glimpse its moments of revelation and feeling. The importance of retaining the notion of the theater's unimportance is fully established in this intangible, imaginative, at times confusingly engaging adaptation.

Critics have generally applauded Kushner's vivid revitalization of Corneille's play. Audiences undoubtedly assume that much of the play's effectiveness—especially in its ruminations on love—springs from Corneille, but as David Richards astutely writes, the play's "cosmic touch springs from Mr. Kushner's fecund imagination, not Corneille's" (C16). *Variety* critic Mart. sniffed that "Kushner's Corneille isn't likely to become a repertory staple" (61), but that is exactly what it has become, with productions at a large number of repertory and regional theaters, not to mention dozens of university, college, and amateur stagings, as well as many international productions.

The *Boston Globe's* critic, Richard Dyer, reviewing a 1995 Trinity Repertory Company production, called it a "brilliant" adaptation with which Kushner spins "his own fantasia" on Corneille's original, producing "a cascade of Kushner's own vernacular theatrical poetry from which emerge his own themes and emphases"

Figure 10: Sara Morsey as Alcandre in Gainesville, Florida's Hippodrome State Theatre 1995 production of Tony Kushner's *The Illusion.* Photo by Randi Batista, Media Image Photography.

("*The Illusion* Connects With the Real Illusions of Life" 37). Reviewing a 1993 Oregon Shakespeare Festival production of *The Illusion*, Barry Johnson called it "a reasonable substitute" for *Angels*, saying it includes "many of the themes, the humor, the sharp contemporary references, the sexuality, the vivacious wordplay and that magic that made *Angels* such an Olympian hit" (K1). When the play was produced at New York's Classic Stage Company in January 1994, however, critic John Simon carped about the mixture of rhymed couplets with prose and of the elimination of the "surefire comic scene of the actors backstage splitting the box office take," but found that "Kushnerized Corneille is a much better deal than the genuine article" in an adaptation that is "both an updating and a throwback" ("Illusions and Delusions" 69). Michael Feingold praised Kushner's "taut and vivid" language, which goes "arrowlike to the heart of a thought, while the original can be fatiguingly ornate" (89), and Jeremy Gerard felt *The Illusion* demonstrated a "fresh, bumptious quality of an intellect brimming with theatrical ideas," and that the play itself was "that rarity, a lively rethinking of a minor classic whose motifs don't seem at all dated and whose dramatic sleight of hand is timeless" (67). Dan Hulbert, reviewing a 1995 Georgia Ensemble Theatre production found that the adaptation "crackles with up-to-the-minute ideas about the dangers/joys of love and the unknowableness of 'reality'" (10P), while Richard Nilsen, reviewing an Arizona Theatre Company production, called it "high art that is greatly amusing" (C1). When *The Illusion* was produced in England, critic Michael Billington described Kushner's adaptation as "recklessly free" (T12), while John Peter found it "elegant, refined and flamboyant, both a poem and a broadside" (25). A May 2000 production at Boston's Center for the Arts inspired reviewer Ryan McKittrick to applaud Kushner's "witty word play and bold poetic license" in a "script that balances comedy with tragedy" (C12).

The Illusion's revitalized multilayered fantasy respects the adaptation's source while avoiding the pitfalls of literary reverence (with much humor satirizing both theatrical and literary traditions) and the heaviness of the realistic tradition to draw the audience into a bittersweet, unsettling romance of the heartbreaks of love in all of its myriad moods. *The Illusion* was optioned by Universal Pictures for a movie version in the early 1990s, and Kushner worked on a screenplay, but it has not been filmed. *The Illusion* may make a fine film, but so much of its strength is in its theatricality. As Kushner states in the program for an Oregon Shakespeare Festival production, "What theatre does is to return the source of magic to the realm of the human" (*Illuminations* 31).

A Play for Lovers: *Stella*

> "We are yours!" "We are both yours," they cried in one voice, "We are yours forever!" And God on His heavenly throne smiled down on their love, and the Holy Vicar pronounced benediction over them from his throne on earth, and their all-embracing love had as its dwelling place but one house, one bed and one grave.
>
> —Cecilia, *Stella. A Play for Lovers* (V.iii.78)

Stella, like *The Illusion*, reflects on matters of love, though in a much less fantastic, seriocomic way. Kushner's attraction to German classical literature drew him to Goethe's little-known play *Stella. A Play for Lovers*, which he completed for a New York Theatre Workshop production in 1987 as his first major adaptation, working from a translation by Robert M. Browning. *Stella*, a delicate play with an intricate romantic plot, underwent significant revision by Kushner in 1997 and awaits a full-fledged production as he continues to hone his adaptation.

Johann Wolfgang von Goethe (1749–1832), the dominant figure of German literature since the eighteenth century, mastered not only the realms of literature and drama, but was also a statesman, scientist, and philosopher of distinction. His *Stella. A Play for Lovers* (1776) is a modest and somewhat uncharacteristic effort as compared to the Homeric standards of his masterworks: *Götz von Berlichingen mit der eisernen Hand* (1773), *Die Leiden des jungen Werthers* (1774), *Iphigenie auf Tauris* (1779), *Clavigo* (1779), *Egmont* (1787), *Wilhelm Meisters Lehrjahre* (1795), *Torquato Tasso* (1807), and especially *Faust, Part One* (1808) and *Part Two* (1832). These are among the most important works in premodern German literature. Goethe's influence has been profound in philosophy, literature, and art, although his plays, largely due to their length and scope, are not frequently produced.

Kushner's passionate interest in German literature and drama from its beginnings through the twentieth century certainly drew him to Goethe, whose ambitions as a writer, grasp of theatricality and language, and interest in history, religion, and human experience is in many respects not unlike Kushner's. The play's subtitle, "A Play for Lovers," points up its place in the dramatic tradition that includes *The Illusion*, as well as those Kushner plays that explore the many faces of love. In many ways, *Stella* seems to be a forerunner of the plays of Arthur Schnitzler, who, in the early twentieth century, similarly attempted to depict the pains and joys of love (and sex) in a mixture of lyrical and cynical, tragic and comic terms. Kushner does not significantly alter the structure, characters, and themes of Goethe's larger-than-life play. Rather, he sharpens and focuses the work, foregrounding contemporarily relevant aspects to revitalize the play and rescue it from the status of dramatic curio.

Kushner calls attention to his adaptive contributions within the first speech of this five-act play when a Postmistress announces that it is a work by Goethe, stressing that it incorporates "the popular legend of the Count of Gleichen, that comes in the last act, the same last act that had to be rewritten in 1806 to make it more suitable for audiences" (I.1). Goethe's own revision provides Kushner with his most significant opportunity to inject a late-twentieth-century perspective into the play—he combines both of Goethe's endings in two short scenes. Otherwise, Kushner's contributions involve the judicious trimming and shaping of the play's dialogue, his use of the Postmistress and the Steward as narrative forces (an effective notion that might be expanded still further to good effect), and in the tweaking of phrases, particularly those with some comic potential, toward a contemporary sensibility. For example, where Lucy comments on the coachman—in a straight translation from Goethe: "We had a happy, good look-

ing young postillion. I'd like to travel all over the world with him" (190)—
Kushner has her say that the coachman is "very attractive. He could take me anywhere" (I.2).

As the play begins in Kushner's most recent draft of the play, Lucy and her
grief-stricken mother, Madame Sommer, who is mourning her abandonment by
her husband (and Lucy's father), arrive at the inn run by the Postmistress. Lucy is a
spirited young woman who remembers "sitting on the little bed in the green room,
crying because you cried" (I.5) when Madame Sommer's husband vanished.

Overhearing their conversation, the Postmistress tells Madame Sommer that
her own husband has recently died and she introduces her daughter, Annie, who
works as a serving girl in the inn. Madame Sommer explains that Lucy is to
become the companion of the local baroness, who lives in a great house across the
road from the inn. Annie excitedly talks of the great kindness of Stella, the
baroness, and she runs off to inform Stella that Lucy and her mother have arrived.
The Postmistress relates that Stella has also been abandoned by her husband and
occupies her time training local girls in the social graces, marveling how "someone so unhappy can still manage to be so friendly and good" (I.8). The baron has
not been seen for three years, the Postmistress explains, a surprising fact since he
was passionately in love with Stella. There are rumors that he and Stella were
never formally married and that the baron was not a churchgoer—something
frowned upon by the locals. Stella's grief has been compounded by the death of
her daughter who is buried in the hermitage of her garden.

Annie returns to announce that Stella wants to meet Lucy at once, while
Madame Sommer retires to her room to rest. Another arriving coach brings
Fernando, a military officer, who, it is soon revealed, is the long-lost baron.
Missing Stella, and certain that her feelings for him have not changed, he longs
for her embrace so that "in your arms I will forget everything" (I.12). He quizzes
the Postmistress about Stella without revealing his identity and she reports that
since the baron's disappearance, Stella has "lived like a nun" (I.14). When Lucy
returns, she and Fernando meet and the Postmistress, bustling about in preparations for dinner—"If I stand still, it all comes to a standstill" (I.17)—leaves them
alone. Fernando casually flirts with Lucy, but, aware of the pains of love that have
affected her mother, she rebukes him for his "unbelievable arrogance. All men
think they're indispensable, but I don't know why, I manage beautifully without
them" (I.18). Fernando admires Lucy's spirit and feeling discouraged about his
own failings, seems to draw strength from her courage—"Yes, my child, it's true,
as you live, so you lose" (I.20)—as the first act ends.

The setting shifts to Stella's house for the second act, which finds her reflecting on loneliness and a "need to fill and fill, more and more till my heart is full"
(II.21) to make up for Fernando's absence and her lost child. Stella's distress
causes her to clutch her heart in pain, a device frequently employed by Goethe—
and underscored by Kushner—to signal the pangs of lost love or emotional distress, throughout the play.

Lucy and Madame Sommer inspire warm feelings in Stella, who shares with
them the story of her abandonment, explaining, "Yes, those days, those first days

of love—No, golden hours, you haven't left for heaven, you're still here, patient in impatient hearts, blossoming when love does" (II.22). Stella is comforted by the similarly bereft Madame Sommer's presence, as she explains in a speech Kushner changes only by making it more personal to Stella's feelings than Goethe's more sterile version. Kushner transforms this reflection on the ache of love's loss into a wrenching cry of pain from Stella:

> Oh God I thank you—another sorrowing creature, who will understand what I say. Who won't look on my sorrows with dry eyes. We can't help the way we are, you and I. What haven't I done, what haven't I tried, and to what end? Useless. I ache for one thing, just one, not for the world, for nothing in the world, just for him. Oh God, my lover is everywhere, and everything is only for my love. (II.23)

Stella goes on at length to describe the ways in which she sees Fernando in every corner of her life, for in the crucible of love, Stella claims, she was "transformed, became a creature composed entirely from head to foot of nothing but heart and desire" (II.25). She talks of trying many things to avoid feeling so alone, adding that the grave of her dead child is another insupportable burden in her sufferings: "I am seized by the thought, seized by it, that I am alone" (II.26). When Stella shows them her husband's portrait, Lucy recognizes the man she has spoken to at the inn. When she tells Stella that Fernando is nearby, Stella does not dare believe her, but sends the Steward to fetch him. Madame Sommer reveals to Lucy that the man in the portrait is her father. Concerned for her mother, Lucy rushes to the inn to make preparations for them to depart before any of this can be revealed, but Madame Sommer waits unseen in the shadows when Fernando enters. She is confirmed in her fears that it is her husband as the second act concludes.

Act 3 begins with Stella happily reunited with Fernando, who admits his ability to once again feel in her presence: "From the fullness of your heart a storm wind blows, bellowing into this parched, torn and tortured breast new life, new hope for love" (III.33). Fernando takes down her long hair and wraps it around his waist as they give in to their passion. When the Steward arrives to report that Madame Sommer and Lucy are departing, Stella sends him back to prevent them from going. Alone with the Steward, Fernando reveals that not only has he kept tabs on Stella, but has tracked his wife and daughter, learning that his wife's fortune was squandered by a merchant friend. The Steward, referring to Fernando's wanderlust—his "old longing for someplace else" (III.42)—reminds the guilt-ridden Fernando of his hard decision about whom to finally leave, "which one, the wife or the angel, were we going to leave and make miserable" (III.41).

When Madame Sommer returns, Fernando does not immediately recognize her despite being stirred, for she "conjures up my most unpardonable offense" (III.43). Pretending that she does not recognize Fernando, Madame Sommer recounts her feelings about being abandoned, "alone in a dream, a terror-filled wasteland," and that a "dead melancholy followed on the heels of shrieking pain" (III.46). Acknowledging her belief that her husband always loved her, Madame Sommer realizes that he "wanted more than my love," and that all she could be to him was a "virtuous little housewife" (III.47). Fernando, suddenly recognizing

Madame Sommer as his wife, Cecilia, is moved to a tearful collapse. He refuses to allow her to leave, claiming that "even in the arms of this angel here no rest, no joy, everything reminded me of you, of your daughter, my Lucy" (III.49). Lucy returns in the midst of this and Fernando is overcome, suddenly convinced that the three of them must escape together. As they go to prepare, he laments to no one in particular, "I abandoned them both, and now at the moment I find them both again, I abandon myself. Oh this is misery! There is a pain in my breast . . . " (III.51).

Act 4 finds Stella alone in the hermitage visiting the grave of her daughter; she has longed to join her child there in Fernando's absence. Now, however, she is "iridescent with joy" (IV.52), and when Fernando enters she lightheartedly recounts their first meeting. Unable to interrupt the torrent of her recollections, Fernando is moved as she talks of the depth of her feelings since "you'd sunk your roots in my soul" (IV.55). They are interrupted by Annie, who announces that Madame Sommer and Lucy are awaiting him in the coach. Shocked, Stella notices that "night's falling so quickly" (IV.59). When Fernando admits that Cecilia is his wife, Stella faints. He flees, but Cecilia and Lucy come to Stella's aid, and Stella vacillates between feelings of affection for Cecilia and her feelings of guilt, shouting, "I can't stand the sight of you! I've poisoned your lives, I stole everything you had! You were in horrible pain while I exulted in his bed!" (IV.61). Kushner's hand is especially evident in this scene, as dropping to her knees, Stella begs forgiveness; Cecilia responds with sympathy and affection, causing Stella to feel "in your lips, in your eyes, unspeakable Holy Grace. Hold me up, carry me, I'm sinking into the earth. She forgives me, she too despairs" (IV.62). Stella speaks of death, insisting that they all leave her alone as her "soul drowns in a boiling sea, disorder, confusion, horror, despair overwhelm me, I swallow great droughts of unspeakable pain" (IV.63). As act 4 concludes, Cecilia prays for God to "look down on your children, see how they suffer, confused, grieving" (IV.63).

The beginning of act 5, which Kushner labels as the "1806 ending," is set in Stella's apartment and it is in this act that Kushner makes his most significant alterations. He brings on the Postmistress to announce this as the play's "first ending" (V.i.64), adding that a variation will follow. Collapsing from a dose of poison she has taken, Stella proclaims, "Everything for love, that was my life's epigram, for love, everything, even death, it's now become my epitaph" (V.i.67).

Cecilia and Lucy pray for Stella's survival, but Fernando takes a pistol and leaves. Moments later a shot is heard and it is revealed that Fernando has killed himself. Stella sends Cecilia to "hear his last sigh" (V.i.70) and, as rose petals fall on the scene, Stella dies. Kushner then brings on the Postmistress and the Steward to announce that the "unacceptable original ending" (V.i.70) written in 1776, which Goethe had changed in his 1806 version to mollify the expectations of his audience, will now proceed. First, however, is the addition of a short scene showing Stella in her apartment holding Fernando's portrait up to the moonlight and lamenting, "Oh if only I could exist without thinking! If I could weep blood until my veins were dry, or release myself from life into a dull unending sleep" (V.ii.71). Pulling Fernando's portrait from the frame, she insists that although he is a seducer who has destroyed her happiness, she loves him too much to destroy the portrait. The next scene (the actual 1776 ending) begins with Fernando alone, grappling with a "demonic confusion" stemming from his feelings of love for Stella, Cecilia, and Lucy, "the most precious feminine creatures in the world," while wondering "what seraphim convene here to make me utterly abject with their blessings" (V.iii.73), a striking image vastly improved by Kushner's lyricism (in a standard translation, Goethe's version is, "What ecstasies unite to make me miserable!" [217]).

As Fernando prepares to end his life with two pistols, Cecilia enters to ask, "Planning a journey?" (V.iii.73). To his amazement, she announces her plan to leave him; she has gained strength from mourning his loss, stressing, "my love for you isn't the selfish kind of love, not the intoxicated adoration of a mistress who will let go of everything to possess the object of her longings" (V.iii.75). Fernando is outraged and insists that as his wife she will always belong to him. What of Stella, she asks? To which he can only respond that Stella will be free of blame if he and Cecilia are reunited. However, having experienced the pain of loss, Cecilia wonders why Stella "should suffer such a harsh penalty?" (V.iii.77).

To make her point, Cecilia recounts a tale of the Count of Gleichen, who went to the Holy Land to battle the Turks. Taken prisoner and enslaved, he is freed by the sympathetic Saracen daughter of his captor, who runs away with him. At the war's end, the Count returns to his wife with his Saracen mistress, presenting her to his wife as a prize, as her "savior" (V.iii.78), for freeing and caring for him. Fernando weeps at this story, which Cecilia completes by explaining that

> the true wife with streaming eyes embraced the Saracen maid, and cried, "Take everything, all that I have. Take half of him who's all yours, take him completely. He of right belongs to you, he of right belongs to me as well; let us not part let us remain together. And," she cried, falling into his arms, "We are yours!" "We are both yours," they cried in one voice, "We are yours forever!" (V.iii.78)

At this point, Cecilia calls Stella forth, paraphrasing the words of the Count's wife: "I give you half of him, who's wholly yours. You saved him, saved him from himself—and given him back to me again," and, as the three embrace, Cecilia cries, "We are yours!" and the Postmistress and Steward reappear to remind the audience of the play's title: "Stella. A play for lovers" (V.iii.79–80).

Despite Kushner's reverently faithful adaptation of *Stella*, the juxtaposition of the two possible endings adds a dimension that, with his continued revisions, will surely expose deeper levels in Goethe's attempt, with the original ending, to move beyond a mere exploration of the sufferings of love and to raise notions outside bourgeois understandings of its complexities. Kushner is certainly drawn to this aspect of the play; as a gay man, conceptions of loving that do not conform to familiar and traditional depictions are compelling. Kushner succeeds in this adaptation—and particularly through the double-ending—in bringing this relatively obscure work by a literary master closer to a contemporary audience. He demonstrates the thematic sophistication of Goethe's original ending of the play—and the pressures of audience expectations Kushner himself can certainly relate to.

Give Me Meaning: *St. Cecilia, or The Power of Music*

> They'll sing in just a little while.
> Their music's hard, a holy trial:
> They are Doomsday's Chanticleer!
> They Crow! And only sinner's fear,
> whom God gave ears but will not hear.
> —Young Nun, *St. Cecilia, or The Power of Music* (I.vi.48)

Kushner's attraction to German classical literature and drama is again evident in *St. Cecilia, or The Power of Music*, an adaptation based on a story by Heinrich von Kleist (1777–1811). Completed by Kushner in 1997 as an operatic libretto to be set to original music by Bobby McFerrin (who dropped out of the project in 1999), *St. Cecilia* was scheduled to open at the San Francisco Opera in November 1999, but by mid-2000 it had yet to be produced. A New York workshop staging of the first act was planned for the summer of 2000 as Kushner pressed on without McFerrin.

Kleist's unique qualities as a writer—and his marginal status among his contemporaries (including Goethe)—may explain, in part, what drew Kushner to his work. Kleist was a playwright, military officer, and journalist who never received the dramatic recognition he desired during his lifetime and continues to be regarded by critics and scholars as a lesser light of the German classical period. Goethe found a "sick" element in Kleist's work, apparently as a result of Goethe's awareness of the traumas of Kleist's life and the uncertain psychological probings of his work. Born into a military family and educated in a military academy, Kleist eventually left the army when he tired of its strict regimens and pursued an education at the university in Frankfort an der Oder. He withdrew in 1800, suffering from nervous strain. The next year he underwent a mental crisis as the result of studying the writings of either Immanuel Kant or Johann Gottlieb Fichte, which had led him to a realization of the impossibility of determining absolutes. Following a broken engagement with Wilhelmine von Zenge, who left him when he insisted she live as his common-law wife in the Swiss woods, Kleist became closely attached to his sister, Ulrike, and they traveled together extensively. Beginning in 1803, and continuing to his death, Kleist worked as a civil servant and journalist while writing a series of plays and novels in which his use of grotesque and surrealist elements seem to support Goethe's assessment of his work. So did his death in a suicide pact with a friend, Henriette Vogel, who was dying from incurable cancer. He shot her, then himself, on the Wannsee shore in Berlin.

Kleist's sensitive probing of the inner workings of the mind attempts to achieve a surprisingly modern understanding of the processes of thinking and creativity, and this aspect of Kleist's work is undoubtedly also part of what drew Kushner to him. Kleist's dramas, including *Die Familie Schroffenstein* (1803), *Der zerbrochene Krug* (1806), *Kätchen von Heilbronn oder die Feuerprobe* (1808), *Robert Guiskard* (1808), *Penthesilea* (1808), *Die Hermannsschlacht* (1809), and *Prinz Friedrich von Homburg* (1811), as well as his adaptation of Molière's *Amphitryon* (1807) and his singular essay "Über das Marionettentheater" (1810), are the major sources of his recognition as a writer, along with some works of narrative fiction. Kleist's story *Die Heilige Cäcilie oder Die Gewalt der Musik*, first published in 1810–11, was written to commemorate the baptism of Kleist's god-child, Cäcilie Müller, and it deals, as do other Kleist stories, with the "inscrutability and potency of religion and supernatural powers" (Brown 161).

The plot of Kleist's story, recounted by a narrator, involves the rising of an aged nun, Sister Antonia, from her deathbed to conduct a mass. Sister Antonia, it is subsequently explained, dies and is replaced by the patron saint of music, St. Cecilia. This is deemed a miracle by the Catholic Church and, in Kleist's final version of this deeply religious story, he presents a "whole range of different perspectives towards the mysterious music" (Brown 162) and the transformations that occur as a result of the miracle of St. Cecilia's appearance. Kushner has boldly adapted Kleist's story, historicizing the piece with reflections on the social questions of its era, on the rise of commerce and capital, and on issues of political activism, while also underscoring the transformative powers of music implied by Kleist and certainly appreciated by Kushner, the son of musician parents.

This theatrical intersection of art, commerce, and politics is set, more or less, in the period in which Kleist wrote his story—the early eighteenth century. However, Kushner highlights many connections to social and religious strains in the present day. Not surprisingly, Kushner's libretto is, in fact, more Brechtian than Kleistian in both its structure and style, and is imbued with the ambivalence and political probings of Kushner's own plays, as well as a lyricism in language and a bold mixture of humor and drama that is typically Kushnerian.

The first scene of *St. Cecilia* is set outside a prison where three incarcerated prostitutes set a menacing mood:

> On the wing the hungry owl;
> There is murder in the wind,
> And the wolf is on the prowl
> And odor in the air ... (I.i.1)

This ominous lyric, reminiscent of some of the nightmarish speeches in *Bright Room*, allows Kushner to establish an uneasy environment as local tensions between merchants, university intellectuals, workers, and the nuns of the convent of St. Cecilia come to a head.

A grieving Dutch Mother, accompanied by her Maid, arrives from Rotterdam in search of her four sons, all of whom left home for Germany some years before to seek their fortunes together. She has heard nothing from them since their departure, so, traveling with her Maid, "unescorted, out-of-carriage, out of doors, through the wars!" (I.i.3), the Dutch Mother has made her way to the German town of Aachen where, she believes, her sons may reside, either alive or dead. Attempting to get information from the prostitutes, all three of whom are Catholic, the Dutch Mother disapprovingly submits, "In Rotterdam, you see, we don't have any Catholics, and hence, consequently, there aren't any whores" (I.i.3). When a policeman appears, the Maid explains their search for the four sons, the eldest of whom was a divinity student at Wittenberg. The sons had hoped to claim an uncle's estate in Aachen, as well as "to fight Catholic perversity" (I.i.5). Making further inquiries of the Prefect of Police, the Dutch Mother is distressed to learn that he is not inclined to help them since they are not Catholic, for "God spared this city from the Iconoclastic craze" (I.i.9) that set Protestants against Catholic throughout the country. He tells her he will not help locate the young men who "tried to stir the people to frenzy" (I.i.9). One of the prostitutes offers to inform on the Dutch Mother to the police, but when the Dutch Mother learns that the prostitute is a mother herself who has taken to the streets to try to feed her children, she insists on paying for her release from prison with the advice that she keep her children "near you, safe from harm, as the shepherd guards the lamb" (I.i.10).

In the next scene, the Dutch Mother rages at a Protestant Minister about her frustrating search. To calm her, the minister persuades her to sing with him— "Music soothes" (I.ii.12)—but he himself becomes agitated while discussing the peace and conformity of Aachen:

> If God did not *want* battle
> why did He make us moral?
> He must have known we'd quarrel!
> And quarreling, faction's what we lust for,
> what we go from dust to dust for. (I.ii.13)

Saddened by the minister's thirst for bloodshed and conflict, the Dutch Mother pleads for information about her sons and the minister agrees to contact a well-connected minister friend in Rotterdam who may be able to help.

Scene 3 finds the Dutch Mother and the Maid lost on an Aachen street where they overhear the "eerie music" (I.iii.18) of a mass at the Municipal Madhouse. A Young Nun, denying knowledge of the sons, offers to lead the Dutch Mother and her Maid to the safety of their inn. Despite the unpleasant sounds emanating from the madhouse, the Dutch Mother finds it a "moving, such a broken lamentation" (I.iii.23), and wonders if the celebrants are insane, to which the Young Nun ominously replies that there is "a different explanation" (I.iii.23).

Kushner next dramatizes an exchange of letters between the Protestant Minister and his colleague in Rotterdam in a cinematic cross-cutting segment not unlike the overlapping scenes in *Angels*. The letters reveal that the Eldest Brother, "a hot one, challenged his betters" (I.iv.24), and, as the letters continue, the four sons magically appear as their youthful selves. The minister finds a letter written by the Youngest Brother enthusiastically proclaiming, "I want to travel all my life!" (I.iv.26), but he realizes that the letter is six years old and wonders what has become of the boy.

The following scene, set in Veit Gotthelf's Clothing Shop, finds commerce in full bloom, with customers feverishly bartering with clerks. The Dutch Mother reveals she has had a frightening nightmare about her sons, who she envisions dead "from plague, and battle wounds, and starved to death" (I.v.29), while the customers and clerks continue to sing about the growing age of industry and mercantilism:

Mighty, mighty Commerce!
We turn the works!
We grease the wheels! (I.v.31)

Veit himself appears to tie together the inextricably interwoven strands of commercial and religious doctrine:

When He sent down among us
His only son incarnated in
weak, temptable Flesh,
the Good Lord was showing us,
Creator of the Material Universe,
that He is Himself a Materialist,
whose Holy Will must first find expression . . . (I.v.31)

To Veit's suggestion that "when flesh wrestles with the mandates of the spirit" (I.v.32), the customers and clerks proclaim that "PROGRESS" (I.v.32) is the result, a doctrine that, Kushner implies, led to the corporate imperatives that dominate the end of the millennium. Reluctantly admitting that he knew the brothers and was once a believer in their cause ("Oh God, my sins return" [I.v.35]), Veit explains that the struggles of the past are over, that "we choose business over battle" (I.v.33), to which the customers and clerks chant, "PROFIT!" (I.v.33) as Kushner offers, through them, a portrait of the merging of business and Christianity:

The Ideal world is figured in the Real,
which any fool can see is not ideal.
The nightingale, the rose, the summer star,
good health and fortune: blessings secular.
God's happy peaceful presence here is shown.
The festering sore, the painful kidney stone,
the mangy dog, the mudslide and the blight,
the pox that comes from sating appetite,
in ugly children, acne, and in shit,
the Devil shows his noisome opposite.
If matter therefore holds both Good and Evil,
If matter houses equally both God and Devil,
then matter matters as a battle-site,
where Christian warriors carry on the Fight.
In former bloodier times, we'd schismatize:
but we've progressed and hence: Free Enterprise! (I.v.33)

Learning that the sons are alive and incarcerated at the madhouse, the Dutch Mother rushes to the Doctor of Lunacy, who explains to her that the brothers are, in his opinion, "incurably mad" (I.vi.41). They are seen sitting silently in monkish garb and the doctor explains they eat only bread and water and seldom speak, only conferring among themselves on "apocalyptic visions of a final flood or fire" (I.vi.43) and on the idea of resurrection. The brothers do not respond to their mother. The doctor adds that they occasionally sing an "uncanny *Gloria in Excelsis*" (I.vi.44) which the sane find excruciating to hear. When the doctor leaves, the Dutch Mother turns angrily on the Eldest Brother who, she believes, is to blame for their unhappy fate. When her anger subsides, she sits in a rocking chair and sings a lullaby, which brings forth a vision of the brothers as happy children joining hands with their mother to sing. Meanwhile, the Maid converses with the Young Nun, who acknowledges that she did not tell the Dutch Mother of the brothers fate—trapped in an "earthly purgatory" (I.vi.47)—out of pity. As the first act ends, the Young Nun promises she will tell all and persuades the Dutch Mother to come with her to hear the sons sing.

Act 2 begins with a recounting of the day the four brothers met their fate. Kushner indicates that the stage be divided into a triptych, simultaneously revealing the modest cell of Sister Antonia, the Chapel of St. Cecilia, and a court-yard outside the convent. The ailing Sister Antonia lies on her sickbed listening with some frustration to the musical preparations for a mass in the chapel. The Young Nun, Sister Antonia's niece, who, at this time, has left the order because she doubts her faith, is nearby trying to comfort the old woman. Sister Antonia attempts to persuade the Young Nun to return to the convent and her duties as a nun, while the brothers, at the head of a mob, appear in the courtyard with Veit Gotthelf debating their objections to Catholic doctrines and their plans for attacking the convent. The Youngest Brother tries to persuade the mob factions to embrace their differences:

> As God's vessel, each man must
> consult his soul on what is just. (II.ii.54)

The nuns on the other side of the courtyard wall fear the coming attack, feeling unfit for battle. As the mob grows, Veit assails the Vatican's "hoarding of wealth" and proclaims: "I want the money I'm making to work for me!" (II.ii.56). The mob develops into four distinct factions: one made up of intellectuals led by the eldest brother; another, led by Veit, represents the merchant class; yet another, led by the Third Eldest Brother, consists of laborers and the poor; and a fourth, led by the Youngest Brother, includes an indecisive and somewhat more moderate force. As the Youngest Brother proclaims:

> God of the Intellect, God of the Bank,
> sometimes I don't know which God I should thank!
> Oh I believe in a God of Compassion,
> Goodness and mercy, though sometimes He's cruel. (II.ii.60)

He cannot conceive that God is not in this holy place, but the poor, led by the Third Eldest Brother, insists on Christ's commitment to the oppressed:

> And Christ came to the poor!
> And Christ came to the meek!
> And Christ the carpenter came for
> the pauper, leper and the whore . . . (II.ii.62)

And as they grow in strength, they resolve:

> Someday wealth will see God frown!
> The stock exchange, the factory town!
> Then shall God's avenger search!
> Pull the Merchant from his perch!
> Till that day for this we pray,
> Father pull the churches down! (II.i.63)

Veit and the merchants are less revolutionary, fearing the impact of total destruction of the status quo on their pocketbooks. Meanwhile, the convent's Mother Superior visits Sister Antonia, who insists on leading the music for the mass. The Mother Superior tries to help the Young Nun keep Sister Antonia in bed, explaining that Sister Antonia labored for many years,

> making music fit to fall
> like blessings on all ears
> of worshipers and angels both;
> we've struggled long to please.
> But life in service to an Art
> wears away the head and heart. (II.i.59)

As the mob factions are about to attack each other over their differences—"I can't march with fools" (II.ii.68) each group insists—they are brought together by their mutual mistrust of the inhabitants of the convent—"a shaved-headed lute-picking gaggle of whores" (II.ii.70)—who are:

> Women artists! Cloistered tight!
> What more needed to indict
> a creed as upside-down as this?
> Our Father's arch-antithesis! (II.i.70)

The mob decides to attack when the vesper bell rings. Some of the nuns resolve to flee, but Mother Superior demands they perform the mass. Sister Antonia, learning of the coming attack and an assault upon a nun who attempts to reason with the mob, insists on conducting the mass. As the convent's Librarian persuades the other nuns that "God is in music" (II.ii.81), they stand their ground. The vesper bell tolls and the Eldest Son turns to the Dutch Mother, who is observing this recounting of the past, to say that at that precise moment his thoughts, "steeled for slaughter, ran homeward to you ..." (II.ii.86), to which his mother protests that they are "shameless butchers armed with guns!" (II.ii.87), but the Eldest Brother, who insists he hoped the nuns would run away before the attack, claims he would rather dance with one of the nuns, that their grudge is misplaced,

> when in fact it's the merchant class they should be watching
> this mercantile bug they've got, it's very catching,
> catching on everything, catching on rapidly—
> half of these nuns are peasant stock, probably,
> come to the cloister to escape the factory.

> That's not divinity. That's not theology.
> That's not a mystery. That's only . . . History. (II.ii.88)

As the vesper bell finishes tolling, the Eldest Brother steps back into his place at the head of the mob, while a peasant, who earlier had stoned the reasoning nun, steps forward to explain that as the music began "it left us all fearing" (II.ii.91):

> A wild terror seized every man's soul,
> Many dropped weapons, and some lost control
> of their bladders—beg pardon—we looked to your sons,
> but they seemed to me the most terrified ones,
> they shook and they knelt and the music played on
> and the last of my sense and reason was gone. (II.ii.93)

They fled in all directions when the music ended, and as a new morning dawned, the peasant explains, the convent glowed like gold and the sons lay frozen in the road "like sleepers," a "perfect caul of silence wrapt them" (II.ii.95). As the story concludes, the triptych of scenes vanishes and the sons and the Dutch Mother are back in the present at the madhouse where the brothers rise to sing their frightening song as the vesper bell tolls and the Dutch Mother flees in horror.

Act 3 begins outside the inn at Aachen as the Dutch Mother and her Maid are planning to leave. Talking to the Protestant Minister and the Doctor of Lunacy, the Dutch Mother asks that her sons be cared for—"I will not see them anymore" (III.i.99)—and sings of her unhappy, anxious memories waiting for word of them. Abruptly, an ostrich appears, chased by a young man who is followed by the prostitute the Dutch Mother bailed out of jail in the first act. The prostitute, recognizing the Dutch Mother, explains that she returned to the streets after leaving jail, but met the young man with the ostrich and has changed her ways.

The Protestant Minister sees the "costly, bellicose, distemprous" (III.i.105) ostrich as a metaphor for the hard times in which they live, and, along with the Doctor of Lunacy and the Prefect of Police, debates the "grotesque spectacle" (III.i.107) of human experience. The prostitute persuades the Dutch Mother that the nuns at the convent may be able to provide a reason for the fate of the sons, so the Dutch Mother delays her departure and goes to the convent.

Encountering the Young Nun, who has regained her faith and returned to her order, the Dutch Mother expresses anger that she did not tell her about her sons. While awaiting the Mother Superior to hear the full story, the Maid examines the musical score performed on that fateful night. The Young Nun explains that written music looks

> like the stars, like sheep droppings on a snowy field,
> or a scattering of ashes, or jet black sparks
> from a fire that eats light, refusing to yield
> its glow. (III.ii.114)

To which the Maid adds, "It's not really human, this scrawl" (III.ii.114), and she derides music in general, which she claims not to trust. As singing is heard in the chapel, the Maid persists:

We must abolish art.
What is it, but a lie?
It fools our eyes and fills our ears
with fantasies of higher spheres—
A baby's lullaby!
But life's not anything like art,
it goes awry and falls apart
and none sufficient to surmise
its truths, its meanings—otherwise
we'd not be busy telling lies! (III.ii.116)

Recounting the events of the night of the riot, Mother Superior explains that immediately following mass Sister Antonia returned to her cell and died. However, the Young Nun remembers it quite differently, claiming that her aunt never made it to the mass at all, that she died at the top of the stairs trying to get there. Puzzled, Mother Superior swears that she herself saw Sister Antonia lead the musicians, at which point they realize that St. Cecilia, in Sister Antonia's image, appeared to lead the music, thus providing salvation from the mob and explaining the impact of the music on the blasphemous sons. As the libretto ends, the Dutch Mother, powerfully impressed by the miracle of St. Cecilia, converts to Catholicism and becomes a nun. The Young Nun, reflecting on the suffering of parents, states that St. Cecilia's "music kills and cures the soul" (III.iii.122). The Maid addresses the audience to explain that the Dutch Mother joined the nuns to "build the Iron City of God" (III.iii.123) and to be near her sons who, as the curtain falls, once again sing their terrible, hypnotic "Gloria in Excelsis."

In *St. Cecilia*, Kushner as adaptor manages to respect Kleist's original story while surrounding it with a Beckettian hopeful despair in the depiction of the Dutch Mother and her sons. Additionally, he weaves in his own socialist political views through his dramatization of the frictions among the church, the merchant class, the intellectuals, and the laborers. This libretto provides a true challenge for a composer to meet its considerable demands.

Into the Desert: *Grim(m)*

I'm tired of hoping. I'm going to try something else.
Despair, for instance. Maybe despair. But.
I ain't ever going back.
—Amanda, *Grim(m)* (38)

In the early nineteenth century, the same period in which Kleist's *Heilige Cäcilie* was written, the celebrated Brothers Grimm, Jacob (1785–1863) and Wilhelm (1786–1859), wrote their fairy tales drawn from Germanic folklore while also making numerous other contributions to German culture and literature. One of Kushner's most intriguing adaptations is actually a screenplay, as yet unproduced, freely inspired by a Grimm fairy tale, "The Two Journeymen." Kushner's title is a word play combining the Grimm name with the word grim, a word that certainly serves as an apt description for this story as well as the wholly original contemporary plot Kushner builds around the fairy tale's central conceit.

Set in the mid-1990s in the Bronx—and against the background of Newt Gingrich's ascension to political power in the so-called "Republican Revolution" of 1994—*Grim(m)* focuses on Amanda, a bright young African-American grammar school teacher struggling to do her job amid the distressing poverty of her minority students, savage school budget cutbacks, and her own anguished dreams. Searching frantically about her apartment for a volume of fairy tales she is reading to her class, Amanda dodges the amorous advances of her husband, Richie, who teaches at an affluent, predominantly white high school, as she overhears a radio broadcast reporting on a demonstration against Gingrich's "Contract With America" at which the demonstrators claim that it is discrimination "against the poor, the sick and the elderly . . . " (4).

Trying to deal with a class so large that there are not enough seats for all of the children and battling with an unsupportive administration, she derisively refers to her husband's school as "Beverly Hills 90210" (4), but she continues to try to make school a positive experience for her students. As Amanda heads to school, this fundamentally realistic scene is transformed into a nightmare when she sees a dead man and his dead dog lying in the street while the radio reports that Gingrich's policies "will not affect the lives of ordinary Americans" (5).

It is plain, however, that the political changes have indeed had an impact. Amanda, and her immediate world, is under siege. At the school's library, the librarian—"a battered old man with yellow eyes who smiles at everything, chain-smoking unfiltered cigarettes" (6)—unearths the only remaining fairy tale book: *Tales for Home and Children* by the Brothers Grimm. Kushner uses the librarian and other supporting characters in the screenplay to illustrate elements of the grotesque fairy tale world of the Brothers Grimm in ordinary "real" life.

Amanda chooses to read a tale called "The Two Journeymen" to her class, joking that "I picked this story 'cause if you don't behave I'm *journeying* outa here" (7). Amanda, an obviously gifted teacher, creates a lesson drawn from the story's title, as she defines a "journeyman" as someone "trying to learn to do something special, like all of you" and that in Gingrich's America, making "do with less than you need" (7) is that special journey they must take. The tale begins with the notion that "God's children will run into one another, the good ones and the bad ones, the nice children and the wicked children, and when they do . . . ," Amanda reads, and one of the children finishes her sentence—"Watch out!" (8)

At night, Amanda has disturbing dreams of seeing herself in a desert. Kushner allows this scene to leak into the urban blight surrounding Amanda's actual life, as elements of the fairy tale creep in as well. Amanda encounters a frail old man in her dream, known only as The Man, who once had marketable skills, but now works as a migrant worker picking brussel sprouts. "Where the fuck did all the money go?" he wonders, and in the dream Amanda imagines she has quit her teaching job and ended her marriage, making ready to embark on a journey. She is waiting for a bus that The Man tells her will never come—city budget cutbacks, after all—and he adds that it is a "Grim fucking planet" (9).

The Man plans to walk across the vast desert—a four day journey—to his next picker job, but Amanda insists she will wait for the bus. Impatiently, The Man accuses her of not paying attention to what is happening in the world around her:

> you are living in the past, someone will take care of you *you think, you assume* and now you're probably going to die. And nowadays no one will come by to pick up your carcass, like before, some tax-paid carcass-picker-upper sent 'round to salvage the remains of morons who can't be bothered to stay *informed* . . . (11)

Stressing that "civilization vanished with the money" (12), The Man is going to walk across the desert dragging a red wagon filled with plastic containers of water. Suddenly, Amanda is back in her classroom and a child is asking, "*Then what happened?*" (12) and, with that, Kushner succeeds in interweaving Amanda's dream, the fairy tale, and the present social reality in an imaginative merging typical of much of his work.

Kushner shifts the action to a meeting between school principals, including Jonathan, Amanda's principal, and the vice chancellor of the city schools, Mrs. Ariosto, who announces that the school system is faced with a $300 million dollar deficit and that there will be 50,000 more children flowing into existing city classrooms. The principals are outraged, but Mrs. Ariosto replies, "The money's gone" (13). Jonathan insists that Mrs. Ariosto stand for an hour to see what she is asking them to require of their students.

At this point, Kushner presents the contrast between Richie's comparatively lavish classroom and Amanda's decaying school as Richie explains to his class the intricacies of the national budget deficit. He explains that tax cuts—and the resulting elimination of services—are the order of the day, to which a student asks if this policy will work. Richie can only reply, "That's . . . a good question" (14), adding that the same policy was tried a few years earlier under Reagan and that it was—and is—"very, very hard on the most vulnerable members of society" (15). Kushner includes a direction for a shot depicting Richie blinking to cause a sudden transformation of his comfortable classroom. It suddenly grows to twice the number of students, with more from poor backgrounds and peoples of color, and, when Richie blinks again, it returns to a clean, well-equipped facility with a predominantly white class.

At the end of the workday, Richie and Amanda argue about an opportunity for her to join the staff at his school, but she resists, considering such a move— and Richie's employment at his school—tantamount to selling out. He turns the tables on her by pointing out that the only reason they are not "broke" (17) is because of his significantly higher salary. Stung by the suggestion that she is being hypocritical, Amanda contends, "Just because I don't walk out on these kids doesn't mean I can't *complain*. Just because I may benefit from your decision doesn't mean I agree" (17).

Back in Amanda's class, she continues to read the Grimm fairy tale, paraphrasing choice bits to make useful points, and, while she reads, the scene shifts to a continuation of Amanda's journey with The Man across the desert. She now appears dehydrated and exhausted, while he remains in good shape thanks to his water supply. He sneers at her condition and when they stop to sleep and she accidentally rolls into him, he nastily demands, "Get the fuck off me, bitch!" (19). This image suddenly morphs into a continuation of Richie's argument with Amanda. She angrily chastises him for calling her a bitch and storms out of the room.

At a meeting of school system administrators, the deputy mayor makes the grim political and economic realities clear in response to Mrs. Ariosto's insistence that there are too many kids in each class: "Crowded classes or roofs on the schools. Schools or hospitals. Firemen or teachers. *Or*, not *both*. Do your job. Make room" (20), he intones. Amanda, still dreaming of the desert, is now completely out of water and turns to The Man for help, but he coldly replies, "Your need as they say endangers me" (21). Suddenly, back in her classroom again, Amanda wants to stop reading the story, but the students plead with her to continue. She does, and back in the desert, she begs The Man for water, but he continues to refuse: "Tomorrow you'll just need more! What's the fucking point? Die. God knows it can't be worse than *this*" (22). Finally, The Man agrees to give her some water if he can cut out one of her eyes (in the original Brothers Grimm tale, the tailor, The Man's counterpart, demands an eye for a bit of bread). Amanda is horrified by the suggestion, but ultimately relents out of desperation.

In a scene in which Kushner underscores the destruction of compassion in economically deprived circumstances, one of Amanda's colleagues, Karen, talks about a student who received a serious cut on her head in a fall from a jungle gym. Despite the seriousness of this painful injury, the child does not cry. It turns out that the student is "retarded, high lead levels in her blood, *and* malnourished" (25). Karen feels guilty for not being more aware of the child's needs, instead of just being happy that she was quiet in her overcrowded class—it "makes me feel like a bad teacher. When they told me how messed up she is, I hated her" (25), Karen cries. Amanda, telling Karen about the Grimm tale, conjures The Man as she repeats a key line, "You have two eyes. Give me another. The price remains the same" (26). The Man leads the now-blind Amanda to a spot under a tree where the corpses of a man and woman hang—"A lynching, or an execution. Civilization" (27), he grunts. Resting beneath the strange fruit of this horrific tree, Amanda compares the sound of the straining of the ropes of the nooses with the bodies swaying in the wind to a sound "faintly like a ship at sea" (28), in a seafaring reference not unlike those Kushner uses in *Hydriotaphia* and *Angels* to depict the frightening journey toward death. Amanda's wounds hurt, but The Man remains unsympathetic in a speech aping the harsh attitudes of Gingrich's brand of conservatism. The Man insists that her own poor judgment "had to be punished somehow, why shouldn't stupidity be punished? Or weakness? Why shouldn't we punish weakness. It disgusts us. It's insufferable to watch. It drags us down" (29).

Amanda halts reading this increasingly disturbing story to her students. The Brothers Grimm, she feels, made up such horrific stories for children when there were "wars, and kids ... didn't live a long time, and life was hard, and ugly, and ... " (30). Pleading desperately with the children to remain quietly in the classroom, she flees and calls Richie on the phone. He is sympathetic, but believes Amanda's problems go beyond "the low level of elementary school funding" (31). While still on the phone with Richie, Amanda sees a junkie, smiling beatifically, almost run down by a taxicab. Hustling to a subway, Amanda continues to read the fairy tale to herself, reaching the point at which the tailor leaves the blind cobbler under the gallows tree. Set against a scene showing Jonathan seated at the head of Amanda's overcrowded class clasping his head in his hands, her voice is heard continuing the tale:

> And as he slept the cobbler heard the two hanged men talking, and one said to the other: "God will provide. The dew which drips from the feet of hanged men in the morning can restore the eyesight to the blind, only who among the living believe this is possible? If people believed in im-possibilities, impossible things might come to pass. Unfortunately there is no such belief, not even among the desperate." (32–33)

Finding herself near the Gowanus Canal in Brooklyn, Amanda stumbles upon a beautiful small garden on an otherwise empty lot. An elderly woman, Annie, invites her into the garden, which, she explains, she organized her neighbors to create. As Annie explains:

> I had to beat up on councilmen, planning commission types, a state senator, I even phoned Washington, I said, I'm Annie, I'm your precinct captain and if you don't give me this empty lot I'm gonna make sure the whole precinct votes Republican! Democrats, you got to scare them and then they'll do what's right by you, they have no spine and no brain and short memories and tiny dicks and the bravest among them are just gutless wonders *at best* but you can scare 'em, and they want people to think they're nice. This Republican mayor, though, now he says we have to *buy* the garden, budget cuts are eliminating subsidies to rent empty lots, so we have to come up with (*screaming:*) SEVENTY-FIVE THOU-SAND DOLLARS DOWNPAYMENT or the bastard that owns this lot gets to take it back and sell it. Of course no one will buy it, who'd want it? And it'll be a trash dump again in a couple of months. Who in God's name has SEVENTY-FIVE THOUSAND DOLLARS? (35–36)

Discussing "The Two Journeymen," Annie posits that the behavior of the tailor is explained by the fact that "the Wicked don't like their victims, and they don't like witnesses," and Amanda interprets the meaning of the restoration of the blind man's eyesight as brought about through a "miraculous intervention and a happy partnership between suffering humanity and the animal kingdom—bees and storks and horses help him get revenge on the bastard who blinded him, he gets rich, marries the king's daughter ... Kid's stuff. The real story comes to rest under the gallows" (37). The little girl with the cut forehead appears and Amanda asks her, "Where did all the money go?" (38) and the little girl points to a covered bucket. Amanda uncovers it to find gold coins that transform into bumblebees. Suddenly, she is back in her apartment with Richie, nursing a bee sting. Suggesting that she has tired of hoping, Amanda decides that despair may be her only option. As the screenplay ends, in one final transformation, the Grimm fairy tale book is seen on the bench in Annie's garden with Amanda's voice heard reading: "The hills and valleys are far apart and never do they meet, but the children of God oftentimes do, and sometimes the Good meet with the bad . . ." (39). As this speech ends, a bee walks across the word "GRIMM," shown in old German Gothic letters, but the typography abruptly changes to reveal the word "GRIM" in modern print.

Grim(m) has yet to be filmed, but unquestionably suggests powerful possibilities for imagery in support of its themes. In *Grim(m)*, Kushner crafts a contemporary fairy tale from the central idea of the Brothers Grimm story. Amanda is like many of Kushner's major women characters—Agnes in *Bright Room*, Dame Dorothy in *Hydriotaphia*, Harper in *Angels*, Bonfila and Katherina in *Slavs!*—who find themselves living through social and personal stresses beyond their capacities. These stresses bring them to a culminating point of crisis, one typically derived from a collision of dreams, hallucinations, and visions with the very hard, very real circumstances of their lives. They survive and if hope is not possible, as it no longer seems to be for Amanda, at least the possibilities of developing a survival strategy and imagining a future, however imperfect, remain.

Between Two Worlds: *A Dybbuk*

> Every living creature has a heart, and every heart a thread.
> And He of Holy Wisdom draws all the threads together.
> From the fiery threads is woven time, and thus new days are
>   made;
> Unto the heart is given, unto the spring is given.
> As the spring pours waters through the days, the heart of the
>   world looks on.
> And so the world continues, until the world is gone.
>
> —Fradde, *A Dybbuk* (41)

The problems Amanda faces in *Grim(m)* are based in a very contemporary reality—a political and social transition that destroys the hope of the disenfranchised. Kushner's *A Dybbuk*, an adaptation of the early-twentieth-century Yiddish theater classic, places the central characters—a pair of star-crossed lovers—in a seemingly insurmountable conflict with the forces of magic, the spiritual realm, and God. Well beyond the Kushnerian yearnings for a utopian world, *A Dybbuk* provides a dark and, at times, terrifying portrait of two worlds: the heartbreaking, brutal world of the living and the frightening and unknowable realm of a place beyond.

Among Slavic and Eastern European dramas of the twentieth century, S. Ansky's *The Dybbuk* (1912–14) is singular. Perhaps the only pre–World War II Jewish play to transcend its cultural niche as folk art, *The Dybbuk* is the most important modern play to emerge from the Judaic culture to stand beside the classics of European drama. As a Jew, Kushner was certainly drawn to its exploration of religious history, myth, and mysticism, but perhaps more to its challenging dramatic issues and the play's elements of the fantastic. Kushner completed the adaptation in 1995 and it was first staged at the Hartford Repertory Theatre in February of that year, prior to a November 1997 production at the New York Public Theatre.

Ansky's *The Dybbuk* is, in practical and aesthetic terms, a problematic play requiring a large cast and the sort of imaginative stylization and theatricality prevalent in the period in which it was written, but that became increasingly rare as the twentieth century progressed toward a more realistic and minimalist theater. This unique drama of obscure Eastern European shtetl life afforded Kushner an opportunity to grapple with his own questions of religious faith and to make use of his abilities as a playwright in the areas of language and theatricality. He is, as well, able to incorporate issues of the dawning of a technologically based, capitalistic world in conflict with the Old World Judaic traditions and the simple, pious ways of a small rural community trying to survive in the face of breathtaking material and social changes. As with *The Illusion* and *St. Cecilia*, Kushner freely adapts *The Dybbuk*—in his published afterword to the adaptation, literary critic Harold Bloom writes that he is "charmed by the freedom" (110) of Kushner's liberties with the play—and his ability to create an adaptation that honors its source, but is, in essence, a new play. Bloom underscores this in his suggestion that with *A Dybbuk*, his title for his adaptation, Kushner "(politics aside) shrewdly is writing his own New Kabbalah" (110).

The Dybbuk's author, S. Ansky, a pseudonym for Shloyme Zanul Rappoport (1863–1920), was born to a well-to-do Jewish family in Vitebsk, White Russia (now Belarus), on November 8, 1863. Ansky received an Hasidic education, although his family was essentially nonreligious. Hasidism, which was founded in the late eighteenth century in southern Poland by Israel Baal Shem Tov, gets its name from the Hebrew word *hasidut*, meaning piety, saintliness, and an extraordinary devotion to Jewish life. The Hasid must have God constantly in his mind even when going about the minutiae of daily life—this is an important quality in *The Dybbuk*. The Hasidic movement grew rapidly throughout Eastern Europe and beyond, but by the end of the nineteenth century some Jews of Ansky's generation found its isolationism stifling. In his youth, Ansky became rather more enamored of the Haskalah (Enlightenment) movement, which was inclined toward greater interaction with Western culture and burgeoning modernity. Becoming a part of the intelligentsia, Ansky learned to speak and write in Russian, worked at various menial jobs and, occasionally, as a tutor. His blue-collar experiences influenced his increasingly socialist beliefs, leading him to St. Petersburg where he became a writer for the Narodniki group's socialist periodical. When St. Petersburg's authorities cracked down on socialists, Ansky emigrated to Paris where he lived in exile during the 1890s.

Ansky returned to Russia to participate in the Populist and Socialist Revolutionary movements, writing the anthem of the Jewish Labor Bund. In 1911, he founded and led the Jewish Ethnographic Expedition, with the goal of recovering stories, myths, music, jokes, and folklore of the Jewish oral tradition. Curiously, despite his personal rejection of Hasidism, Ansky created evocative depictions of that world in most of his writings, undoubtedly as a result of his involvement with the expedition as it traveled throughout Russia and Eastern Europe. His works particularly emphasize the turbulent transitions and challenges facing orthodox Jews in the first two decades of the twentieth century, an interest that parallels Kushner's attraction to periods of social transition.

Ansky had previously experimented with drama and written two one-act plays in 1906, *Foter und Zon (Father and Son)*, set in a small Jewish village during Passover in 1905, and *Der Zeideh (The Grandfather)*, but he was not otherwise disposed toward playwriting. The catalyst came during the Jewish Ethnographic Expedition when he uncovered a rare document that provided the inspiration for *The Dybbuk:* an eyewitness account of a 1755 (pre-Hasidic) exorcism in the small Ukrainian town of Khmelnik. Moving the story to the late nineteenth or early twentieth century, Ansky stressed the collision of the real and the spiritual worlds within a plot involving two lovers living in a shtetl. The important element providing the play with much of its power is the introduction of a dybbuk, which, in Jewish lore, is a soul, "troubled and dark, without a home or resting place, and these attempt to enter the body of another person, and even these are trying to ascend" (54).

Ansky invented two overlapping plots, both of which are retained by Kushner. One focuses on Chonen, a young rabbinical student from Brinnitz who dies for the love of Leah, his destined bride. Many years before their births, the fathers of Chonen and Leah made a pact that their as-yet-unconceived children would one day marry. Chonen's father has been dead for many years, so Leah's social-climbing father, Reb Sender, breaks the old agreement and arranges a more lucrative match for Leah with a ludicrously shy, vapid young man. "She is the light and I am the flame" (37), cries the heartbroken Chonen when he learns of Sender's betrayal. Despondent, he starves himself to death—a spiritually unclean death made worse by his prior search for forbidden knowledge in the Kabbalah and by his blaspheming in calling on God's fallen angels to assist him in his spiritual possession of Leah. Her father, nurse, and other local citizens are horrified and uncomprehending, but Leah understands Chonen and wonders about the fate of those "cheated of long lives" (51) in a powerful addition to Ansky's original play by Kushner:

What becomes of everything they were supposed to do, the tears unshed, the happy days never spent in happiness? The children they never had together, all of that, does all that unspent life have no place to go? Once upon a time there was a boy with a great mind and a soul as tall as the towers of Jerusalem, oh he was beautiful and he would have been beautiful for ninety years more, but he died while he was still a boy, in an instant he was dead. They put him in the ground, in earth that wasn't ready to receive him, with prayers on his lips he never had time to pray, and words for people he didn't have the breath to speak. Fradde, blow a candle out and if it's still tall and straight you simply light it again, you don't throw it out; if a life is extinguished before its vessel has grown frail and broken, it can't be forever, its flame can be rekindled. (51–52)

Figure 11: Julie Dretzin as Leah in the 1995 Hartford Stage Company production of Tony Kushner's *A Dybbuk,* adapted from S. Ansky's Yiddish theater classic. Photo by T. Charles Erickson.

The other plot of *The Dybbuk* deals with the formidable Rabbi Azriel of Miropol. He is called upon by Sender to rescue Leah from the dybbuk. Ansky's Azriel is a tired, deeply religious, somewhat rigid old man tied firmly to his faith and the old ways of his people. Kushner takes this somewhat one-dimensional figure and imagines that Azriel experiences a crisis of faith, struggling with difficulty to understand God's harsh ways, seeming indifference to human suffering, and abandonment of his creations.

Demonic possession, although the stock-in-trade of modern day horror films, is uniquely applied in the play as Chonen's spirit stubbornly refuses to leave the body of Leah, requiring Azriel to literally wrest the dybbuk from her body. Leah dies as she is freed from the dybbuk, but in death she joins Chonen in the other world. In a faraway voice she is heard proclaiming that Chonen "is light and I am flame and we join into holy fire and rise, and rise, and rise ... " (105). Scholars and critics have described *The Dybbuk* as an Eastern European *Romeo and Juliet*, but it is, in fact, a strikingly original dramatic folk fable achieving classically tragic proportions. The parallel with *Romeo and Juliet* is apt in *The Dybbuk's* sensuality and passion, aspects heightened by Kushner, although its two lovers barely come into physical contact, as well as in the inevitability of the play's ultimate transformative tragedy. Also like *Romeo and Juliet*, *The Dybbuk* provides a romantic depiction of the power of love to transcend circumstance and reality, but there are actually two more complex and central themes that Ansky explores: the possibility of redemption and the ultimate justice of the universe—a belief that human matters will eventually right themselves, either in this world or in another.

Ansky wrote *The Dybbuk* between 1912 and 1914. Written in Yiddish, the play was translated into Russian (until 1904, Ansky wrote exclusively in Russian, but switched to Yiddish as his interest in preserving Jewish cultural traditions and folklore in both fictional and nonfictional writings grew). A draft in Russian came to Constantin Stanislavsky's attention in 1914. Impressed with the play, Stanislavsky made some suggestions for changes to Ansky, the most substantial of which was the addition of the Messenger, one of the play's key characters in illuminating its philosophical and religious context (and a character Kushner uses to expound on the struggles of Azriel with his God). However, Stanislavsky became ill shortly thereafter, and his planned production at the Moscow Art Theater, which would have undoubtedly been a triumph for Ansky, was postponed indefinitely.

To make matters worse, Ansky had to flee Russia's Bolsheviks with the rise of Lenin in January 1918. Disguised as a priest, he made his way to Warsaw in severely ill health exacerbated not only by the political changes in Russia, but also by the knowledge that the Bolsheviks had captured many of the Judaic artifacts Ansky had carefully gathered and preserved for his Jewish Ethnographic Museum, the outcome of the Jewish Ethnographic Expedition. Ansky had to leave behind much of his written work—not only early drafts of *The Dybbuk*, but also his four-volume history, *The Destruction of the Jews of Poland, Galicia, and Bukovina* (Ansky also left one unfinished play at the time of his death, *Tog und Nacht* [*Day and Night*], which was later completed by Alter Katzine and staged in Warsaw in 1921, following the success of *The Dybbuk*). Ansky died on November 8, 1920, from diabetes and heart disease without living to see *The Dybbuk* staged and unaware that it would become one of the signal works of modern Jewish literature.

Following thirty days of mourning after Ansky's death, Warsaw's Vilna Troupe staged *The Dybbuk* under its original title, *Between Two Worlds: A Dramatic Legend*, on December 9, 1920. The production was acclaimed and inspired poet Chiam Bialik to translate it into Hebrew, which, in turn, led to a legendary production at the Moscow Art Theater's Habimah Studio. The Habimah, subsequently Israel's National Theater, was founded in 1918 as a strictly Hebrew-speaking theater, a biblical-historical theater, a moral voice for its community, and a high-art theater with the ultimate goal of becoming the national stage of the sought-after Jewish homeland. *The Dybbuk*, along with David Pinsky's drama *The Eternal Jew*, provided the Habimah with the first worthy plays in support of its goals.

The Habimah's production of *The Dybbuk*, which seems to have inspired Kushner as much as the play itself, opened on January 31, 1922, under the direction of Eugene Vakhtangov. It seemed to audiences and critics so authentic a picture of shtetl life that many assumed (incorrectly) that Vakhtangov was himself a Jew. Marc Chagall had been asked to design scenery, but declined fearing that the Moscow Art Theater's connection to the Habimah would mean a strictly realistic production. He need not have worried, for Vakhtangov conceived, by all accounts, a vividly stylized scheme. Designed by expressionist painter Nathan Altman, the production, not surprisingly, featured distinctly expressionistic qualities which, in Kushner's adaptation, are invigorated with his trademark phantasmagoria.

The politically minded Vakhtangov found ways to connect the play's events to the meaning of the Russian revolution. Nick Worrall explains that "the beggars represented the opposition to the bourgeoisie, whilst Chonen and Leah represented a break with established law—the one in his quest for forbidden knowledge, the other in her rejection of the husband who had been chosen for her on the basis of wealth" (122). The Russian theatrical community was profoundly impressed, but Vakhtangov, who had been seriously ill during preparations for *The Dybbuk*, died after barely managing to complete one more similarly impressive production, an inventive staging of Carlo Gozzi's commedia dell'arte–inspired tragi-farce, *Turandot*. Following Vakhtangov's passing, *The Dybbuk* toured around the world, attracting international audiences to the Habimah. *The Dybbuk* is perhaps best-known from its memorable 1938 Polish, Yiddish-language film, a work suffused with haunting and evocative imagery as it plausibly, and occasionally stereotypically, recreates Ansky's depiction of shtetl life (tragically, many of the actors and crew of the film died during the Holocaust within a few years of making *The Dybbuk*). Although the movie maintains many elements from the original play, it is, like Kushner's adaptation, uniquely its own creation. Kushner seems to draw, as Richard Goldstein writes, on "the movie's aura of sexual ambiguity while maintaining the play's sense of elevation and distance. The spirit that enters of the body of this bride is not just the anguished soul of a young mystic, but the unfathomable immanence of the future" (59).

Kushner's adaptation, published by the Theatre Communications Group in 1998, is *The Dybbuk's* most recent incarnation. The parallels between the lives of author and adaptor are important to understanding why Kushner was drawn to this problematic and fascinating play—and essential to appreciating the reasons his treatment is both so effective and more Kushner than Ansky. While working on the adaptation, Kushner found the original play "immensely effective," noting that "most people remember it as this astounding love story, and it's probably the only love story in all of Western literature in which the lovers have, I think, three lines together on the stage. It's really clumsily constructed, because Ansky was an ethnographer and not really a dramatist" (Gold 5). Kushner's adaptation not only attempts to address the structural problems of the play, but to bring its most powerful elements to the foreground, as he did with *The Illusion* and, in fact, most of his adaptations. Kushner approached the task with some caution, calling himself, "Hebrew-and Yiddish-illiterate, I barely know how to pray. Riddled with ambivalence . . . I now approach Judaism as Jews once approached the splendid strangeness of Goyishe Velt" (Goldstein 59).

Kushner's prior plays demonstrate surprising affinities with Ansky's themes. Ambivalent about his own Jewish heritage, Kushner recognizes in Ansky a kindred spirit. Both writers are driven, to a great extent, by deep religious doubts, but both express the power of and the deep-seated need for the spiritual. Their skepticism fuels their political socialism and activism. For Kushner, the play— and his adaptation of it—are

> definitely a product of that struggle. So the play drew me, because it's not this little fairy tale. It's actually more complicated than that. I think very much about a very insular, premodern shtetl world, but one that's already being impacted upon by modernity and the arrival of the nineteenth century, and everything that would come after that. So, I was very drawn to it for that reason. (Vorlicky 224)

Ansky's internal struggle with his religious skepticism and political activism are, for Kushner, central to the play's strengths. Kushner, like Ansky, struggles with the balance of politics and his conflicted need for faith. Kushner senses that Ansky "went toward Judaism by his political convictions," and that his "sense of himself as a political revolutionary was very much at odds with this sort of emotional tie that he had with Judaism" (Vorlicky 224). In fact, Ansky himself described the sole motif of *The Dybbuk* as a "spiritual struggle" (Ansky 24). Kushner, who describes himself as a "queer American agnostic Jew" believes that his generation "is forging new versions of Judaism. The assimilationist experiment has run its course" and that a reevaluation of traditional Judaism emerges from complicated questions arising from "religious barriers erected because of sexual preference and gender" (Solomon, "Seeking Answers in Yiddish Classics," 7, 22). Ansky's play is, to some extent, an homage to shtetl life which, he could easily see, was vanishing rapidly as the technologies and diversities of the modern era engulfed the Old World. This disappearance was tragically accelerated as purges and, as Kushner underscores, the Holocaust, obliterated those aspects of the traditional Jewish life struggling to survive. Kushner and Ansky share an insider-outsider attitude about Judaism—admiring its mystical beauty, its moral imperatives and questions, and its otherworldliness, while also finding themselves at a distance from its rigidities and more primitive aspects.

History is, for both writers, a significant foundation for the play. One element that Ansky added from his ethnographic studies—and that Kushner maintains in his adaptation—is the legend of the murder of a bride and groom by the Cossacks as they stood under the wedding canopy in Brinnitz many years before the time of the play. The couple's grave marker in the town square has created a tradition that "after any wedding, the guests dance around the grave, to cheer up the grieving, martyred dead" (46). This tradition is also a haunted reminder that foreshadows the ultimate tragic reunion in death of Chonen and Leah.

Kushner's reverence for great dramatic works of the past, many of which examine questions of religious faith and social reality, the complexities of politics, and the meeting of past and present, has shaped his entire oeuvre, and explorations of aspects of Judaism appear in parts of *Bright Room, Angels*, and *Slavs!* as well as several of his one-acts. One of Kushner's more interesting experiments in this regard is a one-act play, *It's an Undoing World or Why Should It Be Easy When It Can Be Hard? Notes on My Grandma for Actors, Dancers and a Band*, in which he seems to be rehearsing for *A Dybbuk*. At the very least, it explores some of *A Dybbuk's* themes on a smaller and more personal scale.

Kushner's *A Dybbuk, or Between Two Worlds* was produced at New York's Public Theatre for three months beginning in November 1997, featuring a slightly revised version of a critically acclaimed premiere of the adaptation at the Hartford Stage Company in February 1995 under the direction of Mark Lamos. Working from a literal translation by Joachim Neugroschel, Kushner substantially restructures Ansky's text, making use of the cinematic, episodic style demonstrated in *Bright Room, Angels*, and *Slavs! A Dybbuk* maintains much of the emphasis on the central characters of Ansky's play, especially Leah, Chonen, and, once he arrives on the scene midway through the play, Rabbi Azriel. Kushner's adaptation places significantly greater emphasis on theological skepticism than Ansky does, with Kushner's addition of speeches permitting Azriel to express his doubts more pointedly, as when at the end of act 3, alone with his Scribe, Azriel cries out to his deceased grandfather:

> You have been dead sixty-seven years; in that time I only grow weaker, and the world grows wickeder. But you in Paradise have grown stronger, and I ask you to accompany me now. In Lublin, in Zlotchov, pogroms. The people talk idly of traveling and scientific marvels and don't pray. I'm older than my years, I don't sleep at night. Under my robe, my knees knock together in fear sometimes. (*Softly*) And sometimes, Grandfather, I do not entirely trust God. (*To the Scribe*) Don't write that down. (86)

Kushner also foreshadows the horrors of the coming Holocaust, most obviously in the onstage arrival of Azriel in a railroad box car, a visual reminder of the transportation of Jews and other "undesirables" to concentration camps before and during World War II. Kushner makes this connection frequently in a variety of ways, adding, for example, the telling line: "In a world of electric light, even Jews can ride the trains" (66).

Holocaust imagery can also be found in act 4 during the exorcism of the dybbuk from Leah's body when Azriel's Scribe, recording the events in a record book, is stunned that an unseen hand has filled a blank page with the following:

> Rabbi, only turn the page:
> the wonders of the coming age
> will dwarf your shtetl magic so—
> dybbuks, golems, all you know,
> your writings and the words you say,
> like oven ashes, swept away.
> At some not-very-distant date
> the martyred dead accumulate;
> books of history will contain
> mountain-piles of the slain. (101)

As is evidenced here, Kushner's trademark lyricism can be found throughout *A Dybbuk*, as when he describes the Torah scrolls as "dark men engulfed in shadows, draped in velvet shawls, bent over mysteries" (21).

The play's lovers, Chonen and Leah, are, in Kushner's treatment, far darker and more passionate than in Ansky, despite the fact that they hardly appear together onstage. Chonen is a distracted, intellectually profound young man, described as a boy who has "got a magical mind," but who disappeared from the village for an entire year following his ordination to wander "in exile," and on his return was "not the same boy who left" (15–16). Chonen's interest in the Kabbalah isolates him from his fellow villagers, who find it "dangerous to nose about in such things" (16). Much of his distraction is the attraction of Leah, described as "beautiful" (17) and who is from a rich family, so it is expected that her greedy father will seek for her a better marriage than with the shunned and destitute Chonen. It is with Sender's greed that the plot of *A Dybbuk* is set in motion.

Sender, Kushner explains, brings tragedy to his family because "Jews do badly when they try to pretend to not be Jews" (Vorlicky 218). Breaking his old bond with his deceased friend to attempt to better himself financially by seeking acceptance in the non-Jewish community is catastrophic. Kushner stresses that Ansky's play is

> about interiority and about the Jew's relationship to him- or herself, and Jews' relationship to one another within the confines of the shtetl, that anti-Semitism and Cossacks exist, but never onstage, and they're sort of bad memories, and always [a] threatening possibility. But they're not the big problem. The big problem is a Jewish problem. It's a problem about somebody making an oath and breaking it. And a rabbinical cord. The outside world is threatening, but only as a kind of scent that drifts through the play. (Vorlicky 225–26)

While the play's time period and ethnic specificity matter to Kushner, especially in the social, historical, and sexual connotations he draws from dybbuk folklore, his late-twentieth-century sensibility is also critically important. As he struggles to create an uneasy truce between fundamental religious faith and the secular world, Kushner strives to make the invisible visible on the stage as his focus touches on the historical ravages of the past and the future, on the order of the universe, on the need for atonement and the possibility of spiritual redemption, on honoring the dead, on celebrating the living, and on rebirth in a hauntingly atmospheric setting.

Kushner's orthodox Jewish world is predominantly and authoritatively male in its structure with the doctrines of Judaism—which are particularly patriarchal—controlling the society. This social order, however, is challenged by a breaking down of expected norms and, in fact, a decidedly feminist point of view. This can be seen in the comedy he elicits from the first act's layabout Talmudic scholars who debate women's exclusion from the synagogue floor and by having Leah's comically awkward unwanted groom, Menashe, declare "when we thank God in the morning he didn't make us women, no one's more grateful than I am . . . " (59). Sender's avaricious use of his daughter to better himself financially allows Kushner to comment on the treatment of "women as chattel" (Solomon 121–22) in the world of the play. Other traditional views of this world are challenged, in part, by a mixture of spiritual longing and earthly passion of a highly erotic nature. Critic Ben Brantley, writing of the 1995 Hartford Stage Company production, found that, improbably, the sexiest scene in *A Dybbuk* came with "Leah, lingeringly, kissing the Torah as Chonen watches from a distance" (C13). The adaptation is filled with similar bursts of aching emotion, as when Chonen speaks of his longing for Leah ("I've seen . . . A diamond, perfect, a perfect thing, absolute, hard and . . . I want to hold her, and cry, until my tears melt the diamond and then . . . I'll drink her in, and then . . . " [32]) or when the dead Chonen, exorcised from Leah's body, movingly states that "I left your body to return to your soul" (105).

Kushner stretches the play's stylistic boundaries, maintaining its qualities as a supernatural folktale of crossed worlds, hearts, and historical ages, while also incorporating a critical view of its religious ritual and, most importantly, with its complex depiction of the sensuality of unformed and unutterable longings that lie beyond human governance. The claims of the dead on the living, the merging of the worlds of both (demonic possession is, in Kushner's adaptation, a passion carried beyond life into the realm of death), and the relationship of Jews to each other and to God shatter narrow definitions of gender and history, as in *Angels*.

Fear of the future, moral uncertainty, and a sense of inexplicable loss drive Kushner's tormented and confused characters in all of his plays, and *A Dybbuk* is certainly no exception. An environment of unease is always present for Kushner as he raises questions that cannot be answered either easily or simply. In *Angels*, Ethel Rosenberg, whose image haunts Roy Cohn because he was instrumental in manipulating her execution for treason years earlier, reluctantly joins Louis to chant the Kaddish over Cohn's corpse. Similarly, in *A Dybbuk*, the dybbuk himself demands the Kaddish be chanted for him as he is being successfully exorcised by Azriel. Chonen's suffering and his possession of Leah—and her subsequent death to join Chonen in the next world—are viewed by Azriel as having happened "simply so that we may turn their sufferings into a text—for others to study in the ages to come" (71). Suffering is inevitable and sin can and must be forgiven, Kushner persuasively insists, and faith in a brighter future is essential, despite the harrowing specters of fear and doubt. In the final scene of *A Dybbuk*, Azriel sends the Messenger off with a pointed message for God:

> Though His love become only abrasion, derision, excoriation, tell Him, I cling. We cling. He made us, He can never shake us off. We will always find Him out. Promise Him that. We will always find Him, no matter how few there are, tell Him we will find Him. To deliver our complaint. (106)

Kushner's identity as a gay dramatist brings him into conflict with Judaism, about which he has "a deep ambivalence, because there is a fantastically powerful homophobic tradition within Judaism" (Cohen 226). Alisa Solomon identifies *A Dybbuk*'s "intensely homosocial world" that "vibrates with erotic implication" (121–22), and it is clear that this undercurrent supplies the play with considerable sensuality. For example, Kushner has rabbinical students indulge in an orgiastic dance in the synagogue and Chonen delivers a passionate recitation of the "Song of Songs" for his beloved Leah, but while he does so he is being held by his male friend, Henech.

The sexual is carried through even more potently when, as the dybbuk, Chonen penetrates Leah's body in ways that are simultaneously both spiritual and sexual. When *A Dybbuk* was produced in New York, critics seemed most disturbed by the treatment of sexuality in the play. Particularly at issue were Chonen's androgyny, which suggests "the whole unease about Jewish masculinity" and Leah, who, for Kushner provides the "real queer revolution" of his adaptation in that "she's a good girl, and she's not about to stop her father from arranging a marriage. So how can she resist? By taking on the persona of a man, and then you see the spectacle of a really strong woman—Leah the man-woman—who turns the natural order upside down" (Goldstein 59).

Kushner also points out the connection of Judaism and homosexuality, for both groups have a shared history of "oppression and persecution" that offers

> a sort of false possibility of a kind of an assimilation that demanded as one of its prerequisites that you abandon your identity as a Jew. The possibility of passing which is not, let's say, available to people whose oppression stems from racial difference or gender difference. For me, as I think is true of most Jewish homosexuals, the business of claiming an identity, the business of coming out of the closet, the business of learning one of the central lessons of the Holocaust, which is that, as Hannah Arendt says, it's better to be a pariah than a parvenu. If you're hated by a social order, don't try and make friends with it. Identify yourself as other, and identify your determining characteristics as those characteristics which make you other and unliked and despised. So, it was central to me. (Cohen 218)

As a Jew, Kushner is part of an ethnic heritage that has experienced harrowing losses, and has survived. As a gay man in the latter part of the twentieth century, he is confronted by the terrifying toll of lost lives resulting from the AIDS pandemic. In *A Dybbuk*, Chonen cannot survive the loss of Leah in this world, but he wins her in the next. Hope, knowledge, and transcendence can emerge from loss, as Kushner consistently stresses in his work. Wrongs can be righted, the universe can be put in order, but often the price is unimaginable. When *A Dybbuk* was produced in New York, Kushner explained:

> I would really like to have people see *A Dybbuk* as a gay play, not because I've done things to make it gay, but because there are all sorts of ways this is a play about gender transgression and the refusal of love to obey moral strictures. But I also want homosexuals to come watch Rabbi Azriel [the exorcist] wrestling with God, because I feel that's part of the gay project. (Goldstein 59).

The significance of the play's subtitle, *Between Two Worlds*, is, in part, that the play works on dual levels: "Death resides in life, male in female, the spiritual in the carnal, religious doubt in devotion, evil in goodness, social well-being in private acts, Hasidism in modernity, the holy in the profane. And, in each instance, vice versa" (Solomon 121–22). Kushner uses this duality to explore his fascination with Judaic traditions—both religious and secular—and to reflect on the impact of the spiritual and the natural worlds on the individual. Above all, he is fascinated with Ansky's play's suggestion of the possibility of communing with the dead and ongoing relationships past the grave (as seen in virtually all of Kushner's plays), and of the ultimate righting of wrongs. He adds and eliminates dialogue and abandons antiquated theatrical and literary devices, but his adaptation is not at all cavalier—it is the result of a deep and highly personal exploration of the drama's themes with an eye toward revealing its immediate significances, its aesthetic power, and its emotional force.

Critical reaction to *A Dybbuk* has generally been positive. Of the original Hartford production in 1995, Ben Brantley found that

> those who haven't read *A Dybbuk* recently may not realize just how much Mr. Kushner has altered it, since most of his interpolations enhance the play's inherent imagery and themes already implicit: sexual division, racial self-awareness, and (since this is Tony Kushner, after all) a glimmer of apocalyptic apprehension. (C9)

Markland Taylor viewed the Hartford production as "a work-in-progress rather than a finished product" (84), but David Patrick Stearns found the production "entrancing" (4D). Richard Dyer praised Kushner's "incomparable ear and his vaulting language: *A Dybbuk* doesn't sound like a translation anymore; instead it is poetry, fully realized" ("Kushner Gives *Dybbuk* New Life" 65).

Charles Isherwood, writing of the New York production, felt that Ansky's play was "perfectly suited" to Kushner's "tastes and talents," but he, like a few other critics, felt that the adaptation and/or the production lacked the passion of the original play, that it "impresses on an intellectual level without engaging the emotions" (72). John Simon, one of the few critics to dislike *Angels*, found the New York production of *A Dybbuk* "both new and challenging, and ultimately surprisingly apt. Stock characters now seem quirkier, the principals enlist our full sympathy or horror, and the plot grows and grows in significance" ("Animal Attraction" 110). Alexis Greene called Kushner's adaptation "vital," noting that it "is both more lyrical and more suffused with the kind of folk humor that Ansky prized" (14).

Kushner's interest in East European Judaic traditions continues. Having completed *A Dybbuk*, he is now grappling with another great remnant of Jewish folklore he regards as a counterpoint project, *The Golem*. In preparation, he is studying Yiddish, "a moral imperative" he believes, stressing that it took a thousand years to make the language and "it'd be a shame to let it die" (Senior 83). *The Golem* deals with the old myth that a monstrous giant—the golem—was created as a protector of the Jews, and it is a distinctly urban play, as opposed to *A Dybbuk's* rural qualities. Kushner intends to stress the historical oppression of the Jews in his approach to *The Golem*, and says that his version will ask how to "confront anti-Semitism? How do you confront the genocidal intent of the world without yourself becoming a murderer, and without usurping certain things which are proscribed by God" (Vorlicky 225–26). And, like *A Dybbuk* and much of Kushner's other work, *The Golem* deals centrally with issues of faith versus skepticism, and the search for understanding. Both Ansky's (*The*) and Kushner's (*A*) *Dybbuk* begin and end with the same mystical lyric describing the search for understanding:

> Why did the soul,
> Oh tell me this,
> Tumble from Heaven
> To the Great Abyss?
> The most profound descents contain
> Ascensions to the heights again ... (9, 106–7)

For the World Must Be Happy: *The Good Person of Setzuan*

> Should people be better? Should the world improve?
> Should we have better Gods, or perhaps, none at all?
> Our hands are all empty, our backs to the wall!
> Our only hope now, to redeem this defeat,
> Comes if you, as you sit in your theatre seat,
> Are willing to make it your jobs to defend
> The good of the world, help them make a good end.
> Honored audience, do it, be brave and be just,
> For the world must be happy: It must, must, must.
> —Player, *The Good Person of Setzuan* (185)

The battle for the survival of the soul—and profound questions of religious faith—are at the heart of *A Dybbuk*, but Kushner returns to more earthly concerns in his as-yet-unpublished adaptation of Brecht's 1940 play, *The Good Person of Setzuan*. Socialist critic Raymond Williams writes of Brecht's attentiveness to themes of "the individual against society" (290), and this is seldom more evident than in *The Good Person of Setzuan*, one of the masterpieces of modern political drama. It was inevitable that Kushner would adapt one or more of the plays of Brecht, a dramatist he describes as "one of the great exemplars of what social commitment in the theatre is about" (Mann 22), and his faithful adaptation is instructive in revealing Kushner's understanding of those elements of Brecht's aesthetics and political commitment guiding his own work.

The Good Person of Setzuan is, in essence, an unsettling fairy tale about the attempts of a good woman to retain her morality in a poverty-striken, corrupted society. Brecht's frequent use of parable in deconstructing history is important to understanding his work. This approach allows him, through the bare-bones, linear simplicity of a fable, to emphasize themes and to layer the play with increasingly more complex meanings as it moves forward. A structure of short episodes, with variations and more complex aspects of the central theme revealed in each, is typical of Brecht's approach—and is employed by Kushner, both in this adaptation and in his own plays. As Raymond Williams writes, Brecht's use of fable and history serve the purpose of "distancing, or making strange, comparable to the more evident distancing conventions and techniques" (282) of Brecht's approach. Stressing that this approach to unravelling the central issues of the play allows it to be debated as an "open, critical-objective drama" (284), Williams explains that Brecht's plays, which are typically set in historical periods and not his own time, remain unquestionably contemporary in thematic content.

Brecht uses various historical epochs as distancing devices, with the result that the era in which the play is set helps reveal questions and concerns about the present moment by allowing the audience to comprehend parallels with present day concerns. Brecht explains his approach in "A Short Organum for the Theater," a seminal text for Kushner, who seems to have adopted Brecht's insistence that "the theater's representations must take second place to what is represented, men's life in society" (205). Brecht adds that the "theater has to become geared into reality if it is to be in a position to turn out effective representations of reality, and to be allowed to do so" (186). For Brecht, this is achieved through the construction of his text and through the actor who, in his view, needs to develop a "critical attitude" toward his character, an alienation effect that "allows us to recognize its subject, but at the same time makes it seem unfamiliar" (190–92). The goal is to free the actor and the play from "that stamp of familiarity which protects them against our grasp today" (192) and this is achieved both through the historicizing of the play and the use of alienation—The A-effect—which, Brecht explains,

> allows the theater to make use in its representations of the new social scientific method known as dialectical materialism. In order to unearth society's laws of motion this method treats social situations as processes, and traces out all their inconsistencies. It regards nothing as existing except in so far as it changes, in other words is in disharmony with itself. This also goes for those human feelings, opinions and attitudes through which at any time the form of men's lives together finds its expression. (193)

The changeable nature of situations, individuals, and societies is deeply political and, at the same time, fundamentally dramatic, a fact recognized by Kushner, who shares Brecht's insistence on the idea that the "coherence of the character is in fact shown by the way in which its individual qualities contradict one another" (196). This is taken to its extreme in *Good Person*, in which Brecht allows the central character, the good-hearted Chinese prostitute Shen Te, to adopt a second persona, Shui Ta, who is, in essence, her alter ego. This is a means for Shen Te to balance her generous and compassionate spirit with the protection of an avaricious rigidity as a defense against the overwhelming demands made on her goodness. It is for Brecht—and for Kushner—the exclusive province of the stage to create such contradictions and, as Brecht points out, "the choice of viewpoint is also a major element of the actor's art, and it has to be decided out-side the theater. Like the transformation of nature, that of society is a liberating act; and it is the joys of liberation which the theater of a scientific age has got to convey" (196).

Kushner's adaptation of *Good Person* had its New York premiere in a produc-tion by the Off-Broadway Wings Theatre Company in their little theater on Christopher Street in May and June 1999. This adaptation, which was first pro-duced in a more elaborate production at San Diego's La Jolla Playhouse in the summer of 1994, is largely, even reverently, faithful to Brecht's original. For Kushner, *Good Person* is a parable, or "agrarian folk poetry" (Mann 22), and its simple structure recounting a tale of three gods coming to earth in search of one good and moral person allows Brecht—and Kushner—to explore those aspects of society, mostly economic, which have an impact on morality.

Kushner worried about a "Forrest Gumpism" creeping into the adaptation, feeling that it must not be "essentialism, she must not be 'essentially' good" (Vorlicky 119). He struggled to understand why Brecht felt that Shen Te was a better person than other characters in the play, a dilemma stemming from a speech in which Shen Te attempts to apologize to the Gods in the trial scene as she defends her creation of Shui Ta:

> Your first decree
> To be good and to live
> Split me, like lightning, in two. I
> Don't know how it happened: to be good to others
> And to myself was not possible for me,
> To help others, and myself, was too hard.
> Ah, your world is hard. Too much need, too much despair!
> The hand you extend to the poor
> Is torn from your arm! Help the lost,
> and you're lost yourself. Who
> Can long avoid evil, when people eat, and there's no food? (180)

Kushner notes of this speech that it is "in some way the most obvious, corny thing in the world, and it is also immensely powerful" (Vorlicky 122). Its simple directness, combined with its nearly psychological rendering of Shen Te's pain, combine with its implied call to arms, is the essence of political theater.

In completing his adaptation, Kushner insists that "I've taken almost no liber-ties with the Brecht at all, so I'm nervous about people thinking of it as an adap-tation—it's not me; it's Brecht. I thought the most important function was to be true to Brecht and also playable by American actors" (Mann 22). As previously indicated, the influence of Brecht on Kushner is profound. During Kushner's student days at New York University, his earliest play, *The Heavenly Theatre*, a drama about "this extraordinary historical phenomenon of a revolution that takes place during a carnival," was an attempt to understand "Brechtian dramaturgy" (Vorlicky 111) and to begin to develop his own approach to it. Kushner's first "real, deliberate" attempt to write a play fully in the Brechtian mode was *Bright Room*, but it was written, in essence, as a response to—or argument with— Brecht's *Fear and Misery of the Third Reich*, a play that, like *Bright Room*, examines the impact of the rise of the Nazis on ordinary lives in Germany. Kushner has "very little respect for" *Fear and Misery of the Third Reich* and believes that despite "a lot of interesting moments" its scenes are "fairly mediocre" (Vorlicky 111). Kushner also acknowledges being less moved by *Good Person* than by *Mother Courage and Her Children*, a Brecht play he believes truly views "history as the accumulation of catastrophes and calamity," and which he considers"the greatest play written in the twentieth century" (Vorlicky 119). One critic has described *Mother Courage and Her Children* as a play that "pricks the conscience and challenges the system we think of as civilized society" (Britton, n.p.). Throughout Brecht's work, Kushner deeply admires him for

> an absolutely serious desire to see the world change *now*, as they say in *Setzuan*: "Now, Now, Now." The urgency of that "Now" is something that I go back to Brecht for. So I remind and then I chastise myself if I feel that I am slipping because it is very hard to maintain the commitment. He is incredibly important to me as an origin and also as a goal. In terms of specifics, after having written a different kind of epic with *Angels*, where I went off in new directions for me in terms of creating an epic play, I am interested in going back and in reexamining in the next play [*Henry Box Brown, or The Mirror of Slavery*] that I am writing the epic form in a more traditional way, a more classically Brechtian sense. (Vorlicky 123)

For Kushner, the challenges of Brecht's understanding of Marxist principles inspired his interst in *Good Person*, the notion that Brecht "uses Marx's analysis of the commodity form and marries it to the western theatrical tradition. At the same time, Brecht understands that his is the theatre of capitalism as well" (Mann 22). Kushner's theater is one that is inextricably tied up with the problems of capitalism, too, since it is constructed and performed within a capitalist society. Brecht's play, however, like Kushner's own works, uses Marxist concepts to unearth the aspects of a capitalist culture that oppress individuals and groups within that society—that, counter to its ideals, do not provide all with the opportunity of flourishing, or even surviving, within it. Kushner discovers that Brecht's play, and his conception of it, can be shaped in its universal way to reflect "another reality: where people who are white have money and people who aren't white are frequently struggling economically. I think that the way that race and poverty are frequently conjoined work very well for this play" (Mann 22).

In Kushner's view, the central theme of *Good Person* "is that something is terribly wrong in the world. Goodness is punished severely and wickedness is the only way to survive. What is that? The great villain is an economic system which creates terrible deprivation and want" (Mann 23). The terrible world in which Shen Te lives—and the problems in Kushner's own world—result not so much from a "collapse of morality" (Mann 23), but from overwhelming want and need. For Kushner this is essentially the same, whether it is in Shen Te's world, in Brecht's Germany, or in post-Reagan America. Indeed, these three eras intersect for Kushner in interesting ways, but, for him, the times of Shen Te and Brecht are the historical eras offering opportunities to raise questions about the economic boom of the 1990s—and the ways in which the upper half of the society did well while the lower half slipped further down the economic scale. Here, in Kushner's effort to connect Brecht's play to the sociopolitical concerns of the present, he is at his most Brechtian.

The social commitment of Kushner's own plays, and the influence of Brecht on his evolution as a dramatist, are evident in several aspects of Kushner's major plays, especially, as previously noted, in *Bright Room*, but also in *Hydriotaphia*, *Slavs!*, and *Angels*. In these works, Kushner adopts Brecht's episodic structure and the overt, self-conscious theatricalism typical of Brecht's major plays. More importantly, the political elements of Kushner's plays are as evident as in Brecht's, although the half century separating their writing has changed some of their particular issues. Capturing the world from its "most intimate to the most metapolitical" (Mann 22), as Kushner states, is the challenge he accepts in adapting Brecht. It is a challenge Kushner is well-prepared for, since his own plays function in these realms as well. Cultural clashes between rich and poor, and the eternal struggle of good and evil, are presented in *Good Person* in both personal and cultural ways, and Brecht himself endeavored, as he explains in his journals, to imbue the play with the accidental and transitory nature of life's occurrences. Kushner is, in this case, a most respectful adaptor, as his contributions are more in the direction of easing the play into a contemporary American idiom while, at the same time, building more fully on its inherent strengths.

Without seeming to eliminate anything of significance from the original text, Kushner's efficient and clear adaptation sharpens the play's issues, deepens its characters, and underscores aspects that make contemporary resonances evident. Kushner's eye for the heart of a scene or a speech, and his lyrical way with dialogue, enhance *Good Person*, keeping the play "true to Brecht and also playable by American actors" (Mann 22). Kushner's contributions are most telling in his polishing of Brecht's lyrics and in underscoring the play's thematic highlights. Most effective are the spare, bone dry verses of "In the Company of the Clouds," "The Powerlessness of the Good and the Gods," and "The Day of St. Never-to-Be."

Kushner's light touch with Brecht's lyrics renders a simplicity that permits the meaning to emerge without unnecessary elaboration or the awkwardness of a literal translation. This is a particular accomplishment for Kushner, since his own writing style is far more voluptuous than Brecht's, so he must restrain his natural proclivities. He succeeds in adapting his style to suit the play's, as demonstrated when Shen Te speaks for poor children by imagining her own:

> Oh son, oh pilot! What kind of world
> Are you coming to? Will you too
> Be an ashcan scavenger? Look
> At this grey little mouth! (*She shows the child*) See
> The way you treat your own! Have you
> No feelings for the fruit
> Of your own wombs? No sympathy
> For yourselves, you miserable people! I at least
> Will defend my own, even if I must
> Become a Tiger. Yes, from the moment
> I saw this: I'll cut myself off
> From everyone else and spare myself nothing
> Till my son is safe! At least my son!
> Everything I've learned
> In the gutter-school of my life,
> Fighting and betraying, now
> It will serve you, my son, to you
> I will be good, a tiger, a wild animal
> To all others, if that's how it has to be. And
> It must be. (133)

Within this lyric Brecht and Kushner relate one of the play's fundamental meanings, and Shen Te's cry of determined despair is shifted on to an audience that must reckon with its unanswerable plea.

Kushner's other slight, but effective, adjustments to Brecht's language come in the exchanging of one set of colloquialisms for another, more contemporary variety. Kushner found that the "syncopation and brusqueness of American English and its mongrel quality works well with Brecht, who goes quickly from [formal] German to something very short and choppy and nasal and street—the Berlin hip talk of the '20s and '30s" (Mann 22). He also recognized that there are distinct languages within the play that are important: the rural language that is spoken mostly by Shen Te and the "harsher language of business and the more sophisticated urban cultural rhetoric" (Mann 22).

Kushner's economical lyrics and dialogue are an especially effective aspect of his contribution, as is evidenced in a terse speech given by Shen Te after losing patience with her greedy relatives and the unemployed man. Turning to the audience, Shen Te says:

> They don't talk back now. They stay
> Where you put them, when you dismiss them
> They go quickly!
> Nothing moves them anymore. Only
> The smell of food makes them look up. (79)

As Kushner suggests, the varied colloquialisms distinguish the characters by class and Kushner underscores not only these linguistic differences, but he emphasizes and deepens the few distinguishing personality traits Brecht distinguishes his characters with in an attempt to keep them easily recognizable human types, as opposed to fully dimensioned individuals.

Shen Te is the protagonist of *Good Person*. She is delicate, full-hearted, and exudes an innate gentility, but, as Brecht shows—and as Kushner amplifies—Shen Te demonstrates a strong and unexpected vein of iron while in her disguise as her hard-edged cousin, Shui Ta. Within these characters are merged aspects of Brecht's and Kushner's individual strengths in providing a required duality of character/actor Brecht demands, while also generating considerable sympathy for a human being faced with appallingly harsh choices, a Kushner specialty. The strong empathy Shen Te elicits, and which Kushner's adaptation emphasizes, permits a fuller experience of Shen Te's struggles, while still retaining the intellectual clarity of her complex dilemma. The play's central themes emerge directly through Shen Te's persona: Is it possible to be decent, generous, and good of heart in a world of staggering need, suffering, and self-centeredness?

More than with Shen Te/Shui Ta, Kushner's adaptation sharpens the secondary characters such as the Gods, Wang the water seller (to some extent the play's compere), and, particularly, the young pilot Yang Sun, a character at once both pitiable and menacing. Kushner believes Brecht's characters "have a certain universality and fit very easily" (Mann 22) into a change of cultural idiom, so he encourages the possibility of such a transition through his own command of language. Allowing Brecht's dialogue to retain its full meaning while providing economically sharp language, something not always evident in standard translations of Brecht's plays, and a slight accentuation of the play's inherent ironic humor, allows Kushner, through his restrained, careful adaptation, to refresh the play.

Kushner's sudden fame with the success of the gay-themed *Angels* curiously echoed Brecht's rise to prominence in 1921 with the publication of his homoerotic short story, *Bargan Lets it Happen*, after which he became the dominant figure in the avant-garde theatrical world of 1920s Berlin. Although Brecht rarely dealt with overtly gay themes, Kushner—who did not reinvent any of Brecht's characters in *Good Person* as gay—believes that there is "gender fuck in *The Good Person* because it is about playing around with gender" (Mann 23) and virtually any character in the play could be played by a male or female, straight or in drag. Since Brecht found his characters among those who were marginalized or oppressed within a society, it is possible for Kushner to see the gay or lesbian individual as an inherently Brechtian character—or, perhaps, to at least suggest the possibility through cross-gender casting.

Where Kushner most obviously parts company with Brecht, both in his own plays and in this adaptation, is in the creation of intensely emotional, richly drawn, and empathetic characters. Brecht certainly provides powerful and memorable characters, but Kushner, intentionally or not, will have none of Brecht's alienation technique as far as the main characters are concerned. While some of Kushner's own characters break the fourth wall to address the audience, they always remain "in character" when they do; the actor behind the role is not as evident in his plays as Brecht insists he or she be in his. There is no doubt that

Figure 12: (Clockwise) Gedde Watanabe as Wang the water seller, Charlayne Woodard as Shen Te, and Lou Diamond Phillips as Yang in the 1994 La Jolla Playhouse production of Tony Kushner's adaptation of Bertolt Brecht's *The Good Person of Setzuan*. Photo by Ken Howard.

Kushner is a quintessentially American dramatist and that this is a quintessentially American adaptation. Kushner's work is as indebted to the style of Tennessee Williams and other lyrically inclined American symbolists as it is to Brecht, although in discussing influences on his work, Kushner's tendency is to stress the Brechtian inspiration. In his own plays, Kushner allows the characters to comment on their own circumstances in the Brechtian mode (more often than not as a comic tension breaker), and he endows them with a depth and reality Brecht tends to avoid.

With the characters in *Good Person*, Kushner, through his finely honed Americanized dialogue, manages to both maintain the stereotypical aspects of the characters (as Brecht would certainly prefer), while bringing a depth of humanity and three-dimensionality to them that is more often found on American stages. This is especially true of Kushner's treatment of the play's major characters, like Shen Te and the Water Seller. Kushner is indeed a Brechtian, but he goes well beyond Brecht's didacticism in the humanity and emotionalism with which he imbues the characters. As such, they become individuals, not merely symbols. This combination may at first seem essentially contradictory, but it is also the likely source of Kushner's estimable skills as a dramatist—and the effectiveness of this particular adaptation.

Kushner's adaptation of *Good Person* was first produced at San Diego's La Jolla Playhouse in the summer of 1994, with Kushner adapting from a literal translation by Wendy Arons. The production's dramaturg, Elissa Adams, explained at the time that existing translations of *Good Person* "have either an academic or British flavor" and that Kushner combined his own "sense of the fantastic with the poetic and the political" (Phillips E6). Directed by Lisa Peterson, who also staged regional productions of Kushner's *Slavs!*, the production was set in contemporary Southern California, a place where Latinos, Native Americans, and African-Americans struggle for survival, and where goodness is seen as a liability or a sucker's game. The cast featured ethnically diverse actors and Kushner stressed the significance of a multicultural approach, where "everybody in the play is economically marginal, which I think reflects another reality; where people who are white have money and people who aren't white are frequently struggling economically" (Mann 22). Kushner's Brecht thus presents culture clashes as a way of life.

While Kushner worked on the adaptation for its La Jolla premiere, he compared U.S. President Bill Clinton to Shen Te, a good person who "started out with a genuine impulse to bring America back from the pit that Reagan and Bush kicked it into" (Mann 23). But within a little more than a year into Clinton's term of office the failure of his progressive policies—universal health care, gays in the military, abortion rights, jobs programs, etc.—suggested that his good intentions were not enough to overcome "an economic system which creates terrible deprivation and want" where "there isn't enough money and people don't have good houses and people don't have enough food, people don't have the luxury to develop their souls—people are crushed and tortured by acts of desperation" (Mann 23).

The La Jolla production featured Charlayne Woodard as Shen Te/Shui Ta, Lou Diamond Phillips as Yang Sun, and Gedde Watanabe as the Water Seller, and included original music by David Hidalgo and Louis Perez. Critic Laurie Winer found it a "hip and poetic adaptation" that connects Brecht and Kushner in their "consuming search for decency" (F1). Winer points out that "Kushner can make you cry; Brecht has no interest in tears," and with the addition of Kushner's lyrical emotionalism the play becomes "vividly entertaining" in spanning "two sensibilities, both comically cold and unexpectantly touching" (F4). Reviewer Don Braunagel called the La Jolla production a "superlative presentation" of Brecht's "cynical and sardonic examination of the dichotomy in human behavior," noting that Kushner "pays considerable homage to Brecht while leavening much of his class-struggle preachiness with humor, colloquialisms and street jargon. This Setzuan, in effect, looks and sounds a lot like Tijuana or Spanish Harlem" (74). Michael Phillips found it "a big, unwieldly, oddly becalmed" version of Brecht, and felt that Kushner's faithful adaptation was "a crisp, fairly pungent" version of the play's "discomfiting lessons" ("Too-Casual Air Leaves Play Oddly Becalmed" E1).

The 1999 Wings Theatre production in New York, staged under modest circumstances, made powerful aesthetic use of its reduced circumstances. The setting was a collection of junk—from shopping carts to old umbrellas and broken chairs—emphasizing the abject poverty of Shen Te's world and allowing the actors to use the commonplace debris to imaginatively invent everything from a shelter (approximated with an old golf umbrella) to a factory (represented in silhouette with a sheet and a little back light). The production received a more mixed reception from critics, with Ricky Spears writing that it was "like spending too many hours in a phantasmagoric *Romper Room*" that is "an overstuffed, cluttered mess of a spectacle that barely lets Brecht's play resonate at all" (13), while others found it "a sharply focused, darkly amusing, and imaginatively theatrical adaptation" (Fisher 121).

If, as Kushner claims, his adaptation of *Good Person* is more Brecht than Kushner, it is at least the case that this adaptation points in the direction of Kushner's work from the mid-1990s. *Angels* attracted so much attention because it tapped into issues of gender and sexuality that remain unresolved in American society. As the twentieth century draws to a close, his attention has shifted toward economic issues in works ranging from his screenplay *East Coast Ode to Howard Jarvis* to his in-progress epic play *Henry Box Brown*. For Kushner, *Good Person* is similarly about money and its meanings. As he says,

> What makes me crazy is that nobody can talk about economics anymore. Nobody can talk about capitalism. Nobody can talk about the notion that workers have rights, or that maybe the rich aren't entitled to maximize profit to the moon and have no regard for human life or the environment or jobs. Maybe downsizing is immoral. Maybe these things need to be looked at again. (Vorlicky 203)

It is obvious that Kushner intends to continue to look at these issues and that *Good Person* provides, as one critic stressed, an "opportunity for some long overdue soul-searching as we face the new century" (Britton, n.p.).

Waiting by the River: *Widows*

> Can you smell my breath? I've spent the
> last five hours talking to the dead.
> —Sofia Fuentes, *Widows* (96)

The least important of Kushner's adaptations is a work that is not, in a sense, a true adaptation. When Ariel Dorfman (b. 1942), best known as the author of *Death and the Maiden*, attempted to make a play of his novel *Widows* (a project begun in the early 1980s), he found it difficult. For a time, Kushner provided assistance. Dorfman's novel was published in English translation by Stephen Kessler in 1983, ten years after Dorfman, a novelist, poet, essayist, and journalist, fled Chile following the overthrow of Chilean President Allende. The novel is set in a Greek village in 1940, depicting the impact of abductions carried out by the occupying Nazis who "disappear" dissident citizens. It also illuminates the life of an imaginary Dutch writer and resistance fighter, Eric Lohmann (Dorfman even includes a foreword by Lohmann's "son," Sirgud), who disappeared at the hands of the Nazis. Here the Nazi occupation of Greece provides a metaphor for the brutal Pinochet dictatorship in Chile. The shift of contemporary concerns to the past provides an initial connection between Dorfman and Kushner, but, in this case, it seems a too-obvious attempt to lend additional universality to a situation that is, in its own right, all too tragically universal. The play wisely shifts the action back to Chile and the Pinochet years, focusing on the stubborn, courageous struggle of a woman whose father, husband, and sons were abducted and are among the "disappeared."

Dorfman had completed five collections of essays and a novel before fleeing Chile, and since his exile regards himself as "a professional dictator-molester" (Breslin BW6). Reviewer Dennis Drabelle called *Widows* a "taut novel" written with "piercing intensity" (BW6), and Alan Cheuse, writing for the *New York Times*, found it a "sharply dramatic little novel of large passions" (10). This view was shared by other critics, all of whom made reference to the dramatic possibilities of the work. Dorfman's central character, a peasant woman named Sofia Fuentes, is a complete invention of the author, who explains that "if she could come from my imagination, however, it was because she was inspired by real women who searched for real bodies in a real world more cruel and inhuman than anything I finally described in my fiction" (6).

During the years he continued to revise his stage version of *Widows*, Dorfman also adapted his novel *Death and the Maiden* for theatrical production in 1992, with resulting critical acclaim and a well-received 1994 film version with Sigourney Weaver and Ben Kingsley heading the cast. Subsequent Dorfman films include *Prisoners in Time* (1995) and *My House is on Fire* (1997), which he also directed. The adaptation of *Death and the Maiden*, which took only three weeks to complete, depicts a harrowing encounter years after the fact between a woman, who had been raped and tortured during the period of a repressive dictatorship, and a man she believes was one of her torturers. Creating an adaptation of *Widows* proved to be far more problematic for Dorfman, requiring over seven years of revisions and leading to the involvement of Kushner in what is to date his only writing collaboration.

The plot of *Widows* is simple and the action proceeds chronologically in each of the three versions (Dorfman and Kushner each produced an adaptation, and Dorfman and Kushner collaborated on a final version). In a small Chilean village, the river yields up a man's disfigured body, leading a local woman, Sofia Fuentes, to insist that the body is her missing father. When, some time later, another body in similar condition appears, Sofia claims that it is her husband. The women of the village, led by Sofia, recognize the moral significance of identifying the corpses—a terrible harvest of the "disappeared"—and honoring them.

The military authorities, led by a nameless Captain, are dismissive of Sofia at first, but ultimately come to fear her resolve and the support of the other women in the village whose men are also missing. A battle of wills between Sofia and the Captain demonstrates one of the central themes of *Widows*: the capacity of those who suffer injustice and insupportable loss to return, even from death, to haunt the culpable. Sofia will settle for nothing less than the return of the men—dead or alive—and the punishment of those who took them away and killed them. Sofia's grief and festering hate for those who "disappeared" her father, husband, and sons serves as a moral lightning rod, illuminating issues of loyalty among the villagers, disharmonies among the powerful, and the problems of dealing with the crimes of the past and how to move on without forgetting those who have paid the price of political conflict.

Dorfman uses the style and, to some extent, the structure of classical tragedy. The play is reminiscent of Sophocles's *Antigone* and, more precisely, Euripides's *The Trojan Women*, as the village women evolve into something like a chorus that comments on the action of the play. The women's grief binds them together, but they are at odds, even within Sofia's family, over how to challenge the military as a collective entity. Some of the women, including Sofia's daughter-in-law, Alexandra, fear further reprisals from the military, while others find Sofia simply too bitter and stubborn. The humble rural setting, the Christian values of the women, and the almost ritualistic aspects of the plot call to mind the plays of Federico Garcia Lorca, as well as the classical dramatists. Sofia, like the title character in Garcia Lorca's drama *Yerma*, gives the play its central image and dramatic strength, but attempts by Dorfman to broaden his canvas are somewhat less compelling, although Kushner made some significant contributions to strengthening and broadening the work.

Dorfman received a commission from Los Angeles's Mark Taper Forum to dramatize *Widows* in 1985, and it was staged in two workshop versions that culminated in the first performances of the play in 1988 at the Hip Pocket Theatre in Fort Worth, Texas. This short run was followed by performances at the Williamstown Theatre Festival in August 1988. At that time, and prior to Kushner's involvement, Dorfman discussed the play with *New York Times* writer Peter Applebome:

> There's a symbol that goes beyond just one person who gets abducted. For me the whole idea of disappearance comes to represent the fate of so many millions

around the world who have disappeared from the attention of the overdeveloped world. In a sense, the challenge of the play is that we are bringing to light people who never appear as protagonists of anything, and when they do appear they appear only as victims of catastrophes over which they have no control. Their appearance on this stage is a different sort of appearance. Their appearance is an antidote to disappearance. It's about women who are defying terror, amnesia and moral blindness to say, "We exist." It is a chance for people who are outside history to say, "We exist." They are a symbol of people who won't be silenced no matter what we think. (5)

Dorfman continued to revise *Widows* for a 1990 production at the Taper. However, the director, Robert Egan, postponed it, asking for further revisions by Dorfman. Although Dorfman had some initial discomfort about it, Egan suggested that Kushner be brought in to co-adapt the script. The idea of giving voice to the "disappeared" resonated with Kushner, whose own work, especially in *Angels*, attempts to give voice to the historically invisible gay community in American society—and even more deeply, as it resonated with Kushner's Jewishness and the horrors of the Holocaust. Dorfman, like Kushner, saw a challenge in approaching an American audience which, he believes, has an "innocence, a very dangerous innocence" that he attempts to jar in forcing them to think "about their own history, their own amnesia about history, their incapacity to see what is happening outside their borders, almost the incapacity of Americans, North Americans, to understand evil" (Applebome 5). Tragedy, he stressed after the play was produced at Williamstown—and after the Taper removed it from its 1990 schedule—was "somehow still possible in the Third World. It's almost impossible in the post-modern United States. That may be an abyss we have to jump across" (Shirley F4).

Kushner's central mission with *Widows* was to assist Dorfman in making the piece more stageworthy and he proceeded to do a full-fledged revision of the script himself. Kushner, impressed by Dorfman's novel, found it "immensely dramatic, with a simplicity of narrative that resembles Greek tragedy. I wrote a stage version which was more argumentative than Ariel's. He thought it interesting but wanted a more collaborative process" (Rosenthal 35). Kushner's "top-to-bottom" rewrite led to the two writers getting together for two marathon sessions (each of five days length) at Dorfman's home in Durham, North Carolina, where Kushner attempted, as Dorfman explained, to "explode the old version, and forced me to think from a new dramatic premise" (Koehler C4). As Kushner recalled, "I typed and Ariel paced. We'd write a few lines, read them aloud, then write some more. We changed the opening and the whole rhythm. Whenever we got stuck, we devised solutions that differed from what either of us had originally advocated" (Rosenthal 35).

For purposes of understanding Kushner's contributions, it is instructive to study Kushner's solo effort, which is, not surprisingly, far more spare and Brechtian than either Dorfman's solo version or the Dorfman-Kushner collaboration. Both of these are not without effective elements, but both, in different ways, lack the raw power of Kushner's solo treatment.

Kushner underscores the political significance and almost frightening bravery of Sofia Fuentes and the other simple village women in demanding the return of their men from the brutal and all-powerful military. Sofia's actions are clearly more provocative in Kushner's version, although he somewhat reduces the involvement of some of the other village women (most of whom go unnamed in his treatment). He gives their presence and few speeches the quality of a choric threnody of grief that underscores Sofia's actions, while he also emphasizes Sofia's conflicts with some of the other village women, especially her own daughter-in-law, Alexandra, who bitterly opposes Sofia's provocations of the military fearing further grief for the family. As in *Angels*, Kushner also movingly argues for the commemoration of atrocities through Sofia's insistence that they must continue to demand the return of the men and to confront the authorities despite ruthless counteractions, which conclude in the unarmed village women standing face to face with the guns of the soldiers pointed at them.

Elements of Kushner's characteristic style are evident from the beginning of his version, which features a terse little scene between the Captain and his aide, Emmanuel, who was raised in the region. The Captain hates his rural posting and when Emmanuel enters, he already knows that waiting outside his door is "that old bitch" (1) demanding possession of the body in the river, which, she claims, is that of her father. The Captain has been told that Sofia has not, in fact, even seen the body and wonders how she can know "if she hasn't even seen it?" (4). Sofia's actions are acts of civil disobedience—she is attempting to force the Pinochet bureaucracy, represented by the Captain, to confront the atrocities carried out to bring the dictator to power. The Captain shows little interest in her demands—he even cynically suggests that some of the men of her village might have run off with other women—but Sofia insists, "I will bury my dead" (13).

Later, Sofia, her daughter-in-law Yanina, and her granddaughter Fidelia chant by the river, "Nothing dies but returns to me" (23), while Sofia explains the significance of her crucifix:

> If you put Christ by the candles, like so, as the night comes, it darkens; in the candlelight, He writhes again on the cross, in pain again, He suffers His agonies, this frail young man, hoping to relieve the suffering of the world. But. There was too much suffering, too much sin. So his agonies never end. (23)

Sofia's other daughter-in-law, Alexandra, argues with the old woman, insisting that their riverside chants show that "You're all crazy; you've all gone crazy" (23), but it becomes clear that the Captain and his military colleagues are becoming increasingly concerned about the complaints pouring in about the disfigured "men without faces" (32) washing up in the river. They regard Sofia—"that old hag squatting by the river" (33)—as an increasingly dangerous subversive and attempt to get the local priest, Father Gabriel, to reason with her. However, the priest, who implies some criticism of the Captain's handling of the situation, has no explanations for her actions:

Figure 13: The village women with a body of one of the "disappeared" in the 1991 Mark Taper Forum production of *Widows,* adapted by Ariel Dorfman and Tony Kushner from Dorfman's novel. Photo by Jay Thompson.

It's not for me to judge, Captain. We should not judge each other, that's God's job, ours is to consider . . . the conditions which bring us to do the things we do. Her father, her husband, her two sons. Many other women in this valley have suffered such losses. Look for explanations there, Captain, in the pain these women feel, in the loss that produces the pain. It's simple, really. (39)

The Captain, on the advice of a cold-blooded young Lieutenant from Chile's aristocratic class, decides to arrest Sofia's grandson, Alexis, who is only fifteen years old. Emmanuel, meanwhile, convinces his girlfriend, Cecilia, whose husband, Theo, is also among the disappeared, to claim that the body in the river is actually her husband. Cecilia is ostracized by the village women who call her a whore, so she agrees, but only if Emmanuel will marry her.

In a truly Kushnerian scene, Fidelia talks to her father's chair, which he has tried to paint blue many times, the soft pine wood continually swallowing up the paint. This chair, he believes, is "like the chair waiting for him in heaven, a sky-blue chair" (54). Baked in the sun, the chair became bluer, which he calls "a miracle" (54), but since his disappearance no one will sit in it. His spirit, emanating from the chair, speaks to Fidelia, and the chorus of women reflect on this miracle and others:

That was a miracle; when things are working, who needs miracles? When you paint a chair blue and it stays blue you don't need a blue-paint miracle. And when the spring is mild and the autumn is wet and sharp and the winter rains come and the summer hot and moist then the wheat and the beans and the cane will grow and you don't need miracles of plants. And when the men are next to you in the fields or in bed or working the fields of the big farms south or drinking together in the square they'll come home on their own two legs and you don't need the river to tumble them home, you don't need the miracle of bodies in the river, my husband, brother, uncle, cousin, father, grandfather, lover, son tumbled mile after mile by the water in the river, just to have him back, just to have him come back home. And when people die in their beds as they should you don't need a black miracle like this to make you a widow instead of just someone who waits. And doesn't know. And waits. (55)

With Alexis as a bargaining chip, the Captain plans to convince Sofia to end her resistance to his rule. However, when a second body appears, Sofia insists that this one is her husband's corpse, and Fidelia begins to understand the importance of her grandmother's actions: "The river couldn't bring back all the bodies, there are too many, so it brought back two, and they belong to all the women" (65). Thirty-seven women, in fact, attempt to claim the second body. The Captain, believing Sofia is behind this latest act of resistance, loses patience and considers his options and the various factions manipulating the situation:

There are those, you see, who would like me to unload several crates of bullets into these hags and let that answer their petitions. That's one group. And within that group there are those who would like a pile of bodies because they want to see this situation made tidy, and there are those who want to see bodies because they want the situation to explode, and those factions make one group and then ... there's another group. That wants negotiation. Compromise. No dead women, no bullets. And in that group there are factions, and among the factions, factions. Within and within and within. (74)

Cecilia thinks she sees Theo's body in the river, but it turns out to be merely some rags. Feeling guilt for her actions, she tells Emmanuel about her recurring nightmares, to which he replies, "We all have bad dreams" (79). Alexis is released, but has been tortured and refuses to speak. Yanina's baby also will not talk and only cries. Unrepentant, Sofia dares to taunt the Captain: "Look at your face, worried, like a nervous little monkey in a trap, blink blink, your wrinkled forehead, your frightened eyes. I'm amazed at what you don't know. True I'm twice your age but when I was half as old as you I knew four times as much" (96).

A woman reporter interviews the Captain and he tries to put a positive spin on the actions of "his widows" (98) and speaks of a surprise announcement he will make. Demonstrating the power at his command, he compels the reporter to have dinner with him, and also forces the widows to attend his announcement. It is in the form of a letter from the Minister of Security offering amnesty and cynically suggesting, "We must raise up a garden from the carnage of war" and "let go of the past" (110). As a gesture of "good will," one prisoner will be released and sent home. It turns out to be Alonso, Sofia's son and Yanina's husband, and the reporter is sent to cover the release, but the Captain so carefully controls her interview with Alonso that she gives up.

The release of Alonso, the Captain hopes, will cause Sofia to back down. The Captain and the reporter end up in bed together, where they are interrupted by news that bodies are turning up everywhere and that the women are continuing to come forth to claim them. The local aristocrats are seen worrying about the laxity of the Captain and, as a result, the Captain allows the more brutal Lieutenant to deal with matters. With a squad of soldiers, he goes to the Fuentes house and rearrests young Alexis: "You people . . . You push too much. You think . . . we want this? I have a brother his age. Stop pushing. Or he'll be the next one you fish out of the river. So help me God" (150).

The rearrest of Alexis galvanizes the formerly reluctant Alexandra into action. While the Lieutenant reflects on his actions in the Pinochet era—"I have tortured men. And I have killed men. Strangled them. Put electrical wires to their genitals. Made them bleed. I have raped women" (155)—Alexandra, with Fidelia's help, cuts the Lieutenant's throat.

The Captain tries, once again, to use Alexis's well-being as a leash to restrain Sofia, but she refuses to back down. When the frustrated Captain wonders what it will take, she tells him: "I want the men to come home. And to bury them" (163), adding, "And after that I want the killers found and punished. This is what we all want. All of us. By the river" (163). Sadly admitting, "All I know anymore is my grief" (164), Sofia tries to help Alexis face his inevitable fate by explaining what his suffering can mean:

> Up in the mountains you can see cracks in the rock. In the cold months snow gets packed deep inside, works its way into the cracks, and when the sun hits the rock in the warm months the cold snow deep inside the rock makes the cracks grow bigger. Just snow, but after enough time the snow can split a mountain in two. Do you understand? (165)

Kushner's treatment uses a number of archetypal symbolic speeches like this— and references such as "seed corn" to describe the younger Fuentes family members—inspired by moments in Dorfman's novel. Alexis is too frightened to grasp the meaning of her words, so Sofia adds, "There are villages of the living and villages of the dead crowding around you always. Remember that I said that to you. The living and the dead are always there" (165). As Alexis is dragged away, Sofia returns to the other women at the river's edge. The Captain, leading a squad of soldiers, arrives and orders the guns aimed at the women as the play ends.

Kushner's spare, episodic version of *Widows* underwent significant revision by Dorfman and Kushner. Changes on the order and length of scenes led to a somewhat different structure, with the roles of the chorus of village women expanded (many have names and dialogue in this version) and that of the woman reporter eliminated. The piece as a whole adopts a more realistic style than the drier, theatrical Brechtian approach of Kushner's solo version, which maintains the reality of the character's situations while depending more on a spare symbolism. Later, Dorfman returned to the play to make further revisions for a March 1997 production at Edinburgh's Traverse Theatre, followed by a tour of Great Britain. He made use of the version co-adapted with Kushner, who had told Dorfman, "with his usual generosity—that I should go ahead without him" (Dorfman 6), because, in part, following the runaway success of *Angels,* he did not have enough time to continue to work on *Widows.* Dorfman, following his own success with the stage production of *Death and the Maiden,* stressed that

> Tony's vision might be different from mine, but he was struggling with the same demons of expression, confronting ways in which politics and imagination intersect, how to depict suffering and repression without sinking into hopelessness, how to be colloquial and simultaneously mythical, how to show human resistance and resilience without being propagandistic or doctrinaire, how to recognize that we have the enemy inside and the best people are capable of the most terrible things. If I have deluded myself into believing that I was the bridge the missing had been looking for to enter the world and speak to it, Tony became in effect the bridge I had been looking for to enter the world of theatre and reach the U.S. audience. For the next two years, Tony patiently helped me craft *Widows* into the play it had always promised to be, provided dialogue and characters and rhythm. He is the co-author, its midwife. (6)

Dorfman made additional changes after Kushner withdrew his involvement, particularly the addition of a narrator to frame the play—a Dorfmanesque figure who, like his author, was in exile helplessly watching the suffering in his country from a distance. Most critics found this an awkward device when the play was performed in England.

The critical response had been more positive—although decidedly mixed—for the original Dorfman-Kushner adaptation of *Widows* when it opened at the Mark Taper Forum on July 24, 1991. *Los Angeles Times* reviewer Sylvie Drake felt its dramatic viability "eludes its makers. It remains an exercise in artifice rather than art" (F23), while *Variety* critic Marc Berman lauded the play's epic tragedy and its depiction of the "under-represented" women and "the disappeared" men of Latin America, finding the stories of South America too little examined in the canon of world drama. However Berman and other critics, felt that Dorfman, Kushner, and the director, Robert Egan, struggled with "mixed results" to give "their concerns immediate impact on the stage," with the result that the "first act, in particular, plods and the tone is dogmatically grim," adding that the Dorfman/Kushner version of *Widows* "owes a debt to Brecht, not so much in style as in its elevation of peasant women to heroines as they struggle against a corrupt and repressive regime" (49).

Kushner was certainly drawn to *Widows* for its representation of the unrepresented, a frequent concern of his own drama, from his full-length plays to his impressively diverse one-acts plays which, in short form, visit aspects of the same questions examined in Kushner's major plays and adaptations.

CHAPTER SIX

An Undoing World
Kushner's One-Acts

People will always do surprising things, both good and bad, and the way that people surprise themselves and their audience are the most interesting moments of human behavior. The space between what we'd like to be and what we actually are is where you find out the most interesting things.
—Tony Kushner (Bernstein 59)

During the chaotic success of *Angels in America*, the initial productions of *Slavs!*, and continuing work on various adaptations and new play ideas, Kushner indulged himself in some efforts in the oft-neglected form of the one-act play. *Slavs!* is, in essence, a very long one-act play, although its large cast of characters and the complexity of its themes suggests it should be thought of as a full-length play. Since its completion, Kushner has written several plays that are true one-act plays. For a dramatist known mostly through the Homeric scope of *Angels*—he jokingly calls himself "the James Michener of American drama" (letter to James Fisher, Dec. 28, 1996)—the exploration of the one-act form seems, at first, an odd choice. However, Kushner demonstrates in these short plays, most of which have been produced in a variety of settings, that he is able to maintain the epic scope of his full-length dramas and adaptations while working in this short form.

And Then You'll Know Suffering: *It's an Undoing World or Why Should It Be Easy When It Can Be Hard? Notes on My Grandma for Actors, Dancers and a Band*

In many respects, the most interesting of Kushner's one-acts is the most unusual and personal. *It's an Undoing World or Why Should It Be Easy When It Can Be Hard? Notes on My Grandma for Actors, Dancers and a Band* was completed in 1995 as a project for choreographer Naomi Goldberg, who asked Kushner to write a piece her dance company could perform accompanied by the music of the Klezmatics, a klezmer band that had provided evocative Jewish music for Kushner's *A Dybbuk* during its New York Public Theatre production. Goldberg, wife of stage director Brian Kulick (who had commissioned Kushner's Corneille adaptation, *The Illusion*), staged *Undoing World* with her Los Angeles Modern Dance and Ballet Company. Kushner himself performed as a reader, along with John Fleck, Rachel Rosenthal, Nealla Gordon, Page Leong, and Teresa Tudury. Critic Lewis Segal, facetiously describing the performance as "Kushner on the Roof," felt that the readings "awkwardly paused for formal dance and musical interludes," but that Kushner had delivered a "rambling, whimsical text" about his grandmother's "spontaneous absorption of knowledge through dancing" (3). *Undoing World* was later given a staged reading at New York's Public Theatre as a benefit for a City University of New York's teacher's union. The well-known cast of the reading included Susan Sontag, Larry Kramer, Suzan-Lori Parks, Holly Hughes, Katha Pollitt, Kathleen Chalfant, Lola Pashalinski, and Ellen McLaughlin. The Public Theatre reading was an experience Kushner called "great," although the play remains "a seedling" and he intends to "work it up into something" (e-mail to James Fisher).

Kushner frequently cautions against viewing his characters as mouthpieces of the author, although many of his plays from *Angels* to *Caroline, or Change*, include bits of his autobiography and politics—Kushner, however, sprinkles bits of his own life over the fictive elements of *Undoing World*. What *Undoing World* may or may not ultimately evolve into remains unclear, but as it now stands it not only offers bits of autobiography, but suggests ample opportunities for a fuller development of the characters, the play's central concerns, and the richly textured and complex web of fantasy and reality Kushner weaves into many of his plays. *Undoing World* depicts the immigrant experience, from the highly personal sufferings of those who journeyed to America's shores in the late nineteenth century to the shaping of the immigrant generation's intellectual, moral, and political foundations of twentieth-century liberalism resulting from their extraordinary experiences.

Without a doubt, Kushner feels the pull of the immigrant experience—of the transitions made, of the changes embraced, of the dislocations experienced, of the sorrows felt, and of the discoveries made by those who left an old world for a new one. Sarah, the grandmother in *Undoing World*, is the brave, tragic, feisty, and sometimes absurdly comic traveler of the play. She shares her fading memories—presumably after her death—with her three daughters, all of whom suffer from various stages of breast cancer—"under their eyes are dark rings and their heads are wrapped in brightly colored chemotherapy scarves" (14)—as well as a Solemn Grandchild whose serious manner and precocious questions make the child Kushner's obvious surrogate in the play. These five are found eating around a kitchen table where the past, present, and future overlap in a play that is not linear, but cyclic. Sarah's resemblance to Sarah Ironson, Louis's recently deceased grandmother in *Angels*, is obvious, though her resemblance to Kushner's own grandmother may perhaps be of greater significance. Kushner dedicates the play to his aunt, Martha Deutscher, the Middle Daughter of the play, and his own late mother, Sylvia, is also represented. However, the women are mostly focused on unraveling the truths and fallacies of their mother's story. Kushner is concerned here with the meanings of Sarah's story as they symbolize not only the immigrant experience, but also the impact of the ideas of existence, society, and politics brought from Eastern Europe to America—and the ways in which those ideas permanently burnished the American intellectual and moral landscape. This is not new territory for Kushner, who deals with aspects of it in *Angels*, *Slavs!*, and *A Dybbuk*, but the unique structure and modes of revelation in *Undoing World* are singular. Beyond the Eastern European influence on American life, Kushner similarly explores dislocations and intersections of other cultures in his plays, from *Hydriotaphia* to *Home Body/Kabul*, with the goal of revealing issues of justice, compassion, and human suffering impacted by momentous social transitions.

Undoing World is most obviously complex in both its characters and in the theatrical devices Kushner employs. Sarah is a cantankerous, opinionated, and, at times, confused old woman clinging to a vanishing past she is now unable—or unwilling—to remember with any accuracy. She lives in the past and even talks about her own death and those of her daughters, as they, at times, speak in Sarah's voice, adopting her grammatical errors as though these presumably native English speakers were also of the Eastern European immigrant group whose grasp on a second language is tenuous and eccentric. A boiling teapot whistles out Sarah's unconscious lamentations—"Oooooooyyyyyyyy ... It's an undoing world, I'm telling you" (15)—providing background and narrative bridges, and, when Sarah and the three daughters ("Youngest," "Middle," "Eldest") misidentify places or persons, the teapot provides correction to the crazy quilt of details and gaps in their talk. The Solemn Grandchild, who Kushner explains in his stage directions "never looks happy" (14), raises pointed questions for Sarah who, with the kibitzing of her daughters, recounts her life in Chiroszchjew, a small town near the Russian-Polish border where she was born and spent her earliest years. The Eldest Daughter complains that Sarah's stories are "often unreliable" (15), but although there is much debating over the veracity of particular details, the essence of Sarah's life emerges through the bits and pieces from Sarah, the teapot, the daughters (who also seem, at moments, to be their mother), and the questions of the Solemn Grandchild.

Sarah's father was a Polish innkeeper who sent his young daughter to the cheder in Tarnopol so that she might learn the Jewish prayers and one day say the Kaddish over him because he did not believe his unloving wife would. A young Russian student carries Sarah around piggyback, and from him, "she acquired his knowledge: Through his shirt, through the skin on his back it came: It was Russian words, it was Pushkin, it was botany" (16). Back at her father's inn, Sarah meets a Polish Countess who, during a cold winter night, secretly takes Sarah on a sleigh ride to a pine forest where they dance and Sarah "acquired the Countess's knowledge; through the flesh of the palms of the Countess, through the fine kid gloves it came: fluency in Polish, in Hungarian, French" (17), as well as a few French Christmas carols and skill in embroidery. Sarah wistfully sings a few words of one of the carols, recalling that because of the Countess she always had a Christmas tree in her home despite being a Jew.

Along with these flashes from Sarah's mythic past, she also reflects on the lonely end of her life, complaining, "my eyes are bothering me. My daughters are such bitches. They have left me in this hot hell" (18), referring to the hotel (mispronounced by Sarah as hot hell) room where she died alone. Slipping back into memories of her early life, Sarah and the daughters recall that following the death of Sarah's father she earned her fare to America by doing gold thread embroidery for the Countess and for the Russian navy. Jumping ahead in her story, Sarah tells of meeting Benjamin Nathan Cardozo, the legendary judge, but the Middle Daughter interrupts saying, "She has no sense, of, of *order*. She is *impossible*" (19).

Returning to the story of Sarah's migration to the United States, the daughters describe her crossing of the ocean where, aboard ship, she "danced with the students, she danced with deserters, she danced with fatherless girls," learning from these encounters "cooking skills, sewing skills, and military drinking songs" (19). Kushner indicates in the script a dance should occur here, while the Solemn Grandchild wonders what life was like in America at the time of Sarah's arrival. The Youngest Daughter explains, "It was all goys and goniffs, everyone in America was an actor or a general or a thief" (20). Speaking derisively of her early neighbors, Sarah annoys the Eldest Daughter, who complains that Sarah is "racist, she says wops, she says sheenies, she says schwarzes, later in the sixties when she's seventy something she says spics. What a terrible old woman" (20), but Sarah protests, describing the difficult separations of ethnic groups that existed in her early days in America. In this period, Sarah knew Annie Lazarus, through whom, she claims, she met Emma Lazarus, whose poem emblazoned on the base of the Statue of Liberty is eccentrically recited by the teapot:

> Give me your tired, your poor,
> Your huddled masses abubbadah bubbudah bubbudah
> Yearning to breathe free. (21)

Lazarus, Sarah says, "bought for me the little tin Statue of Liberty" (21) that the Eldest Daughter has inherited after Sarah's death, although the Middle Daughter accuses her of stealing it when Sarah was living in the hot hell. The Youngest Daughter proudly notes that she "inherited the teapot" (21), which subsequently went to the Middle Daughter when the Youngest died of cancer. The Solemn Grandchild points out that Lazarus died the year before Sarah was even born, and the Eldest Daughter warns her to "never tell these stories, they ain't for mass consumption" (22).

From her encounter with Cardozo who, the teapot explains, developed "pragmatical-philosophical inquiries into the highly subjective nature of the Judicial Process" that "paved the way for an Interventionist Activist Court which was what made America decent" (22), Sarah's politics are formed. The historical Cardozo (1870–1938), a Sephardic Jew, had a distinguished career as a liberal New York Supreme Court judge beginning in 1913. He decided civil and criminal cases on the Court of Appeals as the first Jew to sit in that prestigious position, and following the 1932 retirement of Oliver Wendell Holmes, Cardozo replaced his mentor on the U. S. Supreme Court. Despite a relatively short tenure (six years), and thanks to many important legal decisions made throughout his career, he became a seminal figure in both the judicial and academic worlds. Several lectures Cardozo gave at Yale were later published as *The Nature of the Judicial Process*, and during the early years of the New Deal, as the activist policies of the Roosevelt administration bitterly divided the Court over constitutional interpretation, Cardozo often held a key vote in support of action. Cardozo's decisions and his view of the law continue to influence important decisions, such as *Roe v. Wade*, which depend on some of his decisions for their legal foundations. Cardozo's talmudic intellectualism provides *Undoing World* with a strong undercurrent of political liberalism set against the personal experiences of Sarah. In one of the play's most compelling sequences, Kushner includes "Benjamin Nathan Cardozo's Love Song to American Law," in which Cardozo sings:

> When she agrees to be mine,
> More-than-impartial Athena,
> This will become our subpoena:
> The Court must not be a machine!
> Law is Democracy's shrine
> Here in the Gold'ne Medina,
> Where the legal light
> Will dispel the night
> And my goddess of Justice will shine! (23)

The Youngest Daughter connects this to Sarah by explaining that while on the boat to America Sarah secretly acquired "a knowledge of the Law" (23) from a Hasidic student with whom, because of her youth, she should not have been dancing. Sarah's acquaintance with the young Cardozo, whom the Eldest Daughter describes as "a sad and lonely man" who never married because "he was in love with the law" (23), led to Cardozo being impressed by Sarah's interest in the law and, as the Middle Daughter explains, he "wanted to marry my ma" (24). Cardozo's sister resents Sarah and when the San Francisco earthquake occurs, Sarah believes this "augurs bad for America" and "so all the Jews who could manage got back on the boats" (24).

On the ship returning to Europe, Sarah met a Glazier who she later marries and, as the Youngest Daughter tells it, "she would break his glass heart" (25). Kushner's script suggests a dance for the shipboard Glaziers at this point. When Sarah arrives back in Chiroszchjew, she finds that it no longer exists. Burned to the ground in a Czarist purge, the town is gone, although Sarah manages to find her father's grave. Sleeping on it one night, she dances in her dreams with his ghost, from which she gained "knowledge of the Yenne Welt, the land of the dead, and years later in the Home when for ten years she sat alone in the nursing home while two of her daughters died of breast cancer" she "travelled living to the Yenne Welt to seek her father" (25). The Eldest Daughter explains that shortly before Sarah's death she seemed to be "a vegetable"—"wasn't nobody home in there" (25)—but that she actually traveled to the Oylem-Habbe—the World To Come—to be with her father.

Following the purge of Chiroszchjew, Sarah's mother and stepfather moved to Tarnopol, where they sold ice cream and candy. Sarah complains that her mother had never loved her father, so "we never got along" (26). "For me," she explains, "the only mother is the Mother of Exiles" (26), the Statue of Liberty. Sarah subsequently returned to the United States with her mother and stepfather, dancing on the boat with her stepfather—"an ignoramus" (27)—which caused Sarah to forget many of the things she had learned in previous dances. Unable to live harmoniously with her mother, Sarah married the Glazier, but at the wedding could only remember a bit of the Polish Countess's Christmas Carol to sing and, as a result, "the marriage wasn't no good" (27).

The Solemn Grandchild asks if Sarah ever saw Cardozo again, reminding her that Cardozo helped make America "decent," but that "it's not so decent now. Lately it has very indecent gotten" (28). Sarah recalls dancing with Cardozo years later during a World War I rally, but that they did not recognize each other. However, while dancing, the teapot explains that

> And through my arms my wrists my neck-nape my boobies
> And from off the Top of my head in heat it came
> Ribbons of smoke which he breathing in dancing inhaled he
> my secret knowledge, was a song: (29)

And Sarah sings of their passing encounter, of dispossession, of the Statue of Liberty and its meaning to the immigrant "in this undoing world":

> Mother, for your derelicted children from your womb evicted
> grant us shelter harbor solace safety
> Let us in!
> Let us tell you where we travelled how our hopes our lives
> unravelled how unwelcome everywhere we've been. (30)

The Youngest Daughter stresses how Cardozo "helped to add human complication subtlety nuance a sense of history a sense of the tragic by which law is made mobile" (30) to the social decisions of his time, and Sarah explains that in a dream during the early 1930s she danced with the entire Supreme Court (Kushner indicates that a dance be performed at this point in the script). Sarah, yearning for the return of Cardozo, condemns the current Supreme Court—"it's just vulgarians" (30)—believing that they only care for big business and now "it's bad for the immigrants bad for the Jews" (31).

As *Undoing World* draws to its melancholy conclusion, the Solemn Grandchild reports that Sarah died at the age of a hundred and three on the day that Proposition 187 passed in California. She died "strangled in disgust no that ain't true she died before that under Reagan she died it was from the fucking capitalist exploiters" (31), and the Solemn Grandchild wonders why Sarah never returned from her premature death in the Home, so "we make answers up" (31). Through the teapot, Sarah explains she wanted to reside in the little tin Statue of Liberty, but "could not find a doorway in, and so in the Statue I couldn't go. And so instead I went to live in this teapot" (32). As the daughters argue over possession of it, Sarah concludes that whoever gets it will live to be a hundred and five: "Yah. You will live a long time. And *then* you'll know suffering" (32).

Suffering is certainly something that Sarah has known only too well. The Solemn Grandchild tells her grandmother at one point that "your whole life has been women fucking up and letting you down" (25), although it becomes clear that despite Sarah's conflict with her mother, in this play about women it is the men in Sarah's life who have, in fact, let her down. Her father, the emotional support of her young life, died prematurely; her stepfather is an "ignoramus" who drains the knowledge from her; her husband, the Glazier, has a heart of glass; and, even the great Cardozo loves the law more passionately than he loves Sarah. The conflict of human need with the inhumanly immense sweep of history and social change is a recurring Kushnerian theme set against his fantasizing of his grandmother's past cobbled together from the dubious, albeit emotionally and intellectually compelling, details.

Strategies of Resistance: *Notes on Akiba*

Kushner draws again on his Jewish heritage for *Notes on Akiba*, a short and "very silly two-hander" (E-mail to James Fisher) written for the third seder of New York's Jewish Museum. The performance on April 13, 1995, conceived and produced by Neil Goldberg, Joan Hocky, and Alicia Svigals, included choreography by David Dorfman, another performance piece by Hocky, stage design by Goldberg, music by the Klezmatics (who had already contributed music for *Undoing World* and the New York production of *A Dybbuk*), and a play by Sarah Schulman. A typically Kushnerian mixture of humor, history, and sociopolitical concerns, *Notes on Akiba* features Kushner himself in a dialogue with his friend, director Michael Mayer, who staged the national tour of *Angels*. Drawn from a study of his "usual rabbinate" (127), including Harold Bloom and, especially, Ira Steingroot, Kushner effectively twines together the Passover traditions of Judaism with the attributes of the modern skeptic who, despite his skepticism, is searching for meaning and understanding in ancient stories and texts. This search for meaning in his religious heritage inspires much of Kushner's work, from *A Dybbuk* (and his projected plan to adapt *The Golem*) through *Angels* and in elements of other works.

Following introductions, the prologue of this play of "exegis, or elaboration" (115) on Passover is a run-on speech spoken by "Tony," a pronouncement with Beckettian overtones. He apologizes for the play, written in haste "on a fucking AIRPLANE," a work for which "I alone am responsible I alone bear responsibility I cannot bear the responsibility it is insupportable it is impossible it is imponderable" (115–16). "Michael" explains that in traditional Sephardic seders the participants lash each other with leeks, which they proceed to do—"Ow" (116), whines Tony, who is clearly the play's comic relief, while Michael provides clarity on the history and traditions of Judaism. Michael explains that this strange ritual is the result of the Jews complaining to Moses in the desert about missing good food—the lashing is a reminder. Tony gripes about his father typically skipping this portion—"The Fier Kashe"—that everyone skips because, "it's like one of those medieval Jewish numerological things" (117).

Michael explains that "echad," the Hebrew word for the number one, "has letters the numerological value of which add up to thirteen" (117) to symbolize the thirteen attributes of God, "potent emenatory demi-divine entities suffused throughout the world of prayerful visionary journeying as mystical lights as described in Kaballah, Jewish magic" (118). Tony goes off on a rant about his father's chronic omission of the story of the five rabbis, including Akiba, and a competitiveness emerges as it seems to infuriate Tony that his father cannot admit he skips it because *his* father always said *all* of it, "every detour and digression" (118).

Michael attempts to change the subject to tell of a favorite Passover treat of his childhood in Maryland, which involved the breaking up of matzoh in a bowl over which is poured condensed milk and Fox's U Bett syrup. As he explains,

> The matzoh represents the pious deflation of the pridefulness of man and woman as they approach God during this Holy Week of Remembrance, not puffed up with the yeast of their pretensions and their vainglories. Flat. Broken up in pieces in a bowl, the matzoh means basically the same thing as it does whole, in a box. The condensed milk is known as the Milk of Affliction. It represents canned food, the food of haste, the fallout shelters, especially in the 50s and early 60s. The meaning of Fox's U Bett Syrup is obscure. It is not a traditional component of *Shulchan Arukh*, the Prepared Table. (119)

Tony, still obsessed, becomes concerned that his rant about his father, of whom he has said "is like molecularly incapable of conceiving that he maybe does less than his FATHER did because it's like Jewish men, it's this sick thing, isn't it, it's this sick thing, this sick sick sick sick sick thing they have with their fathers" means he is "self-hating" and does not know what to make of the fact that he loves Passover, but hates that his family skips the elaboration—the hard parts of their traditions—and do not "explicate or enumerate or niggle or nit pick" (118–20).

Tony and Michael proceed to discuss aspects of Passover, while Tony criticizes the memorization of Hebrew by small children who "can barely read *Green Eggs and Ham*" (120), but must reproduce the Hebrew flawlessly because if not, the child knows that "like *the whole year to follow and his life along with it will be cursed, the crops will fail and Elijah won't come because YOU FORGOT WHAT COMES AFTER MA NISHTANAH ETCETERA* and like that's not affliction?" (120).

Michael endeavors to return their attentions to the fifteen verses of *Dayenu* and, as Tony, injects, "to read and do exegis on the part everybody skips" (121). This part concerns five rabbis, but essentially the deceased Rabbi Akiba, the "greatest Mishmaic tanna of them all" (121). When Moses received the Ten Commandments he asked God why there were little curlicues on the Hebrew letters, the points and thorns and God said turn around and Moses did and lo, he was looking, two thousand years in the future, looking through a window into Rabbi Akiba's Yeshiva in Bene Berok, and Akiba was doing exegis on the five books of Moses, which Moses of course had yet to write, and Moses turned back around again and God said, "that man Akiba is so smart he will be able to interpret even the curlicues on the letters of the words of the books you will someday write." (121)

As Michael and Tony discuss aspects of Exodus and various historical rabbis, Tony proposes that this part of the Seder is skipped over because of the "tension set up in the form of the Seder between the forward-moving motional urgency of appetite, on the one hand, and the profound reluctance on the other hand of true critical thought to move ahead" (123). The cumulative "genetic memory" (123) of Jews for past Seders, in which fathers and sons competed to *elaborate* the most, may also explain it, Tony suggests.

Michael and Tony further explain that the plague section is another that is typically skipped over because it is "lengthy, confusing, too close to dinner to be endured, and exceedingly blood-curdling" (123), which allows Kushner to raise the background of violence in Judaic history. Tony explains that the discussion of the plagues contains the mnemonic, *Detzakh Adash Beahab*, the letters of which contain the first letters of the ten plagues and which translates, "A scorpion bit my uncle" (123). This led Jewish tribes residing from North Africa to Tijuana, Mexico, to compose a Pesach counting song, "A Scorpion Bit My Uncle," which has been abandoned in the modern era, Michael explains, "due to the arrival of modern insecticides and a concomitant lessening of the anxieties provoked by the mnemonic" (124).

Tony returns to his discussion of "passing over with many a great sigh the imponderably weighty inheritance of millennia of Jewish intellectual, theological, political, historical, mystical *effort*" (124), an unfortunate cultural tendency that imponderability creates as a symptom a desire to skip it, "the elegant uneasy skip of the dilettante" (124). Michael points out the lesson of the story—the importance of understanding even the curlicues—while Tony points to the "ache of insufficiency. The tribal genetically encoded Darwinian anxiety of inexorable decline down through the generations, the entropic cooling down unto Death" (124). Michael notes that the skipping of this "brief odd strobic glimpse" of Akiba and the other ancient rabbis—"these protean daddies"—who raise the question of how the future receives the story of Exodus and "the imponderable burden" of the "unreasonable difficulty" (124–25) of Judaism—is unfortunate. The Jew, Tony explains, must remember everything, an "unappeasably hard" (125) demand, and it must be understood, after which must come a full elaboration on that understanding. The freeing of the slave "only commences the wandering of the now-homeless," Michael explains, the freed slave is still not free, the Exodus is "also an affliction" (125).

Michael asks why the night of Passover is different from other nights: "On all other nights gay Jewish men are channeling their great-great-grandmothers from the Russian Pale" (125). And perhaps, Michael imagines, the rabbis are working out "strategies of resistance" instead of merely recounting the Exodus: "The garrison is weak, that one is vulnerably positioned, we might roll big stones off the tops of those cliffs and bash in the skull of that centurion, this captain, that governor. Is Death a part of the miracle that brings liberation?" (126). Exodus, the act of freeing oneself from one constraint, oppression, or trial, places one within another, so, Kushner argues in *Notes on Akiba*, it is "a liberation and also an affliction" (126). As the play ends, Kushner has Michael say that the frequently skipped Akiba story offers "a quadruple benediction: The Place, God, The Torah, God. Ha-Makon, Hebrew for 'The place,' is one of God's many names" (126). Seeking "the place" is a journey, Kushner allows his dramatic alter ego to stress, "towards which perhaps we are wandering" (126)—and Kushner, as in *Angels* and other works, depicts existence and death as a journeying, not necessarily to a reward, but, in itself, a strategy of existing, of finding meaning, of surviving.

The Transmutation of Horror into Meaning: *Reverse Transcription.* *Six Playwrights Bury a Seventh, A Ten-Minute Play That's Nearly Twenty Minutes Long*

Themes of loss and change are central to Kushner's *Reverse Transcription. Six Playwrights Bury a Seventh, A Ten-Minute Play That's Nearly Twenty Minutes Long*, a 1996 play premiered at the Humana Festival of New American Plays at the Actors Theatre of Louisville. Finding the ten-minute form "preposterous" (Greene 17), Kushner crafted an amusing depiction of fictional playwrights based on aspects of Kushner's peers whose descriptions make some of them familiar to audiences. Although Kushner claimed that he found it "fun to try" the ten-minute format, he added, "I immediately failed" (Greene 17). This play is not without some intriguing elements, particularly as it explores the role and struggles of the artist. This riff on the strains of being a contemporary playwright was called "one big in-joke" (Greene 17) by at least one critic, but it is an interesting opportunity for Kushner to argue, in a somewhat lighthearted tone, about the pros and cons of the dramatist's life, the value of theater in general, the nature of literature, and, as always in Kushner's work, the sufferings of life and the fears and fantasies of death or other, unknown worlds.

Reverse Transcription begins with a sublimely self-deprecating joke told through the recorded Voice of the Playwright (Kushner's own voice at Louisville) that the play includes seven characters, "too many for a ten-minute play. It'll be twenty minutes long! Fuck it. One of them is dead and the others can all talk fast" (117–18). As the action commences, six playwrights find themselves on Abel's Hill, an old Yankee cemetery on Martha's Vineyard, where a seventh playwright, Ding, has asked to be buried following his death from AIDS. Improbably, they have brought Ding's body here for a secret burial. The six live writers are a bold assortment of types, varying in ethnic backgrounds, sexual orientations, and levels of success: some are critically acclaimed, some are unknown; some are rich and frequently produced, some are struggling and comparatively unknown; some are prolific, some are not. The difficulty of developing six characters in such a short form provides a significant challenge which Kushner addresses by allowing each to be a type, requiring the audience to fill in some of the more obvious blanks. Each character announces his or her own particular characteristics and distinguishing sufferings, allowing connections to be made among the characters in their human and professional struggles and yearnings. Curiously, it is the deceased Ding who emerges most vividly, both as an inspiration and as an object of affection to the others. They are drawn together, despite their many disagreements and jealousies, in mutual sadness over losing Ding. The playwrights are a contentious group, and only in the play's final moments, as they finally prepare to break ground to bury Ding, do they come together to share some fleeting insights on their craft and art.

Abel's Hill, an exclusive cemetery where Lillian Hellman and John Belushi are buried, is now "way too expensive for any mortal to get a plot in" (118), so the conspiratorial playwrights are burying Ding illegally at midnight. Hautflote, a thirtyish playwright who writes beautiful plays with little financial success and who was Ding's closest friend, leads the others to the top of a rise to a peaceful spot selected as Ding's final resting place. However, this place is not peaceful for long as the slightly inebriated, bickering group breathlessly arrives behind Hautflote, who carries Ding's corpse wrapped in a winding sheet. Hautflote tries in vain to get the others to begin digging, but all relish, as Kushner suggests in his stage directions, this clandestine adventure while underneath their mirth is "a very deep grief" (116).

One of the group, Ottoline, a fiftyish African-American woman writer of experimental plays who works in relative obscurity, worries over the legality of what they are about to do, while Biff, a "scruffy, bisexual" (115) young writer of somewhat superficial political plays, finds the life of an American playwright lacking in "dignity" (118). Ottoline remarks on the fact that the cemetery is filled with the colonial forefathers of the United States, while Aspera, a lesbian writer who cannot get her works produced in America despite critical acclaim in England, scoffs, "Oh fuck me, 'forefatherly'; John Belushi's buried here," and Flatty, a "good writer, hugely prolific," jokes that Belushi had "enough drugs in him when he died to poison all the waters from here to Nantucket" (117–19).

Ottoline's reduced circumstances cause her to worry about the cost of the trip to Martha's Vineyard, so the financially secure Flatty offers to pay her fare. Biff seizes the opportunity of being in a holy place to pray, "O come to me short sweet simple idea!" (119), and he continues to lament the plight of playwrights. Describing Bertolt Brecht's journey throughout the world following his exile from Germany at the rise of the Nazis, Biff posits that dramatists are actually "Never in exile, always in extremis" (120). Thinking about the contemporary struggles of art and politics, he talks of his recurring dream of "shooting Jesse Helms in the head" (120), but admits that "you do not dream a play, you *write* a play" (120). Falling into self-pity, Biff whines, "I repulse myself, I am not of this earth, if I were more serious I would be an essayist if I were more observant a

Figure 14: The cast of the 1996 Actors Theatre of Louisville production of Tony Kushner's *Reverse Transcription*. Photo by Richard Trigg.

novelist more articulate more intelligent a poet more ... succinct more *ballsy* a screenwriter and then I could buy an apartment" (120).

Some of the playwrights sadly recall Ding's final days battling AIDS, while Aspera picks up on Biff's self-pity, decrying her successful exile in London and the seeming impossibility of getting her plays produced in her homeland. Happy, a bored but rich Hollywood writer whose early plays were much admired, articulates the meaning of the play's title when he explains that HIV "reads and writes its genetic alphabet backwards, RNA transcribing DNA transcribing RNA, hence *retro*virus, reverse transcription," comparing it with reading Hebrew "backwards" (121). Realizing that he has hit upon a "metaphor doomed to fail" (121), Happy explains:

> I mean here we are, playwrights in a graveyard, here to dig, right? So, digging, I think: HIV, reverse transcribing, dust to dust, writing backwards, Hebrew and the Great and Terrible magic of that backwards alphabet, which runs against the grain, counter to the current of European traditions, heritage, thought: a language of fiery, consuming revelation, of refusal, the proper way, so I was taught, to address oneself to God ... (*He puts his hands on Ding's body*) Perhaps, maybe, this backwards-writing viral nightmare is keeping some secret, subterraneanly affianced to a principle of ... Reversals: good reversals and also very bad, where good

meets bad, perhaps, the place of mystery where back meets forth, where our sorrow's not the point, where the forward flow of life brutally throws itself into reverse, to reveal . . . (*He lies alongside the body, curls up to it, head on Ding's shoulder, listening*) What? Hebrew always looked to me like zipper teeth unzipped. What awesome thing is it we're zipping open? To what do we return when we write in reverse? What's relinquished, what's released? (121)

Aspera angrily objects to the equating of HIV with a language ("I'm going to beat you up" [121], she tells Happy), but he assures her that he does not mean to diminish the tragedy of AIDS. Aspera then shifts her rancor to the wealthy Flatty, who matter-of-factly agrees with her derision about his money: "I'm richer than essayists, novelists, at least the respectable ones, and all poets ever" (122).

Ottoline only envies Flatty's flattering reviews, realizing that the dramaturgical path she treads is "perverse": "What I have done no one has ever done and no one does it nearly so well. But what I do is break the vessels because they never fit me right and I despise their elegance and I like the sound the breaking makes" (122). However, she still longs for a hit, not just another Obie Award. Hautflote finally manages to get them all to move toward digging Ding's grave, but before anything can be accomplished ruminations begin on the meanings of the breaking of ground. Happy, continuing to back away from equating AIDS and Hebrew, falls back into considering what writing is:

It's just the words: reverse transcription. *Thinking* about it. Something I can't help doing. Writing began with the effort to record speech. All writing is an attempt to fix intangibles—thought, speech, what the eye observes—fixed on clay tablets, in stone, on paper. Writers *capture*. We playwrights on the other hand write or rather "wright" to set these free again. Not inscribing, not de-scribing but . . . ex-scribing (?) . . . "W-R-I-G-H-T," that archaism, because it's something earlier we do, cruder, something one does with one's mitts, one's paws. To claw words up . . . ! (124)

And with that, Happy drops to his knees to dig with his hands to "startle words back into the air again, to . . . evanesce. It is . . . unwriting, to do it is to die, yes, but. A lively form of doom" (124). Happy continues digging, finally arriving at the conclusion that "It's not about *equation*. It's about the transmutation of horror into meaning" (124).

The others join Happy in digging while Aspera offers a benediction: "Good night old Ding. Rest easy baby and flights of self-dramatizing hypochondriacal hypersensitive self-pitying paroxysmical angels saddlebag you off to sleep" (124). Hautflote describes graves as "centographs," mere "empty tombs, honorifics. Sailors lost on whalers, lost at sea, no body ever found, air and memory interred instead," adding that the other grave markers are "peristalithic to these few empty tombs, whose ghostly drama utterly overwhelms The Real" (124–25). And, as they continue to dig and the play concludes, Flatty brings them back to The Real as he wonders, "Doesn't David Mamet live around here somewhere?" (125).

Mel Gussow, writing about *Reverse Transcription* in its premiere at the Humana Festival, felt it "amusingly represented" (54) the ten-minute form, despite its greater length, while other critics limited their few comments on the play to guessing which character was which real playwright. Although a play unlikely to be frequently produced, Kushner reveals some intriguing attitudes about his chosen profession and his own writing drive in *Reverse Transcription*. As a gay man, a Jew, a political liberal, and an artist in late-twentieth-century America, Kushner belongs to a staggering collection of marginalized, oppressed groups. He is, in essence, the reversed transcription of an American citizen—a role which has led him, as a writer, to evanesce, to attempt to transcribe his world, to strive for the impossibility of capturing the intangible—to transmute horror into meaning.

To Be with You Alone: *Terminating, or Lass Meine Schmerzen Nicht Verloren Sein, or Ambivalence*

Kushner contributed a one-act play, *Terminating, or Lass Meine Schmerzen Nicht Verloren Sein, or Ambivalence,* inspired by William Shakespeare's seventy-fifth sonnet, to a bill of one-acts by several contemporary American playwrights (including Eric Bogosian, John Guare, Marsha Norman, Ntozake Shange, Wendy Wasserstein, and William Finn) called *Love's Fire.* Staged by The Acting Company for a tour of the United States throughout 1997, *Love's Fire* concluded in a month-long run at New York's Public Theatre during the summer of 1998.

Terminating, which is set in a present-day psychiatrist's office, focuses on Hendryk, a bizarrely disturbed and loquacious intellectual who believes himself to be in love with his shrink, Esther, who has recently terminated Hendryk's therapy. Esther is, in fact, afraid of Hendryk, a "godforsaken mess" (47), and she tries to convince him that his feelings of love for her are just transference. He retorts that all love is transference, begging desperately to sleep with her. Esther tries to laugh this off, pointing out that Hendryk is, in fact, gay. When he calls her "a dyke" (51) in response, she tries to deny it, but he insists: "You wear . . . *Harley Davidson boots* and you have short hair" (51).

Esther and Hendryk see visions of their lovers as they continue their serio-comic battle of wills. Esther's domestic partner, Dympha, is younger than Esther and prone to possessiveness, while Hendryk's lover, Billygoat, appears on stage occasionally to spout bits of Shakespearean love poetry—"So are you to my thoughts as food to life" (52)—to distract Hendryk. He tries to ignore these intrusions, shouting, "SHUT UP! I hate the sonnets. Boring boring boring" (52). However, this is not completely true, for the terminally ambivalent Hendryk speaks in an incessant torrent of literary references—a bit of Kushnerian self-mockery, although this is the only aspect of Hendryk that seems at all like his author. Hendryk's speech also reveals a stream of hilarious contradictions and bizarre juxtapositions, underscoring Kushner's central exploration of the power and failure of language to communicate feeling. Other than Billygoat's comic intrusions, Shakespeare is in little obvious evidence in *Terminating,* although the phrase "Possessing and pursuing no delight" permeates its essence. The lyrical language, episodic scene structure, startlingly original characterizations, and universality of themes is typical of the quality of Shakespeare's plays—and of Kushner's as well. Critics have made much of the connections between Kushner's dramas and Brecht's, but the influence of Shakespeare is here exposed to be, in its way, as important in Kushner's work.

As Esther and Hendryk continue to debate, Dympha and Billygoat float in and out of their thoughts as the possessing and pursuing continues. Hendryk persists in pleading with Esther to sleep with him, so she threatens to charge him for this unscheduled visit. He compares her unfavorably with historical analysts who had "unshakable faith" in what they perceived about human nature while she, like most people he sees around him, are mired in "ambivalence" (53):

> So like those priests who wind up sleeping with children, it's not their fault, I mean we should put them in prison of course kill them probably who knows I know that's bad to say but there are days when everyone, um seems like everyone should be killed, you know? In a world in which no structure rests assuredly, with assurancy on a foundation in which nothing comes with a metaphysical guarantee, because even, take even an old atheist like Freud, God was still *watching*, he was *watching* all the way up until so-on-and-so-forth but today, today . . . Well, take me for instance.
>
> *Only you have ever been watching me.* For five years.
>
> And nothing lasts longer than five years. Used to be, used to be . . . ten at least. And so abuse of your . . . of *one's* . . . wards, patients, *inferiors*, subjects. Well it's wrong but not absolutely so because there simply are no absolutes, and. The, uh. (53–54)

Hendryk whines that Esther refuses to sleep with him because he is fat (he also confesses to urinating in his pants on the subway), but his central disorder seems to be his anxiety over the lack of absolutes. Esther is reduced to little more than his foil as Hendryk riffs on the anxieties of life at the end of the twentieth century, making a bizarre leap to explaining that people get tattooed because of their ambivalence—because "tattoos last" (54). He recounts seeing a heavily tattooed man who was "like an epidermatological crisis," adding that the man "must've really enjoyed that suffering, bet he remembers every inky little needle stick. This is how he knows he's been here. Because it hurt to be" (55). For Hendryk, the tattoos are an inscription of existence; the man cannot change the world, but he can change "this small world" (55) of his skin, a metaphor Kushner uses to suggest his own progressive political anxieties about the seeming impossibility of bringing about needed change in the world.

"Ambivalence," Hendryk states, "expands our options" (55), and, as he sees it, the more ambivalent we are, the more free we are. Driving home the point, he insists that we become desperate in our ambivalent existence to find "non-ambivalent things like tattoos," which, despite their apparent permanence are, he believes, mostly "markers of how ambivalent and impermanent we are or feel we are" (55–56). When Esther points out that present-day tattoos are easily removable, Hendryk grumbles as his metaphorical construction collapses, "I hate the way you introduce irrelevancies" (56).

Shifting back to questions of love and relationships, Hendryk announces that he has a boyfriend who is "beautiful and ... has no soul" (56). While discussing the correlations of beauty and evil, Hendryk bursts out that his mother, as Esther has apparently suggested, did not name him Hendryk because it rhymes with Schmendrik—"SHE WAS DUTCH, FOR CHRIST'S SAKE" (56). He accuses Esther of malpractice and ruining his life for making such a suggestion, but she reminds him that his mother *did* call him Schmendrik. Meanwhile, thinking about his own personal satyr, Billygoat, causes Hendryk to spout short bursts of Shakespearean sonnets—he frequently squeals, "All this coil is long for you" (57)—while talking with Esther. They also get into a tongue-twisting debate over rhymes:

ESTHER: The words are practically homonymic.
HENDRYK: Homophonous, actually, is what you ...
ESTHER: Homonym and homophone are ... Homologues. They're homologous.
HENDRYK: They're homonyms, actually, no homologues, though homophony is the precise ...
ESTHER: But if they're homonymous then they're precisely.... (56–57)

This expands to include references to everything from Oskar Homolka to homosexual, although despite ample evidence to the contrary, Hendryk insists that he is not gay—"I have no talent to be" (57)—adding that the thought of anal sex disgusts him, leading to a rant on the "fragrance" of sexual activity, which, he says, is sometimes "malodorous" (58). Billygoat, however, suddenly appears to add that "shit transforms when you're in love" (58). Hendryk wonders if he has ever truly been in love. To him, Billygoat is "a satyr. A Priapist," but he recognizes that Billygoat does love him, marveling that "nothing human is alien" to Billygoat and that, to him, seems "inhuman" (59).

Dympha appears to insist that Esther part company permanently with Hendryk and Billygoat announces his intention to leave Hendryk because, "You don't love me, Hendryk. And that breaks my heart. It makes me want to die" (59). The relationship of Hendryk and Billygoat bears more than a passing resemblance to the more realistic, fully dimensioned relationship of Louis and Prior in *Angels*, while Esther, as a character, has attributes found in Zillah of *Bright Room* and Bonfila of *Slavs!*

Terminating's focus shifts at this point to Esther, whose own battle with depression is explained when she says, "As a lesbian and a feminist and a rational progressive person and everything I am, as lucky as I am, I know it's bad to say this but I don't give a fuck" (60). Her particular brand of ambivalence is tied to a desire to have a baby. Her despair at failing to have a baby makes her hate her own analyst, who has prescribed Zoloft as a solution, but which Esther believes robs her of "my death-desiring depression" (60), which, she believes, is all that exists of her unconceived baby. What keeps her alive is a "complete lack of hope" (61), for she senses that were she to actually feel some level of hope, it would become possible to kill herself.

Meanwhile, Hendryk and Billygoat have continued to debate the merits of anal sex. Hendryk wonders if his revulsion to it—"poo-poo, yuch"—is innate, while Billygoat insists, "With love's light wings did I o'erperch that revulsion" (62). Hendryk accuses Billygoat of lacking a soul and not understanding ambivalence. Ambivalence, he posits, is not understood by animals because, like Billygoat, they have no soul—"ambivalence," he insists, "is the soul" (62).

Esther continues to try to end this hair-raising session, but Hendryk, who has never laid down on her couch in the great cliché of therapy, now insists on doing so. He complains that the pillow always smells, to which Esther responds, "Many troubled heads have been laid upon it" (63). They return to a heated discussion about Hendryk's mother—and motherhood in general—with Hendryk believing that a mother's ambivalence is "lethal" (56), while also sensing that there is no such thing as paternal ambivalence. According to Hendryk, his father "hated me, till he figured out how to swallow me" (63). Hendryk then drifts off to sleep on Esther's couch, and once she is certain that he is soundly asleep, she quietly complains, "I have problems of my own" (64).

Dympha appears to state that "our inability to love one another is humankind's greatest tragedy" (64). "Generosity makes us free," she insists, and wonders, "Why can't people live up to their moral questions?" (64). This statement reflects the dilemma in many of Kushner's plays and characters. Finding Dympha's notion that the embracing of sacrifice and good work will allow "goodness and mercy" to "follow me all the days of my life" to be "a question in a closet," she wraps some keys in a note and leaves them on Hendryk's chest as she departs.

Critic Ben Brantley called *Terminating* a "deliciously convoluted" (E1) play, with other reviewers, led by John Simon, finding it "hilarious" (77). Richard Zoglin called it "a labored sitcom" (92), but John Hammond appreciated *Terminating* as "a masterpiece of ambivalent angst—a Jules Feiffer cartoon come hilariously to life" (13). It is a Kushner one-act likely to have a long life in professional and amateur theaters.

Swimming in Guilt: *G. David Schine in Hell*

G. David Schine in Hell, a very short 1996 Kushner one-act first published in the *New York Times Magazine* under the title *A Backstage Pass to Hell*, is little more than a sketch, written, as Kushner notes, "with apologies to George Bernard Shaw, Philip Roth, God, the Devil and everyone in between" (*Death and Taxes* 229). It gave Kushner an opportunity to bring back the hilarious and frightening vision of Roy Cohn so central to *Angels*, a character so rich in its ability to represent the aggressive hypocrisies of American conservatism that Kushner is clearly reluctant to let him go.

Kushner was inspired to briefly revisit Cohn and other significant figures of his era in response to news of the June 19, 1996 death of G. David Schine (1927–96) in a single-engine plane crash. Schine was a catalyst in one of the most disturbing eras of post–World War II American history, an unwitting central figure (though ultimately insignificant himself) in the political fall of Cohn, and, more importantly, Cohn's boss, Wisconsin Senator Joseph McCarthy (1908–57).

Schine, a McCarthy consultant during the Army-McCarthy hearings in 1953–54—and purportedly the object of Cohn's private desires—became the center of a public storm when McCarthy and Cohn applied inappropriate pressure on the military to get Schine, a private in the Army, preferential treatment and a commission as an officer.

The acrimonious Army-McCarthy hearings, focusing on alleged Communist infiltration of the Army Communications Center at Fort Monmouth, New Jersey, came to a fierce climax when the Army revealed the behind-the-scenes pressures emanating from McCarthy's office and, during testimony, the special treatment Schine had received (including being absent without leave, release from drills, special phone privileges, passes every weekend, and so on). The most damaging evidence unearthed was a doctored photo, presumably manufactured by McCarthy's staff, that added Schine's image to a photo of Secretary of the Army Robert T. Stevens. These hearings—including testimony about Schine—irrevocably damaged McCarthy's public image, eventually leading to the ignominious end of his political career. Following the firestorm of these hearings, Schine continued in the military, rising only to the rank of corporal, after which he left the military and politics to run hotels, theaters, and to serve as executive producer of the 1971 Academy Award–winning film, *The French Connection*.

As *G. David Schine in Hell* begins, Cohn is discovered residing in Hell, much as he is at the end of *Perestroika*. As described by Kushner, Hell is a place resembling "a dinner theater in Orange County California" (231), where Cohn, dressed in a loudly colored tuxedo, holds court while Andrew Lloyd Webber music drones incessantly in the background. Cohn encounters an elderly man newly arrived in Hell, and, after some preliminary misunderstandings, he recognizes the man as G. David Schine, the slow-witted one-time object of his conflicted affections. David, realizing that if Cohn is present, "This *must* be Hell!" insists he belongs in Heaven—"I've been really good, the last fifty years, I mean, not *perfect*, but I produced a hit movie! I married Miss Universe!" (232–33).

Cohn, in the outrageously aggressive manner he exhibits in *Angels*, explains that they are both better off in Hell, for Heaven is "Fulla kvetchy communists" discussing "how the Great Leap Forward turned into the Biggest Bellyflop in History" (233). David asks Cohn who else resides in Hell and Cohn lists: "All Republicans, many Democrats, Jesse Helms—I know he's not really dead but he has a backstage pass" (233). Cohn tells David that he no longer has to look like an old man and, with that, David instantly transforms into his former self as a handsome young man dressed in a G. I. uniform. David asks why Cohn has not transformed himself into a more youthful image, to which Cohn replies, "as the very Embodiment or rather as the Spirit of American Conservatism," he cannot change (234). Cohn is ecstatic to see the attractive young David again—"like the replacement lead in a Tarzan movie"—the man whom Cohn says helped push McCarthy "to perdition" for "our story is epic, it's tragic, it's ... *South Pacific*, Dave, my doomed love for you turned you into history...." (235).

Suddenly, the "Internationale" is heard playing in the background and a third man appears, yet another important figure in the political intrigues of the 1950s, Alger Hiss (1904–96), visiting Hell for "a little comforting conservative certainty" even though, he says, it must be obtained at the price of "an appalling degree of moral shortsightedness" (237). As a diplomat who had accompanied President Roosevelt to the 1945 Yalta Conference, Hiss was accused in 1948 of having been a Communist spy in the State Department during the 1930s. Hiss denied the charges before Congress and in related court cases, but with the testimony of Whittaker Chambers, a onetime Soviet agent, Hiss was convicted and served over three and a half years in prison. Richard M. Nixon, then a junior Congressman, sprang to national attention as a result of his involvement in helping to build a case against Hiss, and the conviction of Hiss provided McCarthy with the necessary credibility to charge that the U. S. State Department was infested with Communists.

In Heaven, Hiss complains, "everyone's swimming in guilt, ideological confusion, and the *questions*, my God!" (237). Many of the questions directed at Hiss are apparently about the meaning of the political struggles of the Cold War era and whether or not Hiss was actually guilty of what he was accused of, but Hiss dismissively protests, "Do I look like Tiresias?" (237). Hiss scoffs at the "endless soul-searching" in Heaven. He says that the conservatives in Hell "haven't got any souls to search" (238). As the three men gossip about old rumors—"You fellows really were queers, huh, it wasn't just gossip?" Hiss asks—they are interrupted by a burst of "Hail to the Chief" as Richard M. Nixon (1913–94), the thirty-seventh President of the United States, fresh from "finishing my 75th volume of memoirs and geopolitical stratagems" arrives, adding that "just because I'm dead doesn't mean I have to stop writing" (239). Nixon gripes about life in Hell—"too many meetings"—and every few words he speaks are interrupted by "(expletive deleted)" (239). Unlike his old nemesis Hiss, Nixon longs to go to Heaven, "where people still believe in Government. I want some (expletive deleted) respect," but Hiss informs Nixon that in Heaven they "despise you" to which Cohn adds, "We hate him down here too. The man's entirely devoid of charm. He's hated everywhere. It's a talent he has," but unphased, Nixon responds, "Bob Dole likes me" (239).

Abruptly, "Glinda's entrance music" is heard playing in the background and a "dumpy man with a face like a Walt Kelly bulldog, wearing a black Chanel dress, hose and stiletto pumps" (240) enters. It is, of course, J. Edgar Hoover (1895–1972), whose drag inspires Nixon to attack the "gender confusion" (240) he finds rampant in Hell. The stunned Schine, recognizing Hoover, turns to Cohn whining, "I'm real confused," to which Cohn flamboyantly replies, "Of course you are, beautiful!" (8) as the play ends.

The connections between *Angels* and this little play extend well beyond the inclusion of Cohn. *G. David Schine in Hell* could easily fit into *Perestroika*, as its mixture of history, fantasy, and outrageous humor coincides with those aspects of *Angels*, as well as Kushner's depiction of the traditional battles between the twentieth century's conservative and liberal political poles.

My Tight-Wound Soul: *And the Torso Even More So*

After premiering *Slavs!* in 1994 and *Reverse Transcription* in 1996 at the Actors Theatre of Louisville Humana Festival of New American Plays, Kushner contributed a brief and amusing trifle, *And the Torso Even More So*, a "T-shirt" play, to the 1999 Humana Festival. In it, Kushner comically reveals that even a t-shirt is held together by the contradictory: the Woof, the horizontal threads, and the Warp, the vertical threads. The Warp is depressed—his "tight wound soul descends; You'll never understand: I'm *deep, bereft*"—while the Woof is weary of "shuttling through this weave," longing to unravel their "sleeve of care" (305) and see the wide world. The Warp begs the Woof not to leave and reveal "naked flesh undressed," so the Woof reluctantly agrees to hang together, "For now," as the Warp continues to be "distressed ... " (305). This lighthearted trifle was written as Kushner revised and prepared for production of another, considerably more substantial, one-act, *Home Body/Kabul*.

Marvelous Dislocations: *Home Body/Kabul*

Home Body/Kabul, which premiered in London in the summer of 1999, is a monologue written in 1997 featuring a single female character and although its tone is far less comic than that of *And the Torso Even More So*—and much of Kushner's one-act work—its central, unnamed woman character, connects to his other women characters, especially Harper of *Angels*, who is similarly isolated and imagines a world far from her own.

First staged at London's Chelsea Theatre Centre from July 12–31, 1999 (it had previously been given a workshop reading at the Chelsea in December 1997 and at the Alley Theatre in Houston, Texas, on June 26, 1998), *Home Body/Kabul* was written for actress Kika Markham, a friend of Kushner's, who gave a virtuoso performance of the play's sole character/narrator. This mesmeric woman admits to talking too much and, as is slowly revealed, she also cares perhaps too much about the history and present circumstances of Afghanistan. The woman, who feels an inability to connect, is first seen immersed in reading an old guidebook about the Afghan city of Kabul, a place, she says, that "as we all know, has ... undergone change" (1). She discusses her impassioned way of researching a subject she finds interesting—and this armchair traveler is fascinated by Kabul. In her studies, she seeks "not the source but all that which was dropped by the wayside on the way to the source": material from magazines, old political tracts, and guidebooks. These, for her, are "irrelevant and irresistible, spooky, dreamy, the knowing what *was* known before the more that has since become known overwhelms" (1). *Home Body/Kabul* is, as critic Sheridan Morley writes, "a memoir, a travelogue, a poem, the history of a nation wrecked by tourism and capitalism and internecine strife and tribal loyalty. It's also a lament for one woman's inability to connect, except of course with us" (42).

For Kushner, "the real heart of what happens in drama is in some kind of dialogue" (Edwardes, n.p.), and in *Home Body/Kabul* that dialogue is between its only character and the audience. The woman, seated alone in comfortable isolation, reads aloud historical facts about Kabul from her guidebook, illuminating the dawn of history there around 3,000 B.C. when "magic beliefs are immensely strong" (2)—before colonization led to the destruction of such beliefs. She talks of the loss of privacy and the necessity for all things to be touched—a process of corruption that she finds disturbing, but she adds that it is always thus to those living through a time: "The Present is *always* an awful place to be" (3). She reasons that the ability to look back over recent decades and sense a "recedence," a loss, is somewhat made up for by the understanding of the sufferings of a time that becomes possible—a distance that provides a period to be "illumined from within" (3–4).

Continuing to read from the guidebook, the woman provides rich descriptions of Kabul's rich and varied historical past, from the conquests of Alexander the Great to various local tribes' wars over territory. Proclaiming, "Oh I love the world" (5), she apologizes to the audience for her way of speaking which, she claims, comes from having read too many books. Noting that even her parents do not speak as she does, the woman attributes it to "an *alien influence*," adding, however, that "my borders have only ever been broached by books" (6). It is apparent that she longs for even further broadening. The isolation in which the woman lives seems to spark her imagination, much as it does with Harper in *Angels*. Harper, trapped in a similarly troubled marriage, floats away on Valium-fueled imaginative journeys to exotic places. Harper spends her trips in Antarctica, while the woman in *Home Body/Kabul* imagines herself to be in the deeply troubled nation of Afghanistan. This country, and the city of Kabul in particular, are used by Kushner to reflect the woman's mental state as it is, a place that is both wondrously exotic and profoundly unsettled. This is a play of paradoxes in which, as critic Robert Hewison writes, Kushner juxtaposes "two ruling attitudes," commingling a "wealthy, civilised West to the underdeveloped, savage East" (20).

The woman describes her husband who, she says, cannot bear her talk or her passionate interest in other cultures, so "I rarely speak to him anymore" (6). They each take different antidepressant drugs, but she worries about the impact of these chemicals on her body. She also occasionally takes her husband's pill instead of her own so that she might "know what he's feeling," adding that he never takes hers and she finds "his refusal to sample dull" (7).

Planning for a party in honor of her husband's "having completed some joyless task at his place of business" (8), she plans to enliven the party with some dazzling fezlike hats she remembers seeing in a shop window. The party, she fears, will be a typical one with "lovely lovely people" who "affect one another, one might even say *afflict* one another," so that "powerful antidepressants are consumed" (9). Discussing the workings of her particular antidepressant, the woman imagines it as a kind of "talented salt" in which her brain floats like a pickle in brine, wondering how it could leaven depression, but finding it a sufficiently "pleasing image which cheers one and makes life's burdens less difficult to bear" (10–11).

As she continues to read the guidebook, the woman repeatedly interrupts herself to consider "these abbreviated fezlike pillboxy attenuated yarmulkite millinarisms, um, hats," she wants for the party, but which she prizes as "doodahs of a culture once aswarm with spirit matter, radiant with potent magic" (12). Struggling to remember where she saw the shop selling these wondrous hats, the woman explains that she ultimately found it and that it was run by Afghan refugees. She shows the audience one of the hats which, she explains, conjures "not bygone days of magic belief but the suffering behind the craft; this century has taught us to direct our imagination however fleetingly toward the hidden suffering: the appropriation, the exploitation" (13). She ponders how, without her sort of research, could the attitudes and feelings of the maker of such a hat— "the product of some variant of slavery"—ever be known or understood. She imagines the village where the hat was made, a place still "resisting the onslaught of modernity" (13). She equates the hats, which "are beautiful; relatively inexpensive; sinister if you've a mind to see them that way; and sad," as "dislocations are. And marvelous, as dislocations are. Always bloody" (14).

Donning the hat, the woman continues to read from her guidebook about Kabul. She explains that little archaeological digging has been done there, but recently "the bodies of two thousand Taliban soldiers were found in a mass grave in northern Afghanistan, prisoners who were executed apparently by soldiers loyal to the overthrown government of Burhanuddin Rabbani, so someone is digging" (15). The guidebook reveals centuries of upheavals, slaughters, and tribal factions, which she compares to the late-twentieth-century tragedies of Afghanistan. As a result, the artifacts in the shop where she buys the hat take on significance as remnants of a decimated culture. In that little shop, she imagines "all the caravanserai camels or elephants or horses" flopping down to die of exhaustion there, "of shock, of the heartache of refugees, the goods simply piled high upon their dromedary bones, just where they came to rest, and set up shop atop the carcasses, and so on" (18). She worries about the obvious fact that, as one critic pointed out, "touching without understanding corrupts" and that "we are doomed to corrupt almost everything we explore" (Halliburton 9).

Returning to her account of purchasing the hats, the woman talks of encountering the shop clerk, an Afghan man approximately her age, who, she notices, is missing three fingers on his right hand. She imagines these have been hacked off by a hatchet blade and tries to avoid staring, but cannot seem to help allowing her mind's eye to "detail that poor ruined hand slipping my MasterCard into the . . . You know, that thing, that roller press thing which is used to. . . . Never mind. Here, in London, that poor ruined hand" (19). Trying to envisage the events that led to the loss of the man's fingers, she can only conclude, "I know nothing of this hand, its history, of course, nothing" (19).

It becomes clear that the woman's fascination with Kabul's turbulent past, and its present, results from skimming through her guidebook for information about nineteenth- and twentieth-century atrocities. She continues through to the period in which Afghanistan is armed by the Soviet Union against Pakistan, an era in which "the U.S. refuses assistance, militant Islamic movements form the seed of what will become the Mujahideen, the U.S. begins sending money, much civil strife, approaching at times a state of civil war, over liberal reforms" leading to the Soviet invasion during which the Soviets "for ten years do their best to outdo the Hephthalites in savagery, in barbarism, then like so many other empires traversing the Hindu Kush the USSR is swept away, and now the Taliban, and ... Well" (21). She decries Afghan poverty and the fact that the nation's infrastructure lies in ruin.

In a typically Kushnerian imaginative leap, the woman realizes that she is suddenly able to speak Pushtu as she pays for her hats. Noticing that the man "is very beautiful" with a face full of "lines inscribed by hardships, siroccos and strife, battle scars, perhaps, well certainly the marks of some battle, some life unimaginably more difficult than my own," she uses her new linguistic skill to ask him what happened to his hand, recalling a Spanish anarchist—a former prisoner of Canovas who spoke in Trafalgar Square to a sympathetic crowd—who held up his hand to show that it had been burned by his former captors and "the crowd fell silent and the bodies of those present swayed together like leaves caught in a breeze, silent, merely at the sight of a pair of scarred palms" (22).

The woman imagines various reasons for the ruination of the man's hand: he was with the Mujahideen or the Russians, he stole bread for his starving family or "stole bread *from* a starving family" (22). The reasons are not clear, which raises questions of culpability. The woman says:

> I have nothing to say about guilt, or culpability, for we are all culpable. Our own individual degrees of culpability being entirely bound up in our correspondent degrees of action, malevolent or not, well-intended or otherwise; or in our correspondent degrees of inertia, which can be taken as a form of malevolent action if you've a mind to see it that way. I do. I've such a mind. (23)

Further issues of guilt are examined through the metaphor of a friend who responds, "Might do," to most questions, leading the woman to consider the "abeyant residual of the tension between the wavering of 'might', which expresses equivocation but also suggests power, doesn't it? As in 'mighty'; and 'do': the hold, 'm-m-m-i-i-i-ght' and the forward charge, 'DO', into action!" (24). Reflecting on the "awful times" of the present, she asks, "What has this century taught the civilized if not a profound mistrust of all those who have nothing to do with, no use for 'might do'? Contempt for those who merely contemplate; the lock-up and the lethal injection for those who Do" (24). She seems to be explaining all this to the Afghan man in whose presence she feels "absolute terror of your censure and disdain" (24). However, as he completes the sale of the hats, he tells someone at the back of the shop that he is taking the rest of the afternoon off and, taking the woman's arm, escorts her on a tour of Kabul. She finds herself seeing the places she has read about in the guidebook and, at the same time, finds that the "scent of the hat merchant takes me by surprise, toasted almonds, and he smiles a broader shy smile which shatters his face into a thousand shards" (26).

She imagines they are in Bemaru, "thought to be the grave of Bibi Mahru, the Moon-Faced Lady, who died of grief when her betrothed was reported slain on the battlefield, but he wasn't slain, he'd only lost his hand" (26). Here, she and the hat merchant "make love beneath a chindar tree" and "he places his hand inside me, it seems to me his whole hand inside me, and it seems to me a whole hand" (27). Suddenly, she is back in the shop and the hat merchant hands her the bag with the hats she has purchased and "a chill wind blows up my bones and I long to be back in the safety of my kitchen" (27). She finds herself wondering whether the dosage of her antidepressant is too strong as she leaves the shop.

The woman reveals she has a child—a girl—for whom "alas nothing ever seems to go well" and that she is at fault, or is at least told so by "my husband the near-mute purveyor of reproachful lids-lowered glances" (27–28). This unhappy woman reveals, "We all loved one another, once, but today it simply isn't so or isn't what it used to be, it's . . . well, love" (28). Describing herself as a narcissist, she returns to her earlier proclamation of love for the world, which, she acknowledges, is "inexcusable and vague, suspect but it's all I can say for myself, I love the world at its most rotund and orbicular, at its most vast and unembraceable" (28), but she realizes that such language is

> merely fog to blur the lineaments of an ugly incapacity. To love, a narcissism which seeks in the outsized and the impossible to clearly comprehend a reflection commensurate with its own oceanic . . . of, well, I suppose of the extent to which the soul excuse me I mean the self is always an insoluble mystery to the narcissist who flatters herself that feeling of vagueness always hanging about her which not a salt in the world can cure is something grand, oceanic, titantically erotic while of course what it really is is nothing more than an inadequately shaped unsteady incoherent . . . quoggy sort of bubble where the solid core ought to be. (28–29)

She explains that the paradox of the narcissist is that she cannot stand being by herself, that "we become lost in our own guidebooks and less able to be rescued by the guidebooks of others" (29). We find ways to "pierce the silence of the private with public utterance, or rather public mutterance, for it's noise and not meaning by means of which all that which is touched and connected, by means of which we connect, and connect only furtively in a kind of conspiracy, a conspiracy to extrude . . . um, the dangers of silent spaces" (29).

As the play ends, the woman says that the hats had the desired effect on her party guests. Chatting with several of her friends, one asks how she even knows that the man who sold her the hats was an Afghan, to which the woman asks, "'Would you make love to a stranger with a mutilated hand if the opportunity was offered you?' 'Might do,' she says" (30). With that, the woman begins singing "It's Nice to Go Trav'ling," a song made famous by Frank Sinatra, "Such an awful man, such perfect perfect music! A paradox!" and returns to her guidebook to read of Kabul, "for only through an encounter with the beautiful and strange may one be moved" (30–31).

London critics commented with some surprise that a Kushner premiere would take place in a small fringe theater, but most applauded the appropriateness of the setting for such an intimate and personal drama. Critics also compared the play, mostly favorably, with Martin Sherman's one-woman play *Rose*, starring Olympia Dukakis, which opened at the Royal National Theatre of Great Britain within days of *Home Body/Kabul*. That play more prosaically deals with the reminiscences of an eighty-year-old Jewish woman, from her experiences in a Ukrainian shtetl to Nazi-occupied Warsaw to present-day Miami Beach. Sheridan Morley found Kushner's play "vastly more multi-layered and complex," adding that "Kushner's lyrical, butterfly mind and his curious talent for finding joy even in dark despair, the commonplace in the extraordinary, keeps his potent verbal avalanche within some sort of context" (10), while Patrick Marmion found it "a mysterious voyage combining the epic and the intimate" (35).

Kika Markham, who, along with the Chelsea Theatre Centre, had commissioned *Home Body/Kabul*, won considerable praise for her performance, with Nigel Cliff writing that she "does full justice to the fierce intelligence of Kushner's script; she establishes just the right arm's-length rapport with the audience" (19). Susannah Clapp called *Home Body/Kabul* a "purposely elusive monologue," but found that there are "unsatisfactory as well as intriguing aspects to this" (9). Reviewer Rachel Halliburton noted the political ramifications of the play, the "accusations about our political attitudes," and the implied contempt the woman and, by logical extension, Kushner, feels for those "who merely contemplate" (9). Mark Shenton found the small Chelsea Theatre space "allows the play to speak with its own quiet authority and Kushner to display his customary dazzling linguistic ability" (47).

Home Body/Kabul reminds Kushner of the central dilemma of the political dramatist, who struggles to understand that "in a situation like Afghanistan where there's a clear need for action of a direct kind, it's more morally defensible to take that action instead of going off to write some strange, drifty little monologue about it. That's always the dilemma. You either give up writing to become an activist or try to do both" (Edwardes, n.p.).

CHAPTER SEVEN

The Great Work Continues

Screenplays, Activism, and Future Projects

> Pessimism of the intellect, optimism of the will. That's still the formula. The planet may cease to exist over the next 100 years, but I can't be a gay man living in 1999, even given all that's still wrong all over the world for lesbians and gay men, and be blind to the fact that so much has changed in such an incredibly short time.
>
> —Tony Kushner (Edwardes)

Tony Kushner is essentially a dramatist, and is likely to remain so despite increasing opportunities to write for film and television. As early as 1990, Universal Pictures optioned Kushner's Corneille adaptation, *The Illusion*, with a screenplay by Kushner for a film that has yet to be made. In 1995, the possibility that Kushner would write a shooting script for a projected Warner Brothers film, *The Mayor of Castro Street*, about the life of Harvey Milk, with Dustin Hoffman in the lead role, was announced, but it did not pan out. Considerable press attention was focused on a possible collaboration between Kushner and legendary filmmaker Robert Altman to film *Angels* as one or two films. Unfortunately, this collaboration ended, after which it was announced that Mike Nichols would be directing the *Angels* film(s) for HBO. As of 2001, production had not commenced, but Kushner had completed another screenplay—also as yet unproduced—providing examples of his theatrical imagination which is, in many respects, cinematic. Kushner worries about a shift to screenwriting, which he sees as "primarily a narrative art":

> I don't think that's true of playwriting, which is dialogic and dialectic, and is fundamentally always more about an argument than it is about narrative progression. I suspect, in fact, that novel writing and screenwriting have more in common than playwriting has with either of the other forms. So, yes, I'm very worried about it,

because I think that a lot of talented playwrights wound up producing much less than they should have, and progressing less surely than they ought to have, because they've spent a certain amount of their creative life doodling around in Hollywood. (Hawthorne)

In his screenplays, Kushner carries over themes, language, and characters, as well as his politics, from his theater work.

Collective Expression: *East Coast Ode to Howard Jarvis*

> I guess I have always felt I pay too much taxes. Right? And I'm like, *for what?*
> —Corrections Officer,
> *East Coast Ode to Howard Jarvis* (1)

Kushner's screenplay, *East Coast Ode to Howard Jarvis*, gets its title from the elderly Californian who, in 1978 at the age of seventy-six, led a grassroots tax revolt. Teaming with Paul Gann, a retired businessman, Jarvis (1902–86) circulated a petition to get a measure on the California ballot to curb burgeoning property taxes. Jarvis and Gann secured enough signatures to get Proposition 13 on the ballot, proposing an amendment to California's state constitution which would slash property taxes by as much as 58 percent. On election day, the proposition passed by a two-to-one margin and Jarvis became a populist icon inspiring similar tax revolts in Massachusetts and Michigan. *East Coast Ode* is actually a "little teleplay in tiny monologues" (*Death and Taxes* 291) that Kushner completed for the cable television station Showtime in 1996, although it has yet to be produced.

Essentially a long one-act play (and a piece likely to work effectively in live theater), *East Coast Ode* is large in scope, calling for sixteen men (roles can be doubled for eight actors) and seven women (doubled by five actors) in a variety of locations suggested rather than staged realistically. Kushner hints that the actors might be shot in closeup in front of a blank photographer's screen.

The action of *East Coast Ode* is set in various locales around New York City between 1991 and 1996. Using fanciful humor to reflect a multitude of attitudes about taxation, the Internal Revenue Service, government, antigovernment militias, and law enforcement, it employs a mock-documentary style fictionalizing an actual mini–tax revolt inspired by a scheme created by a midwestern white supremacist. Instead of developing three-dimensional characters, Kushner uses an array of familiar social types simply identified as: Detective, Housing Police, Environmental Protection Officer, Woman in the Payroll Department, The Supremely Scary Girl Who Knows Practically Everything, and so on. The revelation of the bizarre plot to avoid taxes is accomplished through the recollections of those involved—centrally or peripherally—on both sides of the case. A Corrections Officer on Rikers Island who says, "I guess I have always felt I pay too much taxes" (297), learns from Skinhead Inmate of a scheme devised by one Leonard "Hap" Dutchman, the mastermind of the North American White Mens Freedom and Liberty Council, a white supremacist militia group in Indiana.

Stressing that Dutchman "has proved through Thoreau and shit like that that the IRS is unconstitutional" (298), Skinhead Inmate whets the appetite of the Corrections Officer for finding a way to avoid taxes.

A Housing Detective gets wind of the possibility and is intrigued to know more about "some bunch of armed whackos in Indiana who had figured out how legally to get out of paying taxes" (299). The Housing Detective compels his "seriously disaffected" (299) daughter to use the Internet to contact the NAWMF and LC. She finally succeeds, but tells her father that the organization might be a front for "terrorists" (300). However, he is only concerned with skirting his taxes and the daughter contacts Dutchman under an assumed name "off this book from school last year which no one in the whole class even bothered to read" (301). Dutchman, who refers to the federal government as "the Zionist Occupation Government HQ'd in DC" (302), responds to "Ethan Frome" with the suggestion that on a W-4 form the number 98 should be put in the space provided for exemptions. Reminding "Mr. Frome" that there is no legal limit on the number of exemptions a citizen might claim, Dutchman offers to send literature on the National Rifle Association and adds that the plan will "legally lift from your stooped but proud shoulders the oppressors' contumely, also known as your entire tax bill; and if your claim is initially rejected, repeat the process several times, and if that don't work, Ethan, E-mail me for further instructions" (302).

The Housing Detective files the W-4 through his uncle, an accountant, and as it moves through the process others get wind of the plan and adapt it for themselves. When the Housing Detective's claim reaches a Woman in the Payroll Department, she says she first thought it was a joke and sent it back. When it was filed again, however, she sent it back again to the detective stamped "ITEMIZE" (304) which, she figures, will be "good for a laugh" (304). Returning via cyberspace to Dutchman, the Housing Detective is advised to attach a "secret weapon" (304), a letter, to his W-4 form which, he claims, has worked effectively for "your fellow resistance fighters out here in the ZOG-free liberation Zone formerly known as Crawfordsville" (304). The letter, written in legalize, denies that the Housing Detective is a "citizen or resident of any state and federal conglomerate within your jurisdiction," stressing that since "I am alien to the United States, and am not a resident there" (305) he is not subject to taxation.

When the letter reaches the Woman in the Payroll Department, an African-American, she responds, "Alien to the United States. Baby, I hear what you're saying" (305). She explains that she is in her early fifties and lives in an apartment that "is a box" (305), a thought that causes her to vividly express the disconnection she and others in the screenplay feel in various ways. As the woman says:

> I got no money, I hate my job, I hate this city, I hate my cat, my husband hates his job, this city, the cat, we hate the disappointments, the delays in construction, the bigots, the bozos, the Democrats *and* the Republicans, Newt Gingrich, Bill Clinton, *his* cat, Rudy Giuliani, my insurance company and my boss, the guy playing with himself on the subway at 9AM, the kid with the radio playing at 6AM

and I hate the piss smell in the hallway that I have to inhale. Every day. On my way. To my box. Where I *live*. (305–6)

She sends the letter "uptown downtown all around the town" (306) and enters zero for the state and federal withholding in the Housing Detective's paycheck, sending a "big fat check with no taxes withheld" to the Housing Detective, absolving herself by saying "let *them* sort it out it is *not* my problem" (306).

It soon becomes clear that many of the Housing Detective's colleagues, from a Precinct Captain to a Meter Reader, are trying the same scheme and that he has begun selling copies of the form letter from Dutchman for as much as $2,000. When all of this is reported to Dutchman, he is "pleased to hear that your East Coast rebellion is proceeding apace" (309), but warns against spreading the scheme "too liberally" (309) and bringing down the wrath of the ZOG.

However, the scheme continues to spread until an Attorney for the City of New York begins sending all the characters letters stating that "the status you are seeking as 'non-resident, non-immigrant Alien' does not exist" (311). As the scheme begins to unravel, the Housing Detective tries to get help via the Internet from Dutchman, but the only message is "THIS WEB SITE IS TEMPORARILY UNAVAILABLE" (312). The Housing Detective's Daughter finds out that Dutchman has "been busted in Cincinnati for crossing state lines with a suitcase full of Uzis, and some bullets, and also he wrote some letter to a US Marshall saying he was gonna whack him or something" (313). The next image reveals Dutchman in a jail cell singing "The Impossible Dream," while it is revealed by a United States Attorney that "as few as five hundred and as many as a thousand" (314) New York City employees have been involved in evading their taxes with his scheme. The Supremely Scary Girl Who Knows Practically Everything reflects on the Social Contract, which she describes as

a theory *propounded* (*Big smile, she's proud of that word*) by Thomas Hobbes, John Locke and Jean-Jacques Rousseau, who were French philosophers. Um, part of the deal is, like, the people agree to surrender their power to the state. Some of their power. But it's like, *how much*? And it's like, say you the state and I'm the people, did I "lend" you my power and can I fire you if I don't like what you are doing with my power, did I somehow give up my power at birth and now I just got to hope for the best from you, and um, oh yeah, like, is this a contract between authority and each individual or is it, like, a collective expression of a general will towards civilization? (315)

The Defense Attorney for the police, however, sees their actions as less ideological and, "well, idiocy. Or lunacy. Take your pick" (315), but he fails to address the dissatisfactions reflected by their participation in the scheme. Kushner gives the last word to the Woman in the Payroll Department who worries about what will happen to "those poor stupid people" who evaded their taxes and, she is concerned that "Things coming unglued, that's how it seems to me. Don't it seem like that to you? Everything's just coming apart at the seams. And nobody understands" (316). As she finishes, a video clip of President Clinton's 1996 State of the Union speech shows him proclaiming: "So I join with Congress and my fellow Americans in declaring: The Era Of Big Government Is Over!" (316).

As with most of Kushner plays, the complex collisions of the political with human nature is central to this screenplay. Kushner frequently reads *East Coast Ode to Howard Jarvis* in public presentations at colleges and universities around the country, and these concerns reappear in his more ambitious operatic libretto, *Caroline, or Change*:

Never Oh Never Oh Never Forget: *Caroline, or Change*

> Fixed in black ice, deep and terribly still,
> like coins the stars jingle-bell; we count the cost:
> Who know what it costs, and who knows what it's worth?
> Who knows what it is to be good on the earth?
> Never oh never oh never forget,
> never forget me oh never forget.
> —*Caroline, or Change* (58)

As the twentieth century moved to its end, Kushner completed a first draft for an original opera libretto called *Caroline, or Change* (1998), a work with a story firmly rooted in the middle of the twentieth century. *Caroline, or Change* was workshopped in late 1999 at New York's Public Theatre and Kushner continues to revise it for an as-yet-unspecified major production. In *Caroline, or Change*, Kushner merges history (the Deep South—specifically Louisiana—at the time of John F. Kennedy's assassination) with the personal (a semiautobiographical account of his earliest encounters with the submerged oppressions of middle-class American life and a little boy struggling with the death of his mother and the remarriage of his father) to examine a society of ingrained inequities (the gentile dominance of the white middle-class, the oppression of African-Americans) of American society at a significant moment of transition and in an era of vast social change.

African-American characters appear with increasing frequency in Kushner's plays set in the United States, from Belize in *Angels* to the central characters of his forthcoming *Henry Box Brown, or The Mirror of Slavery*, and the central character in *Caroline, or Change* is an African-American woman. Kushner's Louisiana childhood exposed him to a black population that was "ghettoized and impoverished" and writes that that "anyone black in my hometown was like anyone black anywhere in the United States: feared, subjected to indignity and abuse, dehumanized, Other as Americans understand and have historically responded to the Other—as a negation of good, as Death, as ripe for extermination" ("Copious, Gigantic and Sane" M1).

Caroline, or Change begins in a basement laundry room in the Gellman's upper-middle-class Louisiana home where Caroline Thibodeaux, a black maid, listens to the radio while doing her work. The inspiration for this character undoubtedly came, in part, from Kushner's vivid childhood memory of watching Martin Luther King's funeral on television with his family's maid, Maudi Lee Davis. It is difficult not to see aspects of Caroline Thibodeaux in his recollection:

> Maudi cried throughout the broadcast, and I was both frightened and impressed—I felt her powerful grief connected us, her and me and my quiet hometown, with the struggle I knew was being waged in the world, in history. It was an instant in which one feels that one is being changed as the world is changed, and I believe I was. ("Copious, Gigantic and Sane" 51)

Caroline "contemplates and speculates" about life's questions while the washer, dryer, and radio (broadcasting a trio of voices singing like the Supremes) comment on life in the Deep South of the early 1960s, concluding that "nothing happens underground in Louisiana" (2). Noah Gellman, a small boy (Kushner's alter ego) whose mother has recently died, likes to stay close to the unsmiling Caroline, whom he idolizes:

> Caroline! Caroline Caroline
> Caroline who's always mad!
> Caroline who runs everything!
> Caroline who's stronger than my dad. (3)

Noah goes through his daily ritual of lighting Caroline's once-a-day cigarette while the appliances sing of the oppressive heat emanating from them:

> Heat ain't coming from desire:
> It's the front-load lectric dryer;
> sucking moisture out of the air:
> melt the hairspray in your hair:
> Turn it on, turn on despair! (4)

The despair has to do with Caroline's hard life; divorced and with four children, she makes a mere thirty dollars a week as the Gellman's maid but fantasizes about being swept off her feet by Nat King Cole. Referring to her basement hell, Caroline notes that nothing happens underground in Louisiana except that you are "under water" (7).

Noah is also "under water." His unhappiness at the death of his mother is compounded by his father's marriage to Rose, his late mother's best friend. Rose is a kind woman, but Noah dreams of his dead mother in "her grave, underwater" (7). Only in the "implacable, indestructible" (28) Caroline does he find some relief from his sadness. Noah's father plays a clarinet and his mother "was a sad bassoon" (8)— Kushner's own mother played the bassoon. Also in the Gellman home are Noah's paternal grandparents, who are first seen in a Chevy Impala lamenting the death of Noah's mother from cancer. As Caroline tries to explain to Noah:

> When cancer eat people Noah
> it God eating them;

> God sometimes eat people, like a wolf.
> He make this whole world as a test.
> Cancer was your momma's test,
> and her death is your test, you been tested too. (9)

Noah's test includes his stepmother, who his father has married to "make a new start," but Noah can only "hate her with all my heart" (11) because she is not his real mother. Noah's battle of wills with Rose centers around his habit of carelessly leaving loose change in his pockets. Rose tells Noah that his blasé attitude about money is insulting to Caroline, who has to work so hard for the little she makes. Noah seems not to completely appreciate this point, but Rose tries to temper her frustration with him, as she explains on the phone to her father, an elderly Jewish socialist. Noah, she realizes, does not like her, that he is "a little funny, spoiled and quiet—sad, I guess" (12). Guiltily, she admits that they do not pay Caroline very well, but lamely jokes that "it's against the law, to overpay negroes down here" (12). Her father harangues her about the oppression of Caroline, but she can only chastise him in return for worrying more about the maid than her troubled attempt to integrate herself into the Gellman family.

Throughout the libretto, Kushner uses the word *change* in various ways—to refer to Noah's pocket change, the changes of the moon, the changes in Rose's life, Caroline's increasing unwillingness to surrender her anger and change her attitude, and to the sweeping social changes reflected not only by Kennedy's assassination, but by the vandalizing of a courthouse statue of a Confederate soldier—a symbol of white dominance in the south—that winds up, headless, wrapped in a Confederate flag in the bayou.

Caroline's inability to change is explored in scene 4 as Dotty Moffett, another maid and Caroline's best friend, waits with her for a bus and accuses Caroline of "getting pinched and pruney" because her life "ain't what it should be" (14). Dotty serves as Kushner's mouthpiece to point out the inevitability of change, a theme underscored in a typically Kushnerian gesture of having the moon, watching their conversation, comment:

> Change come fast and change come slow
> but change come, Caroline Thibodeaux. (16)

The bus arrives and it, too, sings, as Kushner notes in his stage directions, "in a terrible voice of apocalypse" (17), bringing news of the murder of President Kennedy. Noah's grandparents, warning of "the venal acts, the mortal sins" (23) to come in the wake of Kennedy's death, sing of this political assassination and of Kennedy's symbolic importance:

> Friend to the colored, friend to the Jew,
> ask not what your country
> can do for you!
> Toleration of all men!
> We shall not see his like again. (19)

Dotty and Caroline acknowledge that Kennedy was too slow in helping blacks, but "he was set to help our cause," and they realize, along with Noah's grand-parents, that "madness will arrive now" (20). The bus, inviting all to step on board, sings

> time for departing;
> into the nightmare,
> towards what lies ahead. (22)

What lies ahead for Noah is a small domestic horror. Rose decides that Caroline may keep any change she finds in Noah's clothes, insisting to Noah that

> in time you'll appreciate
> how I taught you how to care:
> and really, darling, I think it's fair.
> It's not what you're used to, but
> things change.
> Things change. (23)

Back at her home, Caroline is annoyed by her daughter, Emmie, who, on return-ing from what Caroline presumes is a night of fun with her friends, is too disaf-fected to be upset by Kennedy's death. Noah, imagining himself calling out to Caroline from his bedroom window, regards her as his new president. She replies that her laws would include bringing her son safely home from Vietnam, making nights last longer, that little boys would never have to go to bed, and that Nat King Cole would come to her nightly to "stroke my soul" (28).

In scene 6, Noah's father informs him that he has reached an age where he will have more household responsibilities, but that he will receive a larger allowance for his chores. Noah excitedly images what he can buy with the additional change—candy, comic books, and "Barbie Doll Dresses on the sly!" (29)—but his practical father encourages him to save it for a chemistry set. When Caroline keeps some of Noah's forgotten change, she buys candy for her younger chil-dren. Noah tests Caroline by leaving some money purposely and, in his emo-tional neediness, assumes it will mean that Caroline and her family will talk about him at dinner:

> They talk about how my mama died
> they talk about my tragedy
> they wish they could take me in
> and I could live with Caroline. (35)

And, he adds, he could become one of Caroline's children, renamed Noah Thibodeaux. In the next scene, "Ironing," Caroline is at work worrying over whether or not it is a good idea to keep Noah's change. She thinks of the value of the money and how she, her mother, and her grandmother worked hard to earn the equivalent of Noah's overlooked change. She also recalls her marriage to a World War II Navy man, of her anxiety waiting for him to return from the war, of giving birth to their son, Larry, who is now in Vietnam. She also thinks about her divorce—her husband returned changed from the war, could not find meaningful employment, and took to drink, all of which culminated in his physically abusing Caroline. Her memories are interrupted by Rose, who asks Caroline to get Dotty and Emmie to assist with a Channukah party she is planning.

The party is made special by the visit of Rose's father. Mr. Stopnick is a character reminiscent of the old socialists in Clifford Odets's plays and is used by Kushner as a harbinger of change. Stopnick talks of his hope for the long delayed socialist revolution in America he believes must come. He senses a movement afoot:

> The old world's ending!
> Negroes marching!
> Change is coming!
> Down with the filthy capitalist chozzen! (48)

Working in the kitchen with Caroline and Emmie, Dotty reports that the missing Confederate statue has been found headless in the bayou. They discuss the murder of Lee Harvey Oswald on television, but Caroline objects to discussing such brutalities at a holiday party. Emmie gets into a lively debate with Stopnick, insisting that Martin Luther King's nonviolent revolution for blacks is working, but Stopnick warns her:

> Oh Jews can be nonviolent too.
> There's nothing meeker than a Jew!
> Listen girlie, we have learned:
> nonviolence will get you burned. (51)

Emmie insists that King is right, but Stopnick, regarding her optimism as "sweet" believes it "ain't realistic" (52). Caroline is infuriated by Emmie's intrusion into the party and orders her back to the kitchen, insisting that Emmie should not "mouth off round white folk like that" (53). Humiliated and aroused to anger, Emmie fires back at Caroline, mocking her subservience:

> Come on, teach me what you know!
> How to keep my head tucked low. (53)

Dotty steps in to defend Caroline, but Emmie's anger grows as she points out that Dotty is at least attending night school to try to better her life—"You got get-up. You got drive!" (53)—while she finds her mother mired in her meager circumstances. Dotty, however, insists that Caroline is "the proudest woman alive" (54) and that

> The truest hearts can't handle Strange.
> The purest souls can't rearrange.
> The best sometimes the worst with change. (54)

Meanwhile, at the party, Stopnick presents a twenty-dollar bill to Noah, inviting him to "contemplate" (54) its meaning:

> Think of someone who is poor:
> And know, you stole this gold from them.
> Especially here in the Devil's South!
> You rip gold from a starving man's mouth! (54–55)

Noah, a little frightened by the old man's warnings, takes the money and runs to his room. Rose encourages Noah's father to go to him, but Gellman speaks of a distance "as remote as Tibet" that has opened up between them, adding that they each "play solo now, in the key of regret" (57). As Emmie tries, unsuccessfully, to apologize to Caroline, and dreams of the material comforts she longs for, all of the characters join in a lyrical refrain of isolation and longing—and reflection on the tragedies of the past:

> Never oh never oh never forget,
> never forget me oh never forget. (58)

In scene 9, "The Twenty Dollar Bill," Noah, sitting bored in school, daydreams of what he will spend his money for when he suddenly realizes that he has left the twenty-dollar bill in his pocket and that Caroline will take it—"She can't have it! My money! I'll sue!" (60). Caroline does find the money and intends to keep it, but when Noah arrives home he demands that Caroline give it back to him. Her refusal makes him hysterical and, in a scene reminiscent of the climax of Athol Fugard's *Master Harold and the Boys*, the little boy who longs to be part of his black maid's family turns on her using the power of racial oppression:

> President Johnson has built a bomb
> special made to kill all negroes!
> I hate you, hate you, kill all negroes! Really! For true!
> I hope he drops this bomb on you! (62)

Caroline also falls into slurs, angrily retorting that the oppressive heat of the basement is a hell where "Jews go when they die" (63). Leaving the money in the bleach cup where she has always put Noah's change, Caroline storms out. When Rose returns home, Noah cannot tell her what happened and runs to hide in his room. As days pass and Caroline does not return to work, Noah worries, "I did it I killed her, I did it she died" (64). When Rose finds the twenty dollars in the bleach cup she confronts Noah, who claims it is not his twenty because he gave his to a "poor starving Negro kid" (65). Rose is unconvinced and Stopnick, who has observed this scene, takes the twenty-dollar bill, saying that it is his and, adding with irony, "Now everything's fine" (66).

However, everything is not fine. Rose cannot get Caroline to answer her phone calls and when she turns to Dotty for help, Dotty is able to offer little, though she tries to get Caroline to go back to work or to formally resign from the Gellmans. Caroline, realizing that she cannot afford to resign, wants to go to church because, reflecting on her argument with Emmie and her unfortunate scene with Noah, she "said and done some things this week I'm sad about. I need to pray" (68). When Dotty tries to dissect Caroline's dispute with Emmie, Caroline insists that "not everything a person face can be fix by talking" (68). She is most distressed about her feelings of hate, but Dotty tries to convince her that she can "change" and "learn something new!" (68). Caroline, however, feels she cannot change:

> Dot, I can't read.
> Dot, it's too late,
> I hate; that all; except for God;
> I hate.
> That all I do.
> Read Luke 18, verse 32. (69)

She thinks of Lot's wife, who "dwelt upon ruination and she turned to a pillar of salt" (69). Kushner, borrowing again on Walter Benjamin's description of the Angel of History as he did in *Angels*, has Caroline realize that Lot's wife was warned not to look back, but only ahead at the "unruined future" (70). Lot's wife was compelled to "eyeball ruination"—a parallel she makes with her own thinking "too much about ruination" (71).

In scene 12, "How Long Has This Been Going On," the radio trio sings, "I could cry salty tears" (72) in a torch-song lament for Caroline's unhappy return to work. Noah apologizes in one of their imagined nighttime conversations, hoping they can mend their friendship. Caroline, making it clear that they "weren't never friends" (73), says:

> Someday we'll talk again,
> Just gotta wait. (73)

The washing machine hums along decrying "these small domestic tragedies" (73) and Noah worries about his late mother buried underwater in Louisiana. Rose tries to comfort him, but Caroline explains, in a lyric of sad longing for Kushner's own mother, that:

> Underwater, it's like
> the long drawn sob
> of the song of the bassoon;
> like sleeping with the light out,
> like living alone in the dark of the bassoon,
> like burnt brown toast,
> like beautiful bass clef notes,
> beautiful and bitter and
> oh so calm:
> when you stop breathing air you get
> oh so calm,
> no fire down there
> so it's calm calm calm
> and there's never any money
> so it's very very calm
> but you miss
> oh you miss

the sun
and the moon
and the wooden bassoon. (73–74)

In the libretto's epilogue, "Emmie's Dream," Emmie is visited by a large head wearing "the cap of Johnny Reb" (74) who begs for his head to be put back on his body. It turns out that Emmie vandalized the statue of the Confederate soldier and threw it, headless, into the bayou. This symbolic gesture, she hopes, will lead to a brighter future through activism:

> Oh mister copper hidden head,
> things ain't been as right as this
> for years; and now it starts to spread
> across the South, what was amiss
> begins a metamorphosis,
> a word I learnt that mean
> it changing . . .
> For what we done, I ain't the least bit sorry,
> I just wish they hadn't of found your body.
> Evil you been, but you got to go! (75)

And, with her siblings, Emmie proclaims them the children of the Wife of Lot; their mother, she sees, is a woman who "stood alone where the harsh winds blow" and, as protection, she salted the earth "so nothing grow too close," but her "strong blood" (76) flows through them, the next generation, who may indeed bring change.

Kushner has written of his identification with those he calls "the Black Other," and, as a gay man and a Jew, he has wondered by "what magic do people trans-form bitter centuries of enslavement and murder into Beauty and Grace" ("Copious, Gigantic and Sane" 52). Clearly he attempts to address this by looking at Caroline Thibodeaux's otherness, while recognizing the difficulties he faces, as a white man, in writing about the African-American experience:

> As a white writer, when I'm writing a black character, it's clearly going to have some problems because I'm approaching it from the wrong side of the color line. I don't think that means that I shouldn't attempt it. And I don't think it means that a straight writer shouldn't write gay characters. And certainly it shouldn't be the case that straight audiences should stay away from gay theatre. (Gold 24)

The merging of the historical and the personal—in this case, the very personal for Kushner—drives *Caroline, or Change*. As millennium arrives, Kushner ambi-tiously looks forward to some significant projects. One, *Henry Box Brown, or The Mirror of Slavery*, also revisits the black experience in America, this time in the turbulent decades before the American Civil War—another great transition period—to examine its causes, its impact, and the difficult questions that remain over a hundred and fifty years later.

Forget Not the Unhappy: *Henry Box Brown, or The Mirror of Slavery*

> Forget not the unhappy,
> Though sorrow may annoy,
> There's something then for memory,
> *Hereafter* to enjoy!
> Oh! still from Fortune's garland,
> Some flowers for others strew;
> And forget not the unhappy,
> For, ah! their friends are few.
> —Frontispiece, *Narrative of the Life of Henry*
>   *Box Brown, Written By Himself* (1851)

Henry Box Brown, or The Mirror of Slavery is the first play of what Kushner plans as a three-play epic trilogy on economic history that he describes as being "about the relationship between the textile industry in Britain and American slavery that has a more conventionally epic form" (Vorlicky 123) in the Brechtian tradition. Kushner also describes *Henry Box Brown* as a "very big play" that has a "cast of billions of people, so it's going to be huge and expensive, and only a theater the size of the National or of the Public could produce it" (Vorlicky 240). The play has, in fact, been announced for a major production at the Royal National Theatre of Great Britain, where the two *Angels* plays were enthusiastically received, and has already been given a staged reading there in preparation for the production, the dates of which have not yet been announced.

In *Henry Box Brown*—and presumably in the projected trilogy it is part of—Kushner again merges history, the personal, and progressive politics through the extraordinary life of Henry Brown (c.1815–post-1864). In the summer of 1996, Kushner spent time in Todmorden, an English village near Manchester, which provides the setting for the play. While there, Kushner unearthed a considerable amount of useful background information about the textile industry and its dependence on American slavery. Kushner will, as is typical of his earlier plays, make a connection between Brown's life and his role as a player in the greater sweep of historical currents, set against the issues of economics and the moral questions raised by the shameful practice of slavery.

Brown is a useful choice as a central character, in that he was both a slave and a critic of economic policies in his time. Brown's early years were spent working on a plantation with his family in Louisa County, Virginia. Around 1830—not long before Nat Turner led his slave revolt in Southhampton—Brown was sent to Richmond to work in a tobacco factory. In the mid-1830s, Brown married another slave, a woman named Nancy, and they had at least three children before she and the children were sold by her master to another slaveowner in North Carolina. Brown walked several miles with his wife and children as they, shackled, began their journey to their new home. He never saw them again.

This tragic personal experience, all too typical among southern slaves, led Brown to desire his freedom so much that on March 23, 1849, the two-hundred-pound man took the remarkable step of shipping himself in a canvas-lined crate from Virginia to freedom in Philadelphia. Once there, a white shoemaker, Samuel Smith, received Brown in the crate at the office of the Pennsylvania Anti-Slavery Society. Thanks to a pouch of water, a few crackers, and a tool he used to poke air holes in the crate, Brown survived the twenty-seven-hour journey despite the fact that he spent at least two hours upside down resting on his neck and shoulder, causing him to nearly lose consciousness.

News of Brown's remarkable escape from slavery was widely covered in the media, leading Brown to write an autobiography with the aid of Charles Stearns, called *Narrative of the Life of Henry Box Brown, Written by Himself*. The title acknowledged the addition to his name commemorating his odd vehicle to freedom. The first English edition of the book began with a simple verse, "Forget not the unhappy" (Brown frontispiece), a line that resonates with Kushner's work. Brown makes it clear that "while America is boasting of her freedom and making the world ring with her professions of equality, she holds millions of her inhabitants in bondage" and, prophetically, "unless Americans purge themselves of this stain, they will have to undergo very severe, if not protracted suffering" (i). He lays out a general outline of the economic issues that keep slavery in place, while stressing the moral imperatives of ending the practice. This interplay of moral questions within economic forces is at the heart of Kushner's interest in Brown's story.

Response to Brown's autobiography led him to create a panoramic exhibit, "Mirror of Slavery," a moving series of scrolls depicting aspects of the lives of slaves and Brown's dramatic getaway. Brown's American freedom was short-lived as a result of the November 1850 passage of the Fugitive Slave Act permitting the arrest and return to their masters of suspected slaves throughout both free and slave states. Although the Congressional act was a setback in the antislavery movement, publication of Harriet Beecher Stowe's popular 1852 novel *Uncle Tom's Cabin* and subsequent highly successful theatrical adaptations of the book, as well as Harriet Tubman's 1853 foundation of the Underground Railroad to aid escaping slaves, helped fuel growing abolitionist sentiments, culminating in the events that led to the American Civil War and the end of slavery in the United States. Following the passage of the Fugitive Slave Act, Brown traveled to England, where he successfully exhibited "Mirror of Slavery" and helped encourage antislavery activities there. By 1862, Brown began appearing on bills of popular entertainments and lived in Wales around 1864, after which there is no documentation of his life.

While completing the first draft of *Henry Box Brown* in 1996, Kushner told the *New York Times* that he is "drawn to writing historical characters. The best stories are the ones you find in history" (Marks C2) and that, undoubtedly, the play would be like much of his full-scale work, sweeping in scale, theme, characterization, language, and overall ambition. He describes the play being about

> the relationship between the British textile industry and American slavery in the 19th century, and about the international character of capital, in the way that slavery, this bizarre holdover from earlier social formations, was primarily bankrolled

by a foreign country in the interest of supporting an empire. I'm interested in the question of the internationalist solidarity of labor: I think a very good case can be made that the British working class is essentially what kept Britain out of our Civil War. (Hawthorne)

Kushner expresses some concern about being a white author writing about a large cast of African-American characters: "Just the idea of a white writer writing about a former slave, it's offensive to some people. I feel like going back and reading William Styron to figure out what he did wrong, so that I don't repeat his mistakes. But it's absolutely the time to be writing about race, and it's wrong almost to not do it" (Hawthorne).

The scope of the play also concerns him. Acknowledging the obvious, Kushner explains, "I'm not a miniaturist," adding that the plays in this planned trilogy, of which *Henry Box Brown* is the first play, "are somewhat more tightly focused than *Angels*—they're not as kaleidoscopic and they're certainly not these big field paintings. They're focusing on very specific things. But at the same time I like big, splashy, juicy plays, and that's what they're going to be" (Hawthorne).

Pessimism of the Intellect: Politics and Activism

Despite his remarkable productivity as a dramatist, Kushner has also written not only the occasional poem, prayer, or speech, but also essays, newspaper and magazine columns, and frequent letters to newspaper editors in support of various social causes, arts controversies, political events, and individuals. The Theatre Communications Group published Kushner's *Slavs!* along with some of his nondramatic writings, in a volume called *Thinking About the Longstanding Problems of Virtue and Happiness. Essays, A Play, Two Poems and a Prayer* in 1995. The essays published in it, as well as Kushner's occasional columns in the *Advocate*, the *Nation*, the *New York Times*, and the *Los Angeles Times*, among other periodicals, reveal Kushner's activist agenda.

Some of these essays, like one published in a symposium on the state of the theater, were a typically Kushnerian call for an imaginative, politically engaged theater: "What it requires for health and progress is only ever what society itself requires from its citizens: active engagement in the issues of the day, keen analytical intelligence, imagination, the leisure and freedom necessary for creation, and a plentitude of resources which make such things possible." ("The State of the Theatre"14) He imaged a theater that

> addresses political questions, or addresses questions politically. The United States is at present caught up in a social and economic revolution, very dramatic indeed, and upon the outcome of our current struggles, the future of our country, and perhaps the future of the world (since this revolution is truly international) depends. I am vexed and challenged by the difficulties of representing political struggle on stage without embarrassing everyone. I am also wrestling with ways of writing about money for the theatre without sounding like Brecht; modern

money requires a different approach, and so do modern audiences. We have got out of the habit of thinking economically, of things present and to come, of considering the essential artificiality of the economy—how much like theatre the economy is. As times grow increasingly harsh, and reaction is on the rise, this kind of work becomes more difficult, and more necessary, to do." ("The State of the Theatre" 14)

Thinking About the Longstanding Problems of Virtue and Happiness is mostly a collection of essays written by Kushner in the early and mid-1990s. Kushner writes amusingly in "On Pretentiousness" about his method of playmaking, comparing it to the preparation of his mother's recipe for lasagna. "American Things" provides an intellectual autobiography of Kushner, sketching in those events of the last forty years of political and social history in America that have most influenced his thinking, and "With a Little Help from My Friends" offers Kushner's expression of gratitude to the numerous individuals he credits with guiding him toward the completion of *Angels*. Other essays deal with gay-related issues, from Kushner's often comic assessment of the gay theories of Bruce Bawer and Andrew Sullivan to an exploration of what it means to be tolerated. In this last, an essay called "Some Questions About Tolerance," Kushner explains the problem in being tolerated:

> Tolerance can be used to normalize an insupportable situation, or it can serve to warn those groups which lack real power that they exist on sufferance, that they are tolerated. If you are oppressed, if those characteristics which make you identifiable to yourself make you loathsome to a powerful majority which does not share those characteristics, then you are at great risk if your existence is predicated on being tolerated. Toleration is necessary when power is unequal; if you have power, you will not need to be tolerated. (*Thinking About the Longstanding Problems of Virtue and Happiness* 43).

The remaining essays in this volume, as well as numerous published essays, columns, and interviews, present Kushner's trademark mix of the hilarious and the tragic, his political engagement, and the artistic passions so evident in his plays.

Kushner has frequently leapt into debates about various arts-related controversies. In 1995, Kushner responded to the *New Yorker's* dance critic, Arlene Croce, who initiated a firestorm by condemning choreographer Bill T. Jones's *Still/Here*, a performance in which videotapes of actual terminally ill AIDS patients were used. Croce dismissed what she called "these AIDS epics" on the grounds that they milked audience sympathies and, as such, made it impossible to seriously criticize the work. Unfortunately, Croce admitted that she had not seen Jones's program before assailing it, but Kushner focused on the agenda behind Croce's condemnation: "The people Ms. Croce assaults for milking their victim status are in fact fighting for freedom, equality, survival; in the crazy rhetoric of the Right, struggle and anger are transmogrified into irresponsible slacking and whining" ("Letter to the Editor" 11).

Kushner has also written essays for various publications on subjects including the Wim Wenders film *Wings of Desire*, ideas of a utopian theater, the literature of AIDS (he participated in a 1997 Key West Seminar on the subject, sharing the stage with gay playwright-activist Larry Kramer), the dangers of working in Hollywood (a place, he writes, run by "creepy, soulless, right-wing people, who think they're progressive and hip and 'with-it' because they voted for Clinton, but who leave absolutely no room for subversive experimentation or Left political content" [Coe 17]), and Suzan-Lori Parks's challenging play *Venus*. Most movingly, Kushner wrote a piece for the *New York Times* expressing gratitude to the many friends and mentors who aided him in the creation of *Angels*, from director Oskar Eustis, who commissioned the play for San Francisco's Eureka Theatre, to Kimberly Flynn, noting that *Angels* was more the result of "our intellectual friendship than it is autobiography, and her contribution was as teacher, editor, adviser, not muse" ("Is It a Fiction That Playwrights Create Alone?" 31).

When controversy arose when left-wing activist playwright/actor Dario Fo was awarded the Nobel Prize for Literature, Kushner exulted in this triumph for "progressive politics" and noted that Fo's genius is "making everything he touches debatable," and, with the angered response by the Vatican—as well as members of the international literary establishment—to Fo's selection, for "a brief moment, the world becomes a carnival stage; the Fo Effect" ("Fo's Last Laugh—I" 4). In 1998, Kushner caused a small furor within theatrical circles when addressing the Association for Theatre in Higher Education. He called for the abolition of undergraduate theater majors (suggesting no specialized arts training prior to the graduate level), arguing that students are not well-educated on the undergraduate level in the great works of literature, history, and politics.

Angels became a target for various groups bent on censoring gay-themed plays, so it is perhaps not surprising that, when a similar fate befell another playwright's work, Kushner was at the forefront of the debate. In 1999, the Catholic League vehemently opposed the Manhattan Theatre Club's production of Terrence McNally's *Corpus Christi*. This play set off a furor regarding its depiction of a group of gay men putting on a play about Jesus Christ. In response to bomb threats and fearing for the safety of its artists and patrons, the MTC canceled the production. A backlash of pressure from artists and writers, among others, forced the MTC to rescind the decision within days and the production went forward in a hail of protest, media attention, and discussion of the role of the arts. On opening night, Kushner was in the crowd in front of the theater leading demonstrators supporting the production and opposing picketers from the Catholic League. *Corpus Christi* went on for a successful run in New York, but, to illustrate how bizarre these assaults on artistic freedom have become, McNally was symbolically condemned to death by an Islamic fundamentalist group in response to the London opening of *Corpus Christi* a few months later.

Angels made Kushner a leading spokesman for gay issues. He has frequently written on being gay in America, on gays serving openly in the military (as, he points out, a pursuit of social justice), and contributed occasional columns for the gay and lesbian news magazine, the *Advocate*, in the mid-1990s. These featured his sometimes serious, often comic reflections on many subjects, including disagreements with gay activist organizations, voting in the 1996 election (his column was titled "Holding Our Noses"), the tenuous survival of the National Endowment of the Arts, dating in the age of Ken Starr, the deaths of poet Allen Ginsberg (a "real radical" ["The Lawyer, The Poet" 104]), LAMBDA founder Tom Stoddard ("a brilliant, courageous, indefatigable" force ["The Lawyer, The Poet"104]), and singer Frank Sinatra ("At his best, Sinatra's really a 'girl singer'— the most fem, the least butch, the least obnoxiously phallic of male singers" ["Remembering Frank" 136]). Kushner has also written introductions for numerous books, from gay novels to collections of plays by Larry Kramer and Charles Ludlam, but one particular essay, written for the *Nation*, drew a particularly powerful response.

On October 6, 1998, Matthew Shepard, a gay student at the University of Wyoming, was severely beaten by two young men, Russell Henderson and Aaron McKinney, who tied Shepard to a fencepost in a country field where he was left exposed to the elements for eighteen hours before being found. He died days later. The brutal death of Shepard, who emerged as a martyr of late-twentieth-century homophobia, led to an emotionally charged national debate. Kushner rang in with "Matthew's Passion," an essay published in the *Nation*, eloquently expressing outrage not only at Shepard's murder—"crucifixion"—but at the conservative Senate Majority Leader Trent Lott, whose political prominence, in Kushner's opinion, is based, to a large extent, on his promises to the religious right:

> these Gary Bauers and Paul Weyrichs and Pat Robertsons [who expect him to] speak out against the homosexual agenda, without seeming to endorse murder. Trent Lott endorses murder, of course; his party endorses murder, his party endorses discrimination against homosexuals and in doing so it endorses the ritual slaughter of homosexuals. ("Matthew's Passion" 4)

Lott, who had equated homosexuality with kleptomania in a speech, was not Kushner's only target. He goes on to similarly condemn the Pope for the Catholic Church's "cynical political silence" about the murder, adding that "rigorously denouncing the abuse and murder of homosexuals would be a big sin against spin; denouncing the murder of homosexuals in such a way it received even one-thousandth of the coverage his and his church's attacks on homosexuals routinely receive, this would be an act of decency the Pope can't afford" ("Matthew's Passion" 5). However, Kushner reserves most of his anger for those "decent people, straight and gay" who "sort of think" that what happened to Shepard "shouldn't happen out there to those people, and something should be done. As long as I don't have to do it" ("Matthew's Passion" 4). Kushner closes his essay with a call to get up

> out of your comfortable chair to campaign for homosexual and all civil rights— *campaign*, not just passively support—may you think about this crucified man, and may you mourn, and may you burn with a moral citizen's shame. As one

civilized person to another: *Matthew Shepard shouldn't have died. We should all burn with shame.*" ("Matthew's Passion" 6)

In subsequent issues of the *Nation*, which received a voluminous response, Kushner's essay was variously called moving, strong, and powerful. It was also condemned, particularly by William Donohue, president of the Catholic League, and others who felt he went too far in attacking the Pope's silence. Kushner, however, was defiantly unrepentant. He replied by praising Archbishop Desmond Tutu, who, while visiting Colorado, had responded to a student's question on homosexual rights by suggesting that it "is as unjust as apartheid. . . . For me it's a matter of human rights and a deeply theological issue" ("Kushner Replies" 23), and Kushner wrote that someday a Catholic archbishop may say such a thing, but that it did not seem likely under Pope John Paul II.

Optimism of the Will: Future Projects

Aside from the as-yet-unproduced Kushner works *Caroline, or Change* and *Henry Box Brown, or The Mirror of Slavery*, Kushner continues to work on a play about artist Jan Vermeer called *Dutch Masters*, a work he began in the late 1980s. As early as 1991, he described it as "a dramatic history of capitalism over the course of five centuries. It poses a theory on the relationship between light and money" (Winn 1). However, as of 2001 the play has yet to be produced. Jan, or Johannes, Vermeer (1632–75) was renowned for his depictions of everyday life during the seventeenth century, a favorite era for Kushner and the setting of his early play, *Hydriotaphia*. Little is known about Vermeer's life, although he frequently struggled with debt and seemed to have produced comparatively little art, in spite of the quality and significance of what he did produce. That he remains a singular, somewhat isolated figure in the history of art may explain Kushner's interest—in the few known facts of Vermeer's life there is much room for fictionalizing, for imagining the impact of political and cultural forces on the artist in his times, and for relating Vermeer's life and work to the historical events of both past and present.

At the end of the 1990s, Kushner continued to revise his own earliest plays and adaptations, from *Stella*, which was under consideration for production by the Berkeley Repertory Theatre as early as 1996, to *The Heavenly Theatre*, a work he considers his first play, which was written in 1985 and set in the sixteenth century. He has been revising it since the mid-1990s with composer Mel Marvin for a possible production at Los Angeles's Mark Taper Forum. Productions of *Bright Room*, *Hydriotaphia*, *Angels*, and *Slavs!* as well as Kushner's one-acts, continue in professional and amateur theaters through the United States, England, and elsewhere.

Press reports announced in early 2000 that Kushner would write the lyrics for a stage musical version of the popular 1995 Johnny Depp/Marlon Brando film, *Don Juan DeMarco*, about a presumably disturbed young man who believes he is the great lover, Don Juan. Sent for psychiatric care, the patient's lushly romantic view of life begins to filter into the psyche of his doctor. The musical version will feature a libretto by Craig Lucas and music by Jeanine Tesori, and is scheduled to be directed by Kushner's friend Michael Mayer, who staged the national tour of *Angels*. Some reports suggest that the project with Tesori and Lucas will be a piece based on the rock group Queen. These projects, as well as expected productions of his as-yet-unproduced works, occupied Kushner's time at the dawn of the new millennium.

As a new century begins, Kushner continues to be guided by a "pessimism of the intellect, optimism of the will," a mantra encouraging him in his work as a dramatist and political activist. He continues to focus his thinking on the problems of the past that follow us into the future, and to do so with a battered hope and the realization that, as he has said about the evolution of attitudes about gays in recent decades, "so much has changed in such an incredibly short time" (Edwardes). Change *is* possible, Tony Kushner believes, and, at age forty-five, he looks ahead—as any true progressive must—spinning forward into an unknown future, but with a guardedly hopeful and boldly imaginative spirit.

Appendix
Production History

The following is a partial list of the first significant productions of Tony Kushner's full-length plays, adaptations, one-acts, and libretti. It is by no means complete, but provides a quick reference to important English-speaking productions (Kushner's plays, especially *Angels in America, The Illusion, Slavs!,* and *A Bright Room Called Day* have also been staged in various international productions not included here). When only a year appears, the work has either not yet been performed or no additional information was available. The list of productions of works authored by Kushner is followed by a partial list of productions he has directed.

The Age of Assassins

  1982   Newfoundland Theatre, New York, NY

And the Torso Even More So ("T-shirt" play)

  February 1999   Humana Festival of New American Plays, Actors Theatre
                         of Louisville, Louisville, KY

Angels in America. A Gay Fantasia on National Themes. Part One:
Millennium Approaches

  May 1990   Center Theatre Group/Mark Taper Forum, Los Angeles,
                         CA [workshop]
  May 1991   Eureka Theatre Company, San Francisco, CA
  January 23, 1992   Royal National Theatre of Great Britain, London,
                         England
  November 8, 1992   Mark Taper Forum, Los Angeles, CA
  May 4, 1993   Walter Kerr Theatre, New York, NY
  September 25, 1994   Royal George Theatre, Chicago, IL (beginning of nation-
                         al tour)

October 1994	American Conservatory Theatre, San Francisco, CA
1995	Dallas Theatre Center, Dallas, TX
1995	Alley Theatre, Houston, TX
1995	Intiman Theatre, Seattle, WA
September 1995	Alliance Theatre Company, Atlanta, GA
March 1996	Charlotte Repertory Theatre, Charlotte, NC
September 6, 1996	Trinity Repertory Company, Providence, RI
January 1997	Contemporary Arts Center, New Orleans, LA
March 1997	Arkansas Repertory Theatre, AK
April 1997	Open Stage of Harrisburg, Harrisburg, PA
September 1997	Milwaukee Repertory Theatre, Milwaukee, WI
April 1998	Zachary Scott Theatre, Austin, TX
September 1, 1998	Actors Theatre of Louisville, Louisville, KY
May 25, 1999	Signature Theatre, Arlington, VA
October 1999	Connecticut Repertory Theatre, Storrs, CT
February 25, 2000	Pillsbury House Theatre, Minneapolis, MN
March 2000	Buffalo Ensemble Theatre, Buffalo, NY

Angels in America. A Gay Fantasia on National Themes. Part Two: Perestroika

May 1991	Eureka Theatre Company, San Francisco, CA [staged reading]
May 1992	Mark Taper Forum, Los Angeles, CA [workshop]
November 8, 1992	Mark Taper Forum, Los Angeles, CA
April 1993	New York University/Tisch School of the Arts, New York, NY
November 20, 1993	Royal National Theatre of Great Britain, London, England
November 23, 1993	Walter Kerr Theatre, New York, NY
September 1994	American Conservatory Theatre, San Francisco, CA
September 29, 1994	Royal George Theatre, Chicago, IL (beginning of national tour)
October 1994	American Conservatory Theatre, San Francisco, CA
1995	Alley Theatre, Houston, TX
1995	Intiman Theatre, Seattle, WA
September 1995	Alliance Theatre Company, Atlanta, GA
1996	Dallas Theatre Center, Dallas, TX
April 1996	Charlotte Repertory Theatre, Charlotte, NC
September 6, 1996	Trinity Repertory Company, Providence, RI
March 1997	Arkansas Repertory Theatre, AK
October 1997	Milwaukee Chamber Theatre, Milwaukee, WI
July 1999	Signature Theatre, Arlington, VA
March 2000	Buffalo Theatre Ensemble, Buffalo, NY
March 2000	Diversionary Theatre, San Diego, CA
2000	Connecticut Repertory Theatre, Storrs, CT
2001	Pillsbury House Theatre, Minneapolis, MN

A Bright Room Called Day

April 22, 1985	Heat & Light Company, Inc., Theatre 22, New York, NY [workshop]
October 1987	Eureka Theatre Company, San Francisco, CA
July 1988	Bush Theatre, London, England
January 7, 1991	New York Public Theatre, New York, NY
September 16, 1995	Actor's Express Theatre, Atlanta, GA
February 27, 1997	Connecticut Repertory Theatre, Storrs, CT
May 1999	Outward Spiral Theatre, Minneapolis, MN
April 2000	Theatre of Note, Hollywood, CA

Caroline, or Change (libretto)

1998

A Dybbuk, or Between Two Worlds (adapted from the play by S. Ansky)

February 1995	Hartford Stage Company, New Haven, CT
January 1996	Denver Theatre Center, Denver, CO
November 1997	New York Public Theatre, New York, NY

East Coast Ode to Howard Jarvis (screenplay)

1996

La Fin de la Baleine: An Opera for the Apocalypse

| 1983 | Ohio Theatre, New York, NY |

G. David Schine in Hell

1996

The Good Person of Setzuan (adapted from the play by Bertolt Brecht)

| July 1994 | La Jolla Playhouse, La Jolla, CA |
| June 1999 | Wings Theatre, New York, NY |

Grim(m) (inspired by the Brothers Grimm's "The Two Journeymen") (screenplay)

1995

The Heavenly Theatre

| 1986 | New York University/Tisch School of the Arts, New York, NY |

Henry Box Brown, or The Mirror of Slavery

1997

Historiomax

1985

Home Body/Kabul

July 1999	Chelsea Theatre Centre, London, England
2000	Hartford Stage Company, Hartford, CT
2001	New York Theatre Workshop, New York, NY

Hydriotaphia, or The Death of Dr. Browne

1987	Home for Contemporary Theatre and Art, New York, NY
April 1997	New York University/Tisch School of the Arts, New York, NY
March 1998	Alley Theatre, Houston, TX
September 1998	Berkeley Repertory Theatre, Berkeley, CA

The Illusion (freely adapted from the play by Pierre Corneille)

October 19, 1988	New York Theatre Workshop, New York, NY
December 29 1989	Hartford Stage Company, Hartford, CT
March 30, 1990	Los Angeles Theatre Center, Los Angeles, CA
1991	A Contemporary Theatre, Seattle, WA
May 15, 1991	Round House Theatre, Silver Spring, MD
June 1991	Berkeley Repertory Theatre, Berkeley, CA
October 1991	Los Angeles Theatre Center, Los Angeles, CA
1992	Addison Center Theatre, Addison, TX
July 1993	Oregon Shakespeare Festival, Ashland, OR
1993	Portland Center Stage, Portland, OR
January 19, 1994	Classic Stage Company, New York, NY
March 1994	Zachary Scott Theatre, Austin, TX
September 1994	Merrimack Repertory Theatre, Lowell, MA
September 1994	Hunger Artists, Jack's Theatre, Denver, CO
October 1994	Portland Stage Company, Portland, ME
February 1995	Trinity Repertory Theatre, Providence, RI
March 1995	Georgia Ensemble Theatre, Roswell, GA
May 1995	Hippodrome Theatre, Gainesville, FL
August 1995	Berkshire Theatre Festival, Stockbridge, MA
December 1995	Two River Theatre Company, West Long Branch, NJ
1995	Ensemble Theatre of Cincinnati, Cincinnati, OH
September 6, 1996	Carpenter Square Theatre, Norman, OK
September 1996	Fell's Point Corner Theatre, Baltimore, MD
June 1997	Royal Exchange Theatre, Manchester, England
March 7, 1997	Arizona Theatre Company
October 1998	Alabama Shakespeare Festival, Montgomery, AL
April 1999	Broadway Theatre Company, Milwaukee, WI
May 1999	Actor's Gang Theatre, Namaste Theatre Company, Los Angeles, CA
November 1999	San Diego Repertory Theatre, San Diego, CA
May 2000	Boston Center for the Arts, Boston, MA

2000	Actors Collective, San Francisco, CA
2000	American Stage, St. Petersburg, FL
2000	Actors Express, Atlanta, GA

In Great Eliza's Golden Time

| 1986 | Imaginary Theatre Company, Repertory Theatre of St. Louis, St. Louis, MO |

In That Day; Lives of the Prophets

| 1989 | New York University/Tisch School of the Arts, New York, NY |

"It's an Undoing World", or Why Should It Be Easy When It Can Be Hard? Notes on My Grandma for Actors, Dancers and a Band

| 1995 | Los Angeles Modern Dance and Ballet Company, Los Angeles, CA |

Last Gasp at the Cataract

| 1984 | The Yard, Inc., Martha's Vineyard, MA |

Notes on Akiba

| April 13, 1995 | New York Jewish Museum, New York, NY |

The Protozoa Review

1985

Reverse Transcription. Six Playwrights Bury a Seventh, A Ten-Minute Play That's Nearly Twenty Minutes Long

| March 1996 | Humana Festival of New American Plays, Actors Theatre of Louisville, Louisville, KY |

St. Cecilia, or The Power of Music (libretto, adapted from the story by Heinrich von Kleist)

1997

Slavs! Thinking About the Longstanding Problems of Virtue and Happiness

March 8, 1994	Humana Festival of New American Plays, Actors Theatre of Louisville, Louisville, KY
June 6, 1994	Lesbian Avengers Civil Rights Organizing Project, Walter Kerr Theatre, New York, NY
June 1994	Steppenwolf Theatre Company, Chicago, IL
December 12, 1994	New York Theatre Workshop, New York, NY
December 1994	Hampstead Theatre, London, England
January 6, 1995	Center Stage, Baltimore, MD

February 24, 1995	Yale Repertory Theatre, New Haven, CT
1995	City Theatre Company, Pittsburgh, PA
April 1995	Trinity Repertory Company, Providence, RI
September 1995	Studio Theatre, Washington, D.C.
September 1995	Alley Theatre, Houston, TX
October 15, 1995	Mark Taper Forum, Los Angeles, CA
October 1995	La Jolla Playhouse, San Diego, CA
March 1, 1996	Berkeley Repertory Theatre, Berkeley, CA
August 1996	Manbites Dog Theatre, Raleigh, NC
April 2000	European Repertory at About Face Theatre, Chicago, IL

Stella. A Play for Lovers (adapted from the play by Goethe)

1987	New York Theatre Workshop, New York, NY

Terminating, or Lass Meine Schmerzen Nicht Verloren Sein, or Ambivalence (inspired by William Shakespeare's seventy-fifth sonnet)

January 7, 1998	Guthrie Theater Lab, Minneapolis, MN
July 1998	New York Public Theatre, New York, NY
2000	Studio Theatre, Washington, D.C.

The Umbrella Oracle

1984	The Yard, Inc., Martha's Vineyard, MA

Widows (adapted from the novel by Ariel Dorfman)

July 24, 1991	Mark Taper Forum, Los Angeles, CA
March 1997	Traverse Theatre, Edinburgh, Scotland

Yes Yes No No: The Solace-of-Solstice, Apogee/Perigee, Bestial/Celestial Holiday Show

1986	Imaginary Theatre Company, Repertory Theatre of St. Louis, St. Louis, MO

Stage Productions Directed by Tony Kushner:

The Age of Assassins by Tony Kushner

1982	Newfoundland Theatre, New York, NY

La Fin de la Baleine by Tony Kushner

1983	Ohio Theatre, New York, NY

Last Gasp at the Cataract by Tony Kushner

1984	The Yard, Inc., Martha's Vineyard, MA

A Bright Room Called Day by Tony Kushner

1985	Theatre 22, New York, NY

Yes Yes No No: The Solace-of-Solstice, Apogee/Perigee, Bestial/Celestial Holiday Show by Tony Kushner

1986   Imaginary Theatre Company, Repertory Theatre of St. Louis, St. Louis, MO

Golden Boy by Clifford Odets

1986   Repertory Theatre of St. Louis, St. Louis, MO

Hydriotaphia, or The Death of Dr. Browne by Tony Kushner

1987   Home for Contemporary Theatre and Art, New York, NY

In Great Eliza's Golden Time by Tony Kushner

1987   Imaginary Theatre Company, Repertory Theatre of St. Louis, St. Louis, MO

Fen by Caryl Churchill

1987   New York University/Tisch School of the Arts, New York, NY

Mother Courage and Her Children by Bertolt Brecht

1988   University of New Hampshire, Portsmouth, NH

Fen by Caryl Churchill

1988   New York University/Tisch School of the Arts, New York, NY

In That Day (Lives of the Prophets) by Tony Kushner

1989   New York University/Tisch School of the Arts, New York, NY

Learning Play: On Consent by Bertolt Brecht

1990   New York University/Tisch School of the Arts, New York, NY

In the Heart of America by Naomi Wallace

1994   Long Wharf Theatre, New Haven, CT

References

Preface

Barrett, Amy. "The Way We Live Now: 10-07-01: Questions for Tony Kushner." *The New York Times*, October 7, 2001, section 6, p. 230.

Brantley, Ben. "One Woman's Quest, Fraught With Cultural Land Mines." *The New York Times*, December 20, 2001, p. E8.

Franklin, Nancy. "Afghan Tales." *The New Yorker*, January 28, 2002, 92.

Heilpern, John. "Zounds! Kushner's *Homebody/Kabul* Is Our Best Play in Last 10 Years." *The New York Observer*, January 5, 2002, p. 1.

Isherwood, Charles. "Kabul Journeys Across Time, History." *Variety*, December 19, 2001, p. 27.

Kaplan, Fred. "Despite Ambition, Kushner's *Kabul* Lacks Depth," *The Boston Globe*, December 20, 2001, p. D7.

Kushner, Tony, e-mail to James Fisher, March 25, 2002.

Kushner, Tony, *Homebody/Kabul*. Ninth draft manuscript dated February 2002.

Peyser, Marc. "Tales From Behind Enemy Lines." *Newsweek*, December 17, 2001, 68.

Phillips, Michael. "Response to Terror." *The Los Angeles Times*, December 20, 2001, part 1, p. 5.

Pochoda, Elizabeth. "Afghanistan by Stagelight," *The Nation*, February 4, 2002, p. 36.

Poniewozik, James. "What's Entertainment Now?" *Time*, October 1, 2001, 112.

Reston, James Jr., "A Prophet in His Time," *American Theatre*, March 2002, 53.

Introduction

Benjamin, Walter. *Illuminations. Essays and Reflections.* Edited and with an introduction by Hannah Arendt. Translated by Harry Zohn. New York: Schocken Books, 1968.

Blanchard, Bob. "Playwright of Pain and Hope," *Progressive*, vol. 58, October 1994, pp. 42–44.

Fischer, Ernst. *The Necessity of Art. A Marxist Approach.* Translated by Anna Bostock. New York: Penguin Books, 1963.

Kushner, Tony. *Angels in America. A Gay Fantasia on National Themes. Part Two: Perestroika.* New York: Theatre Communications Group, Inc., 1992, 1994.

————. "Notes About Political Theatre," *Kenyon Review*, vol. XIX, nos. 3/4, summer/fall 1997, pp. 19–34.

————. *Thinking About the Longstanding Problems of Virtue and Happiness, Essays, A Play, Two Poems and A Prayer*. New York: Theatre Communications Group, Inc., 1995.

————. "*Yes Yes No No. The Solace of Solstice Apogee/Perigee Bestial/Celestial Holiday Show*," in *Plays in Process. Three Plays for Young Audiences*. Vol. 7, no. 11. New York: Theatre Communications Group, 1987.

Lahr, John. "Angels on Broadway," *New Yorker*, May 23, 1993, p. 137.

————. "Earth Angels," *New Yorker*, December 13, 1993, pp. 129–33.

Pacheco, Patrick., "AIDS, Angels, Activism, and Sex in the Nineties," *Body Positive*, September 1993, pp. 17–28.

Roca, Octavio. "Kushner's Next Stage," *San Francisco Chronicle*, September 6, 1998, p. 32.

Savran, David. "Tony Kushner," in *Speaking on Stage. Interviews with Contemporary American Playwrights*, edited by Philip C. Kolin and Colby H. Kullman. Tuscaloosa: University of Alabama Press, 1996, pp. 291–313.

Shewey, Don. "Tony Kushner's Sexy Ethics," *Village Voice*, April 20, 1993, pp. 29–32, 36.

Szentgyorgyi, Tom. "Look Back—And Forward—In Anger," *Theater Week*, January 14–20, 1991, pp. 15–19.

Vorlicky, Robert, ed. *Tony Kushner in Conversation*. Ann Arbor: University of Michigan Press, 1998.

Weber, Carl. "I Always Go Back to Brecht," *Brecht Yearbook/Das Brecht-Jahrbuch*, vol. 25, 1995, pp. 67–88.

Chapter 1

Bigsby, Christopher. *Contemporary American Playwrights*. Cambridge: Cambridge University Press, 1999, pp. 86–131.

Bloom, Harold. "Afterword," in Tony Kushner and Joachim Neugroschel. *A Dybbuk and Other Tales of the Supernatural*. Adapted and translated from S. Ansky. New York: Theatre Communications Group, Inc., 1998, p. 109.

Coveney, Michael. "A Bright Room," *Financial Times* (London), July 19, 1998, Sec. I, p. 17.

Disch, Thomas M. "Theatre: *A Bright Room Called Day, Dead Mother, Unchanging Love*," *Nation*, March 18, 1991, pp. 352–53.

Feingold, Michael. "Bright Words," *Village Voice*, January 15, 1991, p. 87.

Helbig, Jack. "*A Bright Room Called Day*," *Booklist*, January 1, 1995, n.p.

Hulbert, Dan. "Backstage: Express *Room* Hits Timelier Target," *Atlanta Journal and Constitution*, September 10, 1995, p. 6L.

————. "Theatre Review: *A Bright Room Called Day*," *Atlanta Journal and Constitution*, September 22, 1995, p. 5P.

Kissel, Howard. "*A Bright Room* Called Cliché," *New York Daily News*, January 8, 1991, p. 29.

Koehler, Robert. "Kushner's *Room* Is a Dark Gem," *Los Angeles Times*, March 22, 1996, p. F28.

Kushner, Tony. *A Bright Room Called Day*. New York: Theatre Communications Group, Inc., 1994.

Lord, M. G. "Public Priorities," *New York Newsday*, January 6, 1991, pp. 4–5, 21.

Monji, Jana J. "Berlin Meets L.A.; *Bright Room* Bridges Time, Space to Address Ethics of Indifference," *Los Angeles Times*, April 27, 2000, p. F31.

Preston, Rohan. "*Day* Becomes Long, Clumsy Night," *Minneapolis Star-Tribune*, March 1999, Variety Sec., p. 7E.

Remy. "*A Bright Room Called Day*," *Variety*, January 14, 1991, p. 118.

Rich, Frank. "Making History Repeat, Even Against Its Will," *New York Times*, January 8, 1991, pp. C11, C14.

Richards, David. "Tale of One City Set in Two Times—Both Fearful," *New York Times*, January 13, 1991, pp. 5, 26.

Sander, Roy. "Theatre Reviews: *A Bright Room Called Day*," *Back Stage*, January 18, 1991, p. 48.

Stearns, David Patrick. "Look for Meaning in World Gone Amok," *USA Today*, January 10, 1991, p. 4D.

Szentgyorgyi, Tom, "Look Back—and Forward—in Anger," *Theater Week*, January 14–21, 1991, pp. 15–19.

Weales, Gerald. "Without a Light. *Normal Life* & *Bright Room*," *Commonweal*, February 22, 1991, p. 132.

Winer, Linda, "Evils of Humanity Crowd *Bright Room*," *New York Newsday*, January 8, 1991, pp. 44, 69.

Chapter 2

Arenschieldt, Rich. "Theatrical 'David and Goliath,' " *Houston Voice*, April 17, 1998, pp. 19–20.

Browne, Sir Thomas. *The Major Works*. Edited with an introduction and notes by C. A. Patrides. London and New York: Penguin Books, 1977.

———. *The Works of Sir Thomas Browne*. Edited by Geoffrey Keynes. Second Edition. Four Volumes. London: Faber & Faber, 1964.

De La Viña, Mark. "Kushner's Farce is a Mortal Cinch," *San Jose Mercury News*, September 18, 1998, pp. 29–30.

Evans, Everett. "Kushner Hits Highs, Lows in Epic Farce," *Houston Chronicle*, April 10, 1998, p. D1.

———. "Kushner Still Tweaking *Hydriotaphia Script*," *Houston Chronicle*, March 30, 1998, p. C1.

———. "Last Laughs," *The Houston Chronicle*, March 29, 1998, pp. 10, 20.

Halverson, Megan. "Farce Creatures," *Houston Sidewalk*, April 17, 1998, n.p.

Kushner, Tony. *Death and Taxes*. Hydriotaphia *and Other Plays*. New York: Theatre Communications Group, Inc., 2000.

———. "Three Brief Notes from the Playwright," *Performing Arts*, September 1998, pp. 5–6.

Mader, Travis. "Tony Kushner and Dr. Browne," *Alley Theatre Newsletter*, spring 1998, p. 1.

Post, Jonathan F. S. *Sir Thomas Browne*. Boston: Twayne, 1987.

Roca, Octavio. "Kushner's Next Stage," *San Francisco Chronicle*, September 6, 1998, p. 32.

Rosenstein, Brad. "Unblocked," *San Francisco Bay Guardian*, September 23–29, 1998, n.p.

"Sir Thomas Browne," *Alley Theatre Newsletter*, spring 1998, p. 4.

Stearns, David Patrick. "Kushner's Latest Less Substance Than Style," *USA Today*, September 29, 1998, p. 4D.

Winn, Steven. "Kushner Overreaches In Ambitious But Static *Hydriotaphia*," *San Francisco Chronicle*, September 18, 1998, p. C1.

Chapter 3

"Anxious in America," *New Yorker*, December 26, 1994–January 2, 1995, p. 52.

Benjamin, Walter. *Illuminations. Essays and Reflections.* Edited and with an introduction by Hannah Arendt. Translated by Harry Zohn. New York: Schocken Books, 1968.

Blanchard, Bob. "Playwright of Pain and Hope." *Progressive*, October 1994, vol. 58, pp. 42–44.

Brecht, Bertolt. *Brecht on Theatre. The Development of an Aesthetic.* Edited and translated by John Willett. New York: Hill and Wang, 1957.

Brustein, Robert. "Angles in America." *New Republic*, May 24, 1993, pp. 29–31.

Christiansen, Richard. "Astounding *Angels.* Part I of Kushner Saga Jolts the Emotions," *Chicago Tribune*, September 26, 1994, Arts Plus Sec., p. 1.

Clum, John M. *Acting Gay. Male Homosexuality in Modern Drama.* New York: Columbia University Press, 1994.

Drukman, Steven. "A Standoff in Charlotte. *Angels* Provokes a Legal and Cultural Confrontation," *American Theatre*, May/June 1994, pp. 46–47.

Evans, Greg. "*Angels in America: A Gay Fantasia on National Themes*," *Variety*, November 16, 1992, pp. 69, 73.

Frost, David. *The Americans.* New York: Stein and Day, 1970.

Gelb, Hal. "Theatre," *Nation*, February 22, 1993, p. 246–48.

Graff, Gerald. *Beyond the Culture Wars. How Teaching the Conflicts Can Revitalize American Education.* New York: W. W. Norton, 1992.

Harrison, Gilbert A. *The Enthusiast. A Life of Thornton Wilder.* New Haven, CT, and New York: Ticknor & Fields, 1983.

Harvey, Dennis. "*Angels in America*" *Variety*, October 31–November 6, 1994, p. 99.

Kauffmann, Stanley. "Homosexual Drama and Its Disguises," *New York Times*, January 23, 1966, sec. 2, p. 1.

Kazin, Alfred. "The Writer as Sexual Show-Off: Making Press Agents Unnecessary." *New York Magazine*, June 9, 1975, p. 38.

Kroll, Jack. "A Seven-Hour Gay Fantasia: A Daring and Dazzling Play for Our Time," *Newsweek*, November 23, 1992, p. 83.

Kushner, Tony. *Angels in America, Part One: Millennium Approaches.* New York: Theatre Communications Group, Inc., 1992, 1993.

———. *Angels in America, Part Two: Perestroika.* New York: Theatre Communications Group, Inc., 1992, 1994.

———. "Fighting the Art Bullies," *Nation*, November 29, 1999, pp. 41–42.

———. "Notes About Political Theatre," *Kenyon Review*, vol. XIX, nos. 3/4, summer/fall 1997, pp. 19–34.

———. "The Secrets of *Angels*" (as told to William Harris), *New York Times*, March 27, 1994, p. H5.

———. "Why We Must Fight," *Stage Directions*, June–July 1997, p. 7.

Lahr, John. "Angels on Broadway," *New Yorker*, May 31, 1993, p. 137.

Lazare, Lewis. "*Angels in America*," *Variety,* October 17–23, 1994, p. 173.

Nunns, Stephen. "No *Angels* on Catholic Campus," *American Theatre*, December 1996, pp. 46–47.

Peithman, Stephen. "Stay Focused Under Fire," *Stage Directions*, June/July 1997, p. 12.

Presley, Delma Eugene. "Little Acts of Grace," in *Tennessee Williams. A Tribute*. Edited by Jac Tharpe. Jackson: University of Mississippi Press, 1977.

Quindlen, Anna. "Happy and Gay," *New York Times*, April 16, 1994, p. A21.

Raymond, Gerard. "Q & A with Tony Kushner." *Theater Week*, December 20, 1993, pp. 14–20.

Rich, Frank. "Embracing All Possibilities in Art and Life," *New York Times*, May 5, 1993, pp. C15–C16.

———. "Marching Out of the Closet, Into History," *New York Times*, November 10, 1992, pp. C15, C22.

Savran, David. "Tony Kushner," in *Speaking on Stage. Interviews with Contemporary American Playwrights*. Edited by Philip C. Kolin and Colby H. Kullman. Tuscaloosa: University of Alabama Press, 1996, pp. 291–313.

Shaw, Bernard. "The Two Latest Comedies," *Saturday Review*, May 18, 1895.

Simon, John. "Angelic Geometry." *New York*, December 6, 1993, pp. 130–31.

Swisher, Kara. "Catholic U. Ejects *Angels*," *Washington Post*, September 21, 1996, pp. C1–C2.

Tommasini, Anthony. "Americana Written for Fleming," *New York Times*, May 10, 2000, p. E3.

Welsh, Anne Marie. "*Angels* II Takes Wing at Diversionary," *San Diego Union-Tribune*, March 25, 2000, p. E7.

Wilder, Thornton. *The Angel That Troubled the Waters and Other Plays*. New York: Coward-McCann, Inc., 1928.

———. *The Bridge of San Luis Rey*. New York: Albert & Charles Boni, 1928.

———. *Three Plays. Our Town, The Skin of Our Teeth, The Matchmaker*. New York: Harper Perennial, 1985.

Williams, Raymond. *Resources of Hope. Culture, Democracy, Socialism*. Edited by Robin Gale. With an introduction by Robin Blackburn. London and New York: Verso, 1989, p. 283.

Williams, Tennessee. *Where I Live. Selected Essays*. Edited by Christine R. Day and Bob Woods. With an introduction by Christine R. Day. New York: New Directions, 1978.

Wynn, Leah. "University forbids ads for *Angels in America*. Officials Didn't Want to Endorse Gay 'Lifestyle'," *Washington Blade*, September 20, 1996, p. 1.

Zamora, Lois Parkinson. "The Myth of Apocalypse and The American Literary Imagination," in *The Apocalyptic Vision in America. Interdisciplinary Essays on Myth and Culture*. Edited and with an introduction by Lois Parkinson Zamora. Bowling Green, OH: Bowling Green University Popular Press, 1982, pp. 97–138.

Chapter 4

Arnott, Christopher. "Totally Tony All Over Connecticut," *Hartford Advocate*, March 9, 1995, p. 23.

Billington, Michael. "Postcards from Siberia," *Guardian*, December 15, 1994, p. T8.

Brustein, Robert. *Cultural Calisthenics. Writings on Race, Politics, and Theatre*. Chicago: Ivan R. Dee, 1998.

Canby, Vincent. "In *Slavs!* Kushner Creates Tragic Burlesque," *New York Times*, December 18, 1994, sec. 2, pp. 5, 24.

Dixon, Michael Bigelow. "*Slavs!*—The Interview," *ATL. Actors Theatre of Louisville. News for Subscribers and Special Patrons*, March 1994, pp. 3–4.

Harris, William. "In *Slavs!* Are the Echoes of *Angels*," *New York Times*, December 4, 1994, sec. 2, pp. 5, 36.

———. "The Road to Optimism," *Dance Ink*, vol. 6, no. 1, spring 1995, pp. 28–29.

Johnson, Malcolm. "Kushner Infuses *Slavs!* With Range of Emotions," *Hartford Courant*, March 4, 1995, p. E1.

King, Robert L. "All-American," *North American Review*, vol. 279, July/August 1994, pp. 43–48.

Korn, Eric. "Slavs Are Us," *Times Literary Supplement*, January 6, 1995, p. 18.

Kushner, Tony. *Thinking About the Longstanding Problems of Virtue and Happiness. Essays, A Play, Two Poems and A Prayer*. New York: Theatre Communications Group, Inc., 1995. [*Slavs!* appears on pp. 81–185.]

Lahr, John. "Beyond Nelly," *New Yorker*, November 23, 1992, p. 129.

———. "Hail, Slavonia," *New Yorker*, January 9, 1995, pp. 85–87.

Macaulay, Alastair. "Tony Kushner's *Slavs!*" *Financial Times* (London), December 15, 1994, p. 23.

Marowitz, Charles. *Alarums and Excursions. Our Theatres in the 90s*. Preface by Irving Wardle. New York and London: Applause Books, 1996.

Phillips, Michael. "The Party's Over," *San Diego Union-Tribune*, August 1, 1995, pp. E1, E3.

Richards, David. "History Hung Over: Post-Soviet Aches and Absurdities," *New York Times*, December 13, 1994, pp. C17–C18.

Robinson, Marc, "Reds Scared," *Village Voice*, December 20, 1994, p. 91.

Rousuck, J. Wynn. "Witty Juxtapositions Season the Heavy-Duty, Thought-Provoking Nature of *Slavs!*" *Baltimore Sun*, January 12, 1995, p. E1.

Simon, John. "From *Slavs!* To Slavonia," *New York*, January 9, 1995, pp. 52–53.

Stearns, David Patrick. "*Slavs!*: Deconstructing Soviets," *USA Today*, June 24, 1994, p. 4D.

Tynan, William. "Red Sunset," *Time*, January 16, 1995, p. 73.

Weales, Gerald. "American Theatre Watch, 1994–1995," *Georgia Review*, vol. 49, fall 1995, pp. 697–707.

Weiss, Hedy. "*Slavs!*" *Chicago Sun-Times*, April 18, 2000, p. 32.

Williams, Raymond. *Marxism and Literature*. Oxford: Oxford University Press, 1977.

Winer, Laurie. "Old Bolshevik Resurfaces," *Los Angeles Times*, August 1, 1995, pp. F1, F5.

———. "Questions Unanswered in Kushner's *Slavs!*" *Los Angeles Times*, October 27, 1995, pp. F1, F28.

Winn, Steven. "*Slavs!* Tony Kushner Play at Berkeley Rep Breathes Life Into Soviet Socialism's Last Gasp," *San Francisco Chronicle*, March 9, 1996, p. B1.

Chapter 5

Ansky, S. "The Jewish Folk Spirit and Its Creations," *Collected Works*, vol. XV. Vilna, Warsaw, and New York: Ansk Publishers, 1925.

Applebome, Peter. "Theatre: Echoes of Evil in a Texas Cow Pasture," *New York Times*, July 17, 1988, sec. 2, p. 5.

Berman, Marc. "*Widows*," *Variety*, August 12, 1991, p. 49.

Billington, Michael. "Arts Theatre, Reviews: *The Illusion*," *The Guardian* (London), June 18, 1997, p. T12.

Brantley, Ben. "Talking to the Dead, Yearning for Answers," *New York Times*, February 20, 1995, pp. C9, C13.

Braunagel, Don. "*The Good Person of Setzuan*," *Variety*, August 8–14, 1994, p. 74.

Brecht, Bertolt. *Brecht on Theatre. The Development of an Aesthetic*. Edited and translated by John Willett. New York: Hill and Way, 1957.

Breslin, Patrick. "Ariel Dorfman: A Writer in Exile," *Washington Post*, June 12, 1983, p. BW6.

Britton, Jeff. "Modern Twist Sharpens SD's *Good Person*," *Long Beach Blade*, August 1994.

Brown, Hilda Meldrum. *Heinrich von Kleist. The Ambiguity of Art and the Necessity of Form*. Oxford: Clarendon Press, 1998.

Cheuse, Alan. "The 'Disappeared' and the Jettisoned," *New York Times*, July 24, 1983, sec. 7, p. 10.

Dorfman, Ariel. "To Have and Have Not," *The Guardian* (London), February 22, 1997, p. 6.

Drabelle, Dennis. "Chile, Cartoons and Commitment," *Washington Post*, June 12, 1983, p. BW6.

Drake, Sylvie. "Widows An Exercise in Artifice," *Los Angeles Times*, July 26, 1991, pp. F1, F23.

Dyer, Richard. "*The Illusion* Connects With the Real Illusions of Life," *Boston Globe*, February 17, 1995, p. 37.

———. "Kushner Gives *Dybbuk* New Life," *Boston Globe*, March 15, 1995, p. 65.

Feingold, Michael. "*The Illusion*," *Village Voice*, February 1, 1994, p. 89.

Fisher, James. "Performance Review: *The Good Person of Setzuan*," *Theatre Journal*, vol. 52, no. 1, March 2000, pp. 120–21.

Gerard, Jeremy. "*The Illusion*," *Variety*, January 24–30, 1994, p. 67.

Goethe, Johann Wolfgang von. *Goethe. The Collected Works. Volume 7. Early Verse Drama and Prose Plays*. Edited by Cyrus Hamlin and Frank Ryder. Princeton, NJ: Princeton University Press, 1988.

Gold, Sylviane. "Today's Big-Name Playwrights Are Busy Translating the Past's," *New York Times*, August 3, 1997, section 2, p. 5.

Goldstein, Richard. "A Queer Dybbuk," *Village Voice*, December 2, 1997, p. 59.

Greene, Alexis. "*A Dybbuk*," *In Theater*, December 5, 1997, p. 14.

Gussow, Mel. "A Magical Journey through Life, Love and Art," *New York Times*, January 18, 1990, p. C21.

Hulbert, Dan. "Review: *The Illusion*," *Atlanta Journal and Constitution*, March 3, 1995, p. 10P.

Illuminations, Stories of the Plays of the 1993 Season, Oregon Shakespeare Festival.

Isherwood, Charles. "Review/Stage: *Dybbuk* Impressive," *Variety*, November 24–30, 1997, p. 72.

Johnson, Barry. "*Illusion* a Grand Spectacle," *Portland Oregonian*, December 10, 1993, pp. K1, K3.

Koehler, Robert. "Caretaker of the Missing; Chilean Author Ariel Dorfman Wrote of Los Desaparecidos in his Novel *Widows*; Now He's Preserving Their Memory on Stage," *Los Angeles Times*, July 21, 1991, p. C4.

Kushner, Tony. *The Good Person of Setzuan*. Adapted from Bertolt Brecht. Unpublished first draft (La Jolla Playhouse), 1995, 1997.

———. *Grim(m)*. After "The Two Journeymen" by the Brothers Grimm. Unpublished second draft, August 11, 1995.

———. *The Illusion*. Freely adapted from Pierre Corneille by Tony Kushner. New York: Theatre Communications Group, Inc., 1994.

———. *Saint Cecilia, or The Power of Music*. Based on the story by Heinrich von Kleist. Unpublished first draft, September 1, 1997.

———. *Stella. A Play for Lovers*. Freely adapted from Goethe. Unpublished first draft, July 11, 1996.

———. and Joachim Neugroschel. *A Dybbuk and Other Tales of the Supernatural*. Adapted and translated from S. Ansky. New York: Theatre Communications Group, Inc., 1998.

Mann, Jordan. "The Good Person of La Jolla," *Theater Week*, July 18–24, 1994, pp. 22–23.

Mart. "*The Illusion*," *Variety*, January 17, 1990, p. 61.

McKittrick, Ryan. "Kushner's *Illusion* Made Palpable," *Boston Globe*, May 19, 2000, p. C12.

Nilsen, Richard. "Witty, Gritty *Illusion* Is Exceptionally Real Theatre," *Arizona Republic*, April 1, 1997, p. C1.

Peter, John. "Rest of the Week's Theatre," *Sunday Times* (London), June 22, 1997, sec. 11, p. 25.

Phillips, Michael. "Kushner to Adapt Brecht's *Good Person*," *San Diego Union-Tribune*, January 26, 1994, p. E6.

———. "Too-Casual Air Leaves Play Oddly Becalmed," *San Diego Union-Tribune*, August 2, 1994, p. E1.

Pirandello, Luigi. "Introduction to the Italian Theatre," translated by Anne Paolucci, in *The Genius of Italian Theatre*. Edited by Eric Bentley. New York: Mentor Books, 1964.

Richards, David. "Kushner's Adaptation of a French Classic," *New York Times*, January 20, 1994, pp. C15–C16.

Rosenthal, David. "Back From the Vanishing Point," *Times* (London), March 5, 1997, p. 35.

Senior, Jennifer. "Betwixt and Between," *New York*, November 10, 1997, p. 83.

Shirley, Don. "Stage Watch: *Widows* and *Discovery* Dropped from Mark Taper Season," *Los Angeles Times*, April 12, 1990, p. F4.

Simon, John. "Animal Attraction," *New York*, December 1, 1997, p. 110.

———. "Illusions and Delusions," *New York*, January 31, 1994, pp. 69–70.

Solomon, Alisa. *Re-Dressing the Canon. Essays on Theatre and Gender*. London and New York: Routledge, 1997.

———. "Seeking Answers in Yiddish Classics," *New York Times*, November 16, 1997, Sec. 2, pp. 7, 22.

Spears, Ricky. "*The Good Person of Setzuan*," *In Theater*, June 21, 1999, p. 13.

Taylor, Markland. "*A Dybbuk or Between Two Worlds*," *Variety*, February 27–March 5, 1995, pp. 83–84.

Vorlicky, Robert H., ed. *Tony Kushner in Conversation*. Ann Arbor: University of Michigan Press, 1997.

Williams, Raymond. *Drama. From Ibsen to Brecht*. New York: Oxford University Press, 1969, p. 282.

Winer, Laurie. "A Good Look at the Hard Lessons of *Good Person*," *Los Angeles Times*, August 2, 1994, p. F1.

Winn, Steven. "Success No Illusion," *San Francisco Chronicle*, July 9, 1991, pp. E1–E2.

Worrall, Nick. *Modernism and Realism on the Soviet Stage. Tairov—Vakhtangov—Okhlopkov*. Cambridge: Cambridge University Press, 1989.

Chapter 6

Bernstein, Andrea. "Tony Kushner," *Mother Jones*, July/August 1995, p. 59.

Brantley, Ben. "How Aged These Sonnets, But They Doth Speak Fresh," *New York Times*, June 23, 1998, p. E1.

Clapp, Susannah. "Theatre: If Only We Could Have a Lily Savage in Parliament . . . ," *Observer* (London), July 25, 1999, p. 9.

Cliff, Nigel. "*Home Body/Kabul*," *Times* (London), July 19, 1999, p. 19.

Edwardes, Jane. "Kabul's Eye," *Time Out*, June 30–July 7, 1999, n.p.

Greene, Alexis. "The Humana Festival," *Theater Week*, April 22–28, 1996, pp. 13–14, 16–17.

Gussow, Mel. "The Plays Tell the Tale," *American Theatre*, July–August 1996, p. 52–54.

Halliburton, Rachel. "The Magic of 'Might' and 'Do,'" *Independent* (London), July 19, 1999, p. 9.

Hammond, John. "*Love's Fire*," *In Theater*, July 10, 1998, pp. 12–14.

Hewison, Robert, "*Home Body/Kabul*," *Sunday Times*, July 25, 1999, sec. II, p. 20.

Kushner, Tony. *And the Torso Even More So*, in *Humana Festival '99. The Complete Plays*. Foreword by Jon Jory. Edited by Michael Bigelow Dixon and Amy Wegener. Lyme, NH: Smith and Kraus, 1999, pp. 303–5.

———. "A Backstage Pass to Hell," in *New York Times Magazine*, December 29, 1996, pp. 22–23.

———. *Death and Taxes. Hydriotaphia and Other Plays*. New York: Theatre Communications Group, Inc., 2000.

———. E-mail to James Fisher, March 18, 2000.

———. *Home Body/Kabul*. Unpublished first draft, December 3, 1997.

———. "*It's an Undoing World, or Why Should It Be Easy When It Can Be Hard?*," in *Conjunctions: 25. The New American Theatre*. Guest edited by John Guare. Annandale-on-Hudson, NY: Bard College, 1995, pp. 14–37.

———. Letter to James Fisher, December 28, 1996.

———. "*Notes on Akiba*," in *Too Jewish:: Challenging Traditional Identities*. Edited by Norman L. Kleeblatt. New York: The Jewish Museum, under the auspices of the Jewish Theological Seminary of America, and New Brunswick, NJ: Rutgers University Press, 1996, pp. 114–27.

———. "*Reverse Transcription. Six Playwrights Bury a Seventh. A Ten-Minute Play That's Nearly Twenty Minutes Long*," in *Humana Festival '96: The Complete Plays*. Edited by Michael Bigelow Dixon and Liz Engelman. Foreword by Jon Jory. Lyme, NH: Smith and Kraus, 1996, pp. 113–25.

———. "*Terminating, or Lass Meine Schmerzen Nicht Verloren Sein, or Ambivalence*," in *Love's Fire. Seven New Plays Inspired by Seven Shakespearean Sonnets*. Original works by Eric Bogosian, William Finn, John Guare, Tony Kushner, Marsha Norman, Ntozake Shange, Wendy Wasserstein. Introduction by Mark Lamos. New York: William Morrow, 1998, pp. 45–65.

Marmion, Patrick. "Confucius He Say, It's Hypnotic," *Evening Standard* (London), July 22, 1999, p. 35.

Morley, Sheridan. "Sondheim's Roam Away From Rome," *International Herald Tribune*, July 28, 1999, p. 10.

Segal, Lewis. "Weekend Reviews: Dance: Collaborative Night Belongs to Klezmatics," *Los Angeles Times*, August 14, 1995, p. F3.

Shenton, Mark. "London: Shylock, Lenny & Musicals Galore," *In Theater*, September 6–13, 1999, pp. 46–47.

Simon, John. "Thin Skin," *New York*, July 20, 1998, pp. 76–77.

Zoglin, Richard. "His Play's the Thing," *Time*, July 6, 1998, p. 92.

Chapter 7

Brown, Henry Box. *Narrative of the Life of Henry Box Brown, Written by Himself*. First English Edition. Manchester, England: Lee and Glynn, 1851.

Coe, Robert. "Let's Make a Deal," *American Theatre*, July/August 1994, pp. 14–21, 73.

Edwardes, Jane. "Kabul's Eye," *Time Out*, June 30–July 7, 1999.

Gold, Sylviane, "Seeking a Theatre Varied as a Rainbow," *New York Times*, February 23, 1997, sec. 2, pp. 5, 24.

Hawthorne, Christopher. "Coming Out As a Socialist," *Salon* (online interview [http://www.salon.com/weekly/interview960610.html]), April 18, 1996.

Kushner, Tony. *Caroline, or Change*. Unpublished first draft, June 28, 1998.

———. "Copious, Gigantic, and Sane," *Los Angeles Times*, April 25, 1993, p. M1.

———. *East Coast Ode to Howard Jarvis*. Unpublished third draft, January 8, 1997.

———. "Fo's Last Laugh—I," *Nation*, November 3, 1997, p. 4.

———. "Is It a Fiction That Playwrights Create Alone?" *New York Times*, November 21, 1993, sec. 2, p. 31.

———. "Kushner Replies," *Nation*, December 28, 1998, p. 23.

———. "The Lawyer, The Poet," *Advocate*, May 27, 1997, p. 104.

———. "Letter to the Editor," *New Yorker*, January 30, 1995, p. 11.

———. "Matthew's Passion," *Nation*, November 9, 1998, pp. 4–6.

———. "Remembering Frank," *Advocate*, June 23, 1998, p. 136.

———. "The State of the Theatre," *Times Literary Supplement*, April 28, 1995, p. 14.

———. *Thinking About the Longstanding Problems of Virtue and Happiness. Essays, A Play, Two Poems, and A Prayer*. New York: Theatre Communications Group, Inc., 1995.

Marks, Peter. "On Stage, and Off," *New York Times*, June 28, 1996, p. C2.

Vorlicky, Robert H., ed. *Tony Kushner in Conversation*. Ann Arbor: University of Michigan Press, 1997.

Select Bibliography

Primary Sources

Plays

And the Torso Even More So, in *Humana Festival '99. The Complete Plays*. Foreword by Jon Jory. Edited by Michael Bigelow Dixon and Amy Wegener. Lyme, NH: Smith and Kraus, 1999, pp. 303–5.

Angels in America. A Gay Fantasia on National Themes. Part One: Millennium Approaches. London: National Theatre/Nick Hern, 1992; New York: Theatre Communications Group, Inc., 1992, 1993. The complete play or excerpts also appear in *The Best Plays of 1992–1993*. New York: Limelight Editions, 1993, pp. 233–50; *American Theatre*, June 1992, pp. 1–16; *The Way We Live Now. American Plays and the AIDS Crisis*. Edited by M. Elizabeth Osborn. New York: Theatre Communications Group, Inc., 1990, pp. 129–35.

Angels in America. A Gay Fantasia on National Themes. Part Two: Perestroika. London: National Theatre/Nick Hern, 1994; New York: Theatre Communications Group, Inc., 1992, 1994. The complete play or excerpts appear in *The Best Plays of 1993–1994*. New York: Limelight Editions, 1994, pp. 259–85; *American Theatre*, July/August 1992, pp. 1–13; *Contemporary American Monologues for Men*. Edited by Todd Lincoln. New York: Theatre Communications Group, Inc., 1998, pp. 109–10; *Contemporary American Monologues for Women*. Edited by Todd Lincoln. New York: Theatre Communications Group, Inc., 1998, p. 131.

Angels in America. A Gay Fantasia on National Themes. Part One: Millennium Approaches/Angels in America. Part Two: Perestroika. New York: Theatre Communications Group, Inc., 1994. [A slipcased, paperback two-volume edition of the previously published single play versions.]

Angels in America. A Gay Fantasia on National Themes. Part One: Millennium Approaches/Angels in America. Part Two: Perestroika. New York: Theatre Communications Group, Inc., 1995. [A slipcased, hardbound edition in one volume that includes both *Angels* plays, with a revised version of *Perestroika*, and numerous illustrations of international productions of the play.]

A Backstage Pass to Hell, in *New York Times Magazine*, December 29, 1996, pp. 22–23. [Also known as *G. David Schine in Hell*, this is a short one-act play.]

A Bright Room Called Day. New York: Theatre Communications Group, Inc., 1987, 1992, 1994. The complete play or excerpts appear in *Seven Different Plays*. Edited by Mac Wellman. New York: Broadway Play Publishing, 1988, pp. 181–259; *Contemporary American Monologues for Men*. Edited by Todd Lincoln. New York: Theatre Communications Group, Inc., 1998, pp. 64–65; *Contemporary American Monologues for Women*. Edited by Todd Lincoln. New York: Theatre Communications Group, Inc., 1998, pp. 3–6, 103–4.

Death & Taxes: Hydriotaphia & Other Plays. New York: Theatre Communications Group, Inc., 2000.

A Dybbuk and Other Tales of the Supernatural (with Joachim Neugroschel). Adapted and Translated from S. Ansky. New York: Theatre Communications Group, Inc., 1998.

The Illusion. Freely adapted by Tony Kushner from the play by Pierre Corneille. New York: Theatre Communications Group, Inc., 1994.

It's an Undoing World, or Why Should It Be Easy When It Can Be Hard?, in *Conjunctions: 25. The New American Theater*. Guest Edited by John Guare. Annandale-on-Hudson, NY: Bard College, 1995, pp. 14–37.

A Meditation from Angels in America. A Folding Screen Book. San Francisco: HarperSan Francisco, 1994.

Notes on Akiba, in *Too Jewish?: Challenging Traditional Identities*. Edited by Norman L. Kleeblatt. New York: The Jewish Museum, under the auspices of the Jewish Theological Seminary of America, and New Brunswick, NJ: Rutgers University Press, 1996, pp. 114–27.

Plays by Tony Kushner. New York: Broadway Play Publishing, Inc., 1992, 1999. [Includes *A Bright Room Called Day*, *The Illusion*, and *Slavs! Thinking About the Longstanding Problems of Virtue and Happiness*]

Plays by Tony Kushner. New York: Broadway Play Publishing, 1992. [Includes *A Bright Room Called Day* and *The Illusion*.]

Reverse Transcription. Six Playwrights Bury a Seventh. A Ten-Minute Play That's Nearly Twenty Minutes Long, in *Humana Festival '96: The Complete Plays*. Edited by Michael Bigelow Dixon and Liz Engelman. Foreword by Jon Jory. Lyme, NH: Smith and Kraus, 1996, pp. 113–25; *From the Other Side of the Century II: A New American Drama 1960–1995*. Edited with prefaces by Douglas Messerli and Mac Wellman. With an introduction by Marc Robinson. Los Angeles: Sun & Moon Press, 1998, pp. 1181–92; *Take Ten: New 10–Minute Plays*. Edited by Eric Lane and Nina Shengold. New York: Vintage Books, 1997, pp. 101–16.

Slavs! Thinking About the Longstanding Problems of Virtue and Happiness. New York: Broadway Play Publishing, Inc., 1996. The complete play or excerpts also appear in *Humana Festival '94: The Complete Plays*. Edited by Marisa Smith. Lyme, NH: Smith and Kraus, 1994, pp. 131–78; *Thinking About the Longstanding Problems of Virtue and Happiness. Essays, A Play, Two Poems, and A Prayer* by Tony Kushner. New York: Theatre Communications Group, Inc., 1995, pp. 81–185.

Terminating, or Lass Meine Schmerzen Nicht Verloren Sein, or Ambivalence, in *Love's Fire. Seven New Plays Inspired by Seven Shakespearean Sonnets*. Original works by Eric Bogosian, William Finn, John Guare, Tony Kushner, Marsha Norman, Ntosake

Shange, Wendy Wasserstein. Introduction by Mark Lamos. New York: William Morrow, 1998, pp. 45–65.

Widows (with Ariel Dorfman), in *Lector, Viuda. Teatro 2*. Buenos Aires: Ediciones de la Flor, 1996, pp. 86–191.

Yes Yes No No. The Solace of Solstice Apogee/Perigee Bestial/Celestial Holiday Show in *Plays in Process. Three Plays for Young Audiences*. Vol. 7, no. 11. New York: Theatre Communications Group, 1987, n.p.

Selected Prose

"Advance Praise," quote on cover of *Consider This [Home]*, by Greg Bills. New York: Simon and Schuster, 1994.

"Afterword," for *Gross Indecency: The Three Trials of Oscar Wilde*, by Moises Kaufman. New York: Vintage Books, 1998, pp. 135–43.

"American Things," in *Thinking About the Longstanding Problems of Virtue and Happiness. Essays, A Play, Two Poems, and A Prayer*. New York: Theatre Communications Group, Inc., 1995, pp. 3–11.

"The Art of the Difficult," *Civilization*, Vol. 4, No. 4, August/September 1997, pp. 62–67.

"Copious, Gigantic, and Sane," *Los Angeles Times*, April 25, 1993, p. M1. Also appears in *Thinking About the Longstanding Problems of Virtue and Happiness. Essays, A Play, Two Poems, and A Prayer*. New York: Theatre Communications Group, Inc., 1995, pp. 49–54; *The Routledge Reader in Politics and Performance*. Edited by Lizbeth Goodman with Jane de Gay. London and New York: Routledge, 2000, pp. 178–80.

"Fallen Angels," *New Republic*, June 14, 1993, pp. 4–5.

"Fick oder Kaputt!" in *Thinking About the Longstanding Problems of Virtue and Happiness. Essays, A Play, Two Poems, and A Prayer*. New York: Theatre Communications Group, Inc., 1995, pp. 13–17.

"Fighting the Art Bullies," *Nation*, November 29, 1999, pp. 41–42.

"Fireworks and Freedom," *Newsweek*, June 27, 1994, p. 46.

"Foreword," *Staging Gay Lives. An Anthology of Contemporary Gay Theater*. Edited by John M Clum. Oxford and Boulder, CO: Westview Press, 1996, pp. vii-ix.

"Foreword," in *Two Plays*. The Normal Heart *and* The Destiny of Me, by Larry Kramer. New York: Grove Press, 2000, pp. vii–xxv.

"Fo's Last Laugh—I," *Nation*, November 3, 1997, pp. 4–5.

"Gay Perestroika," *Advocate*, December 23, 1997, p. 72.

"Gays in the Military: The Pursuit of Social Justice," *Los Angeles Times*, January 31, 1993, pp. M1, M6.

"Guest Speaker: Tony Kushner. The *Angels in America* Author on Beauty and Ambivalence," *Architectural Digest*, volume 52, number II, 1995, pp. 28, 32.

"Holding Our Noses," *Advocate*, October 29, 1996, p. 53.

"I Am Your Newt," *Advocate*, June 24, 1995, p. 10.

"I Have a Dream," *Advocate*, October 18, 1994, p. 8.

"Introduction," in *The Mystery of Irma Vep and Other Plays*, by Charles Ludlam. New York: Consortium Books, 2000.

"Introduction," in *Two Plays*. The Normal Heart *and* The Destiny of Me, by Larry Kramer. New York: Grove Press, 2000.

"Introduction," in *Queer and Loathing: Rants and Raves of a Raging AIDS Clone,* by David B. Feinberg. New York: Penguin, 1995, pp. ix–x.

"Introduction," in *Stuck Rubber Baby,* by Howard Cruse. New York: HarperPerennial, 1996, pp. i–iv.

"Introduction," in *Tales of the Lost Formicans and Other Plays,* by Constance Congdon. New York: Theatre Communications Group, Inc., 1994, pp. ix–xii.

"Introduction," in *The Waterfront Journals,* by David Wojnarowicz. Edited by Amy Scholder. New York: Grove/Atlantic, 1996.

"Is It a Fiction That Playwrights Create Alone?," *New York Times,* Nov. 21, 1993, section 2, pp. 1, 30–31.

"Key West Weekend," *Advocate,* March 4, 1997, p. 64.

"Kushner Replies," *Nation,* December 29, 1998, p. 23.

"The Lawyer, The Poet," *Advocate,* May 27, 1997, p. 104.

"Letter to the Editor," *New York Times Magazine,* October 24, 1999, pp. 14, 16.

"Letter to the Editor," *New Yorker,* January 30, 1995, p. 11.

"Matthew's Passion," *Nation,* November 9, 1998, pp. 4–6.

"A Modest Proposal," *American Theatre,* January 1998, pp. 20–22, 77–89.

"Notes About Political Theatre," *Kenyon Review,* vol. XIX, nos. 3/4, summer/fall 1997, pp. 19–34.

"On Pretentiousness," in *Taking Liberties. Gay Men's Essays on Politics, Culture & Sex.* Edited by Michael Bronski. New York: Richard Kasak, 1996, pp. 207–27. Also appears in *Thinking About the Longstanding Problems of Virtue and Happiness. Essays, A Play, Two Poems, and A Prayer.* New York: Theatre Communications Group, Inc., 1995, pp. 55–79.

"One of the Greats," in *Conducting a Life. Reflections on the Theatre of Maria Irene Fornes.* Edited by Maria M. Delgado and Caridad Svich. Lyme, NH: Smith and Kraus, 1999.

"The Other: Being Gay in America," *Los Angeles Times,* April 25, 1993, p. M1.

"Outtakes from *Perestroika,*" *Theater Week,* January 17–23, 1994, pp. 22–25.

"The Play That Matters," *Dramatics,* Vol. 67, No. 9, May 1996, pp. 4–5.

"Poem: (from) The Second Month of Mourning," *Threepenny Review,* spring 1992, p. 13.

"A Prayer," in *Sex, Spirit, Community. Gay Men at the Millennium.* Edited by Michael Lowenthal. New York: Jeremy P. Tarcher/Putnam, 1997, pp. 170–76.

"Problems of My Own," *Advocate,* March 31, 1998, p. 88.

"Rants & Raves," *Advocate,* October 13, 1998, p. 10.

"Remembering Frank," *Advocate,* June 23, 1998, p. 136.

"The Secrets of *Angels*" (as told to Williams Harris), *New York Times,* March 27, 1994, p. H5.

"Sex is Still Worth It," *Esquire,* October 1993, p. 158.

"A Socialism of the Skin (Liberation, Honey!)," *Nation,* July 4, 1994, pp. 9–14. Also appears in "A Socialism of the Skin," in *Perspectives.* New York: The Nation, 1997, pp. 135–42; *Taking Liberties. Gay Men's Essays on Politics, Culture & Sex.* Edited by Michael Bronski. New York: Richard Kasak, 1996, pp. 49–60; *Thinking About the Longstanding Problems of Virtue and Happiness. Essays, A Play, Two Poems, and A Prayer.* New York: Theatre Communications Group, Inc., 1995, pp. 19–32; *The Best of The Nation. Selections from the Independent Magazine of Politics and Culture.* Edited by Victor Navasky and Katrina Vanden Heuvel. Foreword by Gore Vidal. New York: Nation Books, 2000, pp. 307–15.

"Some Questions About Tolerance," in *Thinking About the Longstanding Problems of Virtue and Happiness. Essays, A Play, Two Poems, and A Prayer*. New York: Theatre Communications Group, Inc., 1995, pp. 41–47.

"Some Thoughts About Maria Irene Fornes," in *The Theater of Maria Irene Fornes*. Edited by Marc Robinson. Baltimore and London: PAJ/Johns Hopkins University Press, 1999, pp. 130–33.

"The State of the Theatre," *Times Literary Supplement*, April 28, 1995, p. 14. [Kushner contributes a short essay, along with numerous other current theatrical practitioners, on issues in contemporary theatre.]

"Stroking at the Easel," *The Advocate*, September 2, 1997, p. 72.

"The Theater of Utopia," *Theater*, 1995, vol. 26, nos. 1 & 2, pp. 9–11.

Thinking About the Longstanding Problems of Virtue and Happiness. Essays, A Play, Two Poems, and A Prayer. New York: Theatre Communications Group, Inc., 1995.

"Three Screeds from Key West," *The Harvard Gay & Lesbian Review*, volume IV, number 2, spring 1997, pp. 20–23. Also appears in *We Must Love One Another or Die: The Life and Legacies of Larry Kramer*. New York: St. Martin's Press, 1997, pp. 191–99.

"Tony Kushner vs. Robert Brustein: An Angelic Slugfest," *New Republic*, vol. 208, no. 24, June 14, 1993, pp. 4–5.

"The 20th Century: Good or Bad," *New York Times Magazine*, September 20, 1998, pp. 76–77.

"University or Trade School?," *New York Times*, June 28, 1993, p. A17.

"Who's the Victim?," *New Yorker*, January 30, 1995, p. 11.

"Why We Must Fight," *Stage Directions*, June–July 1997, p. 7.

"Wings of Desire," *Premiere*, October 1997, p. 70.

"With a Little Help From My Friends," in *The Best Writing on Writing*. Edited by Jack Heffron. Two volumes. Cincinnati: Story Press, 1994, 1995, pp. 20–25. Also appears in *Thinking About the Longstanding Problems of Virtue and Happiness. Essays, A Play, Two Poems, and A Prayer*. New York: Theatre Communications Group, Inc., 1995, pp. 33–40. [This essay also appears in the Theatre Communications Groups edition of *Angels in America, Part Two: Perestroika*, pp. 149–58.]

Poetry

"An Epithalamion," in *Thinking About the Longstanding Problems of Virtue and Happiness. Essays, A Play, Two Poems, and A Prayer*. New York: Theatre Communications Group, Inc., 1995, pp. 189–202.

"The Second Month of Mourning," in *Life Sentences. Writers, Artists, and AIDS*. Edited by Thomas Avena. San Francisco: Mercury House, 1994, pp. 247–57. Also appears in *Thinking About the Longstanding Problems of Virtue and Happiness. Essays, A Play, Two Poems, and A Prayer*. New York: Theatre Communications Group, Inc., 1995, pp. 203–13.

Recordings

Klezmatics. *Possessed* (Green Linnet Records, Inc., XENO 4050). [Kushner provided liner notes for this recording, which features music by the Klezmatics used in the New York production of Kushner's *A Dybbuk*.]

Interviews/Profiles

Annas, Teresa. "Meet Pulitzer-winning Playwright," *Virginian Pilot*, October 4, 1996, p. E5.

Armistead, Claire. "Dynamic Slav Driver. As His New Play *Slavs!* Prepares to Open in London, Explains Why He Refuses to Move Into Film," *Guardian* (London), December 7, 1994, p. T4.

Arnott, Christopher. "Tony Winner," *New Haven Advocate*, March 9, 1995, pp. 16–18.

Barnes, Michael. "Master of Moral Matters," *Austin American-Statesman*, April 10, 1998, pp. F1, F8.

Benedict, David. "Arts: A Seriously Funny Writer: High Drama and Big Ideas Made Tony Kushner's *Angels in America* a Worldwide Hit. But Wit Held It Together," *Independent* (London), July 13, 1999, p. 9.

Bernstein, Andrea. "Interview with Tony Kushner," in *The Bedford Introduction to Drama* by Lee A. Jacobus. Third Edition. Boston: Bedford Books, 1997, pp. 1673–76.

Bernstein, Andrea. "Tony Kushner," *Mother Jones*, July–August 1995, pp. 59, 64.

Berson, Misha. "After *Angels*, Kushner Is a Very Busy Man," *Seattle Times*, April 7, 1996, p. M8.

Blanchard, Bob. "Playwright of Pain and Hope." *Progressive*, October 1994, vol. 58, pp. 42–44.

Brown, Tony. "Creator of *Angels*," *Charlotte Observer*, March 17, 1996, pp. 1F, 4F.

———. "Playwright Comments on Play, Charlotte Controversy," *Charlotte Observer*, March 17, 1996.

C. A. "Kushner in Connecticut: Part One: *In the Heart of America*," *New Haven Advocate*, December 8, 1994, p. 47.

Corathers, Don. "Tony Meets the Press," *Dramatics*, vol. 65, no. 9, May 1994, pp. 6–7.

Dodds, Richard. "Winged Victory," *New Orleans Times-Picayune*, January 3, 1997, Magazine Sec., pp. 18, 20.

Goldstein, Richard. "A Queer Dybbuk," *Village Voice*, December 2, 1997, p. 59.

Harris, William. "In *Slavs!* Are the Echoes of *Angels*," *New York Times*, December 4, 1994, sec. 2, pp. 5, 36.

———. "The Road to Optimism," *Dance Ink*, vol. 6, no. 1, Spring 1995, pp. 28–29.

Hawthorne, Christopher. "Coming Out As a Socialist," *Salon* (on-line interview [http://www.salon.com/weekly/interview960610.html]), April 18, 1996.

Hulbert, Dan. "A Conversation With Tony Kushner," *Atlanta Journal and Constitution*, September 1, 1994.

"I Always Go Back to Brecht," *Brecht Yearbook/Das Brecht-Jahrbuch*, Vol. 25, 1995, pp. 67–88.

Jonas, Susan. "Tony Kushner's *Angels*," in *Dramaturgy in American Theater: A Source Book*. Edited by Susan Jonas, Geoff Proehl, and Michael Lupu. New York: Harcourt Brace, 1997, pp. 472–82.

Jones, Adam Mars. "Tony Kushner," *Platform Papers 2: On "Angels in America*. London: Royal National Theatre of Great Britain, 1992, pp. 3–15.

Kelly, Kevin. "*Angels* in Hollywood. Tony Kushner Talks About Making the Move From Stage to Screen," *Boston Globe*, August 8, 1994, pp. 49, 59.

Kuchwara, Michael. "Playwright Focuses on Troika of New Scripts," *New Haven Register*, February 26, 1995, pp. F1–F2.

"Liza Gets Another Tony," *OUT*, July/August 1994, pp. 62–64, 144–45.

Lowenthal, Michael. "On Art, Angels, and 'Postmodern Fascism'," *Harvard Gay and Lesbian Review*, vol. 2, no. 2, spring 1995, pp. 10–12.

Lubow, Arthur. "Tony Kushner's Paradise Lost," *New Yorker*, November 30, 1992, pp. 59–64.

Lucas, Craig. "The Eye of the Storm," *BOMB*, Spring 1993, pp. 30–35.

Mann, Jordan. "The Good Person of La Jolla," *Theater Week*, July 18–24, 1994, pp. 22–23.

Marvel, Mark. "A Conversation with Tony Kushner," *Interview*, February 1994, vol. 24, p. 84.

Matter, Kathy. "Art, Politics and the Gay Fantasia," *Lafayette Journal and Courier*, October 23, 1995, pp. C1–C2.

McLeod, Bruce. "The Oddest Phenomena in Modern History," *Iowa Journal of Cultural Studies*, vol. 14, no. 1, spring 1995, pp. 143–53.

Murray, Steve. "On Wings of *Angels* Epic, Writer Probes AIDS, Politics," *Atlanta Journal and Constitution*, April 25, 1993, pp. M1, M5.

"Outspoken: Tony Kushner." *Mother Jones*, July/August 1995, pp. 59, 64.

Pacheco, Patrick. "AIDS, Angels, Activism, and Sex in the Nineties," *Body Positive*, September 1993, pp. 17–28.

Preston, Rohan. "To Playwright Tony Kushner, Art is Political," *Minneapolis Star-Tribune*, April 15, 1998, p. 1E.

Raymond, Gerard. "Q & A With Tony Kushner, *Theater Week*, December 20–26, 1993, pp. 14–20.

Rengger, Patrick. "An Optimist by Will," *National Post* (Canada), June 17, 1999, p. B1.

Roca, Octavio. "Kushner's Next Stage," *San Francisco Chronicle*, September 6, 1998, p. 32.

Savran, David. "Tony Kushner," *The Playwright's Voice. American Dramatists on Memory, Writing and the Politics of Culture*. New York: Theatre Communications Group, Inc., 1999, pp. 87–118.

———. "Tony Kushner," in *Speaking on Stage. Interviews with Contemporary American Playwrights*. Edited by Philip C. Kolin and Colby H. Kullman. Tuscaloosa: University of Alabama Press, 1996, pp. 291–313.

———. "Tony Kushner Considers the Longstanding Problems of Virtue and Happiness," *American Theatre*, October 1994, pp. 20–27, 100–4.

Shirley, Don. "It's a Heavenly Assignment for Tony Kushner, But Not This Season," *Los Angeles Times*, February 6, 1994, p. 46.

———. "Kushner Finds an Angel at the Taper," *Los Angeles Times*, May 19, 1991, p. 53.

Span, Paula. "Tony Kushner's Railing Big Show. The Playwright Mixes It Up With *Angels in America*," *Washington Post*, July 31, 1992, pp. B1, B6.

Stearns, David Patrick. "A Playwright in the Power of Angels," *USA Today*, November 12, 1992, p. 13.

Stoudt, Charlotte. "The Proust Questionnaire," *The Next Stage at Center Stage*, vol. 1, no. 3, 1995, pp. 16–17.

Szentgyorgyi, Tom. "Look Back—and Forward—In Anger," *Theater Week*, January 14–20, 1991, pp. 15–19.

Tannenbaum, Perry. "*Angels in America*. Creative Loafing Talks With Playwright Tony Kushner," *Creative Loafing* (Charlottte, NC), March 16, 1996, pp. 16–18.

Toppman, Lawrence. "The Play's the Thing For Kushner, Most Questioners," *Charlotte Observer*, March 24, 1996, p. 12A.

Tyson, Ann Scott. "The Playwright Relishes Politics," *Christian Science Monitor*, July 15, 1994, p. 13.

Vorlicky, Robert H., ed. *Tony Kushner in Conversation*. Ann Arbor: University of Michigan Press, 1998.

Weber, Carl. "I Always Go Back to Brecht," *Brecht Yearbook/Das Brecht-Jahrbuch*, Vol. 25, 1995, pp. 67–88.

———. "Ich werde immer wieder zu Brecht zurück finden," *Theater der Zeit*, no. 6, 1997, pp. 42–46.

Winn, Steven. "Success No Illusion," *San Francisco Chronicle*, July 9, 1991, pp. E1–E2.

Selected Secondary Sources

"Acting: The Shoe Method," *New York Times Magazine*, June 26, 1994, p. 12.

Allen, Dennis. "Mistaken Identitites: Re-Defining Lesbian and Gay Studies," *Canadian Review of Comparative Literature/Revue Canadienne de Littérature Comparée*, March–June 1994, pp. 133–48.

Allen, John D. "Can Kushner Keep It Up In Connecticut," *In Newsweekly*, February 19, 1995, pp. 1, 4.

"An Uproar in Charlotte Streets Greets a Play About Gays, AIDS," *Atlanta Journal and Constitution*, March 22, 1996, p. C1.

Andreach, Robert J. *Creating the Self in the Contemporary American Theatre.* Carbondale and Edwardsville: Southern Illinois University Press, 1998.

Andriote, John-Manuel. *Victory Deferred. How AIDS Changed Gay Life in America.* Chicago and London: University of Chicago Press, 1999.

"Angels and the 80s. Tony Winner Soars In Its Social Context," *USA Today*, June 11, 1993, p. D3.

"*Angels* in Court?," *Charlotte Observer*, March 20, 1996, p. 12A.

"*Angels* Opening Postponed," *New York Times*, April 15, 1993, p. C22.

"*Angels* Takes Right Wing in Texas," *Advocate*, November 23, 1999, p. 18.

Anthony, Michael. "Just Like Old Times for Bobby McFerrin," *Minneapolis Star Tribune*, September 9, 1999, p. 5B.

———. "McFerrin Has a Date With San Francisco Opera," *Minneapolis Star Tribune*, March 2, 1997, p. 4F.

"Anxious in America," *New Yorker*, December 26, 1994–January 2, 1995, p. 52.

"Apocalypse Now," *Irish Times*, June 13, 1995, Arts Sec., p. 10.

Arenschieldt, Rich. "April Fools! *Hydriotaphia* Didn't Open After All," *Houston Voice*, April 3, 1998, pp. 14, 21.

———. "Theatrical 'David and Goliath," *Houston Voice*, April 17, 1998, pp. 19–20.

Arenson, Karen W. "3 Playwrights Urge CUNY to Keep Taking Remedial Students," *New York Times*, May 19, 1998, p. B8.

Arnott, Christopher. "Ronny Graham's the Oldest Slav!" *New Haven Advocate*, March 2, 1995, p. 26.

———. "Totally Tony All Over Connecticut," *Hartford Advocate*, March 9, 1995, p. 23.

Ashcraft, Tom. "*Angels in America*—Real Action Was Offstage," *Charlotte Observer*, May 7, 1996, p. 13A.

Auerbach, Mark G. "Hartford Stage to Present the Yiddish Classic *A Dybbuk*," *Jewish Weekly News*, January 26, 1995, p. 11.

Avedon, Richard. "The Faces of *Angels*," *New Yorker*, May 31, 1993, pp. 138–41.

Avery, Dan. "*Slavs!*" Articulate. *Washington & Baltimore's Contemporary Art Review*, Vol. 1, No. 3, October 1995.

Baker, Rob. *The Art of AIDS. From Stigma to Conscience. Music—Drama—Dance—Movies—Media.* New York: Continuum, 1994.

Baldridge, Charlene. "*Illusion* Works Magic on Stage," *Gay & Lesbian Times*, November 11, 1999.

Bales, Harold. "Who Should See *Angels in America*?," *Charlotte Observer*, March 20, 1996.

Barbour, David. "Site of the Iguana," *TCI*, Vol. 28, November 1994, p. 8.

Barnes, Clive. "Angelically Gay About Our Decay," *New York Post*, May 5, 1993.

———. "Magical *Illusion* Altered," *New York Post*, January 20, 1994.

Barnes, Michael. "A Bow to the Ambitious," *Austin American-Statesman*, May 10, 1998, pp. D1, D4.

———. "*Illusion* Grapples With Old Riddle," *Austin American-Statesman*, March 15, 1994, p. F6.

———. "Wilson's Grand *Illusion*," *Austin American-Statesman*, March 11, 1994, p. 18.

Barron, Karl. "*The Illusion* Is An Imaginative Must-See," *Daily Tidings* (Oregon), July 31, 1993, p. 2.

Beard, William Randall. "*Perestroika* Has Heart Where It Counts," *Minneapolis Star Tribune*, April 15, 2000, p. 4B.

Beasley, Jack. "*Angels* Survives As a Great Event, a Good Production," *Charlotte Leader*, March 29, 1996.

———. "Charlotte Rep's *Angels* Productions Take Company to New Level," *Charlotte Leader*, April 26, 1996, pp. 33.

Beim, Norman. "They're No Angels," *American Theatre*, January 1995, p. 4.

Benedict, David. "French Magic," *Financial Times* (London), June 28, 1997, p. 7.

Bercaw, Nancy Stearns. "*Angels* Wings Its Way to Vermont—And Controversy—This Fall," *Seven Days*, September 17, 1997, pp. 13–14.

Berman, Marc. "*Widows*," *Variety*, August 12, 1991, p. 49.

Biemiller, Lawrence. "Notes From Academe: *Angels in America* Challenges Students at Wabash College," *Chronicle of Higher Education*, October 18, 1996, p. B2.

———. "'Shake Out Your Hands': An Actress Seeks to Share Theatre's Sense of Community," *Chronicle of Higher Education*, October 5, 1995, p. A59.

Bigsby, Christopher. *Contemporary American Playwrights.* Cambridge: Cambridge University Press, 1999, pp. 86–131.

Bilderback, Walter. "The Square Root of Queer," *American Theatre*, April 1998, pp. 45–47.

Billington, Michael. "Angels With Restructured Faces," *Guardian* (London), November 22, 1993, p. 7.

———. "Arts Theatre, Reviews: *The Illusion*," *Guardian* (London), June 18, 1997, p. T12.

———. "Crimes That Fail to Disappear," *Guardian* (London), March 8, 1997, p. 2.

———. "Nation Built on Guilt," *Guardian* (London), January 25, 1992, p. 21.

———. "Postcards From Siberia," *Guardian* (London), December 15, 1994, p. T8.

Blanchard, Jayne M. "In the Spirit of the Times," *St. Paul Pioneer Press*, July 16, 1995, pp. 1E+.

Bliss, Gil. "Trinity Rep Startles with *The Illusion*," *Enterprise*, February 17, 1995, p. 30.

Bloch, Felicity. "Award-winning *Angels in America*," *Australian Jewish News*, September 16, 1995, p. 28.

————. "Compelling Drama as AIDS Strikes," *Australian Jewish News*, October 29, 1993, p. 6.

Bloom, Harold. *Omens of Millennium. The Gnosis of Angels, Dreams, and Resurrection*. New York: Riverhead Books, 1996.

————. *The Western Canon. The Books and School of the Ages*. New York: Riverhead Books, 1994.

Blumenthal, Ralph. "McNally Says Play Has Offers," *New York Times*, May 28, 1998, pp. B1, B10.

Borreca, Art. "Theatre Review: *Angels in America, Part I: Millennium Approaches*," *Theatre Journal*, vol. 45, no. 2, May 1993, pp. 235–38.

Bottoms, Stephen J. "Re-staging Roy: Citizen Cohn and the Search for Xanadu," *Theatre Journal*, 1996, vol. 48, pp. 157–84.

Bradley, Jeff. "Mystical *A Dybbuk* Will Have Music to Match Klezmer Trio Another Player in Yiddish Play," *Denver Post*, January 19, 1996, p. G11.

Brantley, Ben. "A *Dybbuk* Foresees 'The Martyred Dead'," *New York Times*, November 17, 1997, p. E5.

————. "How Aged These Sonnets, But They Doth Speak Fresh," *New York Times*, June 23, 1998, pp. E1.

————. "New Plays With Big Ideas, Really Big," *New York Times*, April 4, 1994, p. C13.

————. "Talking to the Dead, Yearning for Answers," *New York Times*, February 20, 1995, pp. C9, C13.

Brask, Per, ed. *Essay on Kushner's Angels*. Winnipeg: Blizzard Publishing, 1995.

Braunagel, Don. "*The Good Person of Setzuan*," *Variety*, August 8–14, 1994, p. 74.

Breslauer, Jan. "The Wizard of *Slavs!*" *Los Angeles Times*, October 22, 1995, pp. 50–52.

Britton, Jeff. "Modern Twist Sharpens SD's *Good Person*," *Long Beach Blade*, August 1994.

Broder, Michael. "Tony Kushner," in *The Gay & Lesbian Literary Companion*. Detroit, Washington, D.C., and London: Visible Ink Press, 1995, pp. 303–7.

Brooks-Dillard, Sandra. "Images in *Dybbuk* a Delight. Mystical Tale Leaves Viewer at a Distance," *Denver Post*, January 27, 1996, p. E8.

Brower, Millicent. "*A Bright Room* Is An Awfully Dim Production," *Town & Village*, January 10, 1991, p. 10.

Brown, Tony. "*Angels* Is Heavenly," *Charlotte Observer*, March 22, 1996, pp. 1E, 4E.

————. "*Angels* is Latest Example of Charlotte's New Arts Wave," *Charlotte Observer*, April 14, 1996, pp. 1F, 6F.

————. "Financing Issue Puts *Angels* in Spotlight," *Charlotte Observer*, July 19, 1996, p. 3C.

————. "Hush, Hush, Sweet Charlotte," *American Theatre*, May–June 1999, p. 48.

————. "*Millennium Approaches*," *Charlotte Observer*, March 15, 1996, pp. 1E, 4E.

————. "Play's Onstage Nudity, As Is, Risks Charges," *Charlotte Observer*, March 19, 1996, p. 4A.

————. "Theatre Aims to Avert Storm Over *Angels* Drama," *Charlotte Observer*, March 6, 1996, pp. 1A, 10A.

———— and Ricki Morell. "Poll: Don't Clip Wings of *Angels*," *Charlotte Observer*, March 24, 1996, pp. 1A, 12A.

———— and Jim Morrill. "Flap Puts *Angels* in Spotlight," *Charlotte Observer*, March 20, 1996, pp. 1A, 6A.

———— and Gary L. Wright. "*Angels* Disputes Move on to Public Agenda," *Charlotte Observer*, March 28, 1996, pp. 1A, 11A.

———— and Gary L. Wright and Paige Williams. "Judge: Let *Angels* Play," *Charlotte Observer*, March 21, 1996, pp. 1A, 10A.

Brozan, Nadine. "Chronicle: Americans Win London Theatre Awards," *New York Times*, February 12, 1993, p. A26.

Bruckner, D. J. R. "17th Century Antics," *New York Times*, November 3, 1988, p. C28.

Brustein, Robert. "Angles in America," *New Republic*, May 24, 1993, pp. 29–31.

————. *Cultural Calisthenics. Writings on Race, Politics, and Theatre*. Chicago: Ivan R. Dee, 1998.

————. *Dumbocracy in America. Studies in the Theatre of Guilt, 1987–1994*. Chicago: Ivan R. Dee, 1994.

————. "The Great Work Falters," *New Republic*, December 27, 1993, pp. 25–28.

————. "*Slavs!*" *The New Republic*, January 30, 1995, pp. 30–31.

Cadden, Michael. "Strange Angel: The Pinklisting of Roy Cohn," in *Secret Agents: The Rosenberg Case, McCarthyism, and Fifties America*. Edited by Marjorie Garber and Rebecca Walkowitz. New York: Routledge, 1995, pp. 93–105.

Campbell, Jackie. "*A Dybbuk* a Gothic Horror Wrapped in Rabbinical Garb," *Denver Rocky Mountain News*, January 25, 1996, p. 66A.

————. "*The Illusion* is Magical Drama," *Denver Rocky Mountain News*, September 16, 1994, p. 10D.

Canby, Vincent. "In *Slavs!* Kushner Creates Tragic Burlesque," *New York Times*, December 18, 1994, sec. 2, pp. 5, 24.

————. "*The Lion King* Earns Its Roars of Approval," *New York Times*, November 23, 1997, pp. 5, 20.

————. "Two *Angels*, Two Journeys, In London And New York," *New York Times*, January 30, 1994, pp. 5, 22.

Cantara, Jamie Smith. "The Millennium Arrives in Austin," *Austin American-Statesman*, April 15, 1998, p. E7.

Carne, Rosalind. "A Text to Match the Catastrophe," *Guardian* (London), January 23, 1992, p. 27.

Carney, Brian T. "Kushner Challenges Audiences With *Slavs!*" *Washington Blade*, January 20, 1995, p. 45.

Chansky, Dorothy. "Theatre on Higher Ground," *InTheater*, April 24, 1998, pp. 34–35.

Chapman, Dan. "*Angels* Dominates Debate," *Charlotte Observer*, May 14, 1996, pp. 1C, 14C.

————. "City Council Member Wants Arts Money Cut," *Charlotte Observer*, May 31, 1996, pp. 1C, 4C.

————. "Council Affirms Arts Support," *Charlotte Observer*, June 4, 1996, pp. 1A, 8A.

Cheever, Susan. "An Angel Sat Down At His Table," *New York Times*, September 13, 1992, sec. 2, p. 7.

Christiansen, Richard. "Astounding *Angels*. Part I of Kushner Saga Jolts the Emotions," *Chicago Tribune*, September 26, 1994, Arts Plus Sec., p. 1.

————. "Heavenly *Angels*," *Chicago Tribune*, October 11, 1994, sec. 2, p. 1.

————. "Keeping Up With the Times," *Chicago Tribune*, September 28, 1997, sec. 2, p. 14.

————. "*Millennium* Fits Times. Drama Treats AIDS, Homosexuality With Sensibility," *Chicago Tribune*, May 5, 1993, p. 30.

Clanchy, Kate. "*Widows*, Cambridge Art Theatre," *Scotsman*, March 7, 1997, p. 17.

Clapp, Susannah. "Theatre: If Only We Could Have a Lily Savage in Parliament . . . ," *Observer* (London), July 25, 1999, p. 9.

Cliff, Nigel. "*Home Body/Kabul*," *Times* (London), July 19, 1999, p. 19.

Clines, Francis X. "A Star's Creed: Look for Work And Then Die," *New York Times*, December 11, 1994, p. 49.

Clum, John M. *Acting Gay: Male Homosexuality in Modern Drama*. Revised edition. New York: Columbia University Press, 1994.

————. *Something for the Boys. Musical Theatre and Gay Culture*. New York: St. Martin's Press, 1999.

Coe, Robert. "Let's Make a Deal," *American Theatre*, July–August 1994, pp. 14–21, 73.

Coen, Stephanie. "Michael Mayer. One of America's Busiest Directors Reveals His Devotion to All Things Garland," *American Theatre*, March 1998, pp. 38–40.

Cohen, Peter F. *Love and Anger. Essays on AIDS, Activism, and Politics*. Binghamton, NY: Harrington Park Press, 1998.

————. "Strange Bedfellows: Writing Love and Politics in *Angels in America* and *The Normal Heart*," *Journal of Medical Humanities*, vol. 19, nos. 2/3, 1998, pp. 197–219.

Colgan, Gerry. "Inspired Direction For a Clash of Ideas," *Irish Times*, June 8, 1995, p. 12.

Colleran, Jeanne and Jenny S. Spencer. *Staging Resistance. Essays on Political Theater*. Ann Arbor: University of Michigan Press, 1998.

Collins, Glenn. "F. Murray Abraham Finds Roy Cohn in Ron Leibman's Formidable Wake," *New York Times*, March 7, 1994, pp. C11, C16.

————. "*Spider Woman* and *Angels* Win Top Honors in Tony Awards," *New York Times*, June 7, 1993, pp. C11, C16.

————. "2 Musicals Each Win 11 Tony Nominations; *Angels* Sets a Record," *New York Times*, May 11, 1993, pp. C13, C15.

Contemporary Authors, Vol. 74. New Revision Series. Farmington Hills, MI: Gale Group, 1999, pp. 250–52.

Contemporary Dramatists. Chicago and London: St. James Press, 1993.

Cooper, Andrea. "Touched by the *Angels*," *Charlotte*, 1997, pp. 43–53.

"Corneille With a Twist of Kushner," *Boston Globe*, July 29, 1994, p. 49.

Coulbourn, John. "The Angels Are On His Side," *Toronto Sun*, September 19, 1996, p. 62.

————. "*Angels* With Creaky Wings," *Toronto Sun*, September 28, 1996, p. 45.

"County Strikes At Arts Council Over Gay Play," *New York Times*, April 3, 1997, p. A17.

Coveney, Michael. "*A Bright Room*," *Financial Times* (London), July 19, 1988, Sec. I, p. 17.

————. "Heavy Metal and Angels of Light," *Observer* (London), November 28, 1993, p. 11.

Cowen, Ed. "*Slavs!* Tony Kushner's Russian Dressing," *Washington D.C. Metro Weekly*, September 14, 1995, p. 37.

C. P. "*Slavs!*" *Washington City Paper*, September 15, 1995.

————. "Critics Circle Names *Angels* Best Play," *New York Times*, May 12, 1993, p. C15.

Danton, Eric R. "Rep Theatre's *Angels* Rises to Challenge," *Hartford Courant*, October 11, 1999.

Davis, Carol. "San Diego Rep's *Illusion* Theatrical All the Way," *San Diego Jewish Times*, December 2, 1999, p. 31.

D. B. "Grand Illusion," *TCI*, November 1995, pp. 9–10.

———. "Slavic Suits," *TCI*, March 1995, p. 7.

Deem, John. "*Angels* Legal Fight: Bad Communications or Publicity Stunt?," *Charlotte Leader*, April 5, 1996, pp. 1, 16.

De Jongh, Nicholas. "Angels, Lost Souls and an Epic Glimpse of Hell," *Evening Standard* (London), November 22, 1993, p. 7.

———. "Magic of the Angels," *Evening Standard* (London), January 24, 1992, p. 7.

De La Viña, Mark. "Kushner's Farce Is a Mortal Cinch," *San Jose Mercury News*, September 18, 1998, pp. 29–30.

Delgado, Maria M. And Paul Heritage, eds. *In Contact With the Gods. Directors Talk Theatre.* Manchester: Manchester University Press, 1996.

Delisio, Ellen R. "CRT's Millennium Issues Worth Experiencing," *Storrs Journal Inquirer*, October 15, 1999.

Demastes, William W. *Theatre of Chaos. Beyond Absurdism, Into Orderly Disorder.* Cambridge: Cambridge University Press, 1998.

Dickinson, Peter. "'Go-Go Dancing on the Brink of the Apocalypse': Representing AIDS. An Essay in Seven Epigraphs," *English Studies in Canada*, vol. 20, June 1994, pp. 227–47.

Disch, Thomas M. "It's Love's *Illusion* Corneille Recalls," *New York Daily News*, January 20, 1994.

———. "Theatre: *A Bright Room Called Day, Dead Mother, Unchanging Love*," *Nation*, March 18, 1991, pp. 352–53.

Dobrzynski, Judith H. "Across US, Brush Fire Over Money for the Arts," *New York Times*, August 14, 1997, p. A1.

Dodds, Richard. "*Angels* Comes Down to Earth at CAC," *New Orleans Times-Picayune*, January 10, 1997, sec. L, pp. 24–25.

———. "In New Orleans, *Angels* Finds a Warm Embrace," *New Orleans Times-Picayune*, January 3, 1997, Magazine Sec., pp. 19–20.

Dolan, Jill. "Arguing with Kushner," *American Theatre*, April 1998, p. 3.

Donnelly, Pat. "*Angels in America* Lands," *Montreal Gazette*, May 9, 1997, section D, p. 9.

———. "*Angels in America* Soars and Inspires," *Montreal Gazette*, May 10, 1997, p. 21.

Dorfman, Ariel. "To Have and Have Not," *Guardian* (London), February 22, 1997, p. 6.

Doughty, Louise. "Angel Delight," *Mail on Sunday* (London), November 28, 1993, p. 30.

Drake, Sylvie. "*Angels* Compels in Tour of Venal '80s," *Los Angeles Times*, November 10, 1992, pp. F1, F9.

———. "*Widows* An Exercise in Artifice," *Los Angeles Times*, July 26, 1991, pp. F1, F23.

Drama Criticism, Vol. 10. Farmington Hills, MI: Gale Group, 1999, pp. 212–83.

"Drama Desk Honors *Kiss* and *Angels*," *New York Times*, May 18, 1993, p. C14.

Drukman, Steven. "A Standoff in Charlotte. *Angels* Provokes a Legal and Cultural Confrontation," *American Theatre*, May–June 1996, pp. 46–47.

Dunne. Stephen. "Astounding *Angels*," *Sydney Star Observer*, March 5, 1993, p. 14.

———. "Bums on Seats," *Sydney Star Observer*, April 8, 1994, p. 15.

———. "Exeunt, Pursued by Realism," *Syndey Star Observer*, December 22, 1993, p. 7.

Dyer, Richard. "*The Illusion* Connects With the Real Illusions of Life," *Boston Globe*, February 17, 1995, p. 37.

———. "Kushner Gives *Dybbuk* New Life," *Boston Globe*, March 15, 1995, p. 65.

———. "Kushner's *Slavs!*: Genius Isn't Enough," *Boston Globe*, April 6, 1995, p. 61.

Eckert, Toby. "*Angels in America* Sparks Devilish Debate," *Focus: Indianapolis Business Journal*, August 5–10, 1997, pp. 17A, 19A.

Edwardes, Jane. "Kabul's Eye," *Time Out*, June 30–July 7, 1999.

Edwards, Christopher. "Flights of Fantasy," *Spectator* (London), February 1992.

Elkin-Squitieri, Michelle. "'The Great Work begins': Apocalyptic and Millenarian Vision in *Angels in America*," *Anglophonia*, No. 3, 1998, pp. 203–12.

Erstein, Hap. "Message Soars on Wings of *Angels*," *Washington Times*, November 15, 1992, p. D4.

Eshom, Daniel. *Canon Querry: Testing Angels in America's Subversiveness*. MA Thesis, English Department, Colorado State University, Fort Collins, CO, 1996.

Evans, Everett. "Great *Ganesh*, *Slavs!* Are Coming," *Houston Chronicle*, September 10, 1995, p. 13.

———. "Kushner Hits Highs, Lows in Epic Farce," *Houston Chronicle*, April 10, 1998, p. D1.

———. "Kushner Still Tweaking *Hydriotaphia* Script," *Houston Chronicle*, March 30, 1998, p. C1.

———. "Last Laughs," *Houston Chronicle*, March 29, 1998, pp. 10, 20.

———. "Redgrave, Markham Scheduled for Alley Appearances," *Houston Chronicle*, June 17, 1998, p. 12.

———. "*Slavs!* Has Some Peaks But Falls Short of *Angels*," *Houston Chronicle*, September 15, 1995, Houston Section, p. 1.

Evans, Greg. "*Angels in America: A Gay Fantasia on National Themes*," *Variety*, November 16, 1992, pp. 69, 73.

———. "*Angels in American, Part Two: Perestroika*," *Variety*, December 6, 1993, pp. 33–35.

———. "*Slavs!*" *Variety*, December 19, 1994–January 1, 1995, p. 86.

Evanson, Laura. "*Angels* They Have Hoisted on High," *San Francisco Chronicle*, October 10, 1994, pp. E1, E2.

Evett, Marianne. "Hitmakers Bat Again; *Jackie* a Satirical Plot," *Plain Dealer*, November 23, 1997, p. 6I.

———. "Hot Playwright Tony Kushner Sharpens His Political Act," *Plain Dealer*, April 3, 1994, p. 9I.

Fanger, Iris. "Ghost Story From the Shtetl," *Boston Herald*, February 23, 1995, p. 47.

———. "Merrimack's *Illusion* is Simply Grand," *Boston Herald*, September 28, 1995, p. 40.

———. "R.I. Theatre Addresses Problem of Happiness," *Boston Herald*, April 2, 1995, p. 37.

———. "*Slavs!* Sends Up Soviet Union's Decline," *Boston Herald*, April 6, 1995, p. 45.

Feingold, Michael. "Bright Words," *Village Voice*, January 15, 1991, p. 87.

———. "Building the Monolith," *Village Voice*, May 18, 1993, pp. 218–19.

———. "Epic Assumptions," *Village Voice*, December 7, 1993, p. 93.

———. "*The Illusion*," *Village Voice*, February 1, 1994, p. 89.

Felman, Jyl Lynn. "Lost Jewish (Male) Souls. A Midrash on *Angels in America*," *Tikkun*, vol. 10, no. 3, May–June 1995, pp. 27–30.

Fennell, Jenifer. "Midnight in America," *Minneapolis Siren*, March 9–22, 2000, p. 26.

Fife, Stephen. "The Boomerang and the Jewish Dentist," *American Theatre*, November 1999, pp. 6–7.

"Finding a Devil Within to Portray Roy Cohn," *New York Times*, April 18, 1993, sec. 2, pp. 1, 28.

Fink, Joel G. "Performance Review: *A Dybbuk, or Between Two Worlds*," *Theatre Journal*, vol. 48, no. 4, December 1996, pp. 516–17.

Fisher, James, "'The Angels of Fructification': Tennessee Williams, Tony Kushner, and Images of Homosexuality on the American Stage," *Mississippi Quarterly*, winter 1995–96, vol. 49, no. 1, pp. 13–32.

———. "Between Two Worlds: Ansky's *The Dybbuk* and Kushner's *A Dybbuk*," *Soviet and East European Performance*, vol. 18, no. 2, summer 1998, pp. 20–32.

———. "Performance Review: *Angels in America. Part II. Perestroika*," *Theatre Journal*, vol. 47, no. 2, May 1995, pp. 291–93.

———. "Performance Review: *The Good Person of Setzuan*," *Theatre Journal*, vol. 52, no. 1, March 2000, pp. 120–21.

———. "Performance Review: *Hydriotaphia, or The Death of Dr. Browne*," *Theatre Journal*, vol. 50, no. 3, October 1998, pp. 371–72.

———. "Troubling the Waters: Visions of Apocalypse in Wilder's *The Skin of Our Teeth* and Kushner's *Angels in America*," *Thornton Wilder: New Essays*. W. Cornwall, CT: Locust Hill Press, 1998, pp. 391–407.

Fleche, Anne. *Mimetic Disillusion. Eugene O'Neill, Tennessee Williams, and U. S. Dramatic Realism*. Tuscaloosa and London: University of Alabama Press, 1997.

Foley, F. Kathleen. "Light and Lively *Illusion*," *Los Angeles Times*, May 13, 1999, p. F28.

Foster, Steven. "Alley-Oop. Tony Kushner Gives the Alley a Farce-Lift," *OutSmart*, April 1998, p. 59.

"Four Artists on Dreams, Egos and the Learning Process," *New York Times*, May 26, 1996, sec. 13, p. 10.

Fowler, Don. "Trinity Conjures Up a Magical *Illusion*," *Cranston Herald*, February 1995.

Frantzen, Allen J. *Before the Closet: Same-Sex Love From Beowulf to Angels in America*. Chicago: University of Chicago, 1998.

Freedman, Jonathan. "Angels, Monsters, and Jews: Intersections of Queer and Jewish Identity in Kushner's *Angels in America*," *PMLA*, vol. 113, no. 1, January 1998, pp. 90–102.

Friend, Tad. "*Avenging Angel*," *Vogue*, vol. 182, November 1992, pp. 158 et seq.

Fritsch, Jane. "Pulitzer Prize to a Play on AIDS and the 1980s," *New York Times*, April 14, 1993, p. B6.

Funk, Tim and Ken Garfield. "*Angels* Puts Pastors on Stage Center of Debate Over Values," *Charlotte Observer*, March 22, 1996, pp. 1A, 4A.

Gale, William K. "Director Revives *Illusion* on Stage at Trinity Rep," *Providence Sunday Journal*, February 12, 1995, p. E3.

———. "*Illusion* Performs Sleight-of-Mind," *Providence Journal-Bulletin*, February 15, 1995, pp. E1, E4.

Gallo, Clifford. "*Angels* Is a Down-to-Earth Epic," *Los Angeles Reader*, November 13, 1992.

———. "Disappearance and Reality," *Los Angeles Reader*, August 2, 1991.

Garmel, Marion. "Phoenix's *Angels* is Dazzling and Intimate," *Indianapolis Star*, September 12, 1998, p. E5.

———. "Phoenix Takes on *Angels* As IRT Drops Gay Drama," *Indianapolis Star*, December 13, 1997, p. E3.

———. "Wabash Cast Triumphant in Play About Fallibility and Forgiveness," *Indianapolis Star*, October 11, 1996, pp. E1, E9.

———. "Wabash Will Produce Indiana Premiere of Acclaimed Drama by Tony Kushner," *Indianapolis Star*, August 20, 1996, p. D3.

Gehman, Geoff. "CT's *Perestroika* Flies Brilliantly Though It Never Quite Transcends," *Allentown Morning Call*, April 19, 1997, p. A48.

———. "Touched by *Angels*," *Allentown Morning Call*, April 11, 1997, pp. D1, D3.

Geis, Deborah R. and Steven F. Kruger, eds. *Approaching the Millennium: Essays on Angels in America*. Ann Arbor: University of Michigan Press, 1997.

Gelb, Hal. "Theatre," *Nation*, February 22, 1993, pp. 246–48.

Gerard, Jeremy. "*Angels in America: Millennium Approaches*," *Variety*, May 10, 1998, pp. 243–44.

———. "*Angels in America: Millennium Approaches, Perestroika*," *Variety*, May 9–15, 1994, p. 196.

———. "*Angels in American, Part Two: Perestroika*," *Variety*, December 6, 1993, pp. 33–35.

———. "Angling for *Angels*," *Variety*, November 16, 1992, p. 69.

———. "*The Illusion*," *Variety*, January 24–30, 1994, p. 67.

Gloster, Gary. "After the Shouts Die Down, Let Us Journey Toward Healing," *Charlotte Observer*, April 8, 1996, p. 11A.

Gold, Sylviane. "Seeking a Theatre Varied as a Rainbow," *New York Times*, February 23, 1997, sec. 2, pp. 5, 24.

———. "Today's Big-Name Playwrights Are Busy Translating the Past's," *New York Times*, August 3, 1997, sec. 2, p. 5.

Golden, Nancy. "*The Illusion*," *Ashland (Oregon) Lithiagraph*, October 1993, p. 19.

Goldstein, Richard. "A Queer Dybbuk," *Village Voice*, December 2, 1997, p. 59.

Gordon, Tom. "*Slavs! Bedlam Theatre*," *Scotsman*, August 18, 1997, p. F15.

Gorman, Brian. "On the Side of the Angels," *Ottawa Sun*, July 10, 1997.

Graham, Chuck. "ATC Mum About *The Illusion*," *Tuscon Citizen*, March 6, 1997, p. 11.

Grecco, Stephen. "Theatre," *World Literature Today*, vol. 69, 1995, p. 144.

Greene, Alexis. "*Angels*: London vs. New York," *Theater Week*, March 7–13, 1994, pp. 21–22.

———. "A Dybbuk," *InTheater*, December 5, 1997, p. 14.

———. "The Humana Festival," *Theater Week*, April 22–28, 1996, pp. 13–14, 16–17.

———. "*Perestroika*," *Theater Week*, December 13–19, 1993, pp. 35–36.

———. "*Slavs!*" *Theater Week*, January 2–8, 1995, pp. 23–24.

Greene, Ray. "Anguished, Poetic Widows," *Village View*, August 2–8, 1991.

Grenier, Richard. "The Homosexual Millennium: Is It Here? Is It Approaching," *National Review*, June 7, 1993, pp. 52–56.

————. "With Roy, Ethel, and *Angels*," *Washington Times*, April 18, 1993, p. B3.

Grode, Eric. "Two Men and a Mormon (And Ethel Rosenberg)," *Theater Week*, September 20–26, 1993, pp. 15–17.

Gross, John. "Family Values and Poshlost," *Sunday Telegraph* (London), January 26, 1992.

————. "Wenching and Outswilling Bacchus," *Sunday Telegraph* (London), December 18, 1994, Arts Section, p. 5.

Grossberg, Michael. "OSU Cast, Staging Give Lift to *Angels* II," *Columbus Dispatch*, November 12, 1999, p. 10G.

Guerra, Joey. "Kushner and Alley Explore Death in Offbeat *Hydriotaphia*," *Daily Cougar*, April 14, 1998, pp. 6–7.

Gunner, Marjorie. "On and Off-Broadway, *New York Voice*, January 19, 1991, p. 25.

Gussow, Mel. "A Magical Journey Through Life, Love and Art," *New York Times*, January 18, 1990, p. C21.

————. "The Plays Tell the Tale," *American Theatre*, July–August 1996, pp. 52–54.

————. "Stage: Goethe's *Stella* In New Directors Project," *New York Times*, November 4, 1987, p. C23.

Hall, Carla. "*Angels* in the Wings. L. A. Opens Curtain on an American Epic," *Washington Post*, November 17, 1992, sec. G, pp. 1, 4.

Halliburton, Rachel. "The Theatre: The Magic of 'Might' and 'Do'," *Independent* (London), July 19, 1999, p. 9.

Hammond, John. "*Love's Fire*," *InTheater*, July 10, 1998, pp. 12–14.

Hanson, Henry. "Back Talk," *Chicago Magazine*, vol. 43, no. 12, December 1994, p. 156.

Harris, John E. "Miracle on 48th Street," *Christopher Street*, March 1994, p. 6.

Harris, Paul A. "SIUE Production of Bright Room Raises Issues of Choices and Political Upheaval," *St. Louis Post-Dispatch*, November 1, 1999, St. Clair-Monroe Post Sec., p. 1.

Harris, William. "*Angels in America*," *New York Times*, March 27, 1994, sec. 2, p. 5.

Harry, Cindy. "Montage: *Angels in America, Part Two: Perestroika*," *Arts Indiana*, November/December 1998, p. 9.

Hart, Franci. "It's No Illusion: Actors Terrific," *Daily Oklahoman*, September 20, 1996, p. 3.

"Hartford Stage's Next Production is *A Dybbuk*," *Fairfield Citizen News*, February 10, 1995.

Hartigan, Patti. "*Angels* Still a Theatrical Miracle," *Boston Globe*, September 13, 1996, p. D12.

————. "Kushner's *Slavs!* Draws Tears and Laughter," *Boston Globe*, January 16, 1995, p. 47.

Harvey, Dennis. "*Angels in America*," *Variety*, October 31–November 6, 1994, p. 99.

Heilpern, John. *How Good is David Mamet, Anyway? Writings on Theater—and Why It Matters*. New York and London: Routledge, 2000.

Henderson, Kathy. "Snake Charmer," *InTheater*, April 12, 1999, pp. 28–29.

Henry, William A., III. "*Angels in America*," *Time*, November 23, 1992, pp. 72–74.

————. "Angels of No Mercy," *Time*, December 6, 1993, pp. 75–76.

Herman, Charles. "Bolsheviks, Babushkas, & Brilliance," *Washington Blade*, September 15, 1995, p. 53.

Hewison, Robert. "*Home Body/Kabul*," *Sunday Times* (London), July 25, 1999, Sec. II, p. 20.

———. "Nights Out for the Boys," *Sunday Times* (London), April 13, 1997, pp. 14–15.

Hilferty, Robert. "In Profile: Klezmatics," *Advocate*, June 10, 1997, p. 66.

Hillis, Crusader. "Making *Angels* Fly," *Melbourne Star Observer*, October 15, 1993, p. 11.

Hilton, Melissa. *The Political Ideologies of Roy Cohn and Prior Walter: Tony Kushner's Political Vision in Angels in America, A Gay Fantasia on National Themes.* MA Thesis, Angelo State University, San Angelo, TX, 1997.

Hirschhorn, Clive. "Herald Angel Dims the Glory," *Sunday Express* (London), November 28, 1993.

Hitchens, Christopher. "*Angels* Over Broadway," *Vanity Fair*, March 1993, pp. 72–76.

Hobson, Louis B. "*Angels* Much More Than a 'Gay Play'," *Calgary Sun*, September 21, 1996.

Hodson, Matthew. "The Most Important Show of the Decade?," *Gay Times*, January 1994.

Hogan, Kate. "*Слаbc! (Slavs!)*: In Any Language (or Accent) It's a Hit," *Baltimore Gay Paper*, January 20, 1995, p. 26.

Horn, Miriam. "Culture: A Broadway Gamble," *U. S. News & World Report*, May 10, 1993, vol. 114, p. 20.

Hornby, Richard. "Dramatizing AIDS," *The Hudson Review*, vol. 46, no. 1, spring 1993, pp. 189–91.

———. "Regional Theatre Comes of Age," *The Hudson Review*, vol. 46, fall 1993, pp. 529–36.

Hulbert, Dan. "*Angels in America, Part II: Perestroika* Comes to the Stage," *Atlanta Journal and Constitution*, September 3, 1995, p. K2.

———. "Backstage: Express *Room* Hits Timelier Target," *Atlanta Journal and Constitution*, September 10, 1995, p. 6L.

———. "Theatre Review: *A Bright Room Called Day*," *Atlanta Journal and Constitution*, September 22, 1995, p. 5P.

———. "Theatre Review: *The Illusion*," *Atlanta Journal and Constitution*, March 3, 1995, p. 10P.

Hurwitt, Robert. "Angels, Devils in an Earthly Habitat," *San Francisco Chronicle*, November 29, 1992, p. D3.

Hutchinson, P. William. "Theatre Review: *Angels in America, Part II: Perestroika*," *New England Theatre Journal*, vol. 8, 1997, pp. 174–78.

Ickes, Bob. "Heaven Sent. Will Tony Kushner's *Angels in America* Rescue Broadway," *New York Magazine*, April 12, 1993, pp. 43–48.

"Illiberal Arts," *The Advocate*, November 12, 1996, p. 20.

"Infernal Alchemy," *The New Yorker*, January 31, 1994, pp. 10–12.

Isherwood, Charles. "Rent Control," *The Advocate*, May 27, 1997, pp. 75–77.

———. "Review/Stage: *Dybbuk* Impressive," *Variety*, November 24–30, 1997, p. 72.

Isser, Edward R. *Stages of Annihilation. Theatrical Representations of the Holocaust.* Madison and Teaneck, NJ: Fairleigh Dickinson University Press, 1997.

Jaques, Damien. "First Half of *Angels* Is Superb," *Milwaukee Journal Sentinel*, September 21, 1997, p. 8.

Jenkins, Jeffrey Eric. "Kushner and the Kabbalah: *A Dybbuk*," *Slavic and East European Performance*, vol. 18, no. 2, summer 1998, pp. 62–65.

Jenkins, Speight. "The Operatic Overtones Of *Angels in America*," *New York Times*, June 17, 1993, sec. 2, p. 25.

Johnson, Barry. "*Illusion* a Grand Spectacle," *Portland Oregonian*, December 10, 1993, pp. K1, K3.

———. "OSF Final Offerings Both Fanciful and Wrenching," *Portland Oregonian*, August 5, 1993.

Johnson, Hope. "Even Without Wings, This *Angel* Has the Power to Fly," *Texas Triangle*, April 30, 1998, pp. 34–35.

Johnson, Malcolm. "Haunting *Dybbuk* Has Room to Grow," *Hartford Courant*, February 20, 1995, pp. E1, E3.

———. "Kushner Infuses *Slavs!* With Range of Emotions," *Hartford Courant*, March 4, 1995, p. E1.

Jones, Abe, Jr. "*Illusion* Blends Modern Times With 1600s," *Greensboro News & Record*, April 25, 1996, p. 3.

Juillerat, Lee. "You're Confused on Purpose If You See *The Illusion* at OSF," *Klamath Falls Herald & News*, October 1, 1993, pp. 10A-11A.

"Kabul's Eye," *Time Out*, June 30–July 7, 1999.

Kanfer, Stefan. "*Angels in America*," *New Leader*, vol. 76, June 14–28, 1993, pp. 22–23.

———. "*Angels in America: Millennium Approaches*," *National Review*, June 7, 1993, pp. 52–56.

———. "Timon, Simon and God," *New Leader*, vol. 76, December 13, 1993, pp. 22–23.

Kape, Michael. "*Angels* at the Alliance," *Southern Voice*, August 24, 1995, pp. 27–34.

Kaplan, Jon. "Letter From Chicago," *Theater Week*, December 26, 1994–January 1, 1995, pp. 25–27.

Karmel, Terese. "Classic Kushner at Connecticut Rep," *Willimantic Chronicle*, February 27, 1997, p. 9.

Kässens, Wend. "Russen aus Amerika," *Theater Heute*, May 1995, p. 60.

Kaufman, Sarah. "The Flip Side of *Slavs!*" *Washington Post Weekend*, September 8, 1995, p. N39.

Kaylin, Lucy. "A New Angle on *Angels*. Director George C. Wolfe Talks About Bringing the Epic *Angels in America* to Broadway," *Gentlemen's Quarterly*, vol. 63, May 1993, pp. 132, 134–36.

Kellaway, Kate. "Wrestling with Angels," *Observer* (London), January 26, 1992, p. 52.

Kelly, Kevin. "Angels, AIDS and Rage," *Boston Globe*, May 5, 1993, pp. 73–74.

Kerekes, Dick. "Gainesville's Hipp Presents *The Illusion*," *First Coast Entertainer*, May 5, 1995, p. 20A.

Khan, N. "Theatre Review: *A Bright Room Called Day*," *Drama Drama*, no. 170, 1988, pp. 35–36.

Kiefer, Daniel. "*Angels in America* and the Failure of Revelation," *American Drama*, 1994, vol. 4, no. 1, pp. 21–38.

King, Robert L. "All-American," *North American Review*, vol. 279, July–August 1994, pp. 43–48.

———. "*Perestroika*," *North American Review*, vol. 279, March–April 1994, pp. 16–17.

———. "Recent Drama," *Massachusetts Review*, vol. 30, 1989, pp. 122–36.

———. "Social Consciousness Onstage," *North American Review*, vol. 277, September–October 1992, pp. 44–48.

Kingston, Jeremy. "Phantoms of the Soap Opera," *Times* (London), June 19, 1997, p. 37.

Kissel, Howard. "*A Bright Room* Called Cliché," *New York Daily News*, January 8, 1991, p. 29.

———. "Falling *Angels*: Gay Epic Fails to Take Wing," *New York Daily News*, May 5, 1993.

———. "Trip in Time Worth Trip to Hartford," *New York Daily News*, January 12, 1990.

Klein, Alvin. "A New Incarnation For a Classic *Illusion*," *New York Times*, December 3, 1995, sec. 13, p. 24.

———. "Taking *Angels in America* to Storrs," *New York Times*, September 26, 1999, sec. 14 CN, p. 6.

———. "A Writer's Torrential Rush," *New York Times*, March 12, 1995, sec. 13 CN, p. 10.

Koehler, Robert. "Caretaker of the Missing; Chilean Author Ariel Dorfman Wrote of Los Desaparecidos in his Novel Widows; Now He's Preserving Their Memory on Stage," *Los Angeles Times*, July 21, 1991, p. C4.

———. "Kushner's *Room* Is a Dark Gem," *Los Angeles Times*, March 22, 1996, p. F28.

Korn, Eric. "Slavs Are Us," *Times Literary Supplement*, January 6, 1995, p. 18.

Kosman, Joshua. "Kushner to Write Opera Libretto," *San Francisco Chronicle*, February 19, 1999.

Kragen, Pam. "Rep Offers Kushner's Take on Classic *Illusion*," *North County (CA) Times*, October 29, 1999, p. 21.

———. "SD Rep's *Illusion* a Magical Theatrical Trip," *North County (CA) Times*, November 12, 1999, p. 29.

Kramer, Yale. "Broadway Acts Up. *Angels* on Broadway," *The American Spectator*, July 1993, volume 26, pp. 18–25.

Krementz, Jill. *The Jewish Writer*. New York: Henry Holt, 1998.

Kroll, Jack. "*Angels in America*," *Newsweek*, May 17, 1993, p. 70.

———. "A Broadway Godsend: *Angels in America*, an Epic of AIDS and Homosexuality, Is a Big Ticket," *Newsweek*, May 10, 1993, pp. 56–58.

———. "Heaven and Earth on Broadway," *Newsweek*, December 6, 1993, p. 83.

———. "A Seven-Hour Gay Fantasia: A Daring and Dazzling Play for Our Time," *Newsweek*, November 23, 1992, p. 83.

Kulig, B. A. "*A Bright Room*," *Bravo*, May 1997.

"A Kushner Coda," *New Yorker*, March 13, 1995, pp. 37–38.

"Kushner Wins First Humana Impact Award," *Back Stage*, April 5–11, 1996, p. 3.

"Kushner Wins Whiting," *American Theatre*, January 1991, p. 54.

"Kushner's Latest, Late," *USA Today*, April 2, 1998, Life Sec., p. 1.

Lahr, John. "Angels on Broadway," *New Yorker*, May 31, 1993, p. 137.

———. "Beyond Nelly," *New Yorker*, November 23, 1992, pp. 126–30.

———. "Earth Angels," *New Yorker*, December 13, 1993, pp. 129–33.

———. "Hail, Slavonia," *New Yorker*, January 9, 1995, pp. 85–87.

———. *Light Fantastic. Adventures in Theatre*. New York: Dial Press, 1996.

Lamont, Rosette C. "*The Illusion*," *Theater Week*, February 21–27, 1994, p. 53.

———. "*The Illusion*," *Performing Arts Journal*, 1994, vol. 9, no. 1, pp. 54–57.

Lane, Laurie. "Hope," *Brother Sister*, September 9, 1994, p. 21.

Larabee, Ann. "Radioactive Body Politics: AIDS as Nuclear Test," *Literature and Medicine*, vol. 13, no. 2, fall 1994, pp. 229–42.

Larkin, John. "Descent of a Darker Angel," *Sunday Age* (Melbourne), October 24, 1993.

———. "Land of the Free, Home of the Scared," *Sunday Age* (Melbourne), September 11, 1994, p. 7.

Lavender, Andy. "Cottage Industry," *New Statesman & Society* (London), November 26, 1993, p. 35.

Law, Philip G. "True Education," *American Theatre*, April 1998, pp. 51–52.

Lawson, Kyle. "Angels From Chaos," *Albany Times-Union*, February 9, 1996, pp. C1, C3.

———. "Angles of Amour Director Brings Light of Hope to Playwright's Dark *Illusion*," *Arizona Republic*, March 30, 1997, p. F1.

Lazare, Lewis. "*Angels in America*," *Variety*, October 17–23, 1994, p. 173.

"Legit Reviews: *A Bright Room Called Day*," *Variety*, January 8, 1991, pp. 69–70.

Lehman, Jon L. "*Illusion* Takes a Complex Look at Love," *Providence (RI) Patriot Ledger*, February 22, 1995.

Lemon, Brendan. "The Arts: No Angels in Wyoming," *Financial Times* (London), May 19, 2000, p. 17.

Litchfield, Robyn Bradley. "Students Take the Stage," *Montgomery Advertiser*, October 11, 1998, pp. 1H, 4H.

Littlejohn, David. "Theatre: *Angels in America*," *Wall Street Journal*, November 20, 1992, p. 20.

Lochrie, Karma. "Apocalyptic Imaginings," *Modern Philology*, vol. 92, 1995, pp. 351–59.

Loney, Glenn. "Survival Strategies in New York Theatres," *New Theatre Quarterly*, vol. 11, February 1995, pp. 79–90.

Lord, M. G. "Public Priorities," *New York Newsday*, January 6, 1991, part II, pp. 4–5, 21.

L. R. "Mini Reviews. New This Week," *Washington Post Weekend*, September 15, 1995.

Lyman, Rick. "On Stage and Off: Along the Way," *New York Times*, May 8, 1998, p. E2.

———. "On Stage and Off: Of Angels and Spirits," *New York Times*, November 7, 1997, p. E2.

———. "Play Reunites Leibman, Kushner," *Plain Dealer*, November 11, 1997, p. 7E.

Lyons, Donald. "The Trouble With *Angels*," *New Criterion*, June 1993, pp. 56–59.

Mabe, Chauncey. "AIDS Writing: Gay Only? Heterosexual Author Takes Heat From Gay Writers, Playwrights at Seminar for Her Reluctance to Address Theme in Her Works," *Ft. Lauderdale Sun-Sentinel*, January 19, 1997, p. 3D.

———. "Cool Response to AIDS Literary Seminar. Playwrights Larry Kramer and Tony Kushner May See Empty Seats in Key West," *Ft. Lauderdale Sun-Sentinel*, December 8, 1996, p. 10D.

Macaulay, Alastair. "Tony Kushner's *Slavs!*" *Financial Times* (London), December 15, 1994, p. 23.

MacLean, Colin. "Awesome *Angels*," *Edmonton Express*, October 18, 1996.

Magruder, James. "The Image Thing. Making the Point With Posters," *American Theatre*, October 1996, pp. 30–40.

Mangan, Katherine S. "College Draws Hellfire for Staging Disputed Play," *Chronicle of Higher Education*, October 29, 1999, pp. A71–A72.

Mani, Thomas E. "*Slavs!* Russians View New World Disorder," *Washington D.C. Pentagram*, September 29, 1995, p. 35.

Marks, Peter. "On Stage, and Off," *New York Times*, June 28, 1996, p. C2.

Marmion, Patrick. "Confucius He Say, It's Hypnotic," *Evening Standard* (London), July 22, 1999, p. 35.

Marowitz, Charles. *Alarums & Excursions. Our Theatres in the 90s.* Preface by Irving Wardle. New York and London: Applause Books, 1996.

Mart. "*The Illusion*," *Variety*, January 17, 1990, p. 61.

Martin, Kellie and Chad Peterson. "*Slavs!* Hits the Mark," *Yale Daily News*, March 3, 1995.

Marx, Bill. "Kushner Classics," *Boston Phoenix*, February 24, 1995, Sec. 3, p. 9.

Mason, Vivian K. "Year of Improvising in the Balkans," in *New Theatre Vistas. Modern Movements in International Theatre.* Edited by Judy Lee Oliva. New York: Garland, 1996, pp. 119–34.

Massie, Alex. "*Widows*," *The Scotsman*, August 22, 1998, p. 8.

Mauro, Lucia. "*Angels in America (Part I: Millennium Approaches)*," *Chicago Sun-Times*, March 1, 2000, p. 48.

———. "*Angels in America (Part II: Perestroika)*," *Chicago Sun-Times*, March 9, 2000, p. 32.

McDonough, Carla J. *Staging Masculinity. Male Identity in Contemporary American Drama.* Jefferson, NC and London: McFarland & Co., 1997.

McDowell, Edwin. "10 Writers Receive $30,000 Awards," *New York Times*, October 26, 1990, p. C32.

McElroy, Jamie. "Offended by *Angels in America*? Here, Try Another Bite," *Charlotte Leader*, May 17, 1996, pp. 1, 15.

McEntyre, Marilyn Chandler. "A Place to Put the Pain: Three Cancer Stories," *Literature and Medicine*, vol. 14, no. 1, spring 1995, pp. 87–104.

McKinley, Jesse. "On Stage, and Off," *New York Times*, July 16, 1999, p. E2.

McKittrick, Ryan. "Kushner's *Illusion* Made Palpable," *Boston Globe*, May 19, 2000, p. C12.

McNulty, Charles. "*Angels in America*: Tony Kushner's Theses on the Philosophy of History," *Modern Drama*, vol. 39, no. 1, spring 1996, pp. 84–96.

McRuer, Robert. *The Queer Renaissance: Contemporary American Literature and the Reinvention of Lesbian and Gay Identities.* New York: New York University Press, 1997.

Meersman, Roger. "*Illusion* Delights," *Washington Journal*, May 24, 1991, p. B5.

———. "*Slavs!* at Studio," *Washington Journal*, September 15, 1995, pp. C3, C31.

Mellnik, Ted. "Police Separate Protest Groups So All Can Have a Say on *Angels*," *Charlotte Observer*, March 21, 1995, p. 11A.

Mendelsohn, Daniel. "We're Here! We're Queer! Let's Get Coffee," *New York*, September 30, 1996, pp. 24–31.

Meyer, Monika. "Life, Death, and Kushner," *Houston Public News*, April 15, 1998.

"*Millennium Approaches*," *InTheater*, November 15, 1999, pp. 34–51.

Miller, Carl. "Dreams of Zion," *New Statesman & Society* (London), January 25, 1992, pp. 31–32.

Miller, Daryl H. "Epic *Angels* Comes to Grips With Life's Agenda," *Los Angeles Daily News,* November 10, 1992, p. 21.

———. "Shadow of Gloom Lingers Over *Widows,*" *Los Angeles Daily News,* July 26, 1991, p. 24.

Milne, Kirsty. "Morals for the Millennium," *Sunday Telegraph,* November 28, 1993, p. 6.

Miracky, James J. "*Angels in America: Millennium Approaches,*" *America,* May 29, 1993, pp. 22–23.

Miracky, James J. "A Vision of Life Past Hope," *America,* vol. 170, March 5, 1994, pp. 12–13.

Mode, Becky. "Seeing Red," *New Haven Register,* February 26, 1995, pp. F1, F4.

Monji, Jana J. "Berlin Meets L.A.; Bright Room Bridges Time, Space to Address Ethics of Indifference," *Los Angeles Times,* April 27, 2000, p. F31.

Montgomery, Benilde. "*Angels in America* as Medieval Mystery," *Modern Drama,* vol. 41, no. 4, winter 1998, pp. 596–606.

Moore, Margo J. "*Illusion* Is Solid Brilliance at Trinity," *Taunton Daily Gazette,* February 16, 1995, p. 17.

Mootz, William. "Theatre Review: *Slavs!/Trip's Cinch,*" *Louisville Courier-Journal,* March 12, 1994, p. 25S.

Morehouse, Ward, III. "*Angels in America* Remains Earthbound," *Christian Science Monitor,* May 18, 1993, p. 12.

Morley, Sheridan. "Angels in Disguise," *Spectator* (London), November 27, 1993, p. 56.

———. "Roman Follies," *Spectator* (London), July 31, 1999, p. 42.

———. "Sondheim's Roam Away From Rome," *International Herald Tribune,* July 28, 1999, p. 10.

Morrison, Bill. "Huddled Mass Appeal," *Raleigh News & Observer,* August 10, 1996, p. E10.

Neill, Rosemary. "Dazzling, Visionary Drama," *Australian,* February 22, 1993, p. 2.

Nelson, Emmanuel S., ed. *AIDS. The Literary Response.* New York: Twayne Publishers, 1992.

Nicholas, Jonathan. "Tony vs. Tonya: Real Fight of the Week," *Sunday Oregonian,* February 27, 1994, p. L2.

Nichols, Nina da Vinci. "Let's Hear It For The Real Thing," *American Book Review,* vol. 16, August-September 1994, pp. 4, 6, 9.

Nightingale, Benedict. "AIDS Stretched to Its Limits," *Times* (London), January 25, 1992, p. 5.

———. "*Angels* Lose Their Direction," *Times* (London), November 22, 1993, p. 33.

———. *Predictions. The Future of Theatre.* London: Phoenix, 1998.

———. "Those Reds Were Nuts," *Times* (London), December 15, 1994, p. 31.

———. "Waiting For Tears," *Times* (London), March 8, 1997, p. 19.

Nilsen, Richard. "Witty, Gritty *Illusion* Is Exceptionally Real Theater," *Arizona Republic,* April 1, 1997, p. C1.

Nixon, Rob. "*Angels in America,*" *ETC,* September 2, 1994, pp. 31–32.

———. "Theatre Review: *Angels in America: Millennium Approaches,*" *ETC,* September 23, 1994, p. 50.

"No $ for Gay Art," *The Advocate,* May 13, 1997, p. 18.

Norden, Barbara. "Angels in the Age of AIDS," *Times Literary Supplement* (London), December 3, 1993, vol. 4731, p. 19.

Norden, Edward. "From Schnitzler to Kushner," *Commentary*, vol. 99, January 1995, pp. 51–58.

Norris, Michael. "*Slavs!* Black Russian Humor Enlivens Grim Reality," *Belvoir Eagle*, September 28, 1995, p. 14.

Nunns, Stephen. "Charlotte Revisited: No Gay Art," *American Theatre*, May–June 1997, p. 42.

———. "Culture Wars, Continued," *American Theatre*, November 1997, pp. 70–71.

———. "Is Charlotte Burning?," *American Theatre*, February 1999, pp. 22–27, 74–77.

———. "No *Angels* on Catholic Campus," *American Theatre*, December 1996, pp. 46–47.

Olb, Suzanne. "*Angels in America*," *Stages*, September 1994, p. 35.

O'Leary, John. "*Angels in America: A Gay Fantasia on National Themes* by Tony Kushner," *Contemporary American Dramatists*. Edited by K. A. Berney. London, Detroit and Washington, D.C.: St. James Press, 1994, pp. 674–76.

Olson, Walter. "Winged Defeat," *National Review*, January 24, 1994, pp. 71–73.

Oppenheim, Irene. "Shedding More Light on *Bright Room*," *American Theatre*, September 2000, pp. 75–77.

"Opponents Were No Angels," *Buffalo News*, March 26, 1996, p. D2.

O'Quinn, Jim. "Ideas Old and New," *American Theatre*, April 1998, p. 60.

———. "The Subject That Won't Go Away," *American Theatre*, April 1997, p. 38.

O'Toole, Fintan. "*Dybbuk* Revisits Jewish Haunts," *New York Daily News*, November 17, 1997, p. 35.

Pace, David. "*Angels* in Utah. At Salt Lake Acting Company, Kushner's Mormon Characters Have Special Resonance," *American Theatre*, March 1996, pp. 49–50.

Pacheco, Patrick. "Flying High," *InTheater*, April 19, 1999, pp. 24–25, 27.

———. "How Well Did *Angels* Fly on Opening Night?," *Los Angeles Times*, May 6, 1993, pp. F1, F7.

Page, Bob. "Hot Plays Boil in Carolina Cauldron," *Variety*, April 1–7, 1996, pp. 59, 61.

Papatola, Dominic P. "Play Successfully Portrays Failure," *World, Saint Paul Pioneer Press*, February 27, 2000, p. 16A.

Peithman, Stephen. "Collector's Choice," *Stage Directions*, November–December 1998, p. 7.

Peter, John. "Apocalypse Any Time Now," *Sunday Times* (London), February 2, 1992, sec. 6, p. 5.

———. "Rest of the Week's Theatre," *Sunday Times* (London), June 22, 1997, sec. 11, p. 25.

———. "Review: *Angels in America*," *Sunday Times* (London), June 13, 1999, sec. 11, p. 21.

———. "Taboo or Not Taboo?," *Sunday Times*, November 28, 1993, p. 23.

Phillips, Bill. "*Angels in America, Part One: Millennium Approaches*," *Adelaide Gay Times*, October 7, 1994, p. 22.

———. "Principally, A Comedy ... *Angels in America, Part 2: Perestroika*," *Adelaide Gay Times*, November 4, 1994, p. 22.

Phillips, Michael. "Kushner To Adapt Brecht's *Good Person*," *San Diego Union-Tribune*, January 26, 1994, p. E6.

———. "The Party's Over," *San Diego Union-Tribune*, August 1, 1995, pp. E1, E3.

———. "Too-Casual Air Leaves Play Oddly Becalmed," *San Diego Union-Tribune*, August 2, 1994, p. E1.

Piccolo, Gina. "*Angels* in Atlanta. Alliance: Drama Much More Than AIDS Play," *Atlanta Journal and Constitution*, September 24, 1994, pp. K1, K4.

Pixler, Joe. "Soviet Union Falls Again at Steppenwolf," *Chicago Sun-Times*, June 3, 1994, p. 7.

"Playwright Calls Southern Critics 'Bigots'," *Rocky Mountain News*, March 24, 1996, p. 41A.

Plough, Cathy. "Devils in America," *Charlotte Christian*, April 1996, pp. 1, 5.

Plum, Jay. "Pleasure, Politics, and the Performance of Community: Pomo Afro Homo's Dark Fruit," *Modern Drama*, vol. 39, no. 1, spring 1996, pp. 117–31.

Pogrebin, Robin. "Pickets, Pro and Con, as Disputed Play Opens," *New York Times*, October 14, 1998, p. A21.

———. "Play That Stirred Outcry Prepares for Its Opening," *New York Times*, September 3, 1998, pp. B1, B5.

Pollock, Robert C. "Haunting Thinkpiece Now Playing at Hartford Stage," *Bristol Press*, February 27, 1995.

Posnock, Ross. "Roy Cohn in America," *Raritan*, vol. 13, no. 3, winter 1994, pp. 64–77.

Poyen, Jennifer. "Reality of *Illusion* Enthralls Artistic Producer," *San Diego Union-Tribune*, November 2, 1999, pp. E1, E4.

Pressley, Nelson. "Chasing the Illusion of a Socialist Utopia," *Washington Times*, January 17, 1995.

———. "Politics and the *Slavs!*" *Washington Times*, September 12, 1995.

Preston, Rohan. "*Day* Becomes Long, Clumsy Night," *Minneapolis Star-Tribune*, May 12, 1999, Variety Sec., p. 7E.

———. "Pillsbury House Offers a Grand, Jolting Production of *Angels*," *Minneapolis Star-Tribune*, March 1, 2000, p. E10.

Purdy, Pamela. "Slavaganza!" *Washington, D.C. City Paper*, January 18, 1995, p. 33.

Quillin, Martha. "*Angels* Unleashed a Demon," *Raleigh News & Observer*, December 14, 1997.

Quindlen, Anna. "Happy and Gay," *New York Times*, April 6, 1994, p. A21.

Quinn, John R. "*Corpus Juris Tertium*: Redemptive Jurisprudence in *Angels in America*," *Theatre Journal*, vol. 48, no. 1, March 1996, pp. 79–90.

Radic, Leonard. "Powerful and Provocative Punch," *The Age* (Melbourne), October 21, 1993, p. 19.

Raidy, William A. "*Bright Room Called Day* Set at Dawn of the Nazis," *Newark Star-Ledger*, January 8, 1991.

Reid, Kerry. "*Dybbuk*," *Back Stage*, February 16, 1998.

Reiss, Al. "Illusion Succeeds in Staging, Not Dialogue," *Medford Mail Tribune* (Oregon), August 1, 1993.

Remy. "*A Bright Room Called Day*," *Variety*, January 14, 1991, p. 118.

Rich, Frank. "*A Bright Room Called Day*," *New York Times*, January 8, 1990, p. C11.

———. "Embracing All Possibilities in Art and Life," *New York Times*, May 5, 1993, pp. C15–C16.

———. "Exit the Critic," *New York Times Magazine*, February 13, 1994, pp. 32–39, 50–53, 62, 66, 79.

———. "Following an Angel For a Healing Vision Of Heaven on Earth," *New York Times*, November 24, 1993, pp. B1, B4.

———. "Making History Repeat, Even Against Its Will," *New York Times*, January 8, 1991, pp. C11, C14.

———. "Marching Out of the Closet, Into History," *New York Times*, November 10, 1992, pp. C15, C22.

———. "The Reaganite Ethos, With Roy Cohn As a Dark Metaphor," *New York Times*, March 5, 1992, pp. C15, C21.

Richards, David. "*Angels* Finds a Poignant Note of Hope," *New York Times*, November 28, 1993, sec. 2, pp. 1, 27.

———. "*Angels in America*. An Epic, All Right, But It's the Details and Future That Count," *New York Times*, May 16, 1993, sec. 2, pp. 1, 7.

———. "History Hung Over: Post-Soviet Aches and Absurdities," *New York Times*, December 13, 1994, pp. C17–C18.

———. "Kushner's Adaptation Of a French Classic," *New York Times*, January 20, 1994, pp. C15–C16.

———. "Tale of One City Set in Two Times—Both Fearful," *New York Times*, January 13, 1991, pp. 5, 26.

Rilling, Lisa M. *Tony Kushner's The Illusion: A Director's Approach*. MFA Thesis, University of South Dakota, 1992.

Rizzo, Frank. "Kushner's *Dybbuk* Ready for the Stage," *Hartford Courant*, February 12, 1995, pp. G1, G4.

Rizzo, Frank. "Kushner Will Be Omnipresent in State Theatres in 1994–95," *Hartford Courant*, May 10, 1994, pp. D1, D2.

Robbins, Jacqueline. "*Angels* Return," *Calgary Sun*, May 22, 1997.

Robinson, Marc. "Reds Scared," *Village Voice*, December 20, 1994, p. 91.

Roca, Octavio. "Kushner's Next Stage: Award-winning Playwright's *Hydriotaphia* Opens Season at Berkeley Rep," *San Francisco Chronicle*, September 6, 1998, p. 32.

Rockwell, John. "American Music of Protest, Politics and Persuasion," *New York Times*, September 18, 1989, p. C17.

Rodriquez, Bill. "Of Love and Life, *Providence Phoenix*, February 17, 1995, sec. 1, p. 1.

Rogers, V. Cullum. "Tempest in a Dixie Cup: *Angels in America* vs. Charlotte," *Back Stage*, March 29, 1996, pp. 3, 37.

———. "Theatre Becomes Aggressor in *Angels* Brouhaha," *Back Stage*, April 26, 1996, pp. 3, 39.

Rogoff, Gordon. "*Angels in America*, Devils in the Wings," *Theatre*, 1993, vol. 24, no. 2, pp. 21–29.

Román, David. *Acts of Intervention. Performance, Gay Culture, and AIDS*. Bloomington and Indianapolis: Indiana University Press, 1998.

Romney, Jason. "Prophets of Doom," *Melbourne Herald Sun*, September 5, 1994, p. 59.

Rose, Lloyd. "From Here to Eternity; *Perestroika* Takes the Long Way to Paradise," *Washington Post*, July 21, 1999, p. C1.

———. "*The Illusion*: Love's Magic Bag of Tricks," *Washington Post*, May 28, 1991, pp. D1, D2.

———. "Many Hands, Light Work; *Love's Fire*: One-Acts by 7 Big-Name Playwrights Don't Add Up," *Washington Post*, March 28, 2000, p. C8.

———. "The Marx Brothers, Groucho and Karl," *Washington Post*, January 14, 1995, p. C1.

———. "*Slavs!*: Groucho Marxists," *Washington Post*, September 13, 1995, p. B8.

Rosenstein, Brad. "Unblocked," *San Francisco Bay Guardian*, September 23–29, 1998.

Rosenthal, Daniel. "Back From the Vanishing Point," *Times* (London), March 5, 1997, p. 35.

Rousuck, J. Wynn. "Witty Juxtapositions Season the Heavy-Duty, Thought-Provoking Nature of *Slavs!*" *Baltimore Sun*, January 12, 1995, p. E1.

Rubio, Jeff. "Details, Depth Help Make for Rich *Widows*," *Orange County Register*, July 26, 1991, p. P23.

Ruocco, James V. "*A Dybbuk* Debuts at Hartford Stage," *Hartford Republican-American*, February 17, 1995, pp. 16–17.

———. "Kushner Takes on Cold War in *Slavs!*" *Hartford Republican-American*, February 5, 1995, pp. 1H, 6H.

Rush, Michael. "Yale Rep Scores With Fabulous *Slavs!*" *New Haven Register*, March 4, 1995.

Ruth, Jim. "*Angels* Gathers Music En Route to Harrisburg," *Lancaster Sunday News*, April 13, 1997, section H, p. 4.

Rutherford, Malcolm. "A Drama Out of a Crisis," *Financial Times* (London), January 25, 1992, section 1, p. 17.

———. "Madness and Trivia," *Encounter*, September 1990, vol. 75, pp. 73–74.

———. "A Spectacular *Perestroika*," *Financial Times* (London), November 22, 1993, p. 13.

Sack, Kevin. "Charlotte's Cultural Tensions Are Laid Bare by a Play," *New York Times*, March 22, 1996, p. A8.

Saltzman, Simon. "Nazi Entrenchment Dominates *A Bright Room Called Day*," *Daily Record* (Morris County, NJ), January 10, 1991, p. C8.

Samuelsen, Eric. "Whither Mormon Drama? Look First to a Theatre," *Brigham Young University Studies*, 1995, vol. 34, pp. 81–103.

Sander, Roy. "Theatre Reviews: *A Bright Room Called Day*," *Back Stage*, January 18, 1991, p. 48.

Sasso, Laurence J., Jr. "At Trinity *The Illusion* Is Elusive But Delicious," *Observer Life* (Providence, RI), February 23, 1995, p. 3B.

Savran, David. "Ambivalence, Utopia, and a Queer Sort of Materialism: How *Angels in America* Reconstructs the Nation," *Theatre Journal*, vol. 47, no. 2, May 1995, pp. 207–27.

Scanlan, Dick. "Theatre: Fall Preview: George C. Wolfe," *Advocate*, September 19, 1995, pp. 53–54.

———. "Theatre: Joe Mantello," *Advocate*, September 20, 1994, pp. 48–50.

Scheck, Frank. "*Christmas Carol, Slavs!* Fall Short in New York," *Christian Science Monitor*, December 19, 1994, p. 13.

———. "Louisville Festival: Experimentation Onstage," *Christian Science Monitor*, April 1, 1994, p. 14.

Schmid, Alexander. *"Only in America . . . ": The Interplay of Theory and Performance in Angels in America.* MA Thesis, Department of English, Miami University, Oxford, OH, 1996.

Schneider, Robert. "IN and OFF at Avignon," *Theater*, vol. 25, no. 2, 1994, pp. 96–97, 104.

———. "Kushner sans Kitsch," *American Theatre*, January 1995, p. 4.

Schock, Von Axel. "AIDS im Film und im Theater," *Theater Heute*, No. 12, December 1995, pp. 35–39.

Schofield, Leo. "Leo at Large," *Sydney Morning Herald*, February 13, 1993, p. 26.

———. "Leo at Large," *Sydney Morning Herald*, February 27, 1993, p. 26.

Schulman, Sarah. *Stage Struck. Theater, AIDS, and the Marketing of Gay America.* Durham, NC: Duke University Press, 1998.

Seavor, Jim. "Pulitzer-winning Playwright: Life is 'Irreducibly Tragic'," *Providence Journal-Bulletin*, November 19, 1998.

Segal, Lewis. "Weekend Reviews: Dance: Collaborative Night Belongs to Klezmatics," *Los Angeles Times*, August 14, 1995, p. F3.

Senior, Jennifer. "Betwixt and Between," *New York*, November 10, 1997, p. 83.

Serlin, David Harley. "Christine Jorgensen and the Cold War Closet," *Radical History Review*, vol. 62, 1995, pp. 136–165.

Shaver, Warren. "Theatre: *Slavs!*" *The Review* (Washington, D.C.), October 1995.

Shenton, Mark. "Shylock, Lenny & Musicals Galore," *InTheater*, September 6–13, 1999, pp. 46–47.

Shewey, Don. "Public Service," *New York*, December 15, 1997, pp. 43–47.

———. "Revelations," *Village Voice*, July 30, 1991, pp. 91–92.

———. "Tony Kushner's Sexy Ethics," *Village Voice*, April 20, 1993, pp. 29–32, 36.

Shinn, Jerry. "Talking Dirty: Don Reid, Meet Tony Kushner," *Charlotte Observer*, March 28, 1996, p. 13A.

Shirley, Don. "All's Angelic at L.A. Drama Critics' Awards," *Los Angeles Times*, April 10, 1993, p. F10.

Siegel, Ed. "Comedies That Enter Twilight Zone," *Boston Globe*, August 25, 1995, p. 85.

Simon, John. "Angelic Geometry," *New York*, December 6, 1993, pp. 130–31.

———. "Animal Attraction," *New York*, December 1, 1997, pp. 108–10.

———. "*A Bright Room Called Day*," *New York*, January 21, 1991, p. 56.

———. "From *Slavs!* To Slavonia," *New York*, January 9, 1995, pp. 52–53.

———. "Illusions and Delusions," *New York*, January 31, 1994, pp. 69–70.

———. "Of Wings and Webs," *New York*, May 17, 1993, pp. 102–3.

———. "Thin Skin," *New York*, July 20, 1998, pp. 76–77.

Sinfield, Alan. *Out on Stage. Lesbian and Gay Theatre in the Twentieth Century.* New Haven, CT, and London: Yale University Press, 2000.

Slater, Eric. "17th Century Experiment Still Going Up in Smoke," *Oregon Daily Courier*, August 7, 1993.

Smith, Dinitia. "Viewing AIDS Writings Through Prism of Hope," *New York Times*, January 13, 1997, p. C11.

Smith, Iris. "Authors in America: Tony Kushner, Arthur Miller, and Anna Deavere Smith," *Centennial Review*, vol. 40, no. 1, 1996, pp. 125–42.

Smith, Jack. "Weekend of Culture Is Music to His Ears," *Los Angeles Times*, August 28, 1995, pp. E1–E2.

Smith, Jeff. "Sea of Desire," *Reader: San Diego Weekly*, November 11, 1999.

Smith, Matthew Wilson, "*Angels in America*. A Progressive Apocalypse," *Theater*, vol. 29, no. 3, fall 1999, pp. 153–65.

Smith, Whitney. "*Angels* II. U of M Staging 2nd Half of Provocative Epic," *Commercial Appeal*, April 7, 1996, pp. G1–G2.

———. "Local Productions Please *Angels* Writer," *Commercial Appeal*, April 7, 1996, pp. G1–G2.

Solomon, Alisa. *Re-Dressing the Canon. Essays on Theater and Gender.* London and New York: Routledge, 1997.

———. "Review: *The Illusion*," *Village Voice*, November 8, 1988, p. 100.

———. "Seeking Answers in Yiddish Classics," *New York Times*, November 16, 1997, Sec. 2, pp. 7, 22.

Sordi, Michele. "Angels, Critics, and the Rhetoric of AIDS in America," in *Reconceptualizing American Literary/Cultural Studies. Rhetoric, History, and Politics in the Humanities*. Edited by William E. Cain. New York: Garland Publishing, 1996, pp. 185–96.

Sourd, Jacques le. "*A Bright Room* Should Be Called Dull," *Gannett/Westchester*, January 8, 1991, pp. C1, C3.

Sova, Kathy. "Born in Louisville: A New Play Gallery," *American Theatre*, July/August 2000, pp. 28–29.

Spears, Ricky. "*The Good Person of Setzuan*," *InTheater*, June 21, 1999, p. 13.

Speizer, Irwin. "Holy War Rages Over *Angels* in Charlotte," *Raleigh News & Observer*, March 22, 1996, pp. 1A, 10A.

Spencer, Charles. "Apocalyptic Visions," *Daily Telegraph* (London), January 27, 1992, p. 15.

———. "Divine Revelation Gives Way to Cosmic Codswallop," *Daily Telegraph* (London), November 22, 1993, p. 17.

———. "Lost Somewhere in the Soviet Union," *Daily Telegraph* (London), December 20, 1995, p. 15.

Spillane, Margaret. "Preserving a Theatrical Tradition," *Chronicle of Higher Education*, June 26, 1998, p. B8.

———. "*Slavs!*" *Nation*, February 6, 1995, pp. 177–79.

Staff, Charles. "*Perestroika* Offers Powerful Emotion," *Indianapolis Star*, October 26, 1998, p. E2.

Stayton, Richard. "An Epic Look at Reagan-Era Morality," *Los Angeles Times*, May 13, 1990, pp. 45–46, 48.

Stearns, David Patrick. "Daffy and Absolutely Divine," *USA Today*, November 12, 1992, p. 13.

———. "*A Dybbuk* Delves Deep in the Soul," *USA Today*, March 7, 1995, p. 4D.

———. "Kushner's Latest Less Substance Than Style," *USA Today*, September 29, 1998, p. 4D.

———. "Looking for Meaning in Worlds Gone Amok," *USA Today*, January 10, 1991, p. 4D.

———. "Playwright Scales Dramatic Heights," *USA Today*, January 26, 1991, p. 4D.

———. "*Slavs!*: Deconstructing Soviets," *USA Today*, June 24, 1994, p. 4D.

———. "Workshop's *Slavs!* Civilizes the End of Soviet Civilization," *USA Today*, December 15, 1994, p. 10D.

Steinhauer, Jennifer. "Chronicle: Valentine of Angel's Wings," *New York Times*, February 8, 1995, p. B4.

Stevens, Andrea. "Finding a Devil Within to Portray Roy Cohn," *New York Times*, April 18, 1993, sec. 2, pp. 1, 28.

Steyn, Mark. "Communism Is Dead; Long Live the King!" *New Criterion*, vol. 13, no. 6, February 1995, pp. 49–53.

Stout, David. "*Angels* Gets Taken to Task in Charlotte," *Q Notes. The Carolinas' Most Comprehensive Gay & Lesbian Newspaper*, April 1996, pp. 1, 20.

Stuart, Jan. "Dressing Up To Battle Ignorance," *Newsday*, April 13, 1997, sec. L, p. 14.

Sullivan, Paul. "Tony Kushner's *A Dybbuk* Performed at Hartford Stage," *Trinity Tripod*, March 7, 1995, p. 13.

Swanson, Jessica. "*Angels in America*: An Epic Success," *Pulse of the Twin Cities*, March 1, 2000, p. 11.

Swisher, Kara. "Catholic U. Ejects *Angels*," *Washington Post*, September 21, 1996, pp. C1–C2.

———. "This Girl Answers to No One," *Washington Post*, September 16, 1995, p. D2.

Szekrenyi, Laszlo. "*Angels* in Avignon," *Theater Week*, September 5–11, 1994, pp. 37, 42.

Tannenbaum, Perry. "Charlotte Theatre After *Angels*. A Roundtable Discussion With Local Theater Leaders," *Creative Loafing* (Charlotte, NC), May 18, 1996, pp. 16–19.

———. "Phallus Victorious," *Creative Loafing* (Charlotte, NC), March 30, 1996.

———. "Spinning Forward," *Creative Loafing* (Charlotte, NC), April 27, 1996, pp. 22–23.

Taylor, Markland. "*A Dybbuk or Between Two Worlds*," *Variety*, February 27–March 5, 1995, pp. 83–84.

Taylor, Paul. "More Than a Chip Off the Bloc," *Independent* (London), December 15, 1994, p. 26.

———. "A Place Where Love and Justice Meet," *Independent* (London), November 22, 1993, p. 21.

———. "A Sense of Illness as Metaphor," *Independent* (London), January 25, 1992, p. 30.

Teicher, Morton I. "Unwanted Spirit," *Jerusalem Post*, May 28, 1999, p. 12B.

"10 Writers Receive $30,000 Awards," *New York Times*, October 26, 1990, p. C32.

Terry, Clifford. "Putting the Anger in *Angels*. Jonathan Hadary's Bitter Roy Cohn Gives Fury a Demonic Human Face," *Chicago Tribune*, October 16, 1994, Sec. 13, pp. 12, 15.

Thomson, Helen. "*Angels in America, King Lear*," *Australian*, October 22, 1993, p. 10.

Tichi, Claire. "Grand Illusion," *Providence Independent*, February 23, 1995, pp. 14, 16.

Tinker, Jack. "*Angels* High on Wit, Risk and Challenge," *Daily Mail* (London), November 26, 1993, p. 52.

Tobin, Suzanne. "Miraculous Transformations in *Angels*," *Washington Post*, August 6, 1999, p. N28.

Tommasini, Anthony. "Americana Written for Fleming," *New York Times*, May 10, 2000, p. E3.

"Tony Kushner's Latest," *New York Times*, March 27, 1998, p. C2.

Toppman, Lawrence. "The Play's the Thing for Kushner, Most Questioners," *Charlotte Observer*, March 24, 1996.

Townsend, John. "Noel's Angelic Triumph," *Lavender Magazine*, February 2000, p. 24.

Trieschmann, Werner. "*Angels* in Repertory: 7 Hours Flying Times Is One Heavenly Trip," *Arkansas Democrat-Gazette*, March 30, 1997, pp. 1E, 6E.

Tucker, Scott. "Our Queer World. A Storm Blowing from Paradise," *Humanist*, November/December 1993, pp. 32–35.

Tuss, Alex J. "Resurrecting Masculine Spirituality in Tony Kushner's *Angels in America*," *Journal of Men's Studies*, August 1996, vol. 5, no. 1, pp. 49–63.

Tynan, William. "Red Sunset," *Time*, January 16, 1995, p. 73.

Tyson, Ann Scott. "Socialism's Failure Haunts *Slavs!*" *Christian Science Monitor*, July 15, 1994, p. 12.

Vaillancourt, Daniel. "Writing His Own Ticket," *Advocate*, March 2, 1999, pp. 59–60.

Vries, Hilary de. "*Angels*: A Flight Into Social Change," *San Francisco Chronicle*, May 9, 1993, p. 20.

———. "A Gay Epic. Tony Kushner's Play Offers a Unique View of America," *Chicago Tribune*, April 25, 1993, pp. B6–B7.

———. "A Playwright Spreads His Wings," *Los Angeles Times*, October 24, 1992, pp. C3, C74, C76.

Wagner, Vit. "Angels Bring Message For the Here and Now. *Angels in America, Part Two: Perestroika*," *Toronto Star*, November 8, 1996, p. D12.

Wainwright, Jeffrey. "Theatre: *The Illusion*," *Independent* (London), June 23, 1997, p. 12.

Walters, Barry. "Gay Jewish Roots," *Advocate*, June 10, 1997, pp. 65–66.

Wardle, Irving. "Faith, Hope and Charity," *Independent* (London), November 21, 1993, p. 26.

———. "When Thinking Big Is Not Enough," *Independent* (London), January 26, 1992, p. 18.

Warfield, Polly. "Theatre Reviews: *Angels in America*," *Drama-Logue*, November 12–18, 1992.

Watson, Louise. "Shakespeare Presents *The Illusion*," *Daily Tidings* (Oregon), July 29–August 5, 1993, Revels Section, p. 1.

Weales, Gerald. "American Theatre Watch, 1994–1995," *Georgia Review*, vol. 49, fall 1995, pp. 697–707.

———. "Serious & Grotesque. Kushner's *Angels*," *Commonweal*, July 16, 1993, pp. 19–20.

———. "Without a Light. *Normal Life & Bright Room*," *Commonweal*, February 22, 1991, p. 132.

Weaver, Neal. "Wings of Desire. *Angels in America* Takes Flight at the Mark Taper Forum," *Village View*, November 13–19, 1992, p. 31.

Weber, Bruce. "*Angels'* Angels," *New York Times Magazine*, April 25, 1993, pp. 27–31, 48, 50, 52, 56, 58.

———. "A Gay Actor's Temptation to Keep Good Health in the Closet," *New York Times*, June 5, 1993, sec. 1, p. 11.

———. "On Stage, and Off: Rebutting Pulitzer Receptions," *New York Times*, April 22, 1994, p. B4.

———. "Passion and Beast Square Off in Tonys; *Angels* Cited Again," *New York Times*, May 17, 1994, pp. C17, C21.

———. "A Theatre Is Selected for *Angels*," *New York Times*, December 11, 1992, p. C3.

———. "Two Wings, A Prayer and Backstage Help," *New York Times*, January 5, 1994, pp. C15–C16.

Weinberg-Harter, George. "*The Illusion* at the Lyceum Space," *Back Stage*, November 11–17, 1999.

Weiner, Wendy. "Ridiculously Radical," *American Theatre*, July/August 2000, p. 7.

Weiss, Hedy. "Kushner's Brilliant *Slavs!* Shines in Lackluster Festival," *Chicago Sun-Times*, March 29, 1994, p. 26.

———. "Kushner's *Perestroika* Opens Door to *Slavs!*" *Chicago Sun-Times*, June 15, 1994, p. 49.

———. "Russia on the Hot Seat," *Chicago Sun-Times*, June 20, 1994, sec. 2, p. 23.

————. "*Slavs!*" *Chicago Sun-Times,* April 18, 2000, p. 32.

Welsh, Anne Marie. "*Angels* II Takes Wing at Diversionary," *San Diego Union-Tribune,* March 25, 2000, p. E7.

————. "Musical *Millie* and Cosmonauts Tale Set for Launch at La Jolla," *San Diego Union-Tribune,* February 14, 2000, p. E3.

————. "A New *Setzuan* Cooking. Playhouse Adaptation Multicultural to the Max," *San Diego Union-Tribune,* July 24, 1994, p. E1.

————. "Playwrights Magically Connect Across Time," *San Diego Union-Tribune,* November 8, 1999, p. E6.

————. "*Slavs!* is a Wake-Up Call Heard Through a Laugh," *San Diego Union-Tribune,* July 23, 1995, pp. E1, E10.

Wexler, Joyce. "Speaking Out: Dialogue and the Literary Unconscious," *Style,* vol. 31, no. 1, spring 1997, pp. 118–33.

White, Vera. "Prize-winning Playwright Speaks His Mind," *Moscow Pullman Daily News* (Idaho), February 19, 1999.

Wieder, Judy. "Kramer vs. Kushner," *Advocate,* August 17, 1999, pp. 90–95.

Williams, Geoffrey. "Theatre," *Brother Sister,* November 5, 1993, p. 16.

Wilson, Edwin. "Tony Kushner's Gay Fantasia Arrives on Broadway," *Wall Street Journal,* May 6, 1993, p. A9.

Winer, Laurie. "A Good Look at the Hard Lessons of *Good Person,*" *Los Angeles Times,* August 2, 1994, p. F1.

————. "Old Bolshevik Resurfaces," *Los Angeles Times,* August 1, 1995, pp. F1, F5.

————. "Questions Unanswered in Kushner's *Slavs!*" *Los Angeles Times,* October 27, 1995, pp. F1, F28.

Winer, Linda. "*Angels* II: Still Playful, and Still Profound," *New York Newsday,* November 24, 1993.

————. "Corneille With Kushner's Help," *New York Newday,* January 20, 1994.

————. "Evils of Humanity Crowd *Bright Room,*" *New York Newsday,* January 8, 1991, pp. 44, 69.

————. "A Good Look at the Hard Lessons of *Good Person,*" *Los Angeles Times,* August 2, 1994, p. F1.

————. "Pulitzer-Winning *Angels* Emerges from the Wings," *New York Newsday,* May 5, 1993.

Winn, Steven. "An Epic Drama Unfolding," *San Francisco Chronicle,* June 4, 1991, p. E1.

————. "*Angels* Finally Lands in L.A.," *San Francisco Chronicle,* November 10, 1992, pp. E1, E4.

————. "*Angels* Gets Even Better," *San Francisco Chronicle,* May 5, 1993, sec. D, pp. 1, 3.

————. "Anything But a Drag; Gay Theatre Takes New Directions and More Risks," *San Francisco Chronicle,* January 9, 2000, p. 33.

————. "Kushner Overreaches In Ambitious But Static *Hydriotaphia,*" *San Francisco Chronicle,* September 18, 1998, p. C1.

————. "Kushner Puts More Worries on Stage," *San Francisco Chronicle,* February 25, 1995, p. 29.

————. "Marvelous *Millennium,*" *San Francisco Chronicle,* May 27, 1991, p. E1.

————. "*Slavs!* Tony Kushner Play at Berkeley Rep Breathes Life Into Soviet Socialism's Last Gasp," *San Francisco Chronicle,* March 9, 1996, p. B1.

Woods, Gregory. *A History of Gay Literature. The Male Tradition.* New Haven, CT, and London: Yale University Press, 1998.

Wright, Charles. "Theatre: *Slavs!*" *A&E Monthly*, March 1995, pp. 15–16.

Wright, Gary L. "*Angels* Legal Issues Not Settled," *Charlotte Observer*, March 22, 1996, p. 4A.

Wynn, Leah. "University Forbids Ads for *Angels in America*. Officials Didn't Want to Endorse Gay 'Lifestyle'," *Washington Blade*, September 20, 1996, pp. 1, 6.

Yeoman, Barry. "Art & States' Rights," *Nation*, June 29, 1998, pp. 31–33.

———. "Southern Discomfort," *Advocate*, March 17, 1998, pp. 35–37.

Zoglin, Richard. "His Play's The Thing," *Time*, July 6, 1998, p. 92.

Index